Nazi Buildings, Cold War Traces and Governmentality in Post-Unification Berlin

Nazi Buildings, Cold War Traces and Governmentality in Post-Unification Berlin

Clare Copley

BLOOMSBURY ACADEMIC
LONDON • NEW YORK • OXFORD • NEW DELHI • SYDNEY

BLOOMSBURY ACADEMIC
Bloomsbury Publishing Plc
50 Bedford Square, London, WC1B 3DP, UK
1385 Broadway, New York, NY 10018, USA
29 Earlsfort Terrace, Dublin 2, Ireland

BLOOMSBURY, BLOOMSBURY ACADEMIC and the Diana logo are trademarks of Bloomsbury Publishing Plc

First published in Great Britain 2020
This paperback edition published in 2021

Copyright © Clare Copley, 2020

Clare Copley has asserted her right under the Copyright, Designs and Patents Act, 1988, to be identified as Author of this work.

For legal purposes the Acknowledgements on p. x constitute an extension of this copyright page

Cover image: Adler, Eagle-Square, Platz der Luftbruecke, Tempelhof, Berlin, Germany (© Arco Images GmbH / Alamy Stock Photo)

All rights reserved. No part of this publication may be reproduced or transmitted in any form or by any means, electronic or mechanical, including photocopying, recording, or any information storage or retrieval system, without prior permission in writing from the publishers.

Bloomsbury Publishing Plc does not have any control over, or responsibility for, any third-party websites referred to or in this book. All internet addresses given in this book were correct on the access dates indicated. The author and publisher regret any inconvenience caused if addresses have changed or sites have ceased to exist, but can accept no responsibility for any such changes.

Every effort has been made to trace copyright holders and to obtain their permissions for the use of copyright material. The publisher apologizes for any errors or omissions and would be grateful if notified of any corrections that should be incorporated in future reprints or editions of this book.

A catalogue record for this book is available from the British Library.

Library of Congress Cataloging-in-Publication Data
Names: Copley, Clare, author.
Title: Nazi buildings, Cold War traces and governmentality in post-unification Berlin / Clare Copley.
Description: London; New York: Bloomsbury Academic, 2020. | Outgrowth of the author's thesis (Ph. D.)–University of Manchester, 2015, under the title: Post-authoritarian governmentality?: renegotiating the 'other' spaces of National Socialism in unified Berlin. | Includes bibliographical references and index. |
Identifiers: LCCN 2020005744 (print) | LCCN 2020005745 (ebook) | ISBN 9781350081536 (hardback) | ISBN 9781350081543 (ebook) | ISBN 9781350081550 (epub)
Subjects: LCSH: Architecture–Political aspects–Germany–Berlin–History–20th century. | Architecture and society–Germany–Berlin–History–20th century. | National socialism and architecture–Germany–Berlin–History–20th century. | Berlin (Germany)–Buildings, structures, etc.
Classification: LCC NA2543.S6 C665 2020 (print) | LCC NA2543.S6 (ebook) |
DDC 720.943/1550904–dc23
LC record available at https://lccn.loc.gov/2020005744
LC ebook record available at https://lccn.loc.gov/2020005745

ISBN: HB: 978-1-3500-8153-6
PB: 978-1-3502-5441-1
ePDF: 978-1-3500-8154-3
eBook: 978-1-3500-8155-0

Typeset by Deanta Global Publishing Services, Chennai, India

To find out more about our authors and books visit www.bloomsbury.com and sign up for our newsletters.

For James and Evelyn

Contents

List of illustrations	ix
Acknowledgements	x
Introduction	1

Part 1 Theoretical approach

1	Governmentality and the politics of the past	11
2	Difficult heritage in Berlin and beyond	28

Part 2 Plurality? Performing post-authoritarian governmentality at the former Aviation Ministry

	Introduction	41
3	Traces of National Socialism and the GDR in the 'mirror of German history'	46
4	Commemorating opposition to Nazism and to the GDR: Harro Schultze-Boysen and 17 June 1953	55
5	Negotiating (in)accessibility at a democratic government building	69

Part 3 Rationality? Negotiating post-authoritarian governmentality at the Olympic Stadium

	Introduction	81
6	Responding to the 'racist cult of the body manifested in stone': The Olympic Stadium's sculpture collection	87
7	Disentangling the Olympic Stadium's layers: The history trail	98
8	(En)Countering the cult of the dead: The Langemarck Hall memorial	111

Part 4 Freedom? Transcending post-authoritarian governmentality at the former Tempelhof Airport

	Introduction	129
9	Closing Tempelhof Airport, Berlin's 'gateway to the world'	133
10	The Columbia-Haus concentration camp and the forced labourer barracks: Exposing Tempelhof's 'other' pasts	144

11 Contesting freedom: The proposed development of the heterotopia of
Tempelhofer Feld 159

Conclusion 176

Notes 181
Bibliography 220
Index 243

Illustrations

2.1	Main entrance to the German Federal Finance Ministry	42
2.2	Construction of a colossus	42
2.3	The re-emergence of the Wehrmacht	43
2.4	Socialist realism?	51
2.5	Challenges to original aesthetics	53
2.6	Rüppel's memorial and Lingner's mural	61
2.7	The memorial to Harro Schulze-Boysen	63
2.8	The view down Niederkirchnerstraße	64
2.9	Challenging the building's 'totalitarian spirit'?	72
2.10	Activities for children at the Finance Ministry's 'open door day'	74
3.1	Berlin's Olympic Stadium	82
3.2	View through the Marathon Gate and back into the stadium	83
3.3	Karl Albiker's 'The Discus Throwers'	88
3.4	Joseph Wackerle's 'Horse Tamer'	96
3.5	The older plaques at the Marathon Gate	103
3.6	The newer plaques at the Marathon Gate	104
3.7	The older 'southern' stelae	107
3.8	The newer 'northern' stelae	108
3.9	The structure containing the Langemarck Hall	112
3.10	Inside the Langemarck Hall memorial	113
3.11	Exhibition 1909 – 1936 – 2006 Historic Site: The Olympic Grounds	121
4.1	The former Flughafen Tempelhof	130
4.2	Inside the former Flughafen Tempelhof	130
4.3	The highly praised technical back of Flughagen Tempelhof	135
4.4	Eduard Ludwig's 'Air Lift Memorial'	138
4.5	Georg Steibert's 'Columbia-Haus Memorial'	149
4.6	Information boards at the site of the Columbia-Haus concentration camp	153
4.7	Tempelhofer Feld	160
4.8	Tempelhofer Feld 'terms of use'	171
4.9	Pioneer projects at Tempelhofer Feld	173

Acknowledgements

This project began as a PhD thesis at the University of Manchester and thanks must first of all go to my supervisor, Professor Matthew Philpotts, for his incredible generosity with his time, his expertise and his encouragement. I must also take this opportunity to show my gratitude to Professor Maja Zehfuss and Professor Matthew Jefferies for their advice and support and to Professor Chloe Paver, Professor Sharon Macdonald and Professor Stefan Berger for their invaluable input into different stages of this work. I am grateful too to the anonymous reviewers of this book proposal, manuscript and related journal articles – their constructive and insightful comments have certainly made this work considerably better than it would otherwise have been. Further thanks must go to the AHRC for providing the scholarship which made the PhD possible and for the additional funding which enabled me to undertake primary research in Berlin. Post-PhD research trips were funded by the University of Central Lancashire and by a Scouloudi Research Grant from the Institute of Historical Research. I am extremely grateful to these institutions for this assistance. Special thanks go to Rhodri, Laura and the team at Bloomsbury for their advice, support and patience throughout this process.

The analysis within this book would have been much less effective without the help of so many of the Berlin-based experts on the case studies who shared their time, knowledge and materials with me: Uwe Pakull, Professor Dr. Harald Bodenschatz, Professor Dr. Wolfgang Schäche, Professor Dr. Hans-Ernst Mittig, Professor Dr. Gabi Dolff-Bonekämper, Volker Kluge, Elke Dittrich, Martin Pallgen, Werner Jockeit, Michael Richter and Professor Dr. Stefanie Endlich to name but a few. Thanks also to Paul Sabin for help with tricky translations and to Professor Stuart Elden for his advice on the theoretical side of things. The archivists at the *Landesdenkmalamt Berlin*, *Bundesarchiv Berlin-Lichterfelde*, *Bundesarchiv Koblenz*, *Landesarchiv Berlin* and the National Football Museum Archive, Preston, have been unfailingly helpful throughout this project and it would not have been possible without their expertise. Any mistakes are, of course, my own. I am grateful also to the members of the interest groups around Tempelhof who were so forthcoming in explaining their campaigns to me: Beate Winzer of the *Förderverein für ein Gedenken an die Naziverbrechen auf dem Tempelhofer Flugfeld e. V.*; Wolfgang Przewieslik of *Das Thema Tempelhof e. V.*; and the members of *Bürgerinitiative Tempelhof 42* and their hosts at Café Romi. Many thanks to Brill for allowing the reuse of material from Copley, C. '"Stones Do Not Speak for Themselves": Disentangling Berlin's Palimpsest', *Fascism*, 8 (2) (2019), 219–49 and to Cambridge University Press for allowing the reuse of material from Copley, C. 'Curating Tempelhof: Negotiating the Multiple Histories of Berlin's "Symbol of Freedom"'. *Urban History*, 44 (4) (2017), 698–717.

Since completing the PhD, I have worked at Birkbeck College, University of London and the Universities of Manchester, Bristol, Sheffield and Central Lancashire, and have benefitted greatly from the insights of colleagues and students at all of these institutions. I have also had the opportunity to present parts of this project at conferences, workshops and seminars in London, Cambridge, Berlin, Rome, Belfast, Manchester, Washington D.C. and Arras among other places and am hugely grateful to the audiences for their observations and suggestions which have helped immeasurably with the development of the project. I am extremely thankful for assistance from the German History Society and the German Studies Association in funding my attendance at some of these events.

Many of the seeds for this project were sown while working as a walking tour guide for the great Terry Brewer, whose love for Berlin and encyclopaedic knowledge of the city has been passed on to the new generation of guides. Thanks to him and to his successors for sharing their vast knowledge and understanding of the city and to all my Berlin-based friends for welcoming me into their homes and social lives on my research trips there.

Closer to home, I would like to thank my friends and family for their encouragement, love and support. My husband James has lived and breathed this book almost as much as I have and has been a constant source of wisdom, humour, caffeine and chocolate. Our beautiful daughter, Evelyn, was born in the very final stages of putting the book together. While she may not have helped in the conventional sense, her arrival certainly helped focus the mind and precluded an endless process of 'final' tweaking and potential *Verschlimmbesserung*. Any errors can be attributed to her and her profound distaste for sleep! I am extremely grateful to James and to my parents, Rhoda and Terry, for their support and for taking care of both of us so well while I finalized the manuscript.

Introduction

When I started giving walking tours of Berlin I always used to enjoy the looks of surprise on my tourists' faces as I asked them to stop behind the relatively nondescript East German apartment blocks on Wilhelmstrasse. Having just seen Checkpoint Charlie, the Topography of Terror and a section of the Berlin Wall, many of them clearly wondered what on earth could possibly be of interest among a fairly mediocre children's playground, some scruffy, dog-dirt laden patches of grass and a quiet car park. After all, this was back in 2005 when there was nothing to indicate that this was one of the very sites that had actually induced many of them to do the tour, nothing to show that, steeped in myth and shrouded in intrigue, this was one of Europe's most infamous sites, no sign explaining that beneath their feet were the remains of Hitler's bunker. There was no secret; since unification the location of the bunker had been fairly common knowledge, was marked on maps and listed in tourist guidebooks.[1] So why, my tourists would invariably ask, is there nothing here to mark the spot? My deceptively simple answer was that the Berlin authorities simply did not know how to deal with the site, fear of the embarrassment that would ensue should it turn into a site of pilgrimage for neo-Nazis mingled with reluctance to be seen to be suppressing the traces of history and with more economic and practical concerns about the development of the site.[2] By the very next summer, however, the interest in the bunker generated by the success of the film *Der Untergang* (Downfall) compounded with the forthcoming influx of visitors for the World Cup compelled Berlin-based historical society, Berliner Unterwelten, to put together and install an information board on the site. Quoted in *Spiegel International*, Dietmar Arnold, head of Berliner Unterwelten, talked of some of the 'absolute rubbish' that some tourists had been told about the bunker and the need to provide comprehensive, accurate information to dispel such myths and demystify the site.[3]

Since unification, scenarios akin to this one have played out across the city of Berlin with varying outcomes and levels of public interest: the tensions around the reuse of the Reichstag, over the demolition of the Palast der Republik and rebuilding of the Stadtschloss, and over the recent removal of a section of the longest remaining stretch of the Berlin Wall are but three particularly prominent examples.[4] Underlying these contests over how the built environment of Berlin should be constituted and interpreted for its inhabitants and visitors are multiple questions about which people and events should be memorialized and how, about which elements of the past should be preserved and which torn down, about how the city's plans for its future should be represented architecturally and about the legitimacy of the process through which all this should be decided. On one level, the issues at stake are not too dissimilar to those that characterize debates around urban development in any Western city: the tension between calls for the preservation of historical traces and the need to make space for the modern city; the difficulty of striking a balance between economic needs to attract corporate investment and citizens' demands for spaces where non-commercial interests can flourish; and contests over how democratic the process is by which decisions over the future of the city are taken. Yet when such debates take place in Berlin there is another level to them, one that situates them specifically within a society which is heavily shaped by its history. This is particularly apparent when, as in the example of Hitler's bunker, it is one of the physical traces of dictatorship which has come into the spotlight. In these incidences, a structure that was designed to fulfil a function within the built environment of the authoritarian city under National Socialism and/or the German Democratic Republic (GDR) needs to be incorporated into the democratic city of the Berlin Republic. The trajectory of Berlin's development means that it is continually arriving at points such as this: junctures where the present needs to determine how to respond to such legacies.

This book will focus on three such encounters between past and present, all of which have involved sites constructed as National Socialist prestige buildings which survived the destruction of the Second World War, went on to be incorporated into the highly politicized narratives of the Cold War and remained in use after unification: the former Aviation Ministry; the Olympic Stadium and the former Tempelhof Airport. The first to be dealt with is the former Aviation Ministry. Bearing the physical traces of the ruptures of twentieth-century German history, the colossal edifice, now named the Detlev Rohwedder House, has been described as a mirror or reflection of that history.[5] Built in 1935–6 on the site of the former Prussian War Ministry to house the National Socialist *Reichsluftfahrtministerium* (Aviation Ministry), it was one of the first National Socialist prestige buildings to be completed. Containing over 2000 offices, Sagebiel's vast stone-clad building featured in National Socialist propaganda as evidence of the new Reich's 'joyful ability to create'.[6] Despite extensive war damage to the surrounding area, the building was sufficiently intact when the Soviets began to develop their administrative infrastructure in Berlin for it to become the home of the Soviet Military Administration in Germany (SMAD). On 7 October 1949, the GDR was founded in the building's main hall and it went on to house several different government ministries, thus earning the name 'House of Ministries'. In 1961 the Berlin Wall was built so close to the building that its southern edge actually jutted into the death strip and ministries were dispersed around the city in order to divert attention elsewhere. After unification, the building was used as an outpost of the Federal Finance Ministry and to house Treuhand, the body set up to deal with the state-owned assets of the former GDR. In 1992 it was named the Detlev Rohwedder House after the assassinated president of Treuhand. When it became clear that the German government would return to Berlin, the fate of the building hung in the balance as it was debated whether or not such a building had any place in the capital of the democratic Germany.

Further west, in the leafy suburb of Charlottenburg-Wilmersdorf, the Olympic Stadium is the second site to be considered and is as layered and complex as the first. The stadium that currently stands there, that built for the 1936 Olympic Games, is the second to have been built on that site. The first, the German Stadium, was constructed by Otto March for the subsequently aborted Olympics of 1916. When it was announced in 1931 that Germany's bid to host the 1936 Olympics had been successful, Otto March's son Werner was given the commission to renovate his father's stadium, extending it so that it could accommodate the 78,000 seats required for the event.[7] When Hitler came to power in 1933, however, he had much more ambitious plans. Recognizing the propagandistic potential of the Olympics he extended Werner March's brief, commissioning him to design a brand new stadium that would replace and stand on the site of its predecessor.[8] This new stadium would become the focal point of the first Olympic Complex of its kind, an ensemble that included a hockey stadium, an open air swimming stadium, a polo field, field for equestrian events and, more unusually for an Olympic stadium, a parade ground named the Maifeld and the Langemarck Hall, a memorial to the German soldiers killed in the First World War and named after the 1915 battle at Langemarck, Belgium.[9] In common with the former Aviation Ministry, the National Socialist appropriation of the site, which took only twenty-seven months to achieve, was heavily written into propaganda as evidence of the decisiveness and power of the Third Reich.[10] After the 1936 Olympics, the stadium became a backdrop for mass events such as Mussolini's state visit in 1937, youth rallies and athletics competitions. In the later months of the war it functioned as a ration depot and as the quarters for the *Reichssportfeld Volkssturm* battalion. In the dying days of the war, Carl Diem, chief organizer of the 1936 Olympic Games, used the domed lecture theatre of the Sport Forum in the north-east corner of the site to make an emotive speech to members of the Hitler Youth which, according to reports, invoked ideas of Sparta to urge them to fight to the death for the 'victorious final battle'.[11] Despite this, the Olympic Complex suffered only minor damage during the Second World War and reopened for athletic events shortly afterwards.[12] The British made the Sports Forum their headquarters until the departure of the Allies in 1994. While the British have been praised for the care they took of the Olympic Complex while they were there, the lack of critical reflection involved in the reconstruction of certain elements of the site during their tenure has been criticized by campaigners pushing for increased engagement with the site.[13] Following unification, the imminent departure of the British from the site and desire for the newly unified country to host large-scale sports competitions provided the impetus for increased intervention into what had now become a somewhat-dilapidated stadium.

In common with both the former Aviation Ministry and the Olympic Stadium, the National Socialist reshaping of Tempelhof Airport, the final site to be addressed, did not involve a total change of function but rather a shift in how that function was performed and represented. After all, Tempelhof's connection with flight can be traced back to the early twentieth century when Tempelhofer Feld hosted pioneering flight demonstrations by the Wright brothers and Armand Zipfel which would attract large crowds. Berlin's first airport was constructed on the Feld in the 1920s as an ensemble comprising Paul and Klaus Engler's terminal building and Heinrich Kosina and Paul Mahlberg's aircraft hangars which drew much praise for its modern, functional design.[14] Germany had been prohibited by the conditions imposed by the Treaty of Versailles from possessing a military air force and successfully sought to establish itself at the forefront of the burgeoning civil aviation industry. Berlin rapidly became the 'cross-roads' of Europe, becoming connected through long-distance flights with

China, New York, South America and Africa and recognized around the world as a key hub in air transport networks.[15] Following the National Socialist seizure of power, Berlin's position as a major hub in international transport networks was to have been consolidated. As part of this, Hitler commissioned Sagebiel, who had won acclaim for his design of the Aviation Ministry, with the building of a new airport at Tempelhof which was to have a capacity of thirty times that of its predecessor and would be large and technologically advanced enough to stay in service until at least the year 2000.[16] It is this terminal building, begun in 1936, which now stands at the site. Intended to function as the 'gateway to Germania', the monumental 'world capital' into which Hitler and his architect Albert Speer envisaged transforming Berlin, Tempelhof is known for its architectural duality: from the front it has similar characteristics to the Aviation Ministry and the Olympic Stadium – over-sized proportions, rigid symmetry, strong axiality and stone-clad walls – yet from the back it boasts modern materials and technical innovations that were cutting edge at the time and continue to attract praise today.[17] As the war wore on, however, materials and labour were increasingly diverted towards the war effort and neither Speer's reordering of Berlin nor the construction of Sagebiel's airport were ever fully realized. Flughafen Tempelhof only began to function as an airport after the Second World War ended and the site was established as the headquarters of the United States Air Force in Berlin. During the Berlin Blockade of 1948/9, the airport served as the central hub for the importation of supplies through the operation known as the Berlin Airlift, a role which discursively transformed Tempelhof into the *Tor zur Welt* or 'Gateway to the World' for Berlin.[18] Even after the lifting of the blockade, to West Berliners and to refugees from the GDR, Tempelhof would continue to represent a link outwards to freedom until unification by providing a springboard from which they could access the rest of the Federal Republic, as well as the wider Western world, without having to engage with East German border guards. After unification, the decision to consolidate all of Berlin's air traffic at one site made Tempelhof's closure seem inevitable. Following years of protest and several stays of execution, Tempelhof ceased to operate as an airport in 2008, leaving the city authorities with a vast site for which they needed to find a function.

By building on a literature that conceptualizes the built environment as a tool in shaping subjectivity and thus enacting particular mentalities of governance, or governmentalities, the argument in this book is that what can be identified in the built environment of Berlin is the construction of a specifically post-authoritarian subjectivity, one formed by a continuous process of assertion, challenge and (re)negotiation within a distinctive but continually influx post-authoritarian governmentality. As a sub-type of the advanced liberalism identified elsewhere in the Western world, the nature of this post-authoritarian governmentality is contingent on the striking of a balance between fostering and delimiting heterogeneity, of countering the legacies of National Socialism through valorizing 'objective' knowledge and negotiating the balance between freedom and control. To an even greater extent than has been identified in existing conceptions of liberal governmentality, plurality, 'objectivity' and individual freedom are prized as key legitimizing features of post-authoritarian governmentality due to the extent to which they distinguish it from its predecessors yet, as the analysis in this book will reveal, they are contained within a continually shifting constellation of structuring frameworks. What also emerges from the analysis are signs of the limited temporal horizon of this particular governmentality as some evidence points towards a possible shift beyond post-authoritarian governmentality towards the advanced liberal governance seen elsewhere in the Western world.

The sites that will serve as case studies, the former Aviation Ministry, the Olympic Stadium and the former Tempelhof Airport, are all characterized by their visible origins as National Socialist prestige buildings, their functionality and their having been in continuous use since their construction in the 1930s. These commonalities give enough links to form a strong, coherent corpus upon which to base this research. The analysis, however, becomes primarily possible because of the key differences between the sites; the Aviation Ministry's incorporation into the narratives of East Berlin and the other sites into those of West; the different functions of the buildings; the different time frame within which each has been tackled; the interplay of power relations and myriad other factors which constitute the sites differently. The diverse range of sources employed within studies of governmentality means that there is no single methodology for approaching them. What unifies the scholarship are the questions it asks of the material, primarily, what it can tell us about the 'how?' of governance – what does it reveal about ways of seeing and perceiving, about the production of truth within a society, about the ways of acting and intervening that constitute a particular rationality and about the ways in which subjects are formed?[19] Before I could begin to consider the 'how?', however, my research needed to address the 'what?'. Following a vast scholarship that uses space and place as a primary source,[20] for each site the research began with the materiality of the building: What is at the site today? What is visible? What is marked? Which aspects of each site's history are communicated via means other than through the trace (i.e. through memorials, information boards, plaques, exhibitions)? The already substantial literature about the history of each building strongly informed this first stage of primary research, enabling me to identify what was absent either from the sites themselves or from the narratives constructed around them.[21] In keeping with other scholars of governmentality and the built environment,[22] it was then time to situate the objects of analysis, the buildings, within a much wider network, to try and make sense of the interplay between the myriad actors and forces that had led to the sites being constituted, both materially and discursively, as they have been. The sources I used could be understood as loosely grouped into three categories: those that gave a 'behind-the-scenes' insight into the post-unification response to the site; those that transmit the official narratives around the sites; and those that challenge, interpret, subvert or disseminate those official narratives. The focus of this research is on the early years of the Berlin Republic: 1990–2012. This covers the period from unification to the unveiling of the first stage of the history trail on Tempelhofer Feld. To provide context, some sources are used from before this period in order to shed light on the buildings' origins, previous uses and earlier responses to them. Similarly, to keep the study as up to date as possible, more recent events such as the 2014 Tempelhof referendum and the housing of refugees at the former airport are discussed and connected to the analysis but are not its primary focus.

The 'behind-the-scenes' insight came from materials which were put together to inform those actively making decisions about the fate of the sites and which were not primarily designed for public consumption. These include architectural reports and recommendations and correspondence and minutes of meetings between key actors. Analysed in conjunction with other sources they enabled me to unpick some of the processes of governmentality, to see the rationale behind decisions, to identify areas of conflict and to identify some of the innumerable factors that informed the post-unification reordering of the buildings. The 'official' narratives were gleaned from the numerous books, pamphlets, leaflets, marketing materials tours, open days and websites produced by, or on behalf of, the Berlin Senate or the federal government. These provided an insight into the 'official' response to the buildings, particularly showing the aspects of their materiality that were highlighted and the elements of their respective histories that would be incorporated into this dominant official narrative. As well as their content, the tone, form and proliferation of these materials gave a very telling insight into the officially sanctioned means of approaching the past. I then used a range of sources to see how these 'official' narratives were countered, consolidated and negotiated through other channels. These include the popular press (national newspapers and magazines); the blogs, websites, leaflets, booklets and other materials produced by citizens' initiatives, veterans' groups and other actors; and articles by experts (architects, planners, historians, curators) in the scholarly, specialist or popular press. This enabled me to assess reactions to the official narratives constructed around the sites and to see how salient a particular issue was. Relevant newspaper articles were found through keyword searches on the online archive LexisNexis Academic, through the clippings kept by key actors and included in their archived papers and through surveying digital and microfilm holdings for major newspapers on and around key dates in the buildings' histories. While this approach does have the disadvantage of potentially masking silences around the topic and suggesting denser coverage than was the case, it does allow a comprehensive survey across the German newspaper landscape. As such, it provided a multifaceted insight into how the buildings were being constructed for the public urban imaginary and how the press functioned as a site where many of the debates around the future of these buildings were not just reported but actually took place. The blogs, websites and leaflets which were produced by various citizens' groups functioned as spaces where these interest groups could express their demands and concerns and their own responses to the official narratives around the sites.

The book begins by expanding on the theoretical approach and situating the research within the wider scholarship on governmentality and on Berlin. In the first chapter I will make the case for the identification of a specifically post-authoritarian governmentality in the Berlin Republic. In the second I explore responses to difficult heritage in Berlin and beyond. The three remaining parts of the book, each containing three substantive chapters, will each use an analysis of post-unification responses to one of the sites in order to explore one dimension of post-authoritarian governmentality. Although there is significant temporal overlap between the chapters, the order in which the sites feature in this book roughly reflects the chronological order within which the interventions into them occurred. Presenting the information in this way, rather than thematically, has two advantages: first, it enables us to recognize the development of post-authoritarian governmentality as a process, as a mentality of government which emerged, was established, was continually restructured and is now entering a transition towards advanced liberal democracy; secondly, devoting an entire section to each site allows us to focus on the strategies of governance deployed to respond to the challenges and opportunities presented by each individual set of circumstances. Arranging the chapters in this way imposes an artificial categorization on them to some extent. After all, each of the tensions which underpin post-authoritarian governmentality could feasibly be explored at any of the three sites. As will hopefully become apparent, however, there is a case for the approach I have chosen as at each site one of the elements of post-authoritarian governmentality seems to be more significant than the others.

Part 2 will use the post-unification response to the former Aviation Ministry to explore the tension between allowing and delimiting heterogeneity in the Berlin Republic. It will show that expressions of an embrace of plurality have featured heavily in the narratives constructed around responses to the past. In this particular case study they are evident in expressed intentions to preserve the layers of the site's history, to incorporate multiple voices into decisions made about the future of the site and to allow access to spaces of political power. The case study reveals the multiple practices, frameworks and strategies that delimit this plurality but also show how these limits are continually resisted, challenged, (re)negotiated and (re)asserted. Part 3 will use the reordering of the Olympic Stadium to both highlight the valorization of objective, evidence-based knowledge in the Berlin Republic and problematize the very idea of 'objective' knowledge. Tracing the debates around the fate of the stadium's sculpture collection, it will show how the countering of the National Socialist legacies through rational commentary emerged as a dominant paradigm for dealing with the past before exploring the reordering of the site in accordance with this through the installation of the history trail. Analysis of this history trail and of the Langemarck Hall will unsettle the notion of 'objective' knowledge by revealing both the contingent nature of its construction and its instrumentalization. Part 4 will use the contests that have surrounded to post-unification use of Tempelhof Airport to highlight the salience of the negotiation of the balance between freedom and control in the Berlin Republic. Exploring the process through which the National Socialist prestige building has been discursively transformed into a 'symbol of freedom', it will reveal some of the ways in which that concept has been invoked and reframed by various actors seeking to realize particular goals for the site. By conceptualizing the site as a heterotopia, the longer final chapter will also show that recent disputes about freedom/control at Tempelhof have not been framed by the politics of the past but by the ordering processes of the advanced liberal city. The book concludes by exploring the idea that Germany may be moving beyond post-authoritarian governmentality.

Part 1

Theoretical approach

1

Governmentality and the politics of the past

The analysis in this book draws on the study of governmentality, an approach that encourages us to unpick the techniques and rationalities which inform how we are governed and which shape our ideas and actions. Developing the concept in his lectures at the *Collège de France* in February 1978, Foucault identifies a shift which took place between the sixteenth and eighteenth centuries from the overt imposition of controls and restrictions upon subjects towards the cultivation of a collective mentality, which would immerse subjects within a particular body of knowledge and truth and shape their behaviour. This shift was, he argued, underpinned by the developing 'art of government' which became necessary as traditional structures were challenged and an increasing need emerged for rulers to derive their legitimacy from elsewhere. According to Foucault, advisers to the rulers became increasingly concerned with 'a problematic of government in general': the questions of 'how to govern oneself, how to be governed, by whom should we accept to be governed and how to become the best possible governor'.[1] Correspondingly, the objective of the exercise of power shifted from the retention by the prince of his territory, and thereby his position, towards economy. Already recognized within the family sphere as the means to securing prosperity through the correct management of individuals, goods and wealth, the introduction of economy into political practice saw the introducing of the 'meticulous attention of the father towards his family into the management of the state'.[2] Population became the object of governance in this new way of thinking, and government thereby had the task of optimizing the utility of this resource. Given the growing realization that 'if one governed too much one did not govern at all',[3] this was to be achieved not through laws and regulations but through the forming of a subject through shaping their comportment, both internal and external, as is aptly summarized in Foucault's oft cited reference to *le conduire des conduits* or the 'conduct of conduct'.[4]

In developing his ideas around governmentality, Foucault aimed to see if it was possible to approach the state in the way that he had done with institutions such as prisons, armies and schools. Here he had moved beyond focusing on the functions of these institutions and instead sought to locate them within wider technologies of power by interrogating the ideas about truth, knowledge and rationality by which they are constituted and which they, in turn, consolidate.[5] In exposing the 'genealogy' of these institutions, he highlighted the plurality and fluidity of the power relations that lie behind them, thus exposing their instability and showing how rather than standing as rigid structures, they can be permeated and modified by a vast range of processes.[6]

In a similar way, a study of governmentality is concerned with moving beyond the functions of the state and revealing the relations of power that lie behind it. To analyse a particular governmentality, then, means to identify techniques of government, to analyse the rationalities and aspirations behind them and, ultimately, to expose the contingent nature of, and perhaps destabilize, the regimes of truth from which they emerge. As Lemke succinctly summarizes: 'It is not possible to study the technologies of power without an analysis of the political rationality underpinning them.'[7]

The concept of governmentality has gone on to inform a vast scholarship across disciplines including sociology, psychology, criminology, history, political science, social policy and urban studies.[8] Rather than a coherent body of work unified by a particular methodology, these studies are connected through the questions they ask of their diverse objects of study and their aims of exposing the rationalities and technologies that shape them. In parallel with this growth of studies informed by governmentality, a literature has also developed which identifies both flaws in Foucault's ideas and shortcomings in the work that is founded upon them. This has, in turn, been met with a vein of scholarship that challenges and rebuts these criticisms. Prominent among the critics of Foucault's work are those who see it as identifying a totalizing form of power which allows no capacity for individual agency or resistance. Scholars with this view argue that if conduct is, indeed, conducted, then any scope for contestation or alterity must be eliminated. Furthermore, if the oft cited 'positive, productive' view of power that Foucault expounds becomes such as it encounters, and then counters, different forms of resistance, this suggests that resistance strengthens rather than weakens the dominant power structure.[9] To Stephen Legg, however, this draws on a 'caricature' of Foucault's work, one that overlooks the nuance of his analysis of 'plebeian' resistance to normalization, forms of counter-conduct and rights as basis for resistance.[10] A second key strand to the criticisms of Foucault's governmentality is the accusation that his focus on the plural nature of power actually underplays the very real power of the institutions of state.[11] Kim McKee counters this by pointing out that what Foucault rejects is not the idea of the state as a key node of power but a conception of 'the state' which sees it reduced to a 'unified and monolithic all-powerful ruler'. Rather, she argues, governmentality pushes us to identify the multiple voices and power relations that constitute 'the state'.[12] This does not necessarily mean, of course, that this is found in all studies using the governmentality concept. Their concurrence with McKee on this issue notwithstanding, Ulrich Bröckling, Susanne Krasmann and Thomas Lemke find that many studies using governmentality do tend to use the state as a source of an 'archaic and repressing form of exercising power' and address this in their own edited volume.[13] A third strand of criticism is that discussed by Pat O'Malley, Lorna Weir and Clifford Shearing who find that too many studies deploying the governmentality framework are so abstract that they overlook the 'messy actualities' of 'what actually happens' on the ground.[14] This then leads to an overlooking of struggle and resistance and limits the capacity of the scholarship to critique what it is exploring, leaving it behind critical approaches such as those informed by Marxism, feminism and queer theory and risking irrelevance. This issue is, the authors say, 'not immanent to governmentality studies' but one which needs to be addressed.[15] While acknowledging that many studies which draw on the governmentality concept do have such blind spots and omissions, Lemke explains how it is in the making visible 'the depth and breadth of processes of domination and exploitation' that governmentality allows for critique.[16] This ongoing conversation about the strengths and limitations of the governmentality concept is a positive one. It compels those who use it in their work to continually reassess both Foucault's ideas and their own application of them while also encouraging ongoing dialogue between scholars with very different worldviews. In using the concept of governmentality to inform a historical study such as that in this book, these concerns are most effectively allayed not through recourse to Foucault's work but through the careful selection and interpretation of the empirical sources which inform the analysis. The sources deployed in this book, as discussed more fully in the introduction, have been chosen to reflect the plurality of voices and power relations that interact in the debates around how the buildings should be responded to while also revealing the 'real world' complexities around the implementation of particular ideas. The issue of resistance is inherent to the analyses of the interactions between different nodes of power and becomes overt in discussions of the work of different memorial activists and citizens initiatives as they challenge the responses or silences constructed around particular elements of the past or (re)configurations of the built environment.

Within the vast scholarship which now draws on and develops Foucault's ideas, various forms of governmentality have been identified: the 'police' form of governmentality of the eighteenth century; the liberal governmentality which emerged in the nineteenth century; the authoritarian governmentality which some states experienced in the twentieth century; and the advanced liberal governmentality which emerged in many Western states in the 1980s.[17] It is not, however, suggested that these mentalities of government are fundamentally different from one another. Rather, they are understood as different realizations of the same technologies and practices; the variation is more of aspiration and extent than means and techniques of governance.[18] Neither should they be seen as static, monolithic categories, and although they are often presented as periodization, they should not be considered to seamlessly segue into one another; even across apparent political, social and cultural ruptures some technologies of governance endure, others are consciously rethought and rendered obsolete, others simply fade away while still others are adapted.[19] The argument in this book is that none of these existing conceptions of governmentality allows us to take into account the extent to which the politics of the past can inform the rationalities, strategies and practices which constitute governmentality in certain states which have within living memory undergone a period of authoritarian rule. It is suggested instead that it is necessary to conceive of a specifically post-authoritarian governmentality and that the Berlin Republic is a prime example of this. It will use the built environment to gain an insight into the nature of that governmentality.

Liberal governmentality

Emerging towards the end of the eighteenth century, 'liberal governmentality' has at its centre the seemingly contradictory objective of governing through freedom.

This paradox of ruling through freedom is realized through the positing of certain spheres, such as the self and the family as being beyond the reach of government while simultaneously employing a range of techniques to structure the conditions within which the exercise of the autonomy of these entities is possible. The technologies of liberal governance can be recognized in almost every arena where individuals interact with each other, with some manifestation of the state or with non-state actors. As Foucault explains, they are seen in the 'thoroughly heterogenous ensemble of discourses, institutions, architectural forms, regulatory decisions, laws, administrative measures, scientific statements, philosophical, moral and philanthropic propositions'.[20] Much of this builds on the techniques and ideas associated with the emergence of 'biopolitics', the production of knowledge about the population itself and the environment within which it lives in order to facilitate the governing of that population.[21] This is manifested in the collection and compilation of calculations and measurements of statistics about births and deaths, health, fertility and illness, which are then collated, analysed, interpreted and presented as constituting an objective 'knowledge' of a population. This information can then inform interventions into that population in order to manage it more effectively. These may take the form of promoting insurance or savings schemes or campaigns for awareness and action around public health or sexual behaviour.[22] Unlike the more regulatory forms of power that had previously prevailed, the aim of such interventions within a liberal governmentality is not to force mere external compliance to law or social mores but to find a balance between freedom and regulation which produces a self-governing subject, instilled with the middle-class values of hard-work, decency, thrift and sobriety. Studies of liberal governmentality expose the power relations within such apparently neutral, objective processes. They reveal that as a territory and its inhabitants becomes subject to the gaze of the statistician, the bureaucrat or the map-maker and then, subsequently to the readers of the statistics, records and maps that they produce, that population or territory becomes visible, knowable and therefore governable from afar.[23]

Advanced liberal governmentality

Since the late 1980s, much of Europe, North America and Australasia have seen the development of what Rose terms 'advanced liberal democracies'.[24] Characterized by a post-war move beyond welfarist government and Keynesian economics towards a critique of excessive government and the valorization of individual freedom and responsibility, this shift has frequently been analysed in terms of neoliberalism.[25] Following the work of Dean, however, scholars of governmentality highlight that neoliberalism is just one of the multiple rationalities of government, alongside neo-conservatism and communitarianism, for example, that is in contestation within contemporary mentalities of government.[26] In short, neoliberalism should be understood as just one ideological strand of advanced liberalism. 'Advanced liberalism' refers to societies where responsibility for governance has gradually been delegated from the state to a range of agents, starting with the individual, whose effective self-governance is seen as the cornerstone of both individual and national well-being and prosperity. This then radiates outwards into multiple social actors such as teachers, parents, bodies of experts, community groups, private companies, trusts and associations. It is, in essence, a move beyond attempts to govern *through* society towards attempting to govern 'without governing society'.[27] This shift has sought to reconfigure the citizen as an active agent, to empower him/her to realize their own potential and fulfil their own needs rather than to depend on the state for assistance: 'the ideal of the "social state" [has given] way to that of the "enabling state"'.[28]

Just as in nineteenth-century liberalism, however, the autonomy of these actors is only considered to be conducive to the well-being of the nation if it takes place within certain parameters. The field of possibilities open to them is therefore delimited through a range of techniques. The power of the expert, for example, whose research, reports and analyses shape aspects of life from education and health to civil engineering and transport, is curtailed by the 'technologies of performance'.[29] Comprised of strategies such as the introduction of performance indicators, benchmarks and the devolution of budget setting, these technologies subject the expert to monitoring and thus ensure that apparently autonomous agents can be assessed and governed and their conduct can be shaped remotely.[30] In addition, the study of 'new prudentialism' identifies the way in which the citizen and the community become responsible for monitoring risk and so it becomes rational and prudent for them to invest in their own security through private health insurance, neighbourhood watch schemes and private pensions.[31] The role of the citizen is further reconfigured through what Dean refers to as the 'technologies of agency', measures that make the individual an active agent in their own governance. Dean illustrates that these technologies are apparent in the increased proliferation of extrajuridical contracts (such as those between a child and their teacher, the unemployed and the state) which configure us as informed and responsible citizens. They are also manifested in the various means through which the citizen is encouraged and empowered to become engaged in the wider processes of governance through partaking in consultations, focus groups, citizens' panels, opinion polls, referenda and other officially sanctioned channels to make their voice heard.[32]

Authoritarian governmentality

Rose's concept of advanced liberalism has informed a significant literature which addresses the processes and technologies of rule in contemporary Europe, North America and Australasia. It has facilitated studies on how shifting perceptions of 'need' and empowerment have affected social and welfare policy[33] and on the ways in which the rise of risk assessment and risk management has affected public policy.[34] It has also enabled the identification of strategies which legitimize some social practices and forms of knowledge and delegitimize others.[35] This does not, however, provide the right analytical tool for a study of governmentality in post-unification Germany. After all, unlike many of the nations studied in the research literature on advanced liberalism, but like countries such as Italy and Spain, Germany has, within living memory, undergone an experience of distinctly illiberal governance. In his reflections on this, Foucault examines the combination of 'generalized biopower', disciplinary power and sovereign power over life and death in Nazi Germany which he sees as having led to both the development of the 'final solution' and Hitler's 1945 plans to destroy Germany's remaining infrastructure.[36] He later touches briefly on governmentality in 'totalitarian' states conceptualizing it as a 'limitation [...] of the autonomy of the state' by the party, thus leading to a form of 'non-state' or 'party' governmentality distinct from that seen in administrative or bureaucratized state of the eighteenth or nineteenth centuries.[37] Since then, however, a considerable scholarship has arisen which builds on the increased availably of primary sources and the development of *Alltagsgeschichte* to provide a much more nuanced picture of these regimes and to challenge the applicability of the 'totalitarian' label.[38] In his study of the technologies and rationalities deployed in authoritarian states, Dean develops the concept of 'authoritarian governmentality' which, he contends, differs from its liberal equivalent through seeking to operate through 'obedient rather than free subjects'.[39] To show that authoritarian governmentality is, however, founded upon the same rationalities and technologies of government as liberal governance, Dean highlights the 'illiberality' of liberal governance, exploring the exclusion of sections of society such as the ill and the insane from the designation of 'free subject'.[40] Legg builds on this in his study of colonial rule in India. While identifying it as the 'darker side of liberal governmentality' rather than a form of authoritarian governmentality, he demonstrates a different balance between freedom and control to that seen in Europe, with the emphasis more towards the latter.[41]

Dean then goes on to locate extensions of the technologies we see in liberal governance within its authoritarian counterpart, for example, the use of scientifically obtained knowledge of the body to enhance torture techniques, or the role of biopolitics in underpinning genocide, particularly the Holocaust.[42] This latter point has also been explored elsewhere; Rose identifies the Holocaust as having been based on the same rationality as that seen in liberal governance but without 'liberal concerns with limiting government and individual freedoms'.[43] Strong similarities can also be identified in the rationalities behind the engagement of the British with the physical landscape of India and other colonies and the reordering of space in the East through German interventions such as draining marshes, planting forests, building roads and creating settlements as they sought to bring the territory under National Socialist control.[44] Underlying this work on authoritarian rule is the recognition that dictatorship is not fundamentally different to democracy. This understanding has been consolidated by various studies which have identified aspects of authoritarian governmentality in a range of contexts, broadening the application of the concept to non-Western forms of governance.[45] This also feeds into a scholarship which sees both National Socialist fascism and state socialism as different articulations of, rather than aberrations of, modernity.[46]

Post-authoritarian governmentality

The argument in this book is that the experience of the Third Reich and the GDR has impacted upon the form of governmentality that we can observe in post-unification

Germany. As a result, what is in operation in the Berlin Republic is a specifically post-authoritarian governmentality, a sub-type of advanced liberal governmentality strongly informed by this experience of dictatorship. What distinguishes post-authoritarian governmentality from more straightforward examples of its advanced liberal counterpart is not that it employs different mechanisms or practices of governance – we would still expect to see the delegation of power to multiple agents and the constraining of that power through various technologies of government, the monitoring of experts through the setting of performance targets, the development of inducements for non-state bodies to take responsibility for risk and the construction of active and engaged citizens. The distinction lies in the requirement in a post-authoritarian society for the conscious reshaping of subjectivities formed under dictatorship and in the re-aligning of technologies of government that were designed to rule through repression rather than freedom. This means that analysing the Berlin Republic simply as an advanced liberal democracy in the same way one might approach Canada, New Zealand or the UK will not yield an adequate insight into the governmentality in operation there. Such an insight cannot be gained simply from an analysis of policy, the constitution or the economy, it requires recognition of the role the past plays in informing the wider political culture within which mechanisms of governance are developed, operated and responded to. In the Berlin Republic this is complicated by Germany's post-war division which meant that, by 1990, subjectivities formed in the former West had already been shaped by forty-five years of democracy while those in the East had been constituted by the experience of two authoritarian regimes. However, as well as uncovering evidence to support the idea of post-authoritarian governmentality, the analysis also finds indications that this is a transitional phase and that, in some respects, Germany can be seen to be moving towards the advanced liberal governance seen elsewhere in the Western world.

Foucault and the Bonn Republic

Formed on 23 May 1949 the Bonn Republic, the unofficial name for the Federal Republic of Germany (FRG) often used to differentiate between its pre- and post-1990 make up, was shaped from the outset by the legacy of the Nazi takeover of power. With input from the Western allies, determination to prevent Germany from succumbing to dictatorship again was enshrined into the 1949 Basic Law. The strengthening of the federal system and the locating of the parliament, Federal Constitutional Court and the Federal Bank in Bonn, Karlsruhe and Frankfurt respectively meant that power was both institutionally and geographically dispersed. Furthermore, later changes to the electoral system, including the provision to ban anti-system parties and the introduction of a hurdle in Germany's proportional representation voting system, as per which parties needed to gain at least 5 per cent of the vote or one (later three) directly elected seats to take their seats in the Bundestag, meant that extremist parties struggled to gain traction and precluded the splintering and fragmentation seen in the Weimar Republic. Along with the onset of the economic miracle in the 1950s and the development of the *Volksparteien* (catch-all parties), these measures contributed to the fact that Bonn Republic was soon characterized by relative material prosperity and political stability.[47]

The impact of the experience of Nazism was not, of course, only realized in the Bonn Republic's institutional and constitutional make up. The politics of memory will be discussed below. Here, the focus is on the potential for past dictatorship to shape contemporary governance. This was explored by Foucault in his 1978–9 lecture series at the *Collège de France* in which he outlined the 'new programming of liberal governmentality' that he identified in the Bonn Republic.[48] Highlighting the challenges of building a state under conditions of occupation, division and with no historical legitimacy to rest on, he argued that the Federal Republic's founders needed to develop a framework where origin was not important. This framework, he argued, would be found in the development of an economic system which guaranteed economic freedom and which would then produce the political signs required for the structures, mechanisms and justifications of power to function and generate a founding consensus through the development of a strong economy. Foucault expected that continuous economic growth would 'take over from a malfunctioning history', positing that 'a reversal of the axis of time, permission to forget and economic growth are all at the heart of the way in which the German political system functions'.[49] His discussion of the GDR is rather briefer and more a consideration of socialism in general rather than its manifestation in East Germany in particular. Here, he considers the extent to which one can speak of a 'socialist governmentality' and discovers it rather limited due to his finding that socialism lacks the intrinsic governmental rationality seen in liberal states, replacing it with adherence to texts.[50]

In some respects, Foucault's analysis of governmentality in the Federal Republic between 1948 and the late 1970s provides a useful approach to studying it in the early years of the Berlin Republic. In particular, he makes explicit the impact of National Socialism on the present: the 'state-phobia' or fear of 'the invasion of humanity by the state' produced by the experience of living under the Nazi dictatorship,[51] and demonstrates how the ideas and approaches of the Frankfurt School and Freiburg School advocates of neoliberalism in Germany were consciously developed in opposition to National Socialism.[52] However, to provide an effective starting point for gaining an insight into governmentality in the Berlin Republic, Foucault's approach would need to be extended. First, his analysis of governmentality in the Bonn Republic centres on the development of neoliberalism, and this foregrounds the economy to the extent that social, cultural and institutional factors are barely mentioned. Secondly, his apparent anticipation of Germany's 'forgetting of history'[53] has yet to be borne out.

Beyond neoliberalism

Foucault's analysis of governmentality in the Bonn Republic focuses primarily on the economy. This is because the purpose of his analysis is to ascertain the extent to which the concept of governmentality can be applied on a different scale to that on which he has used it in the past. In particular, he wanted to test its usefulness for examining the conduct of conduct of the whole social body rather than that of a specific part of the population such as criminals or the ill. He uses the development of neoliberalism in post-war Germany as just one case study in this intellectual experiment.[54] However, a study which takes governmentality in a single state as its primary focus, such as that initiated in this book, must also consider the social, the cultural and the institutional. After all, it is only through analysis of these features of political and social life that we can identify the technologies of authoritarian governmentality which characterized governance in the Third Reich and so it follows that it is to these features that we must also turn in our attempt to make sense of the mentalities of government in the systems that follow it. There is, as will become apparent in the next chapter, a number of excellent studies of different facets of the unified Germany's society, culture and institutional development, yet these do not generally draw on the 'governmentality' scholarship and thus tend to stop short of making explicit the connection between their objects of study and their place within the wider frameworks and techniques of governance. The scholarship which does use governmentality as a means by which to study post-unification Germany and this has yielded some fascinating insights. Social geographer Lanz, for example, utilizes the concept to explore the implementation and impact of various aspects of urban policy and has been able to highlight the deployment of disciplinary technologies of governance when expressions of self-governance (i.e. through referenda) conflict with government objectives.[55] Another group of geographers has used the concept of governmentality to explore the role of Berlin's luxury apartments in governing its population, identifying the recent surge in their construction as part of the reorganizing of urban order and conceptualizing them as places 'where neo-liberalism is produced and "built".[56] Yet these studies tend to identify governance in the Berlin Republic as advanced liberal or neoliberal and thus overlook the extent to which the politics of the past impacts upon the way Germans govern and are governed. Incorporating this dimension into analyses of power and subjectivity can, where relevant, sharpen the analytical tool of 'governmentality', rendering it more effective for the job in hand. There is still a need to bridge the gap between these literatures, recognizing the social, cultural and institutional as sites where power relations are continually consolidated, challenged and (re)negotiated and addressing the continued role that memory politics plays in shaping those relations.

The politics of the past in Germany

Speaking in 1979, Foucault could not have been expected to foresee the development of the current official consensus on the importance of *Vergangenheitsbewältigung* or 'mastering the past' which today plays a prominent role in German political discourses. He would, however, have no doubt been aware of the shifts in German memory culture which had been occurring, especially in the Federal Republic, since the late 1950s. This is already the subject of an extensive literature but a brief summary will be outlined here in order to provide context.

While the scholarship has moved beyond the idea that a state of collective amnesia and silence prevailed across Germany in the early post-war years, there was certainly a slowness to recognize and acknowledge the atrocities committed in the name on National Socialism.[57] In both East and West Germany, a distinction was drawn between the Nazi elites and the mass of ordinary Germans who, it was considered, had been deceived and betrayed by the elites and who had experienced immeasurable suffering through bombing raids and the loss of loved ones. On both sides this extended to those who had served in the army. In the West, the Wehrmacht was seen as having been comprised of brave and honourable boys and men who had simply been doing their duty. In the East, its members were represented as having been 'led astray' but with potential for 're-education' in Soviet Prisoner of War camps.[58] The Nuremberg International Military Tribunal saw the death penalty and lengthy prison sentences meted out to some of the leading Nazis but this was seen by many ordinary Germans as a form of 'victors' justice'.[59] In terms of the rest of the population, there was no way that all 6.5 million former members of the Nazi Party could all be held to account for the regime's crimes, not least because many of these had expert knowledge without which the reconstruction of Germany would have been virtually impossible.[60] The sentences handed out to those citizens who were brought to trial for their activities under National Socialism were notably lenient and would become even more so after the founding of the Federal Republic and the German Democratic Republic. In the East, the governing party, the SED (Socialist Unity Party of Germany) adopted the stance that by this point any major Nazis had either fled to the West or had already been punished and, consequently, Nazism had been 'dealt with'.[61] In the West, Adenauer prioritized stability, democratization and European integration over seeking out those responsible for Nazi atrocities and bringing them to justice.[62] Yet while there was certainly a continuity of personnel within key German institutions after 1945 and the 'denazification' process designed to 're-educate' former Nazis is widely seen as having been largely ineffective,[63] Jarausch finds that the Allies' termination of any organizations associated with the Nazi Party and the thorough discrediting of Nazi ideology did mean that the early post-war period sowed the seeds of fundamental change in political culture.[64]

Both Germanies went on to develop separate official narratives around what had happened between 1933 and 1945, and, given the intensity of international political tensions, it should be no surprise that these diverging narratives sought to assert the legitimacy of the respective states within which they emerged. In the East, capitalism and imperialism were seen as sources of fascism whereas the West focused on the totalitarianism which was presented as underpinning both fascism and socialism.[65] In the two German states, different narratives of victimhood emerged, both of which downplayed the extent and specificity of Jewish suffering in the Holocaust. In the GDR, the emphasis was placed on the fate of communists and anti-fascist resistors while Jews were subsumed into the broader category of 'victims of fascism'. In the Federal Republic, even as Jewish suffering was increasingly recognized following Adenauer's 1951 acquiescence to Israel's request for acknowledgement and the payment of restitutions, equivalence tended to be drawn between Jewish and German victimhood. In both Germanies other groups of victims such as Sinti, Roma, 'asocials' and homosexuals were largely absent from public memory.[66]

While East Germany's official narratives did not go on to deviate significantly from those that had developed in the 1950s,[67] those that emerged in the West would be challenged from a range of angles from the late 1950s onwards. Events such as the 1961 Eichmann Trial and the 1963/4 trial of Auschwitz SS officers in Frankfurt brought the atrocities committed during the Third Reich and particularly the Holocaust, much more firmly into public focus. They found fertile ground among the protest movements of the 1960s. In common with protestors in other countries, the German '68-ers' sought to challenge the inequality, consumerism, patriarchy and racism they considered to be embedded into politics and society. Specific to Germany, however, were the perceptions that the authoritarianism they identified within institutions such as the police service, higher education and the legal system signified continuity with the Third Reich. The protestors accused their parents' generation of complicity with the Nazi regime and began demanding more information about what had occurred during the Third Reich and for those responsible to be held accountable.[68]

This increasing awareness of the Holocaust intensified in the 1970s both through popular culture, such as the 1979 broadcasting of the US television show *Holocaust*, and through the actions of public figures. In some cases, these actions highlighted increased critical engagement with the Nazi past; Chancellor Brandt's kneeling at the Warsaw Ghetto in 1970 and President Richard von Weizsäcker's call for Germans to confront and remember Nazi crimes in his 1985 speech to the Bundestag are two prominent examples. In other incidences, however, the opposite was the case. For example, Chancellor Kohl and US president Reagan's controversial wreath laying at military cemetery in Bitburg which contained SS graves was seen by many as a step backwards in the development of understanding of the nature of National Socialism.[69] Outside of political and academic institutions, the 1970s and 1980s saw growing numbers of amateur and professional historians, students and interested citizens seeking to increase their own and wider public knowledge of the past through engaging in archival research and excavations of local sites as part of the History Workshop movement. One of the most prominent legacies of such activities is that of the dig organized by two citizens' initiatives, the Active Museum of Fascism and Resistance and the Berlin History Workshop in May 1985, at the site of the former Gestapo headquarters in Berlin. Their initial findings would evolve into the Topography of Terror, now a popular museum in Berlin.[70] Conservative and right-wing voices have, however, long fought back against the notion of Germany's collective guilt for the atrocities committed during the Second World War and perceptions of its ongoing responsibility to identify and acknowledge the extent of them. This came to the fore during the *Historikerstreit* or Historians' Debate of the late 1980s which saw the press, commentators and the wider public drawn into arguments between left and right-wing historians over the uniqueness of the Holocaust and its centrality to German identity and memory. Rejection of German guilt has also underpinned the programmes of far-right extremists since the early post-war period and provided one means by which the radical right party, the NPD (National Party of Germany), was able to capitalize on the backlash against the left-wing protests of 1968.[71]

There was hope that unification would see a step forward in contests about how the Nazi past should be remembered. On 9 November 1993, Rita Süssmuth, president of the Bundestag, posited that end of Germany's division would bring about 'the beginning of joint remembrance',[72] that finally the divergent understandings of what had happened between 1933 and 1945 would be reconciled and a shared narrative would emerge that German people could come together and work through. The main hurdle to this is, of course, that there was no single experience of that period and no consensus on how it should be remembered.[73] This is apparent from the memory contests that continued into the Berlin Republic. While the reaction to the Crimes of the Wehrmacht exhibition which was displayed around Germany between 1995 and 1999 and the debates around Berlin's 2005 Memorial to the Murdered Jews of Europe are two of the most high-profile examples, smaller scale and more localized debates continually arise as different actors and groups push for increased awareness of diverse elements of the Nazi past. This may take the form of a campaign for the marking of the sites of overlooked atrocities or heroism or through publicizing and sharing the results of their own research into the actions of different institutions and enterprises during the Third Reich.[74] Furthermore, post-unification memories do not only need to deal with the Third Reich but also need to deal with the period between 1945 and 1990. Germany's Federal Strategy for Memorial Sites which became law in 1999 sets out that it is concerned with ensuring the remembrance of 'the National Socialist reign of terror, Stalinism and the SED dictatorship and [...] commemorating the victims and those who opposed or resisted those regimes'.[75] As this indicates, the GDR became firmly inscribed into the official narratives of the unified Germany as the 'SED dictatorship', listed in the same context as National Socialism and Stalinism. While some historians, politicians and public commentators have tended to highlight the authoritarian structures and gross human rights abuses of the SED regime, others argue that focusing solely on these elements of its history overlooks the realities and complexities of everyday life and the state's 'emancipatory aspirations' and is seen by many of those who lived in the GDR as a continuation of crude Cold War rhetoric.[76] This contributes to anger among many former East Germans about what they see as the dismissal of their own experiences of the GDR and its positive elements. This has been exacerbated by the rapid privatization of the previously state-owned assets of the former GDR which led to unemployment levels reaching above 17.5 per cent in 1993 in some areas, a harsh shock to the inhabitants of a former socialist state.[77] As the prosperity which Kohl promised would accompany unification failed to materialize and the gap in living standards between the two Germanies persisted, these factors fed into conceptions that what had occurred in 1990 was not so much a 'unification' but rather a colonization of the East by the West. East German resentment was, in turn, met with frustration from many West Germans over the amount of public money used to develop and support the former GDR.[78] Nonetheless, in ending the invocation of the Nazi past in the battle for legitimacy between the two Germanies, unification did, as Koshar puts it, 'lift the ideological blinkers' which had prevented Germans from 'mastering the past'.[79] As will be shown in this book, citizens' initiatives, survivors' groups and historians who had been campaigning for increased recognition of particular facets of the past found there was considerably more public interest in their findings and increased political will to support and develop their work. Exhibitions and public talks brought previously neglected elements of Nazi rule and the Holocaust more firmly to the public's attention, generating national conversations about complex topics ranging from the role of ordinary Germans to the groups of victims who had previously been marginalized within commemoration culture. Commemoration was written more prominently onto Germany's urban landscapes through high-profile projects such as Berlin's Memorial to the Murdered Jews of Europe and the burgeoning number of smaller memorials and plaques all over Germany.

Post-authoritarian governmentality in and beyond the Berlin Republic

The focus on the Berlin Republic in this book should not be seen as an indication of that state as unique. Rather, the Berlin Republic is posited as a specific and, possibly extreme, variant of a generic phenomenon and more research would be required to test the concept's applicability to other contexts. The twentieth and early twenty-first centuries saw myriad manifestations of authoritarian rule in states across Europe, Asia, Africa and Latin America, many of which have since transitioned to democracy. However, by no means is post-authoritarian governmentality necessarily the dominant paradigm within any state which happens to have been a dictatorship. A necessary condition for post-authoritarian governmentality is that it operates within states where the political culture is significantly defined in opposition to a dictatorial past. The Bonn Republic from the 'long 1960s' onwards would have been another good candidate for analysis.[80] Foucault draws links between the post-war economic development of Germany and that of post-liberation France but does not as explicitly identify the French case as having developed in direct opposition to experience during the Second World War to the same extent as in Germany.[81] However, in the years since Foucault's death, critical engagement with that period of French history has certainly become more prominent and so post-Vichy France may well be another worthy case study.[82] However, countries such as France in which dictatorship followed foreign invasion are likely to be different to those in which it developed domestically. Despite varying levels of complicity and collaboration among certain citizens and members of the elite, such a dictatorship and any atrocities committed in its name can be conceptualized as having been imposed from outside. If that is the case, commemoration of that past may shape memory and identity but there is not necessarily the same impetus to demonstrate rupture or that lessons have been learnt. Given the complex and fluctuating relationships all former dictatorships have with their own authoritarian pasts and the depth of knowledge and research required to uncover the rationalities and techniques of rule in any given country, specialists on these individual countries would be better placed to advance these studies and examine the extent to which post-authoritarian governmentality can be said to operate, or have operated, within them.

In the first decades of the Berlin Republic it has been possible to speak of a general consensus on the importance of continuous education and awareness about National Socialism and of Germany's moral responsibility for the atrocities that were committed in its name.[83] This does not mean that German memory culture is monolithic or uniform; on the contrary, there are myriad voices seeking to shape what version of the past is remembered and how and there are multiple other issues, ranging from legislation around planning permission for memorials to economic factors that shape how memory culture is constituted. However, the idea that the Nazi past should be acknowledged and confronted has now become a key element of Germany's national identity. This recently became apparent through the public outcry that followed the 2017 pronouncement from Alexander Gauland, the leading electoral candidate of the right-wing Alternative for Germany Party, that it was time for Germans to reclaim not only their country but their history by drawing a line under the Nazi past. This and later remarks in a similar vein were rapidly and angrily countered by many ordinary Germans on social media as well as by mainstream politicians and cultural figures.[84]

The 1999 Federal Strategy for Memorial Sites articulated the official stance that through remembering the dictatorships and their victims, 'we strengthen our own sense of freedom, justice and democracy'.[85] It is this very publicly and overtly expressed desire for the unified Germany to define itself in opposition to authoritarian governmentality, to confront and come to terms with its past and the extent to which a general consensus on this has gone on to characterize German political, cultural and social life which makes the Berlin Republic a paradigmatic example of post-authoritarian governmentality. The extent to which both the technologies of government and responses to them are informed by the past is evident not only when the politics of the past are explicitly being debated, as in the discussions listed above, but also in the interactions between state and citizen in a range of arenas. Pertinent examples include debates around the protection of civil liberties, the collection of personal data and Germany's involvement in military activity.[86]

The analysis in this book will take as its focus three elements of liberal governmentality that have been impacted upon by the past to such an extent that they cannot be subsumed into an analysis of advanced liberal governance and, instead, require us to consider the existence of a sub-type of advanced liberal governance: post-authoritarian governmentality. It will explore these through analysing post-unification responses to the built legacies of authoritarian governmentality. These structures fulfil a complex role in Berlin's urban landscape. They are simultaneously spaces with potential to undermine the newly formulated democratic Berlin Republic, serving as they do as concrete remnants of the undemocratic past, and spaces where the democratic credentials of the present can be actively performed through providing a platform upon which the juxtaposition between past and present can be enacted. The first of these is the tension between allowing and delimiting plurality. Fundamental to the art of liberal governance is the management of heterogeneity, not through seeking to eliminate it but through the use of discursive, regulatory and other frameworks to structure it. Joyce highlights how 'liberal governmentality's claims to universality are made through a series of exclusions' and provides concrete examples such as the nineteenth-century clubs and societies deemed not to be 'improving' enough to be permitted to use the facilities of the town hall, despite its having been presented as being for widespread use, and the exclusion of undesirable elements from ritualized celebrations such as parades and therefore from expressions of municipal identity.[87] As this book will show, the repressive measures that were taken to curtail plurality in the Third Reich and the GDR have led to an increased sensitivity to attempts to quash heterogeneity, silence opposing voices and impose uniformity in the Federal Republic. This becomes apparent through the prominence given to the Berlin Republic's embrace of plurality in the discourse around the sites. Governmentality in the Berlin Republic is thus very much informed by a particularly sensitive negotiation between the incorporation of multiple perspectives and discourses into the governing process and the careful delimiting of the potential output of these voices.

The second aspect of liberal governmentality which takes a distinctive form in the post-authoritarian Berlin Republic is the valorization of 'objective' knowledge.

Nineteenth-century liberal governance prized the production of rational, evidence-based knowledge that could be deemed 'serious, unsentimental [... and ...] led away from extremes [... and would ...] transcend political and religious passions and bias'.[88] Yet as Joyce and many others have highlighted, the notion of an 'objective', neutral knowledge is problematic, shaped as it is by the gaze of the expert. In the Berlin Republic, the communication of an objective, rigorously researched, comprehensive account of National Socialism and the GDR has become the dominant paradigm for approaching the past and demonstrating a will to acknowledge and confront it. The juxtaposition between this and the emotive, sensationalized, selective and even falsified versions of history which prevailed in the Third Reich and the GDR plays a significant part in legitimizing the Federal Republic. The paradox is, of course, that seeking legitimacy through highlighting the instrumentalization of history by a past regime is, itself, an instrumentalization of history.

The third feature of liberal governmentality which has been significantly impacted on by the past in the Berlin Republic is the negotiation of the tension between freedom and control. For liberalism to function, it needs a free but self-regulating subject. The range of technologies through which a subject's conduct is conducted is vast – from the inculcation of certain behaviours through the disciplinary institutions of the school, the barracks and the prison to the cultivation of self-regulation through exposure to the public and official gaze. To Foucault, the striking of this balance between what can and cannot be done and the 'marking out of the limits of a governmental action' is not imposed by one side or the other but is arrived at through a 'series of conflicts, agreements, discussions and reciprocal concessions'.[89] In post-authoritarian Germany, the experience of past attempts at illiberal governance, at ruling and constituting an 'unfree' subject has rendered this balance particularly salient. As will be shown in the coming analysis, reactions to perceived threats to civil liberty and individual freedom are heavily informed by this past and thus have the potential to challenge the legitimacy of the Federal Republic which is derived from its opposition to this past.

Governmentality and the city

While Foucault did consider the disciplinary mechanisms of the urban environment,[90] until the mid-1990s the application of 'governmentality' to the spatial, rather than to the political or social, was relatively sparse outside the discipline of Geography.[91] Academics from various disciplines have now, however, effectively located and established the significance of the spatial in Foucault's work, demonstrating how it underpins his ideas about surveillance, discipline and the segregation of the deviant from the 'normal'.[92] Scholars such as Elden and Hannah have taken this further, arguing that the governance of population cannot be understood without recognition of its relationship to the governance of territory.[93] As a product of this, a considerable scholarship has grown up around the application of 'governmentality' to analysis of the development of the city in a range of temporal and geographical contexts. Social theorists Osborne and Rose demonstrate that while attempts to govern through the built environment can be traced back to ancient Greece, to comprehend contemporary models of urban governance it is to the 'liberal cities' of the nineteenth century that we must turn.⁹⁴ During this period, much of the Western world saw a paradigm shift in the way that cities were experienced, understood and intervened into. The disordered masses of dwellings, businesses, roads and public buildings that had been growing organically, irregularly and inefficiently came to be seen as something that could, and should, be worked upon. The key impetus for increased intervention into the built environment was the rapid industrialization which drew people to towns at a rate never seen before. At the forefront of the Industrial Revolution, Britain is often used as the paradigmatic example: between 1773 and 1821 the total number of houses in what would come to be referred to as the 'shock city' of Manchester grew from 3,446 to 17,257.⁹⁵ Leeds and Birmingham were not far behind. These new cities struggled to cope, as neither the political not the structural infrastructure had been designed for this huge and rapid influx of residents. The lack of planning regulations meant houses were densely packed with little ventilation or sanitation, and working class areas became hotbeds of disease with influenza, tuberculosis and cholera rife in the most deprived districts. To Victorian bourgeois sensibilities, sanitary and moral order influenced one another and the squalor within which many of the working classes lived was seen as contributing to incest, crime, drunkenness and other behaviours symptomatic of moral decay.⁹⁶

In order to combat this, the city was incorporated into the realm of governance, it became subject to a range of initiatives designed to generate 'knowledge' about the city which were considered to lead to a new expertise of the city, 'a *savoir*' of city government'.⁹⁷ The city began to be conceptualized as a 'social body' which could be cured of its ills if it were subject to examination, diagnosis and appropriate treatment.⁹⁸ This 'treatment' was strongly informed by the idea that acting on the urban fabric of the city would be akin to acting on the subject itself. A strong literature has identified the ways in which this was translated into interventions into the built environment: the widening of roads and the installation of gas lamps would improve conduct by bringing the inhabitants of the city into the public, and official, gaze; the grand architecture of the civic institutions would inculcate a respect for knowledge and a will for self-improvement among the working classes; the high visibility of disciplinary institutions such as the workhouse, the gaol and courthouse would serve as constant incentives for orderly, moral behaviour; the development of spaces such as the park or the public square that functioned both as 'omniopticon', where being 'seen' would enhance awareness of one's comportment, and as spaces of emulation, where one could observe and seek to mirror the manner, dress and behaviour of one's 'betters'; the inculcation of ideas about hygiene, privacy and the connection between cleanliness and morality through the management of the circulation of water and sewage; the enforcement of moral self-control through bans on loitering, public drunkenness and 'indecent' behaviour and language.⁹⁹ As Huxley explains, this arrangement of the city is not just about control but about 'fostering the exercise of liberty and choice on the part of autonomous political subjects'.¹⁰⁰ Research on governmentality in contemporary Western cities reveals how the use of new technologies of government, in both senses of the word, is underpinned by similar rationalities. Beckett and Herbert, for example, explore the use of new social control measures to exclude the socially marginal from public spaces in the United States and find them to be part of a broader extension of state surveillance and spatial regulation which constitutes a means of enacting segregation and exclusion in the urban environment.[101] Zuckerwise uses the concept of governmentality to unpick the rationalities behind shifts in official policies around prostitution in early twenty-first century Amsterdam and highlight the technologies used to enact them.[102] Meanwhile, Vanolo reveals how the development of 'smart cities' in Italy have created a 'new geometry of power relations' which places governance of the urban environment in the realm of technology rather than politics.[103]

As Otter explains, just as the technocrat is able to exploit the apparent objectivity of statistics or maps, governing through the built environment facilitates the creation or consolidation of an apparently free society, 'running according to its own laws and patterns [while] the leviathan socio-technical intervention maintaining it remains hidden'.[104] The built environment thus came to be understood as a medium through which particular behaviours and sensibilities could be inculcated and conduct could be conducted. The building of sewers, widening of roads, installing of street lights, civic spaces, public parks and town halls that were part of this process have thus come to be seen not as practical, neutral features of the urban environment but as technologies of government, tools in a wider cache of techniques, practices and processes designed to shape subjectivity, to mould both the individual and the collective into an ideal subject and which are continually countered, challenged and resisted.[105] Vanolo's work updates this for the twenty-first century, revealing how the benchmarking and statistics that reduce individual cities to the single numbers used to rank them neutralize the idea of the city as a single entity, rather than as an assemblage of actors. Furthermore, building on Rose's work on advanced liberalism, he demonstrates that the indicators used to classify and rank cities are a discipling technology, hiding behind the apparent objectivity of league tables and charts.[106]

Yet cities are not comprised solely of passive objects that can be acted upon and governed through. Attempts to rationalize the city and its population are continually challenged by the self-governing actors who inhabit them. Cicchini, for example, reveals how attempts to develop the 'regime of visibility' through numbering houses in late eighteenth-century Geneva were challenged through the nocturnal erasure or covering up of the numbers by residents.[107] Legg highlights how despite the careful mapping and measuring of overcrowding and congestion in Colonial Delhi in the 1930s and 1940s, protests, petitions and downright refusal to be moved thwarted top-down attempts to ease these urban problems.[108] Similarly, Rosol traces resistance to proposed developments in contemporary Vancouver.[109] To Foucault, this contesting of the 'conduct of conduct' through 'counter-conduct' is immanent to governmentality.[110] It hinges on an understanding of power not as domination, as something that is possessed by the state and exercised by its composite institutions on the passive, inert individual, but rather as plural and relational, existing as the 'multiple relations [...that...] traverse, characterise and constitute the social body'.[111] As these relations are met by resistance, a tension which develops as the balance of power is negotiated, power 'produces things, it induces pleasure, forms of knowledge, produces discourse'.[112] It is this positive, productive view of power that posits the individual as a locus of both freedom and resistance, and it is this freedom and capacity to resist that all forms of liberal governance, including post-authoritarian governance, seek to shape.

2

Difficult heritage in Berlin and beyond

As mentalities of government shift and develop, so too do the technologies of government which are employed. Of all of these, those deployed in the built environment are particularly tangible and have significant potential to endure. The city is therefore constituted by layers of multiple attempts to govern through it. Rather than functioning as static, passive, inanimate repositories of history, these traces are in continuous interaction with one another and with the present – while urban designers can choose how they respond to the urban fabric they are presented with, their work is inevitably shaped in one way or another by what was there before. Even when much of a city has been reduced to rubble, as was the case with Berlin in 1945, features such as underground sewer systems and gas lines, existing street patterns and the remnants of buildings influence the processes of reconstruction.[1] While a new system or regime may deliberately attempt to erase the legacies of its predecessors and write over the top of them, traces of the past prevail. In Berlin, where the governmentalities behind the different uses of the built environment have varied to a great extent, this layering process is particularly pertinent. In his analysis of this, Germanist and literary theorist Andreas Huyssen conceptualizes Berlin as a palimpsest, as a 'disparate city-text that is being rewritten while previous text is preserved, traces are restored, erasures documented'.[2] The analogous potential between the palimpsest, a piece of parchment from which the original text has been erased so that it can be reused, and the built environment is clear and has, indeed, been used elsewhere.[3] The salience of the layering process in Berlin, however, makes its application to that city particularly appropriate as is exemplified by sites such as the three analysed in this book.

Each successive occupant of the former Aviation Ministry, Olympic Stadium and Tempelhof Airport used the material fabric of that site as a surface on which to publicly and overtly proclaim the new political direction of that regime and to provide a commentary on the regime(s) that went before it, yet at each apparent historical rupture, continuities persisted which challenged each successive regime's attempts to appropriate and rewrite the sites.[4] All three buildings were incorporated into National Socialist propaganda as evidence of the power and confidence of that regime.[5] However, despite conscious determination to convey power through this supposedly bold and assertive rewriting of the city, none of the buildings was constructed on a tabula rasa and all of them were heavily shaped both by the building styles and techniques that were in use before 1933 and way the land was used before their erection. Aesthetically and technically, Bernd Nicolai, Professor of History of Architecture and Conservation sees all three sites as examples of 'frozen modernism' adapted for National Socialism from the late Weimar Republic.[6] In his analysis of the original construction of the Aviation Ministry in 1935 on the site of the Prussian War Ministry, Matthew Philpotts highlights the continuities that persisted across the 'rupture' that the National Socialists claimed it represented; Sagebiel's adherence to the existing street layout strongly influenced the footprint of the building he designed; the five-storey height matched that of the buildings it replaced meaning the contours of the area were not dramatically altered; a green area within the site was preserved.[7] At the Olympic Stadium, continuity is most evident in stadium's sunken form. This echoes the design of March senior's stadium which was, in turn, a response to the need to avoid obstructing the view of the racetrack which had been at the site first.[8] Traces of the early stadium still remain at the site, in particular, the main entrance which stands on what is now Jesse Owens Allee and the tunnel entrance with its courtyard which is today named the Marchhof, after the architect.[9] March also made a conscious effort to maintain a connection with the German landscape through retaining some elements of the former woodland, such as old pine trees and the arrangement of newer green spaces, throughout the complex.[10] As the second airport to be built on Tempelhofer Feld, the position and form of Sagebiel's construction were shaped by the need for a smooth transition from the use of one to the other. Furthermore, his original plans needed to be curtailed because they would have necessitated the demolition of a celebrated group of apartment buildings constructed by Bruno Möhring in 1910.[11]

After the 1945 surrender, property of the Third Reich was confiscated by the victors and the authority of all German government agencies was passed to the occupying powers.[12] The Allied Control Council issued an order for the removal of overtly National Socialist symbols such as swastikas and inscriptions from buildings. This process, referred to as *Entnazifizierung* by Winfried Nerdinger, led to a public de-nazification of the buildings by their new inhabitants but also to subsequent criticism on the grounds that it meant Nazi constructions such as these could be reused without real engagement and that less overt images and symbols remained in situ, unchallenged and without commentary.[13] Throughout the Cold War each site would go on to become inscribed in different ways by the highly politicized narratives of that time. Unification in 1990 did not, however, create an immediate rupture for any of the sites – at Tempelhof and the Olympic Stadium things would carry on as they had for a while and the former Aviation Ministry underwent a minor renovation for its new occupants, Treuhand, but the impact of unification on each site would take years to be realized. By this point, the layers at each respective site had become interwoven and a significant part of the subsequent engagement with each of the sites would go on to involve unpicking the layers, identifying, labelling and classifying them in order to determine the appropriate response to each of them.

Architecture in the Third Reich and divided Germany

The issue of dealing with the built legacies of National Socialism is not, of course, limited to these sites nor to Berlin. Within the Nazi regime, architecture came to be seen as having the capacity to function as 'words in stone', able to bypass cognitive reasoning and act directly on the senses and emotions of those who encountered it.[14] Fancying himself as an architect despite his lack of formal training or technical understanding, Hitler actively participated in judging competitions for tenders to design high-profile buildings and would intervene throughout the design process. He was keen to project the image of himself as an architect; praise from pre-eminent architects for his sketches and ideas circulated through the media as did photographs of him side-by-side with architects, scrutinizing plans and models.[15] Yet to Robert Taylor, he was a 'dilettante', an 'amateur sketcher of imposing monuments' who focused on their visual impact rather than on how they could be erected.[16] For the realization of his ideas he relied on architects such as Paul Troost or Albert Speer who either shared his predilection for bombastic public buildings or were willing to cater to it.

Hitler's preference for monumental, stone-clad and neoclassical forms and his public expressions of distaste for the 'Bolshevik' or 'degenerate' modern styles associated with the Bauhaus school are well known.[17] However, to speak of a Nationalist Socialist architectural aesthetic is an oversimplification as from the outset the Nazi elite was divided over what the new 'National Socialist style' should be. Barbara Miller Lane identifies four key factions among the makers of official architectural policy: those wishing to invoke the traditions of the German middle ages through neo-Romanesque styles; those wishing to deploy neoclassical forms to represent eternal values; those wishing to reflect the rural character of National Socialist society through *Völkisch* styles; and those wishing to emphasize the newness of the regime with a revolutionary modern aesthetic. Miller Lane finds that rivalries between these factions as well as the prevalence of personal patronage led to a confused and inconsistent building policy and meant that buildings of all of these styles continued to be constructed in the Third Reich.[18] Indeed, high-profile government buildings and prestige projects such as the Nuremberg rally grounds or the House of German Art in Munich were expected to both reflect and perform aspects of National Socialist ideology through their form: their monumentality was to both represent and consolidate the power of the *Führer* and the subjugation of the masses; neoclassical features such as rigid symmetry and columned arcades were to evoke the mythical connection between the Third Reich and the ancient civilizations while the permanence of the regime was expressed through the stone façades. However, the desired aesthetics even for buildings such as these shifted over time. When Speer became General Building Inspector in 1937, for example, he oversaw a move away from such rational architecture and, at around the same time, Hitler's speech at the opening of House of German Art in Munich advocated a turn towards a 'new neoclassicism' which saw a move away from the stone-cut sculptures which had adorned prestige buildings in favour of bronze.[19] Furthermore, many of these ostensibly neoclassical buildings used modern construction techniques and materials and incorporated aesthetic features commonly associated with modern architecture. Throughout the Third Reich, buildings with different functions had other specifications. Industrial buildings, for example, which continued to be built using modern construction techniques and materials and to openly display characteristics of the officially proscribed *Neue Sachlichkeit* or 'new objectivity', were incorporated into National Socialist propaganda as evidence of the technological advancement of the regime, while *Völkisch* features such as pointed roofs were preferred for residential properties.[20] Scholars have also challenged any notion that the forms that emerged in the Third Reich were specific to Germany. Matthias Donath, for example, points out that neoclassicism was a trend across Europe in the interwar period, particularly in the 1930s and that it should not necessarily be considered antithetical to modern architecture but as a current within it.[21] Ultimately, we cannot speak of a single, specifically National Socialist aesthetic: as Jakob Straub and Andreas Fecht explain, 'The uniformity of the architecture was, above all a uniformity of propaganda, not of style.'[22]

While analyses of Nazi buildings are not generally framed in terms of 'authoritarian governmentality', the National Socialist interventions into the built environment tend to be recognized not as passive, neutral, material projects but as playing a role in the active performance of authoritarian governance. Hitler's antipathy towards much of Berlin's built environment has been well-documented; in a distorted echo of Victorian ideas of a link between moral health and the urban environment, he explicitly linked the chaos, disorder and 'foreignness' he perceived in the urban landscape with the decadence, disorder and immorality he perceived in its inhabitants.[23] This is a theme that Linda Schulte-Sasse has identified in National Socialist films whereby Berlin's cosmopolitan side is portrayed as being in 'a state of disintegration and debasement that needed to be overcome by National Socialism'.[24] In his plans for the construction of the new *Welthauptstadt* (world capital city) of Germania, Hitler wanted the chaos and disorder of Berlin swept away and replaced with clean lines, rigid symmetry and axiality and vast, monumental proportions. Urban forms he admired and wished to emulate were those of imperial Rome, Haussmann's Parisian boulevards and Vienna's Ringstrasse.[25] Characterized by vastly proportioned historicist architecture, the nineteenth-century reshaping of Paris and of Vienna are often considered in conjunction with one another, their prioritization of the 'free circulation' of people, vehicles, light and air held up as examples of the ordering of, and through, space.[26] While Hitler identified in these cities elements that he would incorporate into Germania, he also planned to 'improve' on them, making his version bigger, more monumentally proportioned and even more concerned with the ordering of, and through, the space of the city.[27] Taylor suggests that Hitler's ideas about power and architecture may have been influenced by the writings of Viennese architect Gottfried von Semper who claimed that monumental architecture helped to direct and control the 'apathetic, restless masses'.[28] Whereas Vienna and Paris are both products of attempts to govern indirectly through the built environment, Andrew Webber finds that Hitler planned to 'subject the city, and by extension the state, to the idea of a totalised disciplinary space'.[29] Indeed, Brian Ladd finds that while Hitler's and Speer's designs for the reshaping of Berlin 'shared the technocratic rationality of all modern urban societies', it differed from the majority of these in that they had the power to impose their extensive remodelling on an existing large and complicated city.[30] As Paul Jaskot demonstrates, the oppressive nature of these monumental Nazi prestige buildings is not only a result of their aesthetics or their impact on public space but also a result of the way in which the stone for later buildings was obtained from forced labourers in SS-controlled concentration camps.[31] Although Hitler's ideas were never fully realized, the presence of features in the urban landscape of Berlin such as the *Schwerbelastungskörper*, the vast concrete cylinder created to assess the feasibility of constructing Hitler's planned triumphal arch on Berlin's sandy ground, continue to attest to the very real intention to bring these plans to fruition.[32]

After 1945, the divided Berlin became the frontline in the Cold War between East and West as each side sought to use their part of the city as a showcase for the social, economic and political principles that defined their system. The status of East Berlin as capital of a confident and affluent GDR was proclaimed through high-profile flagship architectural projects such as the bombastic and monumental Stalinallee (begun in 1951) and the ultra-modern television tower (begun in 1965) while perceived symbols of imperialism such as the Hohenzollern palace were destroyed.[33] In the centre of East Berlin, the highly visible presence of state institutions in the area around Marx-Engels Platz was designed to attest to the centralism and hierarchy of state socialism.[34] In West Berlin, the first major architectural project was the building of affordable mass-housing complexes in the centrally located Hansa Quarter. In sharp, and highly considered, contrast to the monumentality of Stalinallee, the modernist, non-axially aligned combination of low and high rise buildings was acclaimed by Western politicians as embodying the freedom, individuality and non-authoritarian order of West Berlin.[35] In neither state, however, was there a clear, enduring consensus on a particular architectural style through which it would be best represented. In the early years of the FRG, modernism, with its associations with Weimar democracy and self-effacement, came to be widely conceptualized as the architectural style that most clearly expressed a rupture with the Third Reich. Deborah Ascher Barnstone traces the emergence and gradual proliferation of 'transparency ideology' whereby the use of glass in government buildings, such as Schwippert's 1949 *Bundeshaus* in Bonn, came to be equated with political transparency and thus with the embodiment of democratic values.[36] The preference for modernism was challenged with the arrival of post-modernism in the 1970s and the ensuing 'Architects' Debate' which brought into the public domain debates over the extent to which the form of any building has the capacity to render it inherently 'fascist' or 'democratic'.[37] Nonetheless, the equation between physical and political transparency endured and would go on to shape both the debates around government architecture in the Berlin Republic and their outcomes.[38]

In the early days of the GDR, modernism was openly disparaged by Soviet and East German officials. It was portrayed as indulging the whim of the individual architect rather than providing the population with the architecture it required in terms of adequate living, working and social spaces and in representing a 'national character'.[39] The resultant favouring of the *Nationale Tradition*, which was influenced by Stalinist Moscow and by eighteenth and nineteenth-century German architects such as Gontard and Schinkel, however, began to give way in the 1960s as the leadership of the GDR sought to show off the modernity and technological advancement of the 'future-oriented' East Germany.[40] From the 1970s onwards, this new-found embrace of modernism ran in parallel with a range of neo-historical building projects such as the reconstruction of the *Nikolaiviertel* which formed part of post-*Ostpolitik* attempts by the GDR to reclaim German history.[41]

Difficult heritage

The built legacies of National Socialism and the GDR, along with remnants of dictatorial regimes or traces of atrocities around the world, can constitute 'difficult' heritage for future generations. Sharon Macdonald explains that what she labels 'difficult heritage' is that which is recognized as meaningful but which is contested and may exacerbate social division. Alongside South Africa's Robben Island and Argentina's Parque de la Memoria, examples she cites include the locations associated with the Khmer Rouge in Cambodia, the Gulags in Russia, slavery in the United States and the Holocaust in Europe. She finds that while there is evidence of local specificity in determining what constitutes 'difficult heritage' and how it should be treated, there are parallels between the responses developed to such sites around the world. These connections are seen in shared ideas about the impetus to mark and remember atrocities; activities, campaigns and memorial strategies developed elsewhere; and an awareness of international perceptions and possible impacts on tourism, investment or international standing.[42]

Given the gradual emergence of a general public acceptance that Germany should acknowledge and confront its Nazi past, as well as the complexities surrounding the legacies of the GDR, it should come as no surprise that Germany has produced more memorials, museums, debates, art works and texts about its difficult heritage than any other country.[43] A vast academic literature has emerged which scrutinizes how responses have been developed at places ranging from high-profile sites such as major concentration camps and the Nuremberg Rally grounds to less prominent places of torture, persecution or resistance such as Grafeneck Euthanasia Centre in Baden-Württemberg and the site of the 1943 Rosenstrasse Protest in Berlin.[44] Given the high concentration of National Socialist and GDR remnants in Berlin and that city's centrality to both regimes, a significant proportion of this scholarship focuses on Berlin. This will be explored later. Notable exceptions to this include the contributions to Gavriel Rosenfeld and Paul Jaskot's edited volume *Beyond Berlin* and a range of in-depth studies of single sites or localities across Germany.[45] These highlight the significance of the specificity of place in shaping responses to 'difficult heritage', revealing the impact of different local histories before, during and after the Nazi regime, the range of permutations in the relationships between local, national and international actors and institutions and the plurality of economic, social and cultural conditions across a single nation. In bringing together a range of such studies, Rosenfeld and Jaskot are not only able to identify trends across Germany, such as a broad shift from selective memory to a wider culture of remembrance in the 1980s, but also to reveal variations that challenge attempts to situate diverse cities within a single narrative. A key example of this is the lack of correlation they found between the extent to which a city could be said to be 'burdened' by its association with National Socialism and subsequent of levels of engagement with its difficult heritage.[46]

This level of variation across Germany does, inevitably, beg the question of how representative a study which focuses primarily on Berlin, such as the one undertaken in this book, can claim to be. The answer is, of course, that this depends upon what the study seeks to uncover. Identifying the 'official mnemonic consensus' which has 'found its physical embodiment in Berlin', Rosenfeld and Jaskot set out to explore regional variations in its realization.[47] The aim of the study in this book, however, is to focus on the emergence of this apparent consensus and the rationalities behind it. It will seek to uncover the processes through which it has been established and mediated and the ways in which it has been, and still is, continually challenged, adapted and renegotiated. For this it makes sense to look at where these processes and the challenges they encounter are at their most overt, at the city where the responses to 'difficult heritage' are the most self-conscious and pronounced: Berlin.

Making sense of Berlin

As Germany tried to pull itself into one cohesive whole after unification, the traces of the attempts to reshape Berlin during the Third Reich and the GDR led to widespread feelings that using Berlin as the capital city was not conducive to assuaging international and domestic fears that a unified Germany would lead to a resurgence of German nationalism. There were fears that the move would 'revive images of German megalomania' and 'awaken mistrust and worry about German unification amongst European neighbours'.[48] Norbert Blüm (CDU) expressed his concerns about the move to such a 'domineering' capital in his speech to the Bundestag on 20 July 1991, the day the issue was voted on. To Blüm, relocating to Berlin would undermine the Europeanization and domestic decentralization that are hallmarks of a modern nation-state and that Germany had been striving to achieve.[49] Peter Conradi (SPD), however, anticipated that the move to Berlin would 'accelerate' the growing together of the two German states.[50] Many others embraced the idea that moving to Berlin would bring about a confrontation with all aspects of German history which would finally enable Germans to come to terms with the past and to reinscribe the city with a new meaning.[51] After an 11-hour debate with over 100 speakers, it was decided by a narrow margin of 338 to 320 that Germany's institutions of government would move from Bonn to Berlin within 4 years.[52] Once this had been settled, a raft of new decisions needed to be taken about how the capital of the united, democratic Germany should be constituted.

The subsequent negotiation of the built environment of Berlin has generated a vast scholarship which approaches the city's redevelopment, reshaping and rebuilding from a range of disciplinary perspectives. A substantial portion of this takes, as its starting point, questions around the nature of memory and the role the built environment plays in simultaneously communicating and structuring a society's relationship with its past. Highly influential in the development of our understanding of forms of memory that can be shared by multiple individuals and passed down through generations is the work of Maurice Halbwachs. Introducing the term 'collective memory', Halbwachs highlighted the representation and mediation that underlines even individual memory processes whereby 'no memory is possible outside frameworks used by people living in society to determine and retrieve their recollections'.[53] Another valuable contribution to the scholarship has been the work of Jan and Aleida Assmann, particularly the distinction they draw between 'communicative' and 'cultural' memory. The former refers to varieties of memory based on everyday communication and is thus characterized by a 'high degree of non-specialisation, reciprocity of roles, thematic instability and disorganisation'. Significantly, communicative memories have a limited temporal horizon of approximately 80 to 100 years. Cultural memory, on the other hand, is maintained through 'that body of reusable texts, images and rituals specific to each society in each epoch, whose cultivation serves to stabilise and convey that society's self-image' and can thus be transmitted across generations.[54] The idea that societies construct sites 'where memory crystallises and secretes itself', has strong links with Pierre Nora's celebrated work on *lieux de mémoire*.[55] Nora finds that the impetus for this comes from the breakdown of traditional communities and rituals as a result of globalization and mass-media. This has led to a 'commemorative vigilance' around traces of the past that we fear history will soon 'sweep away'.[56] Despite the connotations of the word 'lieu', Nora is not referring only to physical places or even material objects but to the range of entities which are of symbolic significance to a particular community. His famous cataloguing of French *lieux de mémoire* demonstrates their diversity: they range from *La Marseillaise* to the Eiffel Tower to a widely read children's book *La tour de la France par deux enfants*.[57] A German equivalent of Nora's project, *Deutsche Erinnerungsorte*, coordinated by Etienne François and Hagen Schultze, highlights the challenges to German memory culture by its 'burdened past'.[58] This three-volume work encompasses an even more diverse range of 'sites' than Nora's and incorporates chapters on Hitler's bunker, Auschwitz, the Berlin Wall and the Stasi alongside those on the Grimm Fairy Tales, Goethe and Bavaria's Neuschwanstein castle.[59] While these ideas do not provide the dominant framework through which Berlin's built environment will be explored in this book, they certainly contribute to it. In facilitating analysis of the structuring of a society's relationship with the past and the instrumentalization of this for the legitimization of the present, this literature addresses a fundamental element in the formation of subjectivity and is thus key to developing an understanding of governmentality.

Analyses of Berlin which have been informed by memory studies have highlighted the contingent nature of the memorial landscape. In seeking to explain why some events and people come to be memorialized and others do not, scholars such as Rudy Koshar and Jennifer Jordan reveal the complex interplay between the multiple factors and actors that bring this memorial landscape into being. A particularly useful framework to emerge from this is Jennifer Jordan's identification of 'four forces' which contribute to the success of a memorial project: the involvement of influential 'memorial entrepreneurs'; public resonance; public ownership of the land; and land use which is compatible with memorialization.[60] Other studies of memorialization such as those by John Czaplicka, Anna Saunders and James Young have shown that controversies extend not only to the question of who or what should be marked in the urban fabric of the city but also to the form that a particular memorial should take.[61] A further significant body of work demonstrates that the relationship with the past is consciously and overtly shaped not only through the construction of memorials and plaques but also through responses to its built remnants. The contests around the treatment of the traces of the GDR have featured prominently in this literature which explores the renaming of East Berlin streets, removal of memorials, demolition of key GDR buildings and other ways in which the legacy of the GDR is shaped through selective interventions into its built environment.[62]

Another significant strand of scholarship has highlighted the continuation of the rhetoric that underpinned the Architects' Debate of the 1970s in West Germany which connects some architectural styles and feature with democracy and others with fascism. Prominent within this area are works such as that by Deborah Ascher Barnstone and Wolfgang Pehnt which explore the impact of this politicization of the aesthetic on the discourse around the housing of the political institutions of the Berlin Republic in the new capital city.[63] Closely related to this is the work by scholars including Elke Heckner and Michael Hebbert who have highlighted the 'selective memory' involved in attempts to unify the city through the evocation of a 'mythological past' that predated both the Third Reich and German division through the Critical Reconstruction of the inner city in a style inspired by Berlin's nineteenth-century appearance.[64] This can be understood in conjunction with the work by social and architectural historians such as Tilmann Buddensieg, Wolfgang Schäche and Brian Ladd who have situated the current renegotiation of the urban fabric of Berlin within a much broader historical narrative, tracing the attempts by different regimes to mould the city to project a desired image of themselves.[65]

In the German language in particular, there is a strong thread of those such as Eva Schweitzer, Harald Bodenschatz, Friedhelm Fischer and Engelbert Luetke-Daldrup who consider the more practical side of the problems and possibilities presented by unification to urban planning – namely, how to suture two halves of a city that had been growing apart over forty years back into one, coherent whole. Issues at stake include the questions of how to (re)establish a functioning infrastructure, how to (re)create a city centre which can function as a focal point for the city and how to determine where the new government institutions should feature in that city.[66] This is complemented by work from urban and social geographers and urban planners such as Claire Colomb on the 'staging' of Berlin – the construction of a particular image for the city that would attract tourists and investors and the attempted moulding of Berlin's physical fabric to make it realize and perform that image. Under the CDU-dominated Grand Coalition of the 1990s this was seen in attempts to reconfigure the city as an economic powerhouse through the building of large corporate headquarters on Potsdamer Platz.[67] Under the subsequent Red-Green (1998) and Red-Red (2001) coalitions, the focus shifted to the marketing of the 'poor but sexy' Berlin to the creative industries.[68] Closely linked to this are the cultural geographers and urban sociologists such as Karen Till and Bastian Lange who have taken a more anthropological approach to exploring Berlin's built environment through their engagement with bottom-up appropriations of 'left over' spaces.[69]

To a large extent, this vast and multifaceted literature on post-unification Berlin addresses the social, cultural and institutional aspects of political life overlooked by Foucault and others in their exploration of advanced liberal democracy in post-war Germany. What is missing, however, is the explicit recognition that the diverse objects of study within this literature, whether they be tangible memorials and buildings or intangible policies and campaigns, are invariably elements of the multiple different frames that structure, and are structured by, subjectivity. They shape our experience of, and interaction with, the past, with authority and with society meaning that our subjectivity is informed both by and in opposition to these structures. Not, of course, as simple and top-down technologies of governance but through being constituted in relation to those technologies. They are all sites, both physical and discursive, where the prevailing dominant narratives are asserted, consolidated or challenged. This is particularly true given that the literature tends to focus on the very points where tensions, conflicts and disruptions reveal the dynamic nature of these structures, helping us recognize the interconnectedness of these seemingly disparate objects of analysis and to create a more rounded picture of governmentality in post-unification Germany than the existing, market-centric analyses.

Part 2

Plurality? Performing post-authoritarian governmentality at the former Aviation Ministry

Introduction

Conveniently located between the site of Hitler's bunker and the Topography of Terror, the former Aviation Ministry building (Figure 2.1), now home to Germany's Federal Finance Ministry, features on most walking tours of Berlin. Approaching from the direction of the bunker and standing on the pavement diagonally opposite Sagebiel's monumental construction provides visitors with the best vantage point from which they can start to appreciate the scale of the building. However, it is often not until they proceed to walk alongside it to reach their next destination that its seemingly interminable length and the unrelenting austerity and monotony of its grey stone façade become apparent. Built between 1935 and 1936, the colossal Aviation Ministry was one of the first National Socialist prestige buildings to be completed. Housing over 2000 offices and stretching for an entire city block, Ernst Sagebiel's vast stone-clad building is situated on the corner of Wilhelmstrasse and Leipziger Strasse, at the heart of Berlin's traditional government district. Older buildings such as the Prussian War Ministry or privately owned buildings were simply demolished to make way for the new edifice while the Prussian *Herrenhaus* (parliamentary upper chamber) was incorporated into the new structure (Figure 2.2). The 'tremendous speed' of the construction, the 'enormous dimensions' and the 'huge significance' of the building were lauded in the National Socialist architectural press, as was Sagebiel's apparent refusal to conform to the pre-existing street pattern.[1] This reordering of a city quarter was portrayed as being part of the 'far-reaching' and 'brave' decisions the new regime had taken in recent years and public acceptance of this was billed as evidence of popular 'confidence in [the] new era'.[2] Furthermore, the building's function as Aviation Ministry was a clear statement of the new regime's flouting of the Treaty of Versailles and determination to re-establish Germany as a military power. This was quite literally written onto the building itself through the inscription of a quotation from Adolf Hitler celebrating the re-emergence of the Wehrmacht on the interior wall of the entrance hall (Figure 2.3).

Despite its many modern features which have been discussed at length elsewhere,[3] Sagebiel's austere construction bears many of the hallmarks one would associate with a National Socialist prestige building: its monumentality, grotesque proportions, limestone cladding and axiality are all intended as clear expressions of the indomitable power of National Socialism. Following its completion, the building was not merely used as a symbol of Nazi power but also as a place from which elements of Nazi brutality and repression were coordinated. Given Göring's prominent position in the Third Reich, his Aviation Ministry building proved to be a key site in the National Socialist administration. As well as being the location from which the Luftwaffe's bombing raids, including that of Guernica, were orchestrated, it also hosted meetings at which key decisions about the persecution of Germany's Jews were made. In the aftermath of

42 Plurality? Performing Post-Authoritarian Governmentality

Figure 2.1 The main entrance to the German Federal Finance Ministry, formerly the National Socialist Aviation Ministry, the headquarters of the Soviet Administration in Germany and the GDR's House of Ministries. Building: Ernst Sagebiel (1935–6).

Photograph: By author.

Figure 2.2 Construction of a colossus.

Photograph: Köster, undated photograph (no, 542). Bundesarchiv Berlin R/ 4606 / 3776.

Figure 2.3 The re-emergence of the Wehrmacht.
Photograph: Köster, undated photograph (no, 908). Bundesarchiv Berlin R / 4606/3782.

the Night of Broken Glass, it was here that Göring met with Heydrich, Frick and others and agreed the Jews should pay for the damage themselves and planned many of the measures that would accelerate the exclusion of Jews from German society.[4]

The building incurred some damage during the war but was not beyond repair. Given the urgent need to house the organs of the post-1945 administration, Soviet Major General Barinow ordered work to begin on repairing 'buildings of extraordinary importance' including the former Aviation Ministry as early as June 1945.[5] On 11 August 1945 he issued a further order that stipulated that, in order to ensure the continued operation of the eleven government departments in the Soviet Occupation Zone, they would be moved into existing buildings. As the former Aviation Ministry was so large it was to house six ministries: The Departments for Agriculture; Trade and Supply; Industry; Post and Telegraph; Energy and Fuel; and Transport.[6] From 1947, the Soviet Military Administration in Germany (SMAD) also used the building to house the German Economic Commission. Founded in 1947, this was the main administrative body of the Soviet Zone, and any remaining German organs of state within the Soviet Zone were subordinate to it until it was disbanded on 7 October 1949 with the founding of the GDR.[7] The GDR's inauguration ceremony took place in the former Aviation Ministry's Great Hall. By this point, the swastikas and eagles had been removed and were in the process of being replaced with symbols more appropriate to the new regime. The building continued to house several different government ministries, thus earning the name 'House of Ministries'. On 15 June 1961 Walter

Ulbricht used the building's Great Hall to deliver his infamous assurance to the world's press that 'no one intends to build a wall'. Just two months later, the first permutation of the Berlin Wall was constructed so close to the building that its southern edge actually jutted into the death strip.

After unification, the building was used as a Berlin office for the Federal Finance Ministry while it was still based in Bonn, and to house (Treuhand) Treuhandanstalt, the body set up to deal with the state-owned assets of the former GDR. Seeking to make the former GDR's debt-ridden, technologically inefficient and often heavily polluting industries competitive in a global capitalist economy through rapid privatization, Treuhand's interventions tended to end to result in closures and lay-offs. Trade union figures estimate that unemployment, which had been virtually unknown in the socialist state, reached 3.1 million in the former GDR in 1993.[8] In addition to the economic impact on the former citizens of East Germany, this had wider social repercussions including widespread feelings of bitterness and dislocation within the new Germany. Treuhand thus came to be seen by many former East Germans as an agent in the FRG's 'colonization' of the former GDR and was the target of protests and demonstrations by East Germans and by West German trade unions.[9] Treuhand's president Detlev Rohwedder, a vocal advocate of privatization, was the focus of many of these protests. On 1 April 1991 Rohwedder, was assassinated in an attack believed to have been carried out by the Red Army Faction. In 1992 the building that had been Göring's Aviation Ministry, then the SMAD headquarters, then the House of Ministries was officially renamed the Detlev Rohwedder House in his honour. The building in which the GDR was founded thus came to be named after the man that many of its former citizens associate with its dismantling, adding another layer to conceptions of the erasure of the traces of the GDR's use of the site which will be explored in the coming chapters. Having been heavily incorporated into the propaganda and administrative apparatus of the Third Reich, the Soviet Military Administration and the GDR, the building was at the centre of post-unification debates around the future of the legacies of dictatorship. This prominence meant that it was subject to a particularly decisive, public and extremely self-conscious response after 1990, one that thus has the potential to give us a strong insight into the rationalities of government in the early years of post-Wende Germany.

When it became clear that the German capital would return to Berlin and that the Federal Finance Ministry would be housed in the former Aviation Ministry, that building functioned as a physical space at which the need to negotiate the tension between fostering and delimiting plurality became apparent. Leaving such a site open to interpretation, allowing people who encountered it to engage with it as they saw fit was considered wholly inadequate, akin to an attempt to ignore or shy away from both the building's history and the wider National Socialist and GDR past. On the other hand, the imposition of a monolithic response to the past, one that silences all alternative interpretations and experiences, would jar with the acceptance of heterogeneity and plurality that differentiates the Berlin Republic from the Third Reich and the GDR. An approach to the building needed to be found which would negotiate these two extremes; the site's otherness needed to persist but responses to it needed to be structured.

The three chapters in this section will focus on three elements of the intervention into the former Aviation Ministry: renovation, memorialization and the negotiation of in/exclusion. In doing so, it will highlight the challenges presented by seeking to impose order on to a site while being seen to embrace its plurality and heterogeneity. The first chapter begins at the point when debates over the most 'appropriate' way to deal with the built legacies of dictatorship were raging, highlighting the multiple possibilities that were open for the site's development at that point. Of the three sites considered in this book, however, this would be the one subjected to the most rigorous ordering process. In tracing how the possibilities for the site's development were gradually closed down, the chapter will both destabilize any conception of the current state of the building as having been inevitable, as being the logical endpoint of a rational, objective process and highlight the tension between the celebration and delimitation of plurality which characterized the site's post-unification development. It will show that public pronouncements that the renovation would preserve the site's plurality were undermined by the designation of many traces of the GDR's use of the site as unworthy of preservation and that the disproportionate removal of the remnants of that regime further challenged the presentation of renovation as an objective, rational process. In exploring the end product of this renovation, and responses to it, it will demonstrate that, although painstakingly carried out and characterized by multiple, very self-consciously developed challenges to the original aesthetics of the site, the physical intervention was not considered to go far enough in making post-unification engagement with the past visible. The following chapter will then move on to look at a more overt structuring of a relationship with the past through the commemoration of Harro Schulze-Boysen, who worked in the Aviation Ministry and was executed by the Nazis for his resistance activities, and the demonstrations of 17 June 1953 which culminated at the House of Ministries before being brutally suppressed. Analysis of how these respective memorializing narratives are manifested at the site and the processes by which they came to be constituted in this way will highlight not only the dynamic and contingent nature of the memorial landscape but also the ever-shifting parameters that determine the scope within which that dynamism and contingency can exist. The third and final section of this chapter will analyse attempts to re-encode the relationship between the state and citizen expressed by the building's spatial configuration. It will focus on a range of strategies employed to enhance impressions of the building's accessibility including changes to the physical form of the building, the inviting of citizens inside for open days, tours and other events, an art project installed at the gates of the building designed to give passers-by a glimpse behind the scenes and a video on the Ministry's website. In exploring the various methods undertaken to demonstrate that the political institutions and the political process, of the Berlin Republic, are considerably more accessible than those of the Third Reich or the GDR, it will show that this access is still strongly delimited and that while the technologies of exclusion may be more subtle, they are still in operation. Unpicking the interventions into this site will reveal that even where plurality appears to persist, it has been contained by the wider structuring frameworks within which it was created. Yet, as absolute ordering is not possible in the lived city, there are still gaps which expose the limits to these frameworks.

3

Traces of National Socialism and the GDR in the 'mirror of German history'[1]

'I find it impossible that a German government ministry is housed in this building. It simply radiates its Nazi atmosphere'.

'I find it highly commendable that buildings like this, which are so pregnant with history, can be used in such a way'.[2]

Nicely juxtaposed on a single page and surrounded by remarks about tax and welfare and expressions of thanks for enjoyable visits, these comments left in the German Federal Finance Ministry visitors' book in 2005 neatly encapsulate one of the thorny debates that arose in the months and years following German unification: Should the government of the new, democratic and united Germany reuse the buildings of their Nazi or Socialist predecessors?

Having been used by core elements of the administrative apparatus of both the Third Reich and the GDR, the first debates over the future of the former Aviation Ministry challenged its very existence: Could such a building be incorporated into the built fabric of the capital of the new Germany? And if so, how should it be reconfigured in order to make it an appropriate structure in which to house a democratic government institution? Determined that the formal ending of the anomalous division of Germany should usher in an age of normalization, Building Minister Schwaetzer and other Bonn politicians were keen to emphasize Germany's break with the past and thus called for the demolition of buildings 'contaminated' by National Socialism or the GDR.[3] The former Aviation Ministry was at centre of their attention. For Schwaetzer, a building so tainted by its previous occupants and by its aesthetics had no place in a democratic Germany.[4] This view gained support from fellow FDP politicians, most notably Foreign Minister Kinkel and Minister of Education and Research Möllemann as well as Interior Minister Seiter (CDU) who branded the building a 'musty hulk … burdened by its associations with the Third Reich and the GDR that ought to be demolished'.[5] This view was not universally accepted, however; Berlin Building Senator Nagel condemned what he referred to as a policy of 'coming to terms with the past with a wrecking ball' while Thierse, deputy leader of the SPD, scoffed that, following such logic 'we might as well bomb Unter den Linden'.[6] Highlighting some of the tensions within Germany's federal structure, demolition was particularly vehemently opposed by the Berlin State government and many Berliners to whom it seemed that Bonn politicians were seeking to make Berlin 'a copy of Bonn in terms of buildings and way of life' and that 'without regard for cost, history or urban design it is the will of Kohl's cabinet that the wrecking-ball be swung in the city centre'.⁷ Those in favour of preserving the building saw a need to engage in a critical dialogue with the inherited burdens of such sites, believing that the only way to indicate a true rupture with the past was to publicly demonstrate the ability of the new Germany to acknowledge and come to terms with that past. This could best be achieved through re-appropriating problematic buildings, illustrating that freedom and democracy now inhabit spaces once dominated by repression and terror.

Although a significant force in German politics, the emotive power of memory politics must be reconciled with the rationality of liberal governance – with economic pragmatism, functionality and existing regulatory frameworks. The Federal Cabinet therefore commissioned a leading West German architectural firm, Hentrich-Petschnigg and Partner (HPP), to assess the economic viability of renovating the building as well as two other 'burdened' buildings: the former Nazi Reichsbank and the GDR's *Staatsratsgebäude*. Although HPP reported back that 'with certain limitations' renovation of the former Aviation Ministry would be possible,⁸ its fate seemed sealed when, on 17 December 1992, demolition was provisionally approved. However, reflecting the plural and competing nodes within Germany's official power structure, the Berlin State government vehemently opposed this decision. Challenging the notion that the HPP report should be accepted as an impartial, objective representation of fact, it commissioned architectural consultants Bodenschatz, Geisenhof and Tscheschner to carry out their own assessment of the building.

In declaring the former Aviation Ministry and other former National Socialist buildings which had been earmarked for demolition 'first rank listed buildings' and 'worthy of preservation',⁹ the resultant report called into question the conclusions produced by HPP on two grounds. First, it questioned HPP's actual findings, contending that they were unclear on several details pertaining to the cost and feasibility of demolition and rebuilding, that they had failed to address the historical and architectural significance of the buildings and that they had overlooked the recent practical experience of those who had used the buildings since unification.¹⁰ Secondly, it questioned the foundations upon which the research had been conducted by highlighting the 'limited brief' that HPP had been given, which focused primarily on the economic viability of renovation.¹¹ Making explicit the potential for politicians to influence supposedly independent research by framing the brief in a particular way seriously undermines perceptions of the neutral, objective production of knowledge by experts. It signifies that the experts themselves do not necessarily need to be consciously complicit in the instrumentalization of their work but that their findings will be shaped by the framework within which they are operating, thus exposing the contingency of one of the cornerstones of legitimacy in advanced liberal governance. Rather than reducing the discussion to one of hard facts and figures, the involvement of experts simply highlighted the scope for questioning the production of knowledge in the Federal Republic.

The debate was ultimately resolved when Kohl replaced Schwaetzer with Klaus Töpfer. Considering economic and practical issues as well as memory politics, Töpfer capped the cost of the move at 20 billion deutschmarks and decreed that, following extensive renovations to bring the buildings up to the desired standard, most ministries would be relocated to existing, rather than new, buildings. As a result, 90 per cent of the ministries would be housed in old buildings, most of which would be in Mitte.[12] Among these, the Foreign Ministry would move into the former Reich Bank, the Labour Ministry into the former National Socialist Ministry of Popular Enlightenment and Propaganda, and the Finance Ministry into the former Aviation Ministry.[13] HPP was commissioned with carrying out the renovation for the former Aviation Ministry's new inhabitant; the Federal Ministry of Finance. As well as bringing the ageing building up to the functional and legal standards required of a modern office, the renovation would also address the physical traces of the building's past, (re)configuring them in order to make them appropriate for the present. This renovation therefore provides us with a means by which we can study the formulation of the Federal Republic's official response to its past.

Renovation

This renovation would, however, be complicated through the 1996 addition of Sagebiel's construction to the protected monuments list due to its 'special significance' and 'architectural and historical value'.[14] As a result, any alterations to the building would need to be in compliance with the rules surrounding its new protected status. This would be overseen on behalf of the Office of Monument Preservation of the State of Berlin (the Berlin *Landesdenkmalamt*) by Pitz and Hoh Werkstatt für Architektur und Denkmalpflege GmbH, an architectural practice specializing in historic preservation. The building's listed status would have a profound impact both on the process through which the renovation was carried out and on its final outcome. Just months after the building was on the verge of demolition, a painstaking process began which would produce reams of correspondence and meeting minutes within which everything from the appropriate shades of paint to the safest cleaning products were deliberated.[15] According to the Office of Monument Preservation's regulations, regardless of its connections with the Third Reich and the GDR, the former Aviation Ministry was to be treated no differently to any other protected monument. The principle 'preserve rather than replace' underlined the renovation and the emphasis was placed on maintaining both the building's original materials and its 'feel'.[16] This latter point would prove problematic in the attempt to make the former Aviation Ministry appropriate for use in post-Wende Germany. First, by limiting the scope of any changes to the building and, secondly, by coming into conflict with the plan to preserve its multiple layers.

Renovations of other Nazi buildings such as the Reich Bank, the Berlin Olympic Stadium and the Congress Hall at the former Nazi Party rally grounds in Nuremberg have seen their austerity and monumentality countered through the use of glass, steel and modern features.[17] Early discussions around the development of the former Aviation Ministry building had also included suggestions for subverting, or at least softening, its dominating and exclusionary appearance. However, many of the ideas that were mooted were considered to contravene the building's listed status and were thus disregarded. These are discussed in more detail in Chapter Five. Instead, the renovation team decided the former Aviation Ministry's association with dictatorship would be challenged through preserving its multiple layers and thus ensuring that its complex history be made legible to the public.[18] As such, it would provide a 'visual aid' for critical and self-critical reflection.[19] This extremely self-conscious negotiation of the traces of previous uses of the site is in line with interventions into the building carried out since its original construction. Philpotts looks at the layering that occurred at two earlier moments of what he describes as the site's 'cultural-political appropriation'; the building of the monumental Aviation Ministry within the historic government quarter of Berlin under the Third Reich in 1935/6; and the design and installation of Lingner's 1953 Socialist Realist mural which is discussed later. He shows that despite both of these attempts to use the building as a public demonstration of 'rupture and new beginning', persistent traces of the past continue(d) to interfere with, and undermine, the total claims of the respective regimes.[20] Clear parallels are identifiable in the discourse that surrounded these two points in the site's history and that which surrounded the post-Wende decision to move the Federal Finance Ministry into the former Aviation Ministry. At all three moments, the rhetoric focused on the physical, highly visible (re)appropriation of the site, (re)inscribing and (re)shaping it as an expression of the new direction of each respective new regime. However, at all three moments the persistent traces of the past strongly interfere(d) with and influence(d) the reshaping. Unlike at the previous points in the site's history, however, engagement with these traces after unification did not primarily focus on their erasure and removal or on covering up and masking them. Instead, the renovation can be seen as a very conscious attempt to 'halt' temporality at the building, to look at the traces and layers which had already accumulated and to go back and attempt to reorder them in a manner 'appropriate' for the present. In doing so, however, that process is in turn part of the layering process, an expression of how the past has been (re)presented in the early days of the Berlin Republic.

The remainder of this chapter will explore two aspects of this approach to the renovation. It will begin by highlighting the subjective nature of renovation by unpicking the consequences of the assertion made by Pitz and Hoh that post-war alterations, including those from the GDR or post-unification period, would be reversed only when they were judged to be of no heritage value (*Denkmalwert*).[21] It will then address the renovation as a whole and show how, through the conscious and explicit decision to 'allow' plurality to persist, the nature of that plurality shifted. Rather than traces of the past remaining in the building by default, their continued presence and possible restoration became instrumentalized and incorporated into the use of the site as part of an overt expression of the present's response to the past; yet the complexity of the building, the impact of external factors, such as funding and the building's listed status, and the range of public responses meant that in reality the imposition of this ordering was not so simple.

Subjective renovation

Before a strategy for approaching the renovation could be developed, the building itself needed to be made known; its features and surfaces measured, counted and numbered;

its structure and materials interrogated, their durability and quality analysed. These new, highly detailed insights into the building and its strengths and flaws were then mapped and sketched, generating a whole new representation of the former Aviation Ministry. The reducing of a building to its bare facts and figures means it takes on the appearance of a neutral, apolitical entity subject to a rational process carried out by objective experts. Yet now that the former Aviation Ministry was entering an accelerated state of flux, a whole range of possibilities opened up. Rather than being at the start point of a journey along a set trajectory towards an inevitable endpoint, the site's development was to be the product of myriad factors which would inform the decisions taken at each juncture of the renovation process.

The scope for interpretation in the renovation process is apparent from the above statement from Pitz and Hoh regarding the removal of elements of the site judged to have no heritage value and echoed in other official commentaries on the renovation.[22] The question of value is, of course wholly subjective; who would be judging this value? And by whom would something have to be valued for it to be deemed worthy of preservation? It transpired that many of the traces deemed to be 'of no heritage value' were those of the alterations made to the building's interior under socialism. Just as in the 1990s, these changes had been carefully orchestrated by the political decision-makers of the day in order to mark the re-appropriation of the building and the new political direction that its occupants would take. Following the removal of National Socialist symbols and inscriptions immediately after the war ended, the redecorating of the building's interior was designed to reflect the contemporary style of Stalin's era through the filling-in of the rounded coffering of the entrance halls, the addition of sleeves around the tops of the pillars in the Northern Hall and the complete remodelling of the Great Hall in order to diminish its 'stern heroism'.[23]

In many cases, the post-unification renovation team removed or reversed these socialist additions and alterations: the layers of paint which had been added to the wooden panelling of the Small Hall, for example, were removed to expose the original panelling which was then restored by hand;[24] the Great Hall, the room in which the GDR was inaugurated, was returned to its appearance in 1946 during its brief use by the Soviets and the stage was removed;[25] and the façade is all that remains of the canteen added as a glass extension to the rear of the building in 1960.[26] The official explanation is that the traces left by the GDR were 'generally low quality and poorly thought through [and therefore] undeserving of preservation'.[27] Here we can see how the interpretation of the building's listed status challenges the idea of addressing the historical sensitivities around the building through preserving its multiple layers; the prioritization of the original fabric and a conception of 'value' as intrinsic to a particular element or feature, determined by its craftsmanship, aesthetics or durability, meant that many of the layers that had accumulated over more than forty years of socialist use were thereby dismissed and erased. This can be seen as indicative of the subjective nature of restoration and led commentators to ask 'did the GDR really leave no meaningful marks on the building? Or is it simply that the present refuses to recognise them?'[28] Comments left in the Finance Ministry's guestbook in 2012 echo these sentiments: 'Are there any traces left of the GDR's use? It would have been nice if the building's use from 1949–1990 was recognisable'.[29] The dissonance between the expressed intention to preserve all layers of the site and the removal of most traces of the GDR echoes the treatment of both the intangible and tangible legacies of the GDR in cases ranging from the changing of street names and destruction of the *Palast der Republik* to the devaluing of East German academic and professional qualifications.[30] Jampol explains how this has been connected to a continuation of Cold War rhetoric around the perceived inferiority of the East German built environment and consumer goods and further exacerbates conceptions that unification had turned into the West's 'colonization' of the former GDR.[31]

One trace of the GDR that was not removed was the brightly coloured mural in the colonnade on Leipziger Straße (figure 2.4). Installed in 1953, this mural won a government-led competition to replace a bronze relief of marching Wehrmacht soldiers which had been affixed to the building during its use by the National Socialists.[32] Designed by Max Lingner, the mural entitled 'the importance of peace for the cultural development of humanity and the necessity of struggle to achieve this goal' comprises a collation of scenes from 'everyday life' in the GDR: a joyful procession demonstrating support for socialism; a young family smiling outside *Stalinbau* apartments; and industrial and agrarian labourers of both sexes cooperating with intellectuals. The replacement of Waldschmidt's militaristic National Socialist relief with Lingner's colourful Socialist Realist mural had been a public, visible and material demonstration of the East German re-appropriation of the building. Demonstrating the significance attached to the mural in signifying the GDR's appropriation of the former National Socialist building, Philpotts outlines the intense scrutiny to which Lingner's work was subjected and the significant involvement of politicians in the design process.[33]

Despite the propagandistic overtones of this idealized depiction of life in the GDR, the mural was designated one of the listed elements of the building and was

Figure 2.4 Socialist realism? Mural: Max Lingner (1953).
Photograph: By author.

painstakingly restored by the post-unification renovation team.[34] It would, however, go on to be incorporated into a memorial composition for the victims of the uprising on June 1953, an event which highlights the brutal, oppressive side of life in the GDR and thus contrasts sharply with the images on Lingner's mural. The precise relationship between the mural and the memorial will be explored in considerably more detail in the next chapter. Here, however, it is worth pointing out that the use of the memorial as a response to the mural has been cited as an example of how dealing with historically problematic places does not necessarily need to be done through demolition.[35] Indeed, through the construction of the memorial, Lingner's mural has been undermined far more thoroughly than if it had been simply allowed to fall into disrepair or even removed. This was not, however, the work of the renovation team and, indeed, occurred long after their work had finished and the Finance Ministry had moved into the building. As shown in the next chapter, it is instead the outcome of a process of negotiation between multiple different actors. The point, therefore, is not that the renovation team made a conscious or deliberate decision to remove the traces of the GDR, it is more that despite all of the rhetoric about plurality, what we see is a real lack of that in key parts of the decision-making process. The initial parts of the discussion about the fate of the building and whether it should be reused or demolished were held in the public domain. After that, however, the detail of the renovation, including the questions over what should be preserved and what removed, was largely determined by experts in committees. As a result, we see that perceptions of 'value' tend more towards material quality and the original fabric of the building. If there had been scope for more plurality in this respect, realized through the incorporation of more voices and thus more differentiated perspectives of 'value', then the end product might have been very different.

Instrumentalization

Despite limitations to its realization, the decision to preserve traces of the site's multiple histories features heavily in the narratives constructed around the site in various officially produced pamphlets, books, tours of the building and the Finance Ministry's website. Through these outlets, the building's historical traces and the renovation process are discussed in various levels of detail. In particular, in two books produced by the Finance Ministry a key theme is the focus on how the historical fabric of the building has been engaged with, which features are original, which are new additions and why.[36] The very existence of such detailed accounts of the renovation in volumes clearly aimed at the general public is indicative of the significance of the renovation in forming part of the present's response to the past. This becomes even more apparent on guided tours of the building where the physical traces of the building's former uses play a key role in the evocation of layering, reuse and re-appropriation. Tours generally begin in the Stone Hall, just behind the building's main entrance, where visitors are given a brief overview of the building's origins, the debates over whether or not it should be demolished or preserved and the renovation. Photographs of the different motifs that have been attached to the back wall at different periods of the building's history are used as a jumping off point from which to talk about the building's temporal layers. After ascending the staircase and being ushered into the Great Hall, visitors are informed that they are now sitting in the room in which the GDR was founded. To enhance the talk given by the guide about the use of the building under that regime, images are projected on to a large screen at the front of the room and audio extracts from key interviews or speeches, including Ulbricht's infamous promise that 'nobody intends to build a wall', are played over the room's sound system. On open days this replication of historic events is also played out in the meeting room now named the Euro Hall, where visitors sit around the large table and listen to the reading of an extract from the minutes of the meeting held in the days after the Night of Broken Glass in which it was decided that the Jewish people should be forced to pay for the damage caused.

As they move around the building, visitors have the chance to appreciate the sheer length of the corridors and the different banister designs, the paternosters, the original door handles and wooden safes and bookcases. Beyond the verbal commentary of the guide, however, these features are not otherwise differentiated from new additions. While the layers are visible they are not necessarily apparent. Beyond highlighting the multiple layers of the site, the tours also provide a platform from which the challenges to the building's original aesthetics can be made explicit. Visitors' attention is drawn to the democratic credentials of the art installations both with regard to their abstract forms which, they are told, counter the heaviness of the rest of the building and to the process by which artists' work is selected for display for periods of four years at a time, chosen not, it is emphasized, by the finance minister but by a committee (Figure 2.5). Through the Finance Ministry's website it is possible to do a 'virtual tour' of the building. Using the keyboard to navigate through the rooms it is possible to click on tabs to access more information about a particular feature.[37] On some of these tabs, such as that attached to the row of pillars in the Stone Hall, the virtual visitor can opt to view photographs of particular spaces or surfaces which show how they were

Figure 2.5 Challenges to original aesthetics.
Photograph: By author.

configured at different points in the building's history. In the case of the Stone Hall, for example, we can see how the rows of pillars looked during the National Socialist use of the building and read about the very consciously designed room sequence which will be explored in Chapter Five.

The overt references to the preservation of many of the site's historical layers means it has the appearance of providing a receptacle within which the legacies of dictatorship can be contained, but this is deceptive: the traces that remain have, in fact, been neatly ordered, regulated and are used as a platform upon which the present and past uses are juxtaposed. The physical traces of dictatorship are thus appropriated by the present, are differentiated from their surroundings, marked out as other and used as a counterfoil for the democratic Berlin Republic and, through this, are discursively transformed. They come to represent not (just) dictatorship but the victory of democracy over dictatorship. Head of Conservation for the Berlin region Jörg Haspel expresses this as he wonders if it might be a feature and a virtue of German democracy that it can actually preserve and withstand such legacies of political architecture and totalitarian history.[38] In a similar vein, art historian Matthias Donath sees the refusal to erase National Socialist heritage in favour of using it as a critical stand point part of the fostering of a democratic community.[39] Not everyone agrees with this understanding of the site, however. Among others, town planner and architecture critic Dieter Hoffmann-Axthelm was vocally critical of this particular strategy for dealing with National Socialist government buildings – first, because it leads to these buildings 'which are as authoritarian as they are banal' being restored 'with a degree of care which is totally inappropriate to the building' and secondly because it avoids the 'real task' of 'responding aesthetically to their aggressiveness'[40]. Others concurred that the painstaking reconstruction had made the building as repellent as it was originally intended to look.[41]

Another expressed fear was that the continued use of the building in its original form might be seen as indicating an 'unbroken continuum' since the 1930s.[42] The renovation strategy did seek to counter elements of the building's forbidding, intimidating ambiance through techniques such as flooding the building with light,[43] adorning the walls with abstract art and breaking up the rigid austerity of the exterior through the asymmetric planting of trees and the creation of paths in the courtyards.[44] These challenges are subtle, however, and, like the layering predominantly, only visible within the building. While the nuances of the approach to the renovation have been heavily written into the discourse around the site, they are only really apparent to people who take a tour of the building or who read about them in one of the numerous printed accounts of the process. The multiple physical layers may now be visible but this does not necessarily mean they are legible without a medium that facilitates their interpretation. To this end, an information board has been installed on Wilhelmstraße which provides an overview of the site's history from its use by the Prussians to the Federal Finance Ministry moving into the building in 1999. Yet this account doesn't connect its uses with its physical layers. As such, the site maintains an appearance of uniformity, rather than heterogeneity. Passers-by could thus be forgiven for seeing the renovation simply as reconstruction, and reconstruction does not necessarily mean engagement.

4

Commemorating opposition to Nazism and to the GDR

Harro Schultze-Boysen and 17 June 1953

On Monday 31 August 1942, Harro Schulze-Boysen was summoned to the foyer of the Aviation Ministry where he worked. Once there, he was arrested by the Gestapo and taken straight to its headquarters, just around the corner at 8 Prinz-Albrecht-Strasse.[1] Along with his wife, Libertas, and other friends and associates, Schulze-Boysen had been involved in a resistance network whose activities included transmitting coded messages containing the sensitive information he had access to as an employee of the Aviation Ministry to Moscow. Unbeknown to the group, named the Red Orchestra by the Gestapo, the messages had been intercepted, decrypted and traced. Over the coming days, 130 people were arrested and tortured under suspicion of being part of the resistance network; at least fifty of these, including Harro Schulze-Boysen and his wife Libertas, were then put to death for spying and treason.[2]

Eleven years later, on 16 June 1953, East German workers gathered outside the same building, now the House of Ministries, in order to present their demands to the GDR's leaders. The next day, many of their number would be killed by Soviet tanks or placed under arrest bringing the only mass uprising to take place in the GDR before 1989 to a brutal and rapid close. Stemming from protests about increases in work quotas from 300 workers on a building site on Berlin's Stalinallee, both the numbers of demonstrators and their demands rapidly grew as they marched towards the House of Ministries in order to present their demands to the government.[3] The next day, as news of events in East Berlin spread via Western radio broadcasts, strikes and further demonstrations took place across the GDR. By now, the demands of the demonstrators had expanded to include free elections, the resignation of the government and lower living costs. In East Berlin the protestors were met by Soviet tanks. There is some uncertainty regarding the death toll that resulted from the intervention of Soviet tanks but it is considered to be at least fifty-five in addition to the 'significant number' sentenced to death and thousands arrested and imprisoned.[4]

The analysis of the renovation of the former Aviation Ministry has shown that the complex and entangled nature of the building's layers hinders and subverts attempts to (re)constitute it as one whose democratic credentials are immediately apparent to a passer-by. Memorialization is, however, different. Rather than seeking to structure a relationship with the building's past by intervening into its layers, the groups and individuals behind the site's various memorials have instead sought to provide a commentary on those layers and highlight elements that they do not reveal by themselves. As a result, an additional layer has been added to the site, one whose primary function is to define the present's response to the building's past. This layer provides us with what Lord defines as a 'space of representation' whereby what is on display is not simply an artefact but the gap between objects and concepts within which we can identify the contingency of that representation.[5] The primary object of analysis of this chapter is therefore not the memorials themselves but the processes through which they came to be in their current state. The structuring of this relationship between past and present is necessarily subjective: Which events should be selected for commemoration? What form should that commemoration take? What relationship, if any, should there be between different forms of memorialization at one site.

Exposing the processes through which the current memorialization of the site came about gives us an insight into a different dimension of the negotiation between the celebration and delimitation of plurality in the Berlin Republic, that of the responses to calls from its citizens. The memorials to both Harro Schulze-Boysen and the 17 June Uprising are both the outcomes of grass-roots campaigns by citizens' groups. At face value, this plays a key role in demonstrating that, unlike under the former regimes where the site functioned as a tool in the imposition and consolidation of a monolithic historical narrative, today it is part of a pluralized memorial culture, one in which the interpretation of the past is negotiated by multiple parties. Through closer analysis, however, we see that this plurality is delimited through wider structuring forces comprised of both the intangible discursive frameworks, which give resonance to particular campaigns, credence to the claims of certain groups and credibility to particular means of representing the past, and of the more overt, more concrete regulatory frameworks such as planning regulations which codify who has the right to decide how public space should be constituted. As such, the tension between simultaneously allowing and limiting plurality is revealed.

As acts of resistance against dictatorial regimes, both the connection with Harro Schulze-Boysen and with the demonstrations of 17 June 1953 could be construed as offering a potential 'redemptive' narrative both for the building and for the German people and, given the brutal punishments meted out to the participants as a consequence of their resistance activities, both acts can understandably be considered worthy of memorialization. Indeed, memorialization at the site has largely coalesced around these two aspects of its history. The commemoration of both acts has, however, been passed through the filter of Cold War memory politics and each has been constituted very differently in East and West German narratives of the past: Harro Schulze-Boysen's alleged connections to communism led to him being celebrated in the GDR and incorporated into one of its core legitimizing narratives as is apparent in Hans Maur's 1971 work in which he explained that, after Schulze-Boysen and his associates were killed, anti-fascists 'unflinchingly continued the fight against war and fascism. Their anti-fascist legacy is being fulfilled in the GDR through the building of a socialist society'.[6] At the site itself, a plaque was installed inside the House of Ministries in 1952 and was supplemented with a display in the foyer featuring documents, photographs and letters produced by the group.⁷ The alleged connections with the USSR meant that the so-called Red Orchestra was treated with suspicion in the Federal Republic.⁸ Conversely, the 17 June uprising was virtually absent from official GDR historical narratives and, where it did feature, it was represented as the work of 'saboteurs' and fascists who had entered East Berlin from the West to try and destabilize the East German state.⁹ In the Federal Republic it was hailed as an indication of East Germans' desire to reject the socialist dictatorship and to be reunited with their Western counterparts and was celebrated as a national holiday, German Unity Day, until unification.¹⁰

Since unification, commemoration of both events has been written onto the fabric of the building but at first glance there appears to be a clear difference in how this has been brought about. The commemoration of 17 June seems to be fairly coherent; it is comprised of multiple elements which refer to one another; it is concentrated at one area of the site; and it is highly visible. Its dominance of public space indicates that this is an officially sanctioned memorial and its neatness suggests that it is the outcome of a highly considered, top-down memorializing process. The memorialization of Harro Schulze-Boysen is much messier and much less visible. Occurring in three areas of the site the multiple points of commemoration should be understood more as a disjointed, uncentred memorialization than as a highly visible, coherent presence. It has the appearance of a bottom-up memorialization, the installation of which has been permitted, rather than instigated, from above. A closer analysis reveals, however, that the memorialization of the two events has more in common than is initially apparent. Both are the outcome of a negotiation process between those seeking to inscribe a particular version of the past onto or around the building and wider structuring forces which both facilitate and delimit this.

Commemoration of 17 June 1953

Dominating the northern end of the building on a route with heavy footfall, the commemoration of 17 June is a highly visible memorializing presence. Situated at the intersection of Wilhelmstraße and Leipziger Straße it is contained within a somewhat ambiguous space which is the end point of a repeated spatial pattern that runs across the front of the building. Formed by a cut-away in the lines of the building, this forecourt originally accentuated the connection with the *Preußenhaus* next door.¹¹ Today, the area's relationship to both the public space of the pavement and the 'owned' space of the building is somewhat unclear; the area is distinct from the rest of the pavement due to the change in surface material which echoes the tones and rhythm of the building, yet a narrow, seldom-used access road actually runs between the building and the square's southern side, while on its western side a neat hedge masks the bike stands that run underneath the row of windows on the side wall of the building's northern wing, both severing the space from the building. The expansion of the memorial composition has, however, increasingly tied the space to the building since unification.

On approaching the square, attention is drawn by a vertical post emblazoned with '17. Juni 1953' and by four large, double-sided story boards which contain information in English and German about the events leading to the uprisings, the details of the uprisings themselves and the aftermath. As the passer-by nears the square they will see a bronze plaque on the wall of the building at the corner of Leipziger Straße and Wilhelmstraße which was installed in June 1993 for the fortieth anniversary of the uprising.[12] Although modest, the plaque is still large enough (56 x 35cm) and, standing at head height at a busy intersection, prominent enough to attract the attention of passers-by. Despite the incorporation of the demonstrations into the discourse of the Federal Republic as an uprising from all sectors of GDR society, the focus of the memorial is surprisingly narrow, referring specifically to 'the construction workers from Stalinallee' who gathered 'in this place' on 16 June 1953.[13] The bulk of the text is used to list their demands: reduction of work quotas, resignation of the government, releasing of political prisoners and free, secret elections. It then goes on to say that this was the 'starting off point of the peoples' uprising of 17 June 1953. We remember the victims'. There is no mention of the scale or nature of the uprising or of the number of victims that it created or, indeed, how it led to the creation of these victims. As the event had featured so prominently in the discourse of the Federal Republic, it is quite possible that such things would be assumed knowledge – that the plaque was therefore designed to function more as a mark of the place where the construction workers gathered than as a central memorial for the quashing of the uprising as a whole. Nearby, set into the ground is an enlarged glazed photograph of demonstrators marching, some with their arms linked together. A small plaque tells us that this installation was designed by Wolfgang Rüppel in memory of the uprising on 17 June 1953. There is a clear connection between Rüppel's memorial and Lingner's Socialist Realist mural which was discussed in the previous section, evident through their perfect alignment and identical dimensions (24 x 3m). This relationship is far from accidental and the means by which it came about is particularly revealing about the power relations involved in the structuring of the post-Cold War built environment.

In the months and years just after the 17 June uprising, memorials to its victims sprung up across West Germany.[14] As late as the 1980s, the German Section of the International Society for Human Rights organized a campaign for the construction of a further high-profile memorial. Following a competition, a jury chose a monumental design by Georg Siebel in which the proposed memorial, made of white stone in the form of a bolt of lightning and a chain of people holding hands with the words '17. Juni 1953' at the bottom, towers over a representation of the Berlin skyline. An image of this was used on a postcard produced in order to request donations to fund the memorial's construction. The text on the back indicates that it is intended as a representation of 'free people' building a 'chain against totalitarian powers who divide. Build it with us by making a generous donation'.[15] The intention had been to erect the memorial in time to mark the thirtieth anniversary of the uprising in 1983. However, in an indication of the shift in East-West relations over the thirty years since other memorials had been constructed, they found that the Senate now rejected the idea of installing such a potentially controversial memorial in a time of détente.[16]

After unification, the idea of marking the quashing of the uprising with a memorial came back into the spotlight with the 1994 decision by CDU and SPD politicians to create a central, national memorial to the victims. From the outset, the development of the memorial was dogged with debates about where the memorial should be located, what form it should take and which groups or individuals should be involved in the decision-making process. The very announcement of the plan to develop a memorial garnered reactions from groups who had long been campaigning for the uprising to be marked in some way. The International Society for Human Rights, for example, sent over the information about their own campaign and the memorial that had been designed through it.[17] However, there was also anger from groups who felt their rightful stake in the memorializing process was being overlooked. In particular, a representative of the builders' union, Bau-Stein-Erden contacted the House of Representatives to highlight the connections between their organization and the builders who began the uprising. He expressed annoyance at not being consulted, especially given that the union had organized a big event in 1993 in which the significance of 17 June 1953 for the builders' union had been emphasized, and urged that this should be remedied as soon as possible.[18]

The politicians themselves became mired in debates about the nature of the memorial. One of the first major stumbling blocks was the question of a suitable location for it, which was discussed in the House of Representatives on 7 March 1994. The CDU and FDP representatives both suggested that the memorial to the Red Army on the Tiergarten was no longer appropriate and that the memorial to the 17 June 1953 should be situated either on that site or nearby in order to highlight the complexity of recent history. They suggested that this memorial should include reference to the protests from within the Soviet Army at the events of 17 June too. The SPD representatives protested that the demonstration did not take place in the Tiergarten and that the memorial should be located in East Berlin. The former Stalinallee, the location where the construction workers first downed their tools and the demonstration began, was posited as an ideal location. The PDS representative was in favour of the installation of a memorial but felt that right location would depend on the particular design of the memorial that would ultimately be erected. On the other hand, Alliance 90/The Greens expressed reticence at the prospect of building a memorial, contending that those affected by the quashing of the uprising would be much better served through intensive research about the GDR and the events of 17 June to ensure they never happen again.[19]

In the meantime, the 13 August Working Group (*Arbeitsgemeinschaft 13. August*), which operates the Checkpoint Charlie Museum, along with survivors of the 17 June uprising and their supporters took matters into their own hands and campaigned for the installation of their own banners showing images of the events of 17 June on the outside of the former House of Ministries. This initiative was supported at the State level by the Berlin House of Representatives but as the building was Federal property, consent from Bonn was necessary. As the building had been earmarked for the Federal Finance Ministry, this would need to come from Theodor Waigel (CSU), then Federal Finance Minister. Correspondence between these levels of government suggests different interests and competing priorities within the federal structure. Dieter Biewald (CDU), the Chair of the Berlin House of Representatives Cultural Affairs Committee, wrote to Waigel to express his support for the installation of the banners. He highlighted the visibility of the site and the potential to enable hundreds of passing drivers and pedestrians to remember this 'important place in German history'. He asked Waigel to grant permission for the installation and for the banners to remain in place until the renovations of the building began.[20] Waigel responded by pointing out the plaque that had already been installed on the fortieth anniversary of the uprising. Furthermore, he emphasized that the building was still in use as an office building and had been designated as a ministerial building and would not be suitable to function as a memorial for several months or years. He did, however, concede that if appropriate permissions were granted by the Berlin Senate, the Borough Council and the Office of Monument Protection, and a contract for the costs of installation, removal and public liability could be agreed, then the banners could be installed for a period of four weeks.[21] The banners were installed but this did not bring an end to the disputes, instead, prolonged negotiations about the length of time the banners would remain on display ensued. The proponents of the banners, supported by the Berlin House of Representatives Cultural Affairs Committee, continually pushed for extensions and these were repeatedly resisted by the Federal Finance Ministry who maintained that the installation was not appropriate for ongoing display for various reasons including that the building was in use, the possibility that it contravened the building's listed status and, finally, due to concerns about public safety. However, following sustained pressure from the citizens' groups, the period for which the banners were allowed to remain was extended incrementally and they remained in place until renovation of the façade began in 1996.[22]

The competition for the official memorial, which would be funded by the Berlin Senate, was launched in 1997. The Berlin Forum for History and Present (Berliner Forum für Geschichte und Gegenwart) reports that, because the events had been understood and instrumentalized differently in the two Germanies, it was deemed important that all parties should have a say in determining the location, form and objectives of such a memorial. They thus invited various interested parties to a symposium to discuss how the memorial should develop. Many of the participants discussed the potential for, and desirability of, a memorial which allowed for plurality and scope for critical engagement and determined that each entrant into the competition should decide themselves where their memorial should be situated. These elements were thus incorporated into the brief for the subsequent competition to design the memorial, a competition that was to be judged by an independent jury.[23] The structuring processes which would delimit this plurality become evident through Anna Saunders' work on the role the memorial plays in 'challenging or concretising Cold War memory narratives'. She outlines how, after the first jury found themselves unable to find a suitable winner, a second jury awarded the commission to Katharina Karrenberg in 1998. In keeping with the brief, Karrenberg sought to use her design to challenge the imposition of a monolithic understanding of the events and of conceptions of 'hero'. The veterans' group 17 June Association, however, vehemently rejected Karrenberg's design and threatened legal action, arguing that it undermined the bravery of the demonstrators and that its location, at the site where the protestors were ultimately defeated, was inappropriate. Their protests attracted the support of then mayor of Berlin Eberhard Diepgen (CDU) and other CDU members as well as large sections of the press. An open letter to the Senate signed by academics, historians and artists demonstrating their support for Karrenberg made little impact and the Senate overrode the jury's decision, refusing to grant her the commission and, in February 1999, giving it instead to second-prize winner Wolfgang Rüppel.[24]

Rüppel's memorial was unveiled in 2000 and this is the installation we see today, the glass photograph on the floor perfectly aligned with Lingner's mural celebrating life in the GDR (Figure 2.6). As if the visual symbolism of Rüppel's design were not overt enough, Finance Minister Eichel (SPD) explicitly described the memorial as a 'counterpoint' to Lingner's mural, stating that now 'real and virtual Socialism stand opposite one another', an enduring message primarily aimed at 'those who lapse into *Ostalgie* and are inclined to romanticise the GDR'.[25] The relationship between the photograph and the mural has also been made clear in the literature produced by the Federal Ministry of Finance: 'The two are thesis and anti-thesis. Each comments on the other; combined they show socialist aspirations and reality'.[26] Rather than serving as a marker of one particular act of atrocity, the memorial is thus construed as an indictment of the GDR as a whole and, indeed, the political and economic ideology upon which it was founded. Instead of the fostering of critical engagement and reflection that the memorial had been supposed to promote, the memorial ended up perpetuating the understanding of the 17 June and, by extension, the GDR, which was rapidly becoming the established paradigm for conceiving of that particular past.

This still did not go far enough for the veterans' group and for some CDU politicians who considered Rüppel's memorial to lack visibility and thus continued to campaign for additional signage and banners so that there would be no space for ambiguity in the present's response to Lingner's mural and to the GDR.[27] To address this, four

Figure 2.6 Rüppel's memorial and Lingner's mural.
Photograph: By author.

information boards were installed in 2007. As well as informing readers about the event itself, one of the boards also explains the history of the commemoration of that event. It strongly identifies Rüppel's piece as part of the present's response to the building's past through situating it within the longer history of the building and through the inclusion of photographs of Waldschmidt's completed relief, in situ in the colonnade, and abstracted details from Lingner's first and third drafts for the mural. After a paragraph about Lingner's mural, the connection between it and the later memorial is made explicit to German readers who are told:

> Diesem propagandistischen Bild stellt der Künstler Wolfgang Rüppel den mehrfach bearbeiteten Ausschnitt eines dokumentarischen Fotos gegenüber. Das Denkmal erinnert an die Ereignisse des 17. Juni 1953 und ist den Aufständischen gewidmet.

English readers, however, are informed:

> The artist, Wolfgang Rüppel, hung this propagandist picture opposite a detail, which had been repeatedly reworked, taken from a documentary photograph. The monument, which commemorates the events of 17 June 1953, is dedicated to the insurgents.

Although the boards seem to have been designed to reduce the any scope for ambiguity around the mural and the memorial, errors in the word order of the translation lead to confusion for English readers. Most significantly, the 'propagandist' appears to refer to Rüppel's work rather than Lingner's mural. While the effectiveness of the content of this board is somewhat undermined by these flaws in its realization, the mere fact of its existence and the form it takes gives the commemoration gravitas; this and the other information boards dominate public space near a government building, indicating they are clearly sanctioned, if not instigated, from above. This impression that they tell an officially supported version of events is enhanced by the high production quality of the boards and the explicit reference to the fact they were financed by the Mayor of Berlin and by the Berlin Senate.

Commemoration of Harro Schulze-Boysen

The memorialization of Harro Schulze-Boysen is not awarded the same prestige. The clearest, most visible reference to him is also on an information board; however, in this case the board is not dedicated solely to him and his resistance activities but instead provides an overview of the history of the building. This board is situated on Wilhelmstraße, not far from the junction with Leipziger Straße but far enough away so that it continues to stand distinct from the growing commemoration of the 17 June. Placed in a recess in the exterior lines of the building, the large (1.8m x 0.7m) self-standing storyboard is not an obstacle to passers-by but is still fairly visible. The overview of the history of the site is written in both English and German and begins with details about its significance in Prussian and Weimar Berlin and ends with the

Figure 2.7 The memorial to Harro Schulze-Boysen.
Photograph: By author.

Federal Finance Ministry moving in 1999. While the resistance activities carried out by about Schulze-Boysen and his colleagues are briefly referred to, there is no mention of his capture and execution by the Nazis.

The memorial dedicated to Schulze-Boysen is located at the southern end of the former Aviation Ministry, affixed to an external wall on Niederkirchnerstraße (Figure 2.7). In German only it says:

Wenn wir auch sterben sollen,
So wissen wir: Die Saat
Geht auf. Wenn Köpfe rollen, dann
Zwingt doch der Geist den Staat.
Harro Schulze-Boysen
2.9.1909-22.12.1942
Glaubt mit mir an die gerechte Zeit, die alles reifen last

There is no explanatory panel accompanying this text, nothing to explain who Schulze-Boysen was, how or, indeed, why he died or that the inscription on the wall is an extract from the final letter he wrote to his parents and a verse from a poem that was found hidden in his cell in the Gestapo prison, signed with his name and dated 1942, the year that he was executed.[28] Aside from his year of death, the memorial gives no indication to those without prior knowledge to suggest that he was in any way connected with resistance to National Socialism. Historical circumstance has had a significant impact upon the configuration of space around the memorial, affecting its visibility and, therefore, its effectiveness. Given that he worked within the Aviation Ministry itself and upon his arrest was taken to the Gestapo quarters across the road, it was decided that the plaque should most appropriately be affixed to the external Aviation Ministry wall directly opposite where the main entrance to the now-destroyed Gestapo headquarters was estimated to have been.[29] The border between the GDR and the Federal Republic would go on to be drawn down that very road, the site of the former Gestapo headquarters (now the Topography of Terror) in West Berlin and the former Aviation Ministry in East Berlin. Today, the second longest remaining stretch of the Berlin Wall continues to run down one side of the street. Consequently, the plaque, as well as having the misfortune of being attached to a wall that people walk parallel to, must compete with the Berlin Wall and the Topography of Terror for visibility (Figure 2.8).

These two references to Schulze-Boysen make a gesture towards fulfilling two very different functions. The board is primarily informative, providing the best key available to the passer-by to help them unlock the temporal layers of the whole site and Schulze-Boysen features as a detail in this wider history of the building. However, there is no personal information about him, no photograph or reference to his fate or anything else that would be likely to generate an emotive response in the reader. The memorial, however, has the potential to be extremely evocative on three levels. First, it highlights

Figure 2.8 The view down Niederkirchnerstraße. The southern wall of the former Aviation Ministry with the memorial to Harro Schulze-Boysen on the left and the Berlin Wall on the right.

Photograph: By author.

the very human tragedy of an imprisoned son writing a final letter to his parents before his execution; secondly, the words themselves show Schulze-Boysen's willingness to sacrifice himself for the fight against fascism; thirdly; they provide a medium through which Schulze-Boysen's sentiments can be communicated to, and possibly inspire, the wider world. The poignant and individual nature of the memorial is increased through its positioning and, as will be discussed below, by the succession of personal dates on which the memorial has been (re)installed and renewed at ceremonies attended by close family members. Yet the lack of contextualizing information robs the memorial of this emotiveness and thus of its potential efficacy.

The installation inside the building draws the two threads of information and of evocativeness together; it comprises three large rectangular display boards suspended from the ceiling. Down the left-hand side of each there is detailed factual information about Schulze-Boysen and Erwin Gehrts, another employee of the Aviation Ministry who worked with Schulze-Boysen in his resistance activities and met the same fate. This text, written only in German, tells us about the backgrounds and family lives of the two men, their resistance activities and their arrest and sentencing to death. In addition to the text, a range of images features on each board. These include personal documents such as photographs of the two men with their families, wives and friends before their arrest, legible images of the handwritten farewell letters they wrote before their executions and of the poem found in Schulze-Boysen's cell after his death. As well as these we see traces of their resistance to the National Socialist regime in the images and extracts from newsletters and flyers that they put together and distributed. These are supplemented with the extracts from the official documentation at the trial at which they were sentenced to death. However, as well as having a limited audience through being only visible from within the Finance Ministry building, the effectiveness of this memorialization is further limited by the use of the space around it. In the centre of the southern wing of the Stone Hall, the display is certainly in a position of optical dominance but the nature of the display, that is the large quantities of text, photographs and images of historical documents, requires the viewer to be standing very close to it and to spend a few minutes there. The organization of space at the Finance Ministry means, however, that visitors are not actually allowed to access the Stone Hall until they have been collected by a member of staff. Until that point they must wait in a small anteroom beside the porter's cabin. This means that by the time the visitor is in the space within which the display is situated, they are already being led elsewhere. The display would appear to be less visible but would conversely be much more effective were it situated in the much less prestigious location of the anteroom itself where visitors awaiting collection would have time to look at it and would perhaps welcome something to read.

Structuring memorialization?

While the memorialization of Harro Schulze-Boysen, situated as it is around and within a government building, has evidently been granted permission from above, it has also clearly been fitted in around existing spatial paradigms. In contrast to this, the commemoration of the 17 June uprising has been allowed to interrupt and rewrite the building's spatial relationship with public space. The difference in status awarded to the two memorialization projects could potentially be explained through reference to the politicization of post-Wende memory narratives. A closer analysis of how the two events came to be memorialized, however, suggests that this does not tell the whole story and that the two have more in common that is immediately apparent. This analysis also reveals how the apparent plurality of the memorial landscape is, in fact, structured by the dominant existing paradigm within which certain groups are able to determine how public space should be constituted and how the relationship with the past engendered by a particular memorial landscape should be shaped. Within this framework, memorial projects which deviate from or detract from the desired understanding of the past can be filtered out through recourse to administrative procedure, often manifested in a refusal to grant funding or planning permission. These structuring processes can be and are continually countered, however, and they must frequently adapt or even yield to such challenges or else risk becoming too visible and strengthening resistance against them.

A fundamental issue is the question of who has the right to speak on a particular topic – whose calls for memorialization will be given credence? While survivors or veterans are generally considered to have the right to speak on how events with which they have such a personal connection should be commemorated, Saunders does not consider the Senate's acquiescence to the demands of the 17 June Association over the Rüppel memorial to signify a concession to a legitimate claim but rather to indicate an overlap in how the veterans and the group of CDU politicians wished to see that particular past represented.[30] Where this overlap does not occur, the structuring frameworks are challenged and tested when memorial entrepreneurs take memorialization into their own hands and operate outside of those dominant frameworks. The citizens' initiative, the Berlin Bridge Association (*Verein Berliner Brücke*), for example, installed the first incarnation of the current external memorial to Schulze-Boysen 'without permission' in December 1992 on the fiftieth anniversary of his death.[31] This memorial was removed, some say 'stolen', by unknown individuals in 1993.[32] A provisional replacement with the same text was installed on 26 July 1994, what would have been Harro and Libertas Schulze-Boysen's fifty-eighth wedding anniversary. Although this version of the memorial had not been officially approved due to the tight time frame,[33] it was marked with a ceremony which included speeches from siblings of Harro and Libertas.[34] The Federal Finance Minister did, however, endorse the re-installation of the plaque on 20 November 1994, what would have been Libertas Schulze-Boysen's eighty-first birthday.[35] The installation of this plaque was followed by a service in the chapel in Schloss Liebenberg where the couple had married and the renaming of the chapel as the 'Libertas Chapel'.[36] The final, officially sanctioned, version was erected in 1995.[37] This persistence signifies a rejection of the idea that any one group should have the power to determine how public space and the memory landscape should be constituted and a sustained effort to compel that group to adapt to their demands. While this attempt was ultimately successful, the Berlin Bridge Association continued to challenge the boundaries; in 1996, on what would have been the couple's sixtieth wedding anniversary, an additional plaque was erected for Libertas Schulze-Boysen, again without official permission, at a ceremony attended by her brother Johannes Haas-Heye and her brother-in-law, Hartmut Schulze-Boysen.[38] At this point, the structuring processes were reinforced as the authorities demanded the removal of this unauthorized memorial. The transparent plaque, which bore an extract from a poem Libertas Schulze-Boysen had written while in custody in 1942, was subsequently moved to the chapel in Liebenberg where Libertas and Harro had married.[39]

The citizens' groups campaigning to make the memorial to 17 June more visible have also brought about compromise through resorting to unorthodox methods. Having found Rüppel's memorial to be too inconspicuous, the Working Group 13 August, with support from Alexandra Hildebrandt, director of the Checkpoint Charlie Museum, renewed their campaign to increase the visibility of 17 June at the site. In 2003, the fiftieth anniversary of the uprising, they again installed banners on the exterior of what was now the fully operational Federal Finance Ministry. In an echo of the 1994–6 disputes, the campaigners again rebutted repeated requests from the Federal Finance Ministry to remove the banners, arguing that they were necessary as a further response to Lingner's mural.[40] This very public clash represents an uncomfortable conflict between two forms of legitimacy in the Federal Republic: that of the survivor or the family members of victims of a particular event to have a say in how that event is commemorated versus codified regulatory frameworks such as a building's listed status and public planning directives which expressly prohibit such activity. When tensions reach this point the structuring forces become visible as they strive to assert themselves. Ultimately, administrative procedure won out and a court order for the removal of the banners was issued on 20 June 2005.[41]

This may have quashed one particular challenge but, in triggering a demonstration at the site by the 17 June Association, it gave rise to another. Reiterating Hildebrandt's claim that Rüppel's memorial was not sufficient and that without the banners the commemoration of 17 June was not visible enough, the leader of the Association, Carl-Wolfgang Holzapfel, began a spontaneous hunger strike outside the Ministry building.[42] The blog of the 17 June Association explains that Holzapfel's nine-day hunger strike ended when CDU General Secretary Frank Henkel and politician Roland Gewalt (CDU) expressed their support for renaming the square to commemorate the demonstrations.[43] The square was renamed *Platz des Volksaufstandes von 1953* on the sixtieth anniversary of the demonstrations. The event was also marked by a temporary exhibition comprised of large boards attached to the inside of the columns of the arcade within which Lingner's mural is situated. Named 'Wir wollen freie Menschen sein! Der DDR-Volksaufstand vom 17. Juni 1953', the exhibition simultaneously took place in town halls, libraries, museums and other community buildings at over 260 locations across the country.[44] Listing the different elements of the memorial composition – Rüppel's memorial, the information boards erected by the State of Berlin, the temporary exhibition and a planned information panel – the Finance Ministry website tells us that these components 'now counter the idealism of Lingner's mural' and that 'together with the renaming of the square the ensemble will provide a dignified space for commemoration of the events and victims of 17 June 1953'.[45] This statement from the Finance Ministry suggests an expectation, or a hope, that the appropriate commemoration of the 17 June uprising has now been achieved.

The exploration of how Harro Schulze-Boysen and 17 June came to be memorialized at the site reveals the dynamic, contingent nature of the memorial landscape but also the ever-shifting parameters which determine the scope within which that dynamism and contingency can exist. The analysis of both the layers and the memorialization at the site has shown the negotiation of freedom/control and plurality/uniformity in an abstract sense. The next chapter will show how that is extended into the physical through the negotiation of (in)accessibility at the site.

5

Negotiating (in)accessibility at a democratic government building

In addition to responding to the building's layers, part of making the former National Socialist Aviation Ministry appropriate for use by a government institution of the Berlin Republic meant reconciling it with expectations for government architecture in the Federal Republic. To a significant extent, this meant subverting the original aesthetics and symbolism of the building described as having been 'hermetically sealed to the public' while functioning as Göring's Aviation Ministry.[1] One strategy for 'dealing with' high-profile National Socialist buildings elsewhere has been to develop architectural solutions which counter their original aesthetics. At the former Nazi Party rally grounds in Nuremberg, for example, the glass and steel of Günther Domenig's new Documentation Centre is described in the official literature as a 'stake [...] making a deconstructive slice through the building ... and so breaking [its] monumentality and strong geometry'.[2] Back in Berlin, not far from the former Aviation Ministry stands Wolff's former Reich Bank which now houses the Federal Foreign Office.[3] Since 1999, the former Reich Bank's stone-clad monumentality has been countered through the glass and travertine of Müller and Reimann's extension. The same width as the older building, the airy and modern new addition obscures the Nazi construction when viewed directly from the front and provides an architectural juxtaposition when viewed at an angle. Containing publicly accessible facilities such as a café, and a visitors' centre, the extension has been praised as a 'convincing gesture of democratic renewal',[4] and as a 'modern, metropolitan, appropriate new interpretation' which provides a 'pleasing contrast to the old building'.[5]

The formidable form cut by Sagebiel's Aviation Ministry, however, continues to both isolate and other it in the urban landscape of Berlin; its austere, heavy lines stretch unbroken for the length of an entire block and, where respite is given from the sheer grey stone of its façade, the view is framed by heavy black metal railings that indicate that a speculative visit would not be welcomed. The ceremonial entrance is midway down the Wilhelmstraße stretch of the building, framed by the stone Court of Honour. Still separated from the pavement by a high, wrought-iron fence with two pillars, each of which was once topped with an eagle clutching a swastika in its claws, the Court of Honour is enclosed on three sides by five storeys of stark, grey stone. At one end of the courtyard the building's main doors are recessed into a columned arcade from which they themselves are hardly visible from the pavement, let alone what lies beyond them. Above the arcade is a long low stone balcony which provided Göring and other members of the National Socialist elite a vantage point from which to see and be seen as military parades took place in front of the building. The still discernible grid-pattern in the courtyard's stone floor provided a visual guide for those taking part these displays.[6] Behind the balcony a row of windows, each stretching three storeys high, attests to the grandeur of the Great Hall within. This small insight marks the extent of accessibility that the original fabric of the Aviation Ministry permitted the average passing citizen from this main entrance point; the unremitting regularity of the fenestration around the rest of the Court of Honour provides little indication of the function, or indeed internal layout of the remainder. Encoded into this composition is the exclusion of the citizen, both from the building itself and from the political processes at work within it.

The performance of (in)accessibility

Such outright exclusion of the citizen from a political building does not sit comfortably in a liberal democracy. In his work on the development of the 'liberal city' of eighteenth- and nineteenth-century Britain, Joyce identifies a far more nuanced and complex approach to the negotiation of (in)accessibility in state architecture which becomes, he argues, 'a direct representation of the troubled relationship between authority and freedom in liberalism'.[7] His analysis of the physical manifestation of this tension in the architecture of the nineteenth-century town hall provides an interesting reference point from which the (in)accessibility of the former Aviation Ministry can be explored. In contrast to the symbol of National Socialist power constructed by Sagebiel, the architecture of the town hall was designed to reflect that it belonged to the citizen rather than to the state. The grand entrances were designed to 'initiate a process of invitation' which continued as the visitor progressed through the grand and ornate spaces within the building. Yet the apparent openness of this invitation was deceptive and the town hall was in fact characterized by a 'dialectic of inclusion and exclusion'.[8] In shaping the post-authoritarian liberal city, the government of the Berlin Republic is faced with the dual task of establishing its own particular balance of inclusion/exclusion and recoding the built legacies of the Third Reich to express it.

To a significant extent this meant subverting the original aesthetics and symbolism of the building. The exclusion of the citizen is written right through the fabric of the building, from the stone cladding that has been described as completely 'encasing' the exterior walls and thus emphasizing the 'closedness' of the building,[9] through to the shaping of the space in the building's interior. Just as at the entrance to the nineteenth-century town hall, the visitor's experience as they progress through the building has been carefully designed. Unlike the 'emphasis upon the invitation of the citizen into the building' that Joyce finds is supposed to appear to be extended by the elaborate and ornate lobbies, staircases and halls of the town hall,[10] the Aviation Ministry was labelled by Donath as a manifestation of 'the principle of architectural uncertainty', designed to disorient and thus intimidate the visitor.[11] Donath considers stepping through the gates and into the Court of Honour as the first part of the evocative, powerful room sequence that culminates in the Great Hall.[12] After crossing through the vestibule the visitor would find themselves in the Stone Hall, a large entrance hall in which the rows of pillars and dim lighting appear to have been designed to disconcert and intimidate the visitor while dramatic lighting highlighted the imperial eagle and quotation from Adolf Hitler attached to the back wall of the monumental staircase which is the focal point of the room. After ascending this, the visitor would find themselves at the entrance to the Great Hall within which the dramatic and evocative interior design was continued through the pillars, reliefs, marble-clad floor indirect lighting and, in particular, in the gigantic ceramic imperial eagle which dominated the rear wall. In common with most nineteenth-century town halls, however, the Aviation Ministry's ceremonial entrance was not designed for use by everyday office traffic. At the town hall smaller, less conspicuous entrances were designed to provide access for civil servants and members of the public with municipal business to attend to.[13] Similarly, at the former Aviation Ministry an alternative, less formal entrance is located on the Leipziger Straße side of the building for everyday use. Rather than fulfilling a purely practical function, however, the motif of disorientation and intimidation continues here. As with the main entrance, the Leipziger Straße entrance is tucked into the shadows of a columned arcade, a 'dark zone [which] underlines the heaviness of the building'.[14] Unlike the main entrance, however, the door is not in the centre of the arcade as the axiality and symmetry of the rest of the building would suggest but is instead tucked away in a corner. In keeping with the prevailing narrative that emphasizes the exclusionary properties of National Socialist architecture, Donath finds the positioning of the door to be the first step in another room sequence designed to disorient and thus intimidate the visitor.[15]

In order to reconfigure the interplay of (in)accessibility at the building, its materiality would need to be reformulated. In their 1993 report which made the case for the building's preservation, Bodenschatz, Geisenhof and Tscheschner made several suggestions about how this could be achieved. One such suggestion was that to detract from its functional monotony, the bottom floor of the former Aviation Ministry and whatever building should be constructed opposite be opened up for civic use. Additionally, they recommended that the renovators consider opening up the Court of Honour by removing the fence, reconfiguring the courtyard and introducing architectural accents to break up its stark axiality of the courtyard. They also suggested the addition of architectural accents to the area at the corner of Wilhelmstraße and Leipziger Straße and on the long façade along Leipziger Straße.[16] Yet the signification of accessibility needed to be reconciled with the requirements of the building's listed status and ultimately, this precluded these alterations. Among the recommendations made in their own report into the protected elements of the building, Pitz and Hoh included the preservation of the existing configuration of the Court of Honour and restoration of the fence to its original colour as well as the restoration of the façade to as close as its original appearance as possible.[17] The evocative room sequence was considered to be integral to the building's character and was therefore also to be preserved throughout the renovations. Some concessions were made to the need to convey political change. For example, internal art installations were seen as an ideal way to strike a balance between the 'totalitarian spirit' of the original building and its contemporary 'liberal ethos',[18] as was the idea of flooding the building's interior with light.[19] Official publications about the renovation celebrate the breaking up of the rigid

Figure 2.9 Challenging the building's 'totalitarian spirit'? The view into the gardens from Wilhelmstrasse.
Photograph: By author.

austerity of the exterior through the asymmetric planting of trees and the creation of paths in the courtyards behind the building (Figure 2.9).[20] However, correspondence between the landscape architects and Pitz and Hoh reveals that they had developed more ambitious plans for challenging the building's 'totalitarian spirit' but were constrained by the listed status of the gardens.[21]

The Aviation Ministry's accessibility has been shaped by a combination of the political impetus to increase its appearance of openness, respect for the building's protected status and adherence to contemporary security requirements. Accordingly we see the building's 1930s character has been interrupted by more modern materials and concerns; for example, the original steel doors still hang on the walls in the Court of Honour, protected by their listed status, but they but have no function today as people enter the building through a revolving glass door. As with the layering, the small changes that were made to the building's accessibility were made only following careful consideration by the parties involved in the renovation[22] and were incorporated into the discourse around the building with particular aspects, such as the use of transparent glass and the brightening up of the internal corridors, seized upon as being analogous to the building's new, democratic use.[23] Also in common with the layering, however, these changes are fairly subtle and the vast bulk of the building still attests to the National Socialist relationship with their citizens. In this respect, the renovation of the former Aviation Ministry can be seen as less effective in facilitating critical reflection than that of other former National Socialist prestige buildings which have been challenged aesthetically as well as discursively.

Beyond the performance of (in)accessibility

The appearance of (in)accessibility does not, of course, translate to actual (in)accessibility. Analysing the 'dialectic of exclusion and inclusion' in the actual use of the town hall, Joyce highlights the gap between the 'invitation' indicated through the materiality of the building and the actual level of access afforded to citizens. Entrances were guarded and movement within the building tightly controlled; access to council meetings was by invitation or advance arrangement only and the small size of the public galleries can be seen as an indication that the emphasis was on spectatorship rather than involvement.[24] At the renovated former Aviation Ministry, the appearance of accessibility is just as illusory as the appearance of plurality; the revolving door may be transparent but is designed to slow the flow of entrants to one at a time and, before progressing any further into the building, visitors need to show identification to the porters who sit behind a glass and metal partition.[25] Similar glass and metal security devices have been installed in the Leipziger Straße side entrance.

However, that the (in)accessibility of political buildings is not reducible to the spatial or to the material becomes apparent in an analysis of accessibility at this building. The Finance Ministry makes considerable gestures towards transcending the building's still overwhelmingly inaccessible appearance and granting ordinary members of public access to the building's interior. As well as ad hoc events such as the 'Musik. Zeit. Geschehen' series, groups can contact the visitor service to arrange a guided tour or can attend the 'Open Door Day' at which they can listen to music, talks and interviews, visit stalls dedicated to areas of the Finance Ministry's work and take guided tours of the building. Since its inception in 1999 the federal government's 'Open Door Day' (*Tag der offenen Tür der Bundesregierung*) has become an annual event. For one weekend over the summer the government issues an 'invitation to a state visit' to the general public. Free shuttle buses are provided to ferry visitors between Berlin's fourteen government ministry buildings, the government press and information office and the Chancellor's Office. At each site the visitor can choose to learn more about the work of the particular institution by attending talks and visiting the various stands or can simply enjoy the music and refreshments on offer. This is just one strand of a wider 'open house' initiative in Germany, from the 'day of open mosques' to the 'day of open monuments', a diverse range of institutions open their doors on a semi-regular basis to allow members of the public an insight into areas which they are not generally able to access.

At the Finance Ministry, the opportunity is used to try and counter the inaccessibility encoded into the building's architecture: visitors are ushered into the garden where ministry staff mingle with the throngs of people bustling about the refreshment stands or drinking beer at the picnic tables, creating a relaxed, convivial atmosphere; the bright, colourful bouncy castle provided for the children contrasts sharply with the cold grey stone of the walls behind it; and the music from the bands offering entertainment between the talks and interviews on the stage bounces off the five-storey building (Figure 2.10). Inside the canteen a variety of stalls provide visitors with access to information about themes such as the Euro, taxes, coins and the federal budget. From here visitors can collect a ticket which allocates them a place on a free tour through

Figure 2.10 Bright colours and activities for children at the Finance Ministry's 'open door day'.
Photograph: By author.

the building. As well as informing visitors about the building's history, the tours also give an insight into the rooms that form the backdrop to economic decision-making in Germany: visitors can sit around the table in the Euro Room, occupying the seats of the officials and advisers who negotiate international and domestic economic policy there; in the Great Hall they sit in the rows of chairs used by delegates, facing the podium with the crossed European and German flags and are encouraged to feel that they are gaining an insight into what the political elite who might attend talks there experience; and they can even peek into, but not enter, the finance minister's office.

A less conventional means of countering the inaccessibility written on to the building was attempted through an installation by artist Jochen Gerz at the entrance to the Court of Honour on Willhelmstraße. Comprised of two small screens, one embedded into each gatepost, it was designed so that passers-by could push a button and watch videoed interviews with Finance Ministry employees, all answering the question 'money, love, death or freedom – what counts more in the end?' Gerz explains that his project is concerned with the individualization of the people that work in the building, a challenge to the subjugation of the individual through both the aesthetics of the building and the regimes that occupied it on the past.[26] Yet despite having been designed specifically in response to the severe, alienating aesthetics of that part of the building and to address individual engagement with it, the effectiveness of the project is undermined by a combination of the form of the installation, the materiality of the building and the effect of that on the individual. Given its appearance and position, the screen-and-button combination could easily be mistaken for an intercom and thus seen as something only to be pressed by those who have business at the Finance Ministry. Furthermore, the installation is not particularly visible and those who do notice it and realize its purpose may be unlikely to proactively engage by pressing the button and then stand to watch the video in such a conspicuous and exposed location. Even the literature produced by the Finance Ministry admits 'the button is rarely pressed. The building is evidently still not inviting'.[27] Perhaps as a result of this, further insight into the people working in the building is provided by the six minute-long 'Behind the Scenes' video on the Finance Ministry's website. Showing various employees going about their work in the Finance Ministry and explaining how their role fits into the wider function of the Ministry, the short film was made because 'for many outsiders the Federal Finance Ministry is an unknown place in the Berlin Government district and people know even less about the work that is done there'.[28] The video seems to be designed to fulfil a similar function to that intended for Gerz's video installation. The insight it provides into daily life in the Ministry both normalizes the Finance Ministry and its employees; by starting in the post room the Ministry is identified early on as a generic workplace with systemic and functional communalities with other office-based institutions. As well as seeing staff go about their daily tasks, we see them interact with one another as one would expect of colleagues in any organization, from exchanging pleasantries as they pass in the corridor to communicating on work-related issues. After telling us about their jobs, the employees are filmed as they pose for 'still' photographs, enabling the viewer to see them as they prepare for the shot to be taken. This is an effective way of humanizing the subject – unaware that they are, in fact, being filmed rather than photographed, their guard is momentarily let down and they betray the uncertainty and amused reluctance at being photographed that most people can relate to. As we recognize our own traits in the employees they are endeared to us, we feel we are seeing more of them than a very polished, highly directed piece would give us. In shifting this portal to 'behind the scenes' access away from the physical site and into the virtual realm, conceptions of (in)accessibility are further severed from the spatial.

The video goes beyond the Gerz installation in fulfilling a more overtly pedagogical function. As higher-level staff explain their roles and situate them in the wider work of the Finance Ministry, the video informs people about how the ministry works. Furthermore, as well as seeing behind the scenes of the working office building, the viewer is also given an insight into high-powered events. We are informed that the meeting we are about to see is of the Stability Council (*Stabilitätsrat*) which is comprised of the Federal and Land level finance ministers, but even those with little understanding of the German political structure would be left in no doubt as to the seniority of the people they are seeing as they exit the fleet of black cars that has swept straight to the front door of the ministry building. Here another technique is used that suggests that the video provides us with enhanced access to the inner-workings of the ministry: as well as candid shots of the delegates arriving at the meeting room, greeting one another, reading through the papers and writing on a smart phone, we actually see the photographers taking their pictures. The perspective that we are gaining seems to be from a more privileged position than that which the other photographers are occupying. This enhances the viewer's impression that they are gaining a greater insight into proceedings than would be gained via conventional information channels such as the television or printed news. The video cuts from this high-powered meeting to a group of young people sitting on the steps of the Stone Hall, chatting and taking photographs of one another. We see them take a tour and then go into a meeting with then Minister of Finance Wolfgang Schäuble (CDU) at which he begins to tell them about the importance of the Euro. The students are shown listening intently to Schäuble; the message is clear that these are bright, articulate young people who wish to engage in the political process and that the Finance Ministry facilitates and encourages that engagement. At the very end of the building the viewer is encouraged to engage further themselves by visiting the website for more information.

This valorization of proactive individual engagement which is so characteristic of advanced liberalism runs right through the discourse around accessibility at the site today. As well as the spatial aspect to the Open Door Days, the allowing of the public into physical spaces into which they are not usually granted access, citizens are encouraged to use such occasions as an opportunity to engage with the political process and with the political elite. In her greeting on the flyer produced for the 2013 event, Chancellor Angela Merkel informs the reader that 'if you look behind the scenes of government you can build for yourself a clear image of where and how we work and the goals we pursue'. The impetus here is clearly on the citizen to allow the dialogue to take place. This is continued throughout the flyer – the respective ministries are described as 'offering', 'inviting', 'showing' and 'informing' certain things, in each case, the action is being performed by the ministry but its completion requires the proactive response of the citizen – they must accept the 'invitation' or the 'offer' or allow themselves to be 'shown' or 'informed'. On the government website an article on the Open Door Day reports that guests 'used the opportunity to inform themselves'.[29] Through initiatives such as the Open Door Day, the virtual tour or the 'Behind the Scenes' video, the former Aviation Ministry becomes a space of representation, a stage on which 'good' governance is played out. Here, governmental legitimacy in the Berlin Republic is presented as a two-way street, one in which a 'good' citizen is one who wishes to engage, to seek to inform themselves and to give themselves access to the political process. Just as millions of Victorians would never have set foot in a town hall, millions of Germans will never attend an Open Door Day at a government ministry. The key difference is that in the latter example there are distinct efforts being made to undermine the mechanisms of self-exclusion which might deter particular social groups from seeking to enter sites of power.

Despite the overt expressions of accessibility, however, we see at the former Aviation Ministry the same nuancing of the idea of accessibility as that identified by Foucault in South American farms where, he explains, travellers were granted access to, and accommodation in, certain rooms while being excluded from the living quarters actually inhabited by the family. The visitor thus never transcended the status of 'guest in transit' to become 'invited guest', the apparent inclusion is, in fact, therefore an 'illusion' as within that very space the visitor is simultaneously excluded.[30] An analysis of (in)accessibility at the former Aviation Ministry reveals the site as a space into which visitors are welcomed and indeed actively encouraged but from which they are simultaneously excluded. Yet the binary of inclusion/exclusion that Foucault draws is along a specifically spatial dimension and is therefore not sufficient for exploring the realization of power relations in government architecture. What is key to our analysis is not the question of depth of access but of its regulation. Access to the rooms, whether physical or virtual, does not, of course, equate to access to the political processes that take place there. The insight gained through the video is clearly tightly framed by the director and editors and even on the physical tour the movement of visitors is closely regulated. This is particularly apparent when approaching the finance minister's guarded office door where visitors must put all camera equipment away and are discouraged from lingering by the building staff. Once at the door itself, the exclusionary message conveyed by the rope across the doorway, indicating that visitors should not try to cross the threshold and actually enter the room, is underlined by the presence of security guards. Tours are carefully timetabled around key meetings and conferences and the areas of the building to which visitors will be granted access have all been preselected and cleared of any content that would provide the visitor with any greater insight into the political process than it has been predetermined that they should have. Similarly, although visitors are encouraged to use the opportunity of the Open Door Day to inform themselves about the workings of particular ministries, they will not be privy to information that is unavailable elsewhere in the public domain. The information provided is about the existing political process, about how well it functions and about how citizens can work within the existing system to express their own views. Just as with the tours, the information provided has been selected and framed in such a way that it casts the existing system in a positive light. There is still a significant distinction between the levels of access to both space and information granted to visitors to the building and people who work there. At the former Aviation Ministry, just as at the nineteenth-century town hall, we see the dialectic of inclusion/exclusion that underpins liberal governmentality; the simultaneous appearance of freedom and its delimitation; the impression of plurality and the frameworks that structure it and the gesture of accessibility and its regulation. That this is framed so consciously around the politics of the past enables us to see how these techniques of advanced liberal governance are shaped by the post-authoritarian governmentality within which they operate.

Part 3

Rationality? Negotiating post-authoritarian governmentality at the Olympic Stadium

Introduction

Arriving at the Olympic Stadium on a day when no football match or event is taking place can be an eerie experience. When alighting at S-Bahnhof Olympiastadion, the row of empty platforms jars with the small handful of people who exit the S-Bahn here, attesting to crowds that the site anticipates but which are difficult to visualize. On match days, however, the S-Bahn platform is an extension of the stadium; excitement is palpable as fans in their team colours, interspersed with souvenir sellers and touts, make their way through the bustling crowds towards the entrance to the stadium. Strengthening the connection between the stadium and the S-Bahnhof are the stone columns of the stadium, only just visible over the trees in front.

Most visitors head towards the main entrance, the East Gate. It is upon arriving here that they will first be able to appreciate some degree of the scale and the axial alignment of Werner March's composition: the long rectangle of Olympia Platz is lined with flagpoles, the black bars of the main gate are flanked by two square, stone pillars which frame both the stadium as a whole and its cavernous main entrance. The allusions to ancient Greece and the origins of the Olympic tradition are clear in this neo-classicist construction with its shell-limestone façade and in the almost two dozen sculptures which are strategically positioned across the Olympic Complex. The stripped-back, reduced form of these warrior-like stone athletes alludes to the classic sculptures of the ancient world while also attesting to the Nazi cult of the body and connections between sport and the military. This connection between ancient Greece and the Third Reich is intensified for visitors who know the names of the different elements of the site: The Langemarck Hall, Maifeld, Friesenturm, Frankenturm, and Schwabenturm are intended to lend a 'symbolic geography' to the site in which Greek and Germanic motifs are connected.[1]

Upon entering the stadium area, the visitor is presented with a choice of paths that form concentric circles: that which runs around the outer extreme of the stadium takes the visitor past two rows of squat, stone stelae engraved with the names of German Olympic champions and punctuated with the larger-than-life, muscular forms of Karl Albiker's statues, the Discus Thrower and the Relay Runners; the path along the rim of the stadium itself takes the visitor around the vast structure either beside or underneath its covered arcade, punctuated with square stone columns; finally, the path within the stadium enables the visitor to encounter for themselves the spatial dynamics of a stadium designed to reflect National Socialist hierarchy through the subjugation of the masses and the subsumption of the individual into the collective.

The stadium is just one element of the expansive Olympic Complex. Originally named the Reichssportfeld, the vast, 132-hectare site also encompasses separate stadia for swimming, hockey and horse riding; an open air stage, originally named the

Figure 3.1 Berlin's Olympic stadium.
Photograph: By author.

Dietrich Eckart stage after the anti-semitic writer (1868–1923) but which has since been renamed the Waldbühne; administrative buildings housed in the German Sports Forum; the Maifeld, which was to be used for parades, rallies and mass-demonstrations with up to 250,000 participants; a bell tower; and a memorial to the German youth who lost their lives in the First World War. This, the first such Olympic Complex in the world, is structured around two cross-cutting axes, the dominant one runs from East to West, beginning from at the East Gate, cutting through the stadium via an open section at the back, named the Marathon Gate, with which the bell tower is perfectly aligned (Figure 3.2).

Designed by Werner March for the 1936 Olympic Games, this was not the first stadium on this spot which was once in the heart of the Grunewald forest. Having been designated by Kaiser Wilhelm II as a place to be used for the leisure and enjoyment of the people, a horse racing track was constructed there between 1906 and 1909.[2] In 1913, Otto March was commissioned to add to this by building a stadium in which Germany could host the 1916 Olympics. Named the German Stadium, it had a sunken pitch so that the racetrack would still be visible from the stands, yet due to the onset of war, the 1916 Games were never held. In the 1920s, Otto March's sons Werner and Walter March were commissioned with building the German Sport Forum, set slightly away from the stadium itself; this would house a Physical Education High School to train sports teachers and medical and technical research into sports as well as sports-related administrative offices and sports facilities.[3] In 1931 the success of Germany's bid to host the 1936 Olympic Games was announced and Werner March was commissioned with the construction of the stadium, initially this was to be an expansion of the

Figure 3.2 View through the Marathon Gate and back into the stadium from the top of the bell tower.

Photograph: By author.

existing stadium built by his father. However, when Hitler came to power, he demanded March create something much more monumental which would reflect the power and durability of the Third Reich.[4] As with other such high-profile buildings, Hitler took an active interest in the design of the Olympic Stadium. Referring to the completed stadium as 'our Führer's magnificent creation' following its completion in 1936, Wilhelm Frick, Reich Minister of the Interior, reflected on the meeting on 5 October 1933 in which Hitler had made him and his colleagues aware of his plans to erect an Olympic Complex at the gates to Berlin that would 'reflect Germany's honour and the dignity of the Olympic idea' while also providing a 'splendid and enduring site for the cultivation of German physical education'.[5] In his memoirs, Speer famously claimed that the design March first showed Hitler comprised glass partition walls and enraged Hitler to the point of telling State Secretary Pfundtner to cancel the Games on the grounds that he would 'never set foot in a glass box like that'. Speer goes on to explain that he amended March's designs overnight, replacing the glass with a natural stone cladding and incorporating huge cornices. Speer's alterations allegedly pleased Hitler who agreed to increase the budget to allow for the additional costs Speer's design would entail and the games were held as planned.[6] This account is, however, disputed by historians. In particular, in a 1994 interview art historian Hans-Ernst Mittig dismissed Speer's version as a 'fairy tale' which suited both Speer and March in the post-war climate. To Mittig, Speer was happy to admit to anything that would not cost him his life, and taking responsibility for various buildings would have far less severe consequences than explaining his other activities in Nazi Germany, whereas March's priority was for the continuation of his career after the war.[7]

The Olympic Games opened on 1 August 1936 with great drama and spectacle. Setting the precedent for a tradition that continues today, the world's first Olympic torch relay saw 3,400 torch bearers carry the Olympic flame from Greece to Germany.[8] Reflecting on the Opening Ceremony itself, British football referee Arthur Willoughby Barton, writes in his diary about the experience of marching into the stadium with his teammates as 'the Olympic bell tolls "ich rufe die Jugend der Welt" [I call the youth of the world]; all the flags hoisted on flag poles at the same time'. Hitler, he writes, was greeted with a 'terrific reception' as he entered the stadium to the Horst Wessel song and *Deutchland über alles*.[9] However, despite Nazi efforts to hide the escalating persecution of German Jews and their martial ambitions by portraying this as the 'peace games',[10] the militarism seems to have filtered through as Willoughby Barton recorded in his diary that his team's placard bearer, a 'handsome German of 21 years of age' appeared 'destined to become an army officer.'[11] After the Olympics, the stadium continued to play a role in Berlin's cultural life, even during the war. Each year it hosted between twenty and twenty-five large events such as sports competitions and rallies, held largely as a distraction from the political situation, until it shut in autumn 1944.[12] From 1938, underground areas of the stadium were used as munitions factory by Blaupunkt.[13] However, while the stadium did incur some war damage, particularly from bomb blasts which affected the Marathon Gate and parts of the stands in late 1944, the stadium wasn't fundamentally damaged.[14]

After the war the stadium was part of British-administered Berlin. They initially used it as a sports ground but, because of Blaupunkt's activity in the bunkers, it was designated a military site and temporarily closed for general use.[15] The British established their headquarters in the German Sports Forum in the northern part of the site and this would remain inaccessible to the general public until their departure in 1994. On 12 May 1949 the British handed authority of the rest of the stadium back to the West Berlin Magistrate so there would be useable sports facilities for German citizens. However, on 4 September 1954, this agreement was terminated as the Basic Law stipulated that all former property of the Third Reich was now Federal, rather than State, property. This led to years of conflict between the Federal and State governments but did not impact upon public access to the stadium.[16] In 1963 an agreement was finally signed between the federal government and the State of Berlin which awarded much of the running and decision-making authority to the State of Berlin. However, this wasn't a simple handing over of the site; caveats were put in place to ensure the federal government had oversight of financial matters and the overall use of or alterations to the site.[17]

In the divided Berlin, the stadium continued to play a significant role in cultural and social life. In 1963 it became the home ground of Berlin football team, Hertha BSC, and hosted a range cultural and sporting events. To Donath, many of these either directly or indirectly reflected German politics. These would include church events which would emphasize the unity of East and West Germany, Police Sports Days which were a way of highlighting links between West Berlin and the British, French and US protective powers and domestic football competitions reinforcing the connection between West Berlin and the rest of the Federal Republic.[18]

In 1974 Germany hosted the FIFA World Cup and the stadium was used for some of the qualifying games. The preparation for this involved the updating of the building in order to meet the requirements of a modern stadium. Particularly contentious issues included plans to roof the inside of the stadium and to install floodlights. Having heard about the proposed alterations in the press, Werner March wrote to the Federal Treasury to express his reservations about the roofing of the stadium which would, he argued, ruin the spatial affect by closing up the site's East-West visual axis.[19] March's objections generated a significant amount of correspondence between different Federal departments and between the State and Federal level.[20] Eventually, March's original contract from 1934 was retrieved and consulted in order to determine his rights as the original creator of the stadium.[21] In doing so, the authorities found that the German state did, in fact, have the right to make changes without his agreement and, as they could find no indication that March had sign the contract under duress, it was considered that there was little likelihood of a successful appeal on those grounds.[22] Nevertheless, an amicable solution was preferred by all parties and March ultimately agreed to work with the renovation team to resolve any current problems and to sit on the jury to judge entries into the competition for roof designs.[23]

Despite the continuous use of the Olympic Stadium and various interventions to modernize and maintain it, by the time Germany unified it was clear it required much more intensive renovation and repair. After unification, the impending departure of the British from their headquarters in the northern part of the site and the growing call for Berlin to begin bidding to host high-profile international sports competitions brought the fate of the dilapidated Olympic Stadium to public attention. Much like at the Aviation Ministry, the debates around the future of the stadium were informed by a combination of economic concerns, practical and function considerations and memory politics and so they pitted Berlin sports clubs and those who insisted that Berlin needed a modern sports facility that could compete on the world stage, against those who saw the opportunity to develop a coherent response to this relic of Nazism. Throughout the 1990s, a range of suggestions was put forward for 'dealing with' the Olympic Stadium: adhering to its listed status and carrying out a careful renovation of the site which would include the erection of a new roof; gutting and then rebuilding the interior of the stadium as the so-called *Barcelona-* or *Reichstag-Lösung*; demolition of the existing stadium and building a new one on the same spot, the so-called *Wembley-Lösung*; or building a brand new stadium on the Maifeld.[24] In 1998, Gerkan, Marg und Partner Architekten (gmp) were finally awarded the commission to renovate the stadium in time for the 2006 World Cup. Their design was picked because it would both create a modern stadium and respect its listed status.[25]

Just as at the former Aviation Ministry, the renovation of the Olympic Stadium was carried out with painstaking attention to the preservation of the original form and the retention of authentic materials where possible.[26] Yet while the discussion around the fate of the Aviation Ministry was largely already structured around a demolition/renovation binary when it entered public discourse and left the public realm once renovation had been decided upon, the approach to the question of how the traces of dictatorship at the Olympic Stadium should be dealt with was much more nuanced. Rather than simply addressing the site, and the solutions, in their totality, some elements were identified as more problematic than others and multiple possible ways of dealing with those traces were publicly debated.

This part of the book will explore attempts to make the Olympic Stadium perform post-authoritarian governmentality through reconfiguring it as a site at which objective, evidence-based knowledge counters the legacies of National Socialism. In common with analysis of the former Aviation Ministry it will begin at a point when the possibilities for engaging with the traces of dictatorship were still open; however, rather than exploring debates around the site as a whole, it will focus on those surrounding the site's sculpture collection. Problematized through its perceived embodiments of aspects of National Socialist ideology, the ensemble has weathered calls for the removal, covering up, re-arrangement and 'museumization' of its components. These debates first came to the fore in the early nineties during Berlin's Olympic bid and, having died down when the bid failed, rose up again in the run-up to the 2006 World Cup. The different nature of these two sets of debates, which becomes apparent through analysis of how they played out in the national press, means that we can identify the countering of National Socialist legacies through rational, evidence-based knowledge emerging as a dominant paradigm through which the traces of dictatorship would be dealt. The second section of this chapter consolidates this by showing how, unlike at the Aviation Ministry, the response to the site's temporal layers was not to be inferred from their preservation but to be made explicit and highly visible through the installation of a history trail. Providing a reasoned, methodically researched, pedagogical commentary on the site's past, the trail would be an expression of the Federal Republic's response to the past, one founded upon thorough engagement with the past and framed in terms of rationality and objectivity. However, analysing the actual realization of this reveals a gap between intention and fulfilment; the extent and effectiveness of this (re)ordering of the site was curtailed by multiple factors ranging from pragmatic issues regarding funding to those created by the strength of the original configuration of the site. The third section will, however, show how the complexity of one area of the site, in particular, the Langemarck Hall, in turn challenges our attempts to impose an order on the Federal Republic's response to the past. Analysis of the post-unification renovation of that structure and the exhibition installed there in 2006 reveal this as an area of the space which simultaneously sets up and challenges multiple binaries which both consolidate the 'othering' of the National Socialist layer elsewhere at the site and call that 'othering' into question.

6

Responding to the 'racist cult of the body manifested in stone'[1]

The Olympic Stadium's sculpture collection

Before the official Opening Ceremony of the 1936 Olympic Games, Werner March contemplated the visual spectacle that would ensue once his creation came to life; he envisaged the flags flying against the backdrop of the Olympic Stadium replete with its towers and statues and how all of these features would combine to make a lasting impression on the crowds gathered in the stadium and those seeing it from home via the world's media.[2] This coming together of the different elements of the site was a key part of March's design. The Olympic Complex was not supposed to be reduced to its individual components but experienced as a whole, a *Gesamtkunstwerk*, within which all of the different components worked together to create an overall effect. While the crowds were also considered as part of the design process, this unity between architecture and sculpture would not only be visible during atmospheric packed sports games but would be immanent to the composition as whole.

The statues to which March referred comprise an array of almost two dozen neoclassical sculptures carefully positioned around the complex. Mostly carved from shell limestone and ranging from five to six metres high inclusive of plinths, these clear allusions to antiquity are largely figurative representations of semi-naked muscular athletes or, as in the case of the Goddess of Victory who is wearing a robe with a snake around her feet, draw links to the symbol and myths of the ancient civilizations (Figure 3.3). While March had decided from at least as early as 1934 that the complex needed sculptures in order to offset its rigidly symmetrical and tightly composed buildings and to 'imbue the site with soul',[3] he was not sure from the outset exactly what form this would take. In 1934, he initiated discussions about the nature of the artistic decoration of the Olympic Complex and options at this point included an exhibition of replicas of antique works or marble statues influenced by the *Foro Mussolini* in Italy.[4] Yet March would go on to consider a 'homogenous arrangement' of sculptures such as that at Mussolini's stadium 'out for the question' for the Reichssportfeld. First, on the basis that it would fail to reflect the wealth of diversity within German sculpture and secondly, because it would not meet the architectural needs of the site as the different locations within which the statues would be situated required bespoke designs to complement them.[5]

Figure 3.3 Karl Albiker's 'The Discus Throwers' (1936).
Photograph: By author.

March worked with a committee of so-called leaders and aficionados of the German arts which had been formed by the Interior Ministry specifically for the purpose of developing a plan for the decoration of the Reichssportfeld.[6] In the publicity materials about the Olympic Complex, March is, however, keen to highlight that the designs of the statues themselves were not imposed from above. He states that there was no initial agreement about artistic content, rather the committee's focus was on the role each piece would play in the overall design and, as such, the function it would play in structuring the site, emphasizing certain aspects, axes, entrances or other elements. This meant that only the scale and the materials would be stipulated as this was necessary in order to ensure each sculpture fit in with the specific surroundings for which it was designated.[7] Indeed, with the exception of Georg Kolbe's Decathlete and Josef Thorak's Boxer, all of the sculptures were specifically designed to stand in the position in which they were placed and where they continue to stand.[8] Even today, visitors can see that the height and bulk of Karl Albiker's Discus Thrower and Relay Runners strengthen the impact of the columns that surround the body of the stadium and the pillars that mark its key access points; Joseph Wackerle's Horse Tamers accentuate the axis that runs through the Marathon Gate towards the bell tower and connect the Maifeld with the stadium; outside the House of German Sport on Jahnplatz, Arno Breker's Decathlete and Female Victor echo the pillars of the colonnade in which they are standing; Willy Meller's Victory Goddess marks the passage from the northern area of the site into the stadium proper; and, in an area of the site that is no longer accessible to the general public, Josef Mages' comrades in sport frame the view from the March Tunnel in the southern section of the site.[9] Yet this apparent embracing of cooperation, diversity and the artistic freedom of the sculptors seems to have been more limited to the propaganda about the site rather than the reality. Bettina Güldner and Wolfgang Schuster highlight how all of the sculptures were seen as playing a part in the elevation of the Reichssportfeld to a site of ritual and that March warned that sculptures that did not contribute to this would be deemed inadequate.[10] Indeed, they contend that rather than encouraging diverse creations from the artists, in order to maintain the unity of the composition, the committee only chose fairly uniform shell-limestone structures with slight differences in the actual composition and subjects.[11]

The sculptors whose work would be incorporated into the Olympic Complex were selected through competitions with financial prizes as well as the honour of inclusion. Several of the successful entrants, including Karl Albiker, Joseph Wackerle and Georg Kolbe, had already been well known before they were awarded the commission for this work and the competitions attracted considerable attention within the upper echelons of the Nazi Party with both Goebbels and Hitler being shown some of the designs.[12] Displaying work in such a high-profile arena was, of course, a highly prestigious honour for the sculptors and, for many, would mark the beginning of a very successful artistic career under National Socialism. This is particularly the case for Arno Breker, Josef Thorak and Adolf Wamper who would go on to become celebrated sculptors in the Nazi regime. Thorak, for example, would complete assignments for Hitler's New Reich Chancellery and the Nuremberg Party Rally grounds and Breker would produce work for the Chancellery and contribute to designs for Speer's plans for Germania.[13]

In post-unification debates over how to deal with the site, the statue collection became the locus for discussions around the continued presence of National Socialism at the site. Endlich attributes this to a disjucture between popular recognition that the sculptures were Nazi constructions which needed to be responded to in some way and perceptions of the rest of the site which, despite its clear monumentality and relation to stuctures such as the Nuremberg Rally grounds and the plans for Germania, was understood by many, including some experts, not as an expression of Nazi ideolgy and propaganda but as an impressive and modern construction. As a result, debates in the 1990s focused almost exclusively on the scupltures.[14] This was frustrating to many experts such as art historian Magdalena Buschart who found that the burden of history seemed to have been pushed onto the statues so that the rest of the site could be dealt with less self-consciously. Pointing out that sculptures are relatively easy to remove, she expressed her fears that they would be 'victims of the prevailing pressure for change' and, like several pieces before them, 'end up in a farmyard somewhere'.[15] The focus on the sculptures largely centred on their embodiment of elements of National Socialist ideology: Conceptualized as 'racial fanaticism hewn in stone',[16] the muscular, athletic builds and determined facial expressions of the Discus Throwers and Relay

Runners have been said to represent the 'ideal image' of a Nordic-Germanic race and to have played a role in furthering the connection between militarism and sport;[17] the Horse Tamers, which stand next to the *Maifeld* and would go on to feature in Leni Riefenstahl's film *Olympia*, are seen to represent the power of man over nature and to be allegories for the notion of strong statesmanship;[18] the Female Victor has been considered to symbolize victory over the enemy whereas the comrades have been said to stand for loyalty within the new Reich.[19]

In a 1992 report into the history and condition of the site which was commissioned by the Berlin Senate in preparation for Berlin's bid for the 2000 Olympic Games, the sculptures are established as key to the expression of the site as a symbol of National Socialism. Compiled by a working group led by Reinald Eckert and Wolfgang Schäche, the report emphasizes that, at the time of its writing, the sculptures were still simply standing at the site in a form of 'permanent exhibition' and that Berliners and the Olympic organizers were becoming increasingly conscious of them. Rather than prescribing a course of action, however, the report's authors call for a serious discussion over how to deal with the statues and how to avoid their symbolism being misunderstood without simply hiding them away. Engaging with this would, they say, provide Berlin with a unique opportunity to make the spatial and ideological functions of the sculptures better understood.[20] Controversies around statues are, of course, hardly unique to the Berlin Republic. As key tools in the celebration of individuals, commemoration of events and expression of ideas, they are highly visible symbols of the values of the systems that erect them. Should these values go on to be called into question, statues are frequently at the centre of contests over how the ideas they represent should be redefined. This can follow sudden regime change, as seen in the debates around the future of communist statues in the former Eastern bloc or a more gradual shift in ideas, as manifested in the ongoing discussions around statues celebrating figures connected with colonialism or the slave trade in the UK. Analysis of these debates has been used as an entry-point into explorations of memory politics in a range of contexts.[21] The contests surrounding the statues at the Olympic Stadium provide a useful insight into the trajectory of the development of post-authoritarian governmentality in the Berlin Republic, largely because the public conversation advocated by the report's authors would enter public discourse at two key points in the site's post-unification history. The first time was in the early nineties during the preparation of Berlin's bid for the 2000 Olympic Games and again in the run-up to the 2006 World Cup. Although the issue at stake was the same thing, the need to respond to the statues, the two sets of debates played out very differently both in terms of the solutions put forward and the nature of the debates. While the earlier discussions were underpinned by an embrace of openness and plurality, the later ones indicate that, by 2006, a particular response to the legacies of National Socialism had been formulated and divergences from it were not welcome. Analysis of these two different sets of discussions indicates that between 1993 and 2006, Germany saw the emergence of an increasingly distinct and self-conscious post-authoritarian governmentality which, by the end of that period, had led to the establishment of a dominant paradigm through which the response to the past was structured and from which alternative narratives would be marginalized and excluded.

The sculptures and the run-up to Germany's bid for Olympia 2000

The first set of debates around the statues was largely instigated by Hilmar Hoffmann. Having worked as Frankfurt's Head of Cultural Affairs, Hoffmann took the post of Cultural Commissioner for the Berlin Olympic bid team and quickly made clear that he had taken the role only on the condition that Olympia 2000 would facilitate 'appropriate engagement with the legacy of the 1936 Olympic Games'.[22] To Hoffmann, Olympia 2000 should offer Germany's new capital the chance for a critical and creative revision. In particular, he announced, the 'disastrous misalliance between art and sport which took place in 1936 must be made visible and a clear and irreversible caesura between dictatorship and democracy, between cult and culture, must be established'.[23] Consequently he envisaged an extensive programme of exhibitions, public discussions and symposia forming part of the pre-program for the Olympics.[24] One of Hoffmann's primary concerns was the question of how the statues, which he labelled the Nazis' 'racist cult of the body manifested in stone' should be dealt with.[25]

In keeping with the protected status of the statues which would allow only temporary alterations, he put forward three suggestions: The first involved temporarily moving the statues and rearranging them on the Maifeld where they could be juxtaposed with a 'counter aesthetic' achieved either through the display of work by artists such as Alfred Hrdlicka or Fritz Cremer, whose art depicts the form of those marginalized and oppressed by the veneration of a particular physical form, or by displaying replicas of pieces included in the Nazis' Degenerate Art exhibition such as those by Käthe Kollwitz and Ernst Barlach; the second suggestion was to turn the statues into exhibits in a museum by installing glass cases around them with a museum-like plaque giving key information about each piece; the third suggestion was to commission the artist Christo to wrap the sculptures with a transparent cover in a similar installation to that which he had done at the Reichstag. Hoffmann did, however, express concerns from the outset that wrapping the statues might be misconstrued as increasing the significance of the statues or that as the wrapping might only be see through to those with good eyes it may risk being perceived as at attempt to cover up the past.[26]

What these suggestions have in common is that they would all employ a strategy of physically 'othering' the statues; they indicate that the sculptures comprise a layer of the site that should not remain entangled with the other layers but should be made distinct and clearly visible in its isolation. Each technique for dealing with the statues would, however, have different implications. Rearranging the figures on the Maifeld would mark the most significant rupture with the site's origins; it would involve physically reordering and re-appropriating the sculptures, changing both the composition of the site and the status of the statues. The erection of museum-like windows would alter temporality at the site in a different way; it would 'freeze' the statues, abstracting them from the space/time of the rest of the site. It represents an idea of containment, of 'isolating' these problematic sculptures, preventing them from contaminating the rest of the site. This idea of containment also underpins the notion of wrapping, but the latter goes much further; as well as isolating the statues it would be a public act of partially gagging or muffling them, indicating that their message was not fit for public consumption. This would have the dual effect of both problematizing the statues and calling into question conceptions of the public's ability to withstand the messages of the statues. Hoffmann's ideas all comprise different ways of appropriating the physicality of the statues to alter their function and thus how people experience and respond to them. Rather than imposing a monolithic narrative, they all leave considerable scope for interpretation. The re-encoding of the statues would be achieved through adjusting their spatial configuration and their surroundings rather than through explicitly situating them within a particular narrative. Underlying Hoffmann's suggestions is, however, a fundamental contradiction. In the public discourse around the debates he makes it clear that, in contrast to the 1936 Olympics, he is keen to ensure that any art connected to the 2000 Olympics should be 'free of any form of instrumentalisation'.[27] This very conscious, public declaration that any art on display at the Olympic Stadium would not be political is, of course, problematic: in seeking to make a statement through the de-politicization of the art at the Olympic Stadium, that art necessarily becomes political. Contrary to his statement, Hoffmann is advocating the 'instrumentalization' of art to convey a political message, only the message he is using it to convey is one that defines the FRG in opposition to the Third Reich. The failure to recognize this is indicative of the strength of the structuring framework within the Berlin Republic whereby the overt challenging of one type of regime is not seen as a political act but is normalized.

To kick-start the debate Hoffmann asked a range of public figures to critically discuss the issue, either by engaging with his suggestions or by giving their own ideas.[28] Reactions to his suggestions varied. Several high-profile figures such as Jean-Christophe Amman, director of the Museum of Modern Art in Frankfurt am Main, and Eberhard Diepgen, then mayor of Berlin, wished to see the sculptures left as they were, for reasons that include respect for the building's listed status; avoiding giving the impression that the Germans were only seeking a temporary solution for the duration of the period for which the eyes of the world were upon them; and allowing the people to see the relics of the ideology that led to the Holocaust. Others, such as Ignatz Bubis, leader of the Central Council of Jews in Germany and Willi Daume, president of the German Olympic Committee, with various caveats, preferred the idea of countering the statues with a counter aesthetic. Others still, such as Björn Engholm, leader of the SPD, were adamant there should be 'no Olympic Games against the backdrop of dictatorship'.[29]

Hoffmann's suggestions generated significant coverage in the press where Hoffmann himself is generally represented as credible, respected and qualified to speak on such issues.[30] Although *Der Spiegel* considers his suggestions to be 'odd', his objectives themselves are seen as 'commendable'.[31] *Die Tageszeitung* emphasizes some of the limitations to potential interventions, highlighting that any response to the past would necessarily be strongly shaped by the legislative structuring frameworks operating within the Berlin Republic. More specifically, given the building's listed status, any alterations made to the statues needed to be temporary and reversible.[32] Yet to several key actors, it was precisely the temporary and reversible nature of Hoffmann's suggestions that made them problematic, especially given the acute awareness that the

Nazis used the 1936 Olympic Games to try and deceive the world into thinking that Germany was a peace-loving democracy. In *Der Spiegel* it is reported that if the means found for dealing with the sculptures was only limited to the period of the Olympic Games then the 2000 Olympic Games might be seen as a historical parallel to 1936.[33] The *Berliner Morgenpost* reported Berlin Mayor Eberhard Diepgen's warning that all temporary and reversible measures risked being perceived as mere 'window dressing'.[34] This focus on international perception underlined much of the coverage, indicating the self-consciousness with which Germany was developing its response to the past. *Der Spiegel* reports the expectations of the consultants working on the 2000 Olympic Bid that 'embarrassments are guaranteed' as they anticipate that should Germany be awarded the Olympic Games, images of how the Olympic Stadium looked in 1936 would fill international newspapers and Leni Riefenstahl's films would be shown on television worldwide.[35] In *Die Tageszeitung*, heritage conservationist Jörg Haspel is quoted stressing the importance of creating a critical distance from the material in order to avoid international perceptions of continuity, rather than new beginnings after the war.[36] Diepgen's view that the wrapping of the statues would be tantamount to a 'tortured suppression' which would be 'laughable' in the eyes of the world is quoted in the *Berliner Morgenpost*.[37]

As well as reporting that discussions over the fate of the sculptures were occurring, the popular press actually became a site where the debates on the issue took place. Lengthy articles written by academics, politicians and other experts were given considerable column inches and readers' opinions on the issue featured in the letters pages. As such, the general reporting in the popular press indicates engagement with the discussions and brought academic and expert debate into the public sphere. A lengthy interview with Jörg Haspel, for example, featured in *Die Tageszeitung*. Here, Haspel explained that given the far-right activity of the last few months one could not assume any kind of fundamental immunity to the National Socialist social and human ideals expressed by the Olympic buildings and sculptures.[38] While he expresses his own preference for a concept that left the sculptures in their historical places and created the possibility for a critical commentary on them, he does not dismiss Hoffmann's suggestions out of hand.[39]

Art historian Tilmann Buddensieg was given sufficient space in the *Tagesspiegel* to engage in a fairly detailed exploration of the extent to which Werner March's stadium could actually be considered 'National Socialist'.[40] A few months later, art historian and curator Ursel Berger was allocated a similar amount of space in the same newspaper for her interrogation of 'how National Socialist are the 1936 sculptures?'[41] Publisher and writer Wolf Jobst Siedler uses the *Frankfurter Allgemeine Zeitung* to make his case that such discussions are 'superfluous'. He questions the extent to which considerations of the site should be temporally and spatially bound to Nazi Germany, highlighting that it was before 1933 that March was awarded the contract to redesign the grounds for the 1936 Olympic Games and asks to what extent it can be connected with the fact 'a decade later something monstrous happened'. He goes on to put the site into context, drawing parallels with neoclassical buildings in France, Scandinavia, Britain and the United States which were constructed at a similar time but which have not been associated with fascism. He concludes that Hoffmann's ideas about adding museum windows or pieces that would provide a counter aesthetic would themselves be a 'nightmare'.[42] Buddensieg then uses the letters page of that newspaper to respond to Siedler, arguing that Siedler had overlooked the fact that while similar styles did develop elsewhere, it was only in Nazi Germany that aesthetics were so rigidly controlled from above and that experimentation was suppressed.[43] Other readers also used the letters pages to express their own views: the crimes of Germany's past should not be trivialized or forgotten, writes one reader, a Hans Borgelt, but if Hoffmann's suggestions are really considered necessary, where will Berlin find the courage to actually bid for the Olympic Games?'[44] Later, a Dieter Prelinger points out that the statues were not put up by Hitler but by renowned artists and argues that the problem Hoffmann is trying to tackle is out of date.[45]

The sculptures and the run-up to the 2006 World Cup

When the Olympic bid failed, public interest in the fate of the sculptures subsided and they largely remained as they had been until 2005 when they and other National Socialist traces at the Olympic Stadium were incorporated into a new history trail. The development of this will be addressed in Chapter 7. Unlike the suggestions put forward by Hoffmann, this solution to the statues made the features that rendered each one problematic explicit by outlining them on an information board erected nearby. On these information boards, the pieces are treated as 'art' through the provision of information of the type and format one would expect to find in a gallery: a simple list of artist; date; height; material. Yet each information panel also contains a body of text which challenges each piece's claim to be considered as art. The control of the artist from above is frequently referred to: the Relay Runners, for example, 'show how closely sculptors "adhered to the master plan" as demanded by March' and mention is made of how the art committee suggested changes to ensure the austerity and uniformity of the pieces; the panel beside Breker's *Decathlete* and *Female Victor* also highlight the 'repeated revisions' demanded by the art committee; and beside the Discus Thrower it is made explicit that 'Nazi leaders urged artists to create images of powerful, healthy bodies'.[46]

Wider context is also given, both in terms of a particular sculptor's role in the Third Reich or the role a particular piece plays in enhancing the aesthetics of the Olympic Stadium complex: the boards explain that the Relay Runners, for example, 'reiterate in a different form the columns of the stadium and the twin towers of the gate' while the composition around Jahnplatz is designed to create a 'ceremonial setting' reminiscent of a 'medieval tournament area'. The most significant use of the boards is to communicate how the piece fits into a particular element of National Socialist ideology: it is highlighted that the reliefs outside the *Waldbühne*, for example, are designed to establish a link with ancient culture; the Relay Runners are 'meant to express the ideological notion of a supra-personal community'; the naked bodies of Breker's *Decathlete* and *Female Victor* were supposed to represent ideals the youth should strive to emulate; that as well as providing a link to classical antiquity, the Horse Tamers sought to show 'the power of human beings over nature and state leadership' specifically, 'subordination to the *Führer*'; the Victory Goddess was designed as a 'reminder that sport should be for the benefit of the Fatherland'; and the 'regime's inhumanity and racist ideology' can be seen in the promotion of the 'Nordic Race' as the 'ideal of beauty' through the Discus Throwers. The overriding theme here is the attempt to neutralize these 'problematic' sculptures through making what was implicit explicit. Evidence of this is also found in the captions beneath the photographs, beside the Discus Throwers, for example, it is stated that 'National Socialist leaders saw art as a form of propaganda'. In a similar vein, a copy of a 1936 photograph of the Relay Runners is accompanied by a short paragraph that explains that the Nazis dramatized photographs of the sculptures by taking them from below and using dramatic lighting effects. The efforts to undermine the impact of the statues can also be seen in the photographs which accompany the texts: the photograph showing the Relay Runners surrounded by scaffolding when under construction, for example, serves to denaturalize it and sever any connections with 'timelessness' or 'antiquity'; and the photographs from the 1936 Olympics showing picnicking crowds around the Relay Runners, paying it no attention whatsoever, and the girls in swimming costumes posing playfully in front of the Resting Athlete and The Boxer diminish their monumental austerity and suggest that even in 1936 the sculptures were not necessarily treated reverentially. In contrast to previous suggestions, this signifies an attempt to deal with the statues through constructing a narrative around them, rather than purely through their materiality. While the sculptures themselves have not been physically altered during this process, their materiality is affected by the information boards which are generally situated within close proximity to the corresponding sculpture (Figure 3.4). As well as instantly identifying the related piece as 'problematic', the boards affect the spatial configuration around the sculptures, often mitigating their monumentality or diminishing their function in highlighting the axiality of the overall composition of the Olympic Complex.

In the run-up to the 2006 World Cup, the discussions over the statues were brought back into the public domain. On this occasion, Lea Rosh, journalist and one of the key initiators of the Berlin Memorial to the Murdered Jews of Europe, and the journalist and writer Ralph Giordano were the most vociferous proponents of the idea that something needed to be done about the sculptures. In an interview with the newspaper *B.Z.* that was widely reported elsewhere, Rosh stated that Breker was a 'leading Nazi' (*Obernazi*) and that his sculptures had no place in public space, and that at the very least, his figures on Jahnplatz should be covered up and an explanation for this posted nearby. Giordano went even further, arguing that the statues should be 'removed and destroyed, quickly and without trace ... to just cover them up would be merely symbolic and would actually symbolise how Germany confronts its past – namely, not decisively enough'.[47]

Analysis of the mainstream press in the days after this interview reveals a distinct commonality in the reaction to Rosh's and Giordano's ideas – namely, that they are not considered to represent a productive, rational means of dealing with the site. This is conveyed through the ways in which the protagonists are presented and the different levels of credence they are given. Occasionally, their previous contributions to similar discussions are used to undermine them; Rosh's suggestion that the tooth of

Figure 3.4 Joseph Wackerle's 'Horse Tamer' (1936) with information board (2005/6). *Photograph:* By author.

a concentration camp victim be incorporated into Berlin's Memorial to the Murdered Jews of Europe was particularly highlighted as evidence of irrationality.[48] Although their argument about the statues is generally communicated using their own words, largely through extracts from the interview above, it is then often paraphrased in such a hyperbolic way that people would find it difficult to support. *Bild*, for example, states that that the measure would be undertaken 'to spare World Cup visitors from across the world from glimpsing the controversial statues'.[49] In the *Berliner Zeitung* the invocation of (ir)rationality is particularly pronounced, Rosh and Giordano's suggestions are equated with a move towards 'mystification' and they are accused of drawing on the idea of art possessing 'magic properties'. In response, the paper posited that hiding or removing the statues would not rob them of their power, rather, that this would be achieved through the provision of information about their histories and their creators.[50] Similarly, in the *Tageszeitung*, Rosh and Giordano's thinking is seen as running contrary to the 'power of knowledge' which has informed the Western world since the eighteenth century.[51] In *Die Welt*, Rosh and Giordano's credibility is even more overtly undermined by claims that the duo do not have the intellectual capacity to understand the complexity of the issue,[52] while in the *Berliner Zeitung* they are even accused of advocating the very suppression they have spoken out against.[53]

Rosh and Giordano's intervention did, however, generate some wider engagement with the topic: in *B.Z.* it is wondered whether the sculptures have become 'scapegoats';[54] and, as in 1993, questions are asked in *Bild* regarding the extent the statues are, in fact, 'Nazi art';[55] and the *Welt am Sonntag* printed pictures of 1930s and 1940s sculptures from France, Germany and the United States and invited readers to see if they could identify the 'Nazi art'.⁵⁶ Yet Rosh and Giordano failed to have any significant, lasting impact and are instead accused of acting as though the debates of the early 1990s had never happened.⁵⁷ Reporting on the development of the history trail for the *Gedenkstättenforum* (Memorials Forum), an online platform for the exchange of information between organizations involved in Berlin's rapidly evolving memorial landscape, Endlich comments on how in launching her campaign for the statues to be removed or covered up on the grounds that international visitors would not expect to encounter 'unmediated Nazi art' in this way, Rosh seems to have overlooked the panels standing in front of each sculpture.⁵⁸

The case against Rosh and Giordano's argument is further strengthened by the use of expert opinion. In some cases, that of the same experts who engaged in the 1993 debates. In contrast to the comprehensive earlier coverage of expert opinion, here it tends to be limited to a couple of sentences and to be somewhat dismissive of the premise of the discussion. Berger, at this point director of Georg Kolbe museum, draws links to the older debates and to 'a clear lack of balance'.⁵⁹ International experts such as Professor of Art Ernst Fuchs are also quoted. To Fuchs, Rosh and Giordano's objections are 'nonsense [...] no better than the book burning of the Nazis' and John G. Bodenstein, director of the Museum of European Art in Cologne also draws parallels with 'the machinations of totalitarian regimes'.⁶⁰ The Central Council of Jews also designated the call to remove the statues 'completely misplaced'.⁶¹ Christoph Stölzl, historian and vice-president of the Berlin House of Representatives, is given a platform from which to explain that the connection between the statues and the cult of the body is more complicated than is being portrayed; that there were both left- and right-wing variants of the concept.⁶² The articles tend to close with this input from their various expert sources. As such, those arguing against, or simply dismissing, Rosh and Giordano's argument are seen to have the final word. The debate is therefore opened and closed within the same article; it is as though further discussion is not called for and the issue of how these material traces of the Third Reich should be dealt with has been resolved.

What this analysis reveals is a distinct difference between the debates around the development of an 'appropriate' response to the past in the years immediately after unification and in 2006. Commenting on Rosh's suggestion, Endlich highlights that since the fall of the wall, a public consensus has developed that democratic societies deal their pasts consciously, not through destroying listed monuments.⁶³ And, indeed, the reactions to Rosch's and Giordano's suggestions do indicate that by 2006 there is a clear and established sense that removing or covering up the traces of dictatorship is not an appropriate or adequate response. Rather, these pieces of difficult heritage should be preserved, left on display and countered through the provision of clear, succinct, rational information.

7

Disentangling the Olympic Stadium's layers

The history trail

In 2005–6 a new layer was added to the Olympic Complex. In common with that added to the site in 1934–6, this new layer was very self-consciously designed to impose a new ordering of space and time on the site and to project contemporary conceptions of national identity onto it. Unlike in 1936, however, this layer was not to be brought about by the destruction of a pre-existing structure, nor from the erection of bombastic, monumental and axially aligned new buildings. Rather it would reflect the political climate of the Berlin Republic: highly considered public engagement with the legacies, both physical and otherwise, of National Socialism which sought to firmly establish the dictatorial past as wholly 'other' to the democratic present. This layer was a history trail comprised of forty-six information boards which would strive to make sense of the jumble of historical traces at the site by identifying and labelling the different temporal layers, rendering them distinct from one another and making their origins and functions clear. As with the former Aviation Ministry, the site itself, of course, defies this attempt to impose any kind of ordering on it, primarily through the density and complexity of the layering at certain points but also through the strength of the composition that already exists. Furthermore, although a dominant paradigm was emerging which posited confrontation with the legacies of dictatorship through their preservation and incorporation into rational commentary as the optimal response to the past, there was no single, coherent top-down force which pushed this through or informed how it should be realized. Rather, the history trail which today stands at the former Olympic Stadium is the product of a long and complex process of negotiation between multiple politicians, academics and citizens' groups which also needed to account for the materiality of the site, economic limitations and other priorities such as the up-coming World Cup. As a result, although a relatively coherent response to the past had been formulated, multiple factors would interact with attempts to translate conceptions of that response into reality leading to a significant gap between intention and realization.

Interest in the stadium's history, particularly its use under National Socialism, and its architectural significance had been growing since the 1980s. After unification, Hans-Ernst Mittig was heavily critical of the extent to which the overtones of the 1936 Olympic Games seemed to have been forgotten and that the Olympic Complex was now 'hardly recognised as a Nazi propaganda piece' and was instead 'blithely used both as a sports facility and as a symbol to promote the State of Berlin and its businesses'.[1] He called for the original intentions behind the design and construction of this item of propaganda to be challenged, not through destruction but through critical engagement with it. For this reason, he argued, the stadium should be preserved as didactic material.[2] His call was very much in line with that of other architects, historians and initiatives such as the Active Museum of Fascism and Resistance, Berufsband Bildener Künstler (BBK) and the Deutscher Werkbund who had also been campaigning for the development of a critical commentary of the site's history.[3] The site's architectural and historical significance was recognized by the Office of Monument Preservation who, in 1998, devised a programme of critical conservation to limit alterations to the site which was agreed by the Senate of Berlin in May of that year.[4] However, the key impetus for developing critical engagement with the site proved to be the decision that the stadium would host the 2006 World Cup final. The Senate departments for Education, Youth and Sport; Science, Research and Culture; and Urban Development agreed that rather than using the €980,000 art budget for installing additional art works, it would be used to fund the installation of a permanent, outdoor, historical commentary on the existing site.[5] This commentary would, announced a press release from the Berlin Senate, be put together by professionals and form part of the Berlin City marketing campaign.[6] This news was welcomed by the groups who had campaigned for such an intervention into the site but in the coming months and years, the development and installation of this commentary threw up a range of challenges, some relating to the site itself and the complexity of the issues it brought to the fore, others stemming from more practical issues such as finance and organizational structure.

Underpinning the practical challenges faced by the history trail's developers was the system of funding and authorization with which they were presented. Concerns about the renovation and operational costs had led the State of Berlin to seek out a public–private partnership with commercial enterprises who would bid for the franchise to operate the facilities and manage the renovation.[7] It was eventually awarded to a consortium including Walter Bau AG, Germany's fourth largest construction company. Walter Bau AG's contract with the State of Berlin stipulated that the development of the site must incorporate a 'historical commentary'. The construction firm then commissioned the Berlin Forum for History and Present with developing and delivering this due to their previous experience with other similar projects. The Forum in turn established a working group comprised of Monica Geyler-von-Bernus, Beate Rossié and Stefanie Endlich which would be supported by a five-member advisory council made up of Professor Reinhard Rürup of the Topography of Terror Foundation, architectural historian Professor Wolfgang Schäche, art historian Professor Hans-Ernst Mittig, sports historian Professor Hans Joachim Teichler and architect Helga Schmidt-Thomsen who would represent the Office of Monument Protection.[8]

Having been commissioned by a private company rather than by the state, the working group encountered several challenges. Most seriously, and very nearly fatal to the development of the history trail, was the financial arrangement. The Senate paid the money for the history trail to Walter Bau AG for them to distribute as they saw fit. Endlich explains that the consequence of this was that although it funded with public money, spending on the project was at the discretion of a private building company rather than the state, and the Berlin Forum for History and Present essentially become a contractor of Walter Bau AG. Endlich reflects on how, from the outset, Walter Bau AG seemed reluctant to spend the allocated funds and was instead continually driving down costs at the expense of quality. Then, in February 2005, the firm declared insolvency.[9] This was reported in the national press and the timing was terrible. The information boards were in very final stages of production, and as suppliers either hadn't been paid at all or had only been given their first instalment they refused to surrender their products. There were initial hopes at being able to retrieve the public money but this was also incorporated into the insolvency funds. Finally, after a five-month delay and following intense negotiations with suppliers, the information boards were released and the first stage of the history trail could proceed. This did, however, jeopardize the planned second stage which was supposed to comprise twenty-five more stations including the Sport Forum, Maifeld, Langemarck Hall, Bell Tower and Waldbühne.[10]

Developing the new layer

In designing the trail itself, one of the most fundamental issues the committee had to address was the identification of precisely which elements of the site warranted a commentary and should be incorporated into the trail, and which should be excluded. In preparation for the first meeting, members of the expert committee were sent an overview of forty-one potential stations put together by the Berlin Forum for History and Present and were invited to give their input. As well as basic details about each of the features, such as its location, artist and material, a 'keyword' was provided which indicated the theme(s) that the commentary could address at that particular point. Some of these keywords, such as those at the Olympic Bell or at the Marathon Gate, focused directly on the relevant feature of the site whereas others would be used as a spring board from which to elucidate broader topics such as elements of National Socialist ideology or the overall composition of the Olympic site. The pair of sculptures named the Discus Throwers, for example, was connected to the veneration of particular body forms under National Socialism while the board beside the southern tower of the Olympic Gate would be put forward as an opportunity to talk about the axiality of the site's composition.[11]

Underpinning the discussions over which features should be included was the question over the total number of 'stations' that should constitute the trail. Minutes of meetings and supplementary information sent to panel members show that in the early days, the suggested numbers fluctuated between twenty-five and forty-one,[12] with members of the committee keen to avoid installing too many panels or particular areas of the stadium becoming 'swamped'.[13] One suggested way of reducing the number of boards was through keeping an eye out for any opportunities for 'aggregation', or explaining multiple elements on one board.[14]

Particularly complex elements generated lengthy discussion. A key example is the Podbielski Oak. Named after the former President of the Imperial Committee for Physical Exercise and the Imperial Committee for the Olympic Games who is generally credited as being behind the construction of the first stadium on the site, the Podbielski Oak is the most visible remnant of the forest which once stood on the site of the Olympic Stadium. As well as symbolizing a connection with the German *Urwald*, March saw it as creating a link between the Third Reich and the olive trees outside the temple of Zeus. It was supposed to be used for victors' wreaths during the 1936 Olympics although it is doubtful that this actually happened.[15] The main issue the committee found was that whereas it would be very hard to convey that tree's 'symbolic power' in a short commentary, merely to characterize it as 'German tree' would be 'banal'. Another point for discussion was whether these elements should be left out of the trail altogether in order to increase the trail's impact elsewhere.[16] The extension of this set of discussions is that the history trail medium might not be fully appropriate for features such as this. Furthermore, the difficulty in making this kind of decision was exacerbated by the lack of a clear source of funding for the continuation of the trail beyond the immediate vicinity of the stadium.[17] Even before the Walter Bau fiasco, committee members could not be certain that a future expansion of the trail would enable them to incorporate the outlying features such as the Langemarck Hall, the Maifeld, the Sport Forum and the swimming stadium and, as such, were unsure how they should address these elements, particularly those visible from the main stadium, in the first stage of the trail.[18] These deliberations reveal the contingent nature of the ordering of the site and the extent to which the historical narrative constructed there was informed by multiple factors not necessarily connected with original events or even the creators' understanding of them but which would nonetheless go on to shape future understandings of those events.

These more fundamental discussions could have been held around the construction of a historical commentary at any site. The more detailed discussions reveal, however, that this ordering becomes more complex at sites such as this precisely because of the post-authoritarian governmentality within which it takes place. Some elements warranted discussions that would not be necessary in most liberal democracies; the use of the term *deer Sieger*, or 'German victors', for example, engendered some debate even though it was recognized that the honouring of national Olympic champions in their home stadium was common international practice.[19] One area which gives a particularly strong insight into the challenge presented by the question of how to impart rational, evidence-based information about the Third Reich is the issue of the inclusion of images, a topic on which the working group explicitly asked the expert committee for advice. The discussion was predicated on the assumption that whereas a narrative can be relatively tightly constructed and communicated through the written word, there is a greater gap between how a visitor is 'supposed' to engage with a visual image and how they actually do so. Within this gap lies a perceived potential for ambiguity and subversion which the committee wished to avoid. The very idea of including pictures was introduced from the outset with certain caveats already in place: the primary function of any pictures would be to support the body of text; all pictures would be accompanied by a brief caption in both English and German; and the use of pictures which recreated the atmosphere of the 1936 Olympics or reproduced the aesthetics of that time would be only be used if appropriate contextualizing information was given.[20]

The main point for the committee to consider concerned the use of photographs which show National Socialist protagonists, symbols or orchestrated displays. The committee papers show that while the use of such photographs in a publicly accessible, unsupervised display was considered problematic, such images were also seen as having the potential to aid historical understanding.[21] Several examples are given of the planned use of pictures on the boards and the text that would accompany them. The discussion of the use of images was given its own item on the agenda for the second meeting on 25 November 2003. The minutes show that while the committee agreed that photographs should be included, the following rules were agreed on unanimously: the photographs should be left in black and white; the total surface area of the photographs should not be larger than that of the text; and that photographs of the National Socialist elite, National Socialist symbols or orchestrated displays should not be used on the information boards inside the stadium area because the focus was to be on the built ensemble itself and not on the 1936 Olympic Games.[22] The committee determined that the viewer's experience of the image should therefore be framed by the written word, either through the broader context provided by the main body of text or through the short caption accompanying each photograph. The problematization of the unsupervised display of certain images suggests a fear over what effects the images might have if encounters with them are not tightly framed. The detail of these deliberations is strongly indicative of the extent to which the committee wanted to shape visitors' engagement with the information boards and, therefore, with the site. However, such rigid ordering does not necessarily only consolidate dominant power relations but also offers the potential for their challenge – in this case, in constructing the narratives too tightly there is an increased chance of disagreement with a particular element and thus undermining the authority of the historical commentary as a whole.

The negotiation between freedom and control is rather different in the narratives contained within the actual text on the boards. Here, the constructors of the narrative show an awareness of the risks of imposing too rigid an order. Linguist Mona Baker explains that through 'selective appropriation' elements of a narrative can be 'suppress[ed], accentuate[d] or elaborate[d]' through 'patterns of omission and addition'.[23] As will be shown in the coming analysis, on several of the information boards it is through omission that the narrative is strengthened. The historical commentary gains its legitimacy through its communication of 'truth' through clear, succinct, provable facts. In this way it is differentiated from the irrationality of National Socialism and the distortion of truth under the Third Reich. In order to maintain that distinction, the writers of the history trail must retain an air of scientific objectivity. A clear line is therefore drawn between informing a visitor about the relationship between National Socialism and a particular feature or individual which can be demonstrated and authenticated, and the imposition of a normative narrative. However, a combination of facts may be framed in such a way that it encourages the reader to reflect upon what they have read. In this respect, the history trail performs a post-authoritarian governmentality by not imposing a closing narrative on the site but rather opening up the possibility of more informed reflection and debate.

Implementing the new layer

As well as the negotiations which determine the form the ordering should take, the actual implementation of that order is heavily informed by the site itself. The minutes and meeting reports show several examples of ways in which the sheer scale and complexity of the site confounded attempts to construct a clear, legible narrative around it. This is mainly evident in areas of the site where the interaction between multiple temporalities is particularly complex and where the committee considered there to be a strong impetus to unpick them. Two examples are the arrangement of plaques on the two walls of the Marathon Gate and the stelae erected on either side of the East Gate entrance to honour German Olympic gold medal winners. Using minutes and meeting reports we can see the contingent nature of the ordering that was ultimately imposed by the history trail on these multiple temporalities.

Despite bearing distinct similarities in style and content and being arranged as a single, coherent composition, the seven plaques which line the walls of the Marathon Gate constitute one of the areas where the site's layering is at its most complex. The plaques on the right-hand side as you face the pitch bear the names and three-dimensional representations of key figures in the building of the German Stadium and the organizing of the aborted 1916 Olympic Games: the architect of the German Stadium, Otto March; the president of the German Olympic Committee Viktor von Podbielski; the Olympic committee member Willy Gebhardt; and the commissioner of the building of the German Stadium, Graf Egbert von der Asseburg (Figure 3.5). Facing them are plaques dedicated to the honour of the organizers of the 1936 games:

Figure 3.5 The older plaques at the Marathon Gate.
Photograph: By author.

Figure 3.6 The newer plaques at the Marathon Gate. Carl Diem's is the noticeably newer one in the centre.
Photograph: By author.

president of the organizing committee of the 1936 Olympic Games, Theodor Lewald; secretary general of the organizing committee of the 1936 Olympic Games, Carl Diem; and architect of the 1936 stadium, Werner March (Figure 3.6). At first glance, the collection appears to be just that, an ensemble of plaques created to honour key individuals in the stadium's history. Closer inspection, however, reveals that some elements in this composition are, in fact, considerably older than others. The first set, that on the right-hand wall, was constructed between 1913 and 1926 to adorn Otto March's original construction, the German Stadium, and the plaques were displayed at various locations around its 1936 replacement. They were only brought together and assembled beside the Marathon Gate during the renovation carried out in the early 1960s.[24] The plaques opposite them were also installed during this renovation at the instigation of Werner March. They represent a tradition which was to have begun in 1936 of honouring the key figures behind the Olympic Games, rather than just the athletes. The middle plaque, that dedicated to Carl Diem, is a replica of the original and is thus considerably newer looking than its neighbours. This is because the 1960s plaque dedicated to Carl Diem was 'kidnapped' in the early nineties by activists protesting against the Berlin 2000 Olympic bid. An undated pamphlet produced by one of the groups involved in the 'Olympic city' movement reported that an unknown individual, or group of individuals, removed the 120cm × 84cm bronze plaque. S/he or they then sent a ransom note signed 'Kommando Lutz Grüttke', a reference to the head of Olympia GmbH, demanding that Berlin withdraw its bid for the 2000 Olympic Games or the plaque would be melted. The ransom demands were not met and the commemorative plaque was replaced with a replica. Neither the perpetrators nor the original plaque were ever found.[25]

The area is therefore product of both an assimilation and a simulation. The first is the consequence of the 1960s reordering of the site, the physical bringing together of different temporalities and displaying of them as one. The simulation is both of a tradition that was never fully realized in its own time and of a contemporaneity that does not exist. The committee sought to unpick this assimilation and highlight the simulation. The initial overview of the stations that would make up the historical commentary indicates that there was an intention to separate the plaques into two sets by giving each their own respective information board. The first, provisionally entitled *Fünf Gedenktafeln* (five plaques), would provide a commentary on the older plaques and a nearby panel which had been installed during the 1960s renovation to provide information on these plaques. The keyword associated with this information board was to be 'history of the former German Stadium' and would therefore have clearly identified this part of the ensemble as belonging to the site's pre-1933 layer. A second information board, to be entitled *Drei Gedenktafeln* (three plaques), would tackle those dedicated to Theodor Lewald, Carl Diem and Werner March. The focus here was to be Carl Diem's role as sports functionary before, during and after the National Socialist era.[26] However, by the time a report dated November 2003 was produced, the plaques had all been assimilated into one board, entitled *Acht Gedenktafeln* (eight plaques) for which the keyword would be 'the complexity of the ancestral portrait gallery'. A note in the minutes states that the two stations were being brought together because of the density of key features in that area and the need to minimize disruption to the spatial configuration of the site.[27] This indicates a preparedness to make compromises in the reordering of the site to avoid disturbing elements of the original composition. In the final realization, the plaques are covered on one board, *Die Gedenktafeln im Marathontor* (the plaques at the Marathon Gate). This means that the plaques are, in fact, represented in a fundamentally different way to that originally intended by the committee. The suggestion in the first draft would have tackled the entanglement of this display head-on, untangling and identifying the traces as belonging to two distinct layers. The final realization, however, consolidates the artificial grouping together of these elements. Consequently, although none of the plaques was erected during the Third Reich, and five of them actually predate National Socialism, they are all woven into a narrative constructed in response to that period.

The critique is not, however, solely aimed at the National Socialist layer but also at the failure of subsequent interventions into the site, particularly those carried out in the 1960s, to critically engage with it. The text on the information board begins by problematizing the collection as a whole, situating it within a tradition initiated in 1936 of honouring politicians and organizers connected with the Olympic Games as well as the Olympic champions. It also points out that the later plaques do not date from the 1930s but from the 1960s and that they were Werner March's idea. In the context of other work by the creators of the history trail, this can be read as an implicit criticism of the lack of critical engagement with the site in the Bonn Republic, especially seen in Werner March's apparently unproblematic involvement in the site's reconstruction.[28] The body of the text contains a brief summary of Werner March's career before, during and after the Third Reich. That someone who received 'commissions including major public contracts under the Nazi regime' would go on to work as 'Professor for Town and Estate Planning at the Technical University, Berlin' is not explicitly problematized; however, the information is merely provided so that visitors may reflect on it to varying extents. This approach is also seen in the treatment of Theodor Lewald on the same information board. His support for the Weimar Republic is mentioned, as is the fact that under National Socialism he was 'defamed' for his Jewish origins and 'discharged from all his official sports posts in Germany'. Yet we also learn that his 'international recognition as a respected member of the International Olympic Committee' meant that he kept his position as the president of the organizing committee of the 1936 Olympic Games. Enough information is provided for the contradictions immanent to National Socialism to become apparent, but they are not made explicit here, allowing space for readers to mull over this in their own time.

Conversely, Carl Diem is overtly problematized; a greater level of detail is given of his involvement in the Third Reich, including his ideology and an account of a specific incident in which he was involved – his 'pathos-filled speech' delivered to the members of Hitler Youth to incite them to fight to the death in the last days of the war. An additional paragraph informs the reader that Carl Diem is 'considered one of the most controversial figures in German sport' and that his and other plaques were kept as 'historical documents'. That this controversy actually extended to affect the very materiality upon which the information board is providing a commentary is, however, not mentioned. In the list of key details about the plaques we can see that the installation date of the Carl Diem plaque is 1965 and that a replica was installed in 1993 but the fate of the original plaque is not referred to. The differentiation between the traditional function of such a plaque, that of honouring the individual depicted, and retaining it as a 'historical document' to show that the individual in question was once honoured is a complex one and one that is not particularly visible to those who encounter the plaques but do not pay close attention to the information boards. Here we see one of the fundamental limits to the efficacy of the history trail as a medium. We have established that information boards can have an impact even if they are not read, through visibly problematizing a feature. In this incidence, however, that simple 'problematization' would be misleading as the retention of the plaque as a 'historical document' does not, in fact, provide a commentary on the Third Reich as might be assumed. Rather it reflects upon the system(s) within which the plaque was actually made and installed without critical reflection: the Bonn Republic and, with regards to the replica, the early Berlin Republic. That the older plaques are not referred to in any particular detail in the body of the text but a nearby explanatory panel, installed in 1967 to provide a commentary on the older plaques as part of the 1960s renovation, is mentioned; the status of this explanatory panel has therefore shifted and it has become a historical trace in itself. This is an indication of the history trail's role in providing an overriding commentary on the totality of the layers that constitute the site and in highlighting that part of the site's past is the lack of critical engagement with it before now. This goes some way towards initiating the othering process that the commentary on the Carl Diem plaque falls short of, one that indicates that today's Germany is defined in opposition not only to its dictatorial past, but also to the previous lack of confrontation with that past.

The interaction between different temporalities is even more complex and evident at the stelae erected to honour German gold medallists. These twenty-five stone stelae are 2.4 metres tall and each is engraved with the year of the Olympic Games it represents – the names of all German gold medal winners that year and images depicting the sports in which the Germans won medals. Nine stelae were installed in 1936 to honour the German Olympic champions of each Games from 1896 to 1936 (Figure 3.7). The tradition was continued in 1957. Including the retrospective honouring of champions in 1952 and 1956, stelae have thus far been erected for every Olympic Games in which the Federal Republic has won gold medals up to Athens 2004 (Figure 3.8). In 1998 it was decided that East German gold medal winners should also be honoured in this way and four stelae were accordingly erected for this purpose.²⁹ Lining the path around the perimeter of the stadium complex, the stelae form a broken semicircle that echoes the curve of the stadium. The arc is interrupted by the East Gate entrance which separates the stelae installed in 1936 from those constructed after the war. As you enter the complex, the original nine stelae are on the left-hand side, those constructed after 1945 on the right.

On one level, the arrangement is a manifestation of a specifically Olympic temporality; time here 'begins' in 1896 with the first modern Olympic Games and is demarcated as existing in four-year blocks. This representation of time interacts with Germany's political temporality within that period; the silences and absences within the ensemble attest to periods of war when the games were not held, to the times Germany was banned from competing and to the West German boycott of the 1980

Figure 3.7 The older 'southern' stelae erected in 1936. Albiker's 'The Discus Throwers' (1936) is in the background.

Photograph: By author.

Figure 3.8 The newer 'northern' stelae, erected 1957–2010. Albiker's 'The Relay Runners' (1936) is in the background.
Photograph: By author.

Moscow Olympics. The addition of the four stelae containing the names of East German Olympic champions can be seen as an incorporation of the more positive elements of GDR history into that of Germany as a whole. Yet the GDR medallists are not given the same status as their West German counterparts; all 348 names are crowded onto 4 stelae on which there is no room for images.[30] The site's natural temporality has also left its mark on the stelae; the older ones are weathered and so worn that they are almost illegible whereas the words and images engraved into the newer ones are still clear. The newer ones have been chemically treated which means they are unlikely to weather to the same extent as their older counterparts.

Much like the plaques at the Marathon Gate, at first glance there is uniformity to the ensemble which unites both the pre- and post-war elements: they are of similar dimensions, are arranged in similar ways and have a similar layout and content (i.e. date, names and images). On closer inspection, however, the different temporal origins of the stelae are apparent from the stylistic differences between the images that they incorporate. Whereas the images on the stelae erected in 1936 are very stark, militaristic and representative, those installed after the war use more rounded, almost cartoon-like images to show a particular sport. Further in common with the plaques, the categorization that would be imposed on the stelae was by no means certain from the outset. Initially it was proposed that the stelae be addressed on three different information boards: one, entitled *Neun Siegerstelen*, (Nine Victory Columns), would inform the reader about those erected between 1935 and 1936, tying them into the National Socialist layer of the site; another, entitled *Vier Siegerstelen* (Four Victory

Columns), would focus on those erected in 1998 to retrospectively honour the GDR Olympic Champions, further differentiating them from their Western counterparts; whereas *Zwei Siegerstelen* (Two Victory Columns) would elucidate those erected in honour of the 1992 and 1994/6 champions.[31] In the November 2003 redrafting of the plan these latter two were assimilated onto one station. As with the plaques, a note in the meeting minutes highlights this, explaining that because this area of the stadium was at risk of being 'overwhelmed' by commentary and because these stelae were made by the same artist and 'ask thematically similar questions', it was considered both desirable and feasible to aggregate this information.[32] Ultimately, the categorization that was applied to the stelae corresponded to their position in the site; one information board now addresses *Die nördlichen Stelen der Olympiasieger* (The Northern Columns for Olympic Champions); another *Die südlichen Stelen der Olympiasieger* (The Southern Columns for Olympic Champions) This means that the stelae are, by virtue of their physical arrangement, still organized temporally in the history trail and that those installed under the Third Reich are dealt with separately to those added later.

On the information board, the older, southern stelae are introduced as 'Hitler's idea' and it is pointed out that in the retrospective commemoration of all German Olympic champions since the modern games began in 1896, the Jewish Flatow brothers who went on to be murdered in Theresienstadt are honoured for their success in gymnastics. As we saw in our analysis of the plaques, although it is not made explicit, sufficient information is provided here to allow the reader to identify the internal contradictions of National Socialism. Elsewhere in the body of text, however, the narratives around the images on the stelae are particularly tight. They inform the reader that the images 'embody central motifs of Nazi art' and it is explicitly pointed out that 'the rowers, for example, look like marching horses and the riders resemble horse tamers'. These military undertones are not alluded to but are specifically highlighted in a level of framing of the reader's experience of the visual which indicates an attempt to significantly narrow the space available for individual interpretation of the image. The northern stelae are conceptualized somewhat differently. Just as with the plaques, these post-war additions are clearly considered in relation to the earlier National Socialist use of the site. Here, however, they are placed within a legitimizing narrative as we instantly learn that the continuation of the tradition was at the behest of Miss Ella Kay 'former resistance fighter against the National Socialists and Berlin Senator for Sport'. This assertion makes clear that the impetus for the continuation of both a tradition and an architectural feature that was, apparently, Adolf Hitler's idea came from someone with clear anti-Nazi credentials. The continuation is therefore discursively 'dealt with'. Informing us of Kay's professional post reminds us that the site is (also) a sports stadium, dedicated to athletic achievement. Again, the narratives around the images on the stelae themselves are tightly constructed in the main body of the text. The body of the text highlights the contrast between 'rigid athletic nudes and martial motifs' of the older stelae and the 'flowing lines and movements' of the newer ones. To further emphasize the point, a photograph of a relief from each of the two sets of stelae are juxtaposed beneath the text, the purpose of this is explicitly stated: it is put forward 'as a comparison'. Just as the National Socialist reliefs were used to reflect and perform one idea of national sporting identity, so too are the more recent ones: in this case an identity constituted by a very public demonstration of the extent to which the National Socialist past is 'other'.

The analysis within this chapter reveals that even though key actors shared a clear understanding about what the response to the past should be, how it should be communicated and that it should be founded on the provision of clear, coherent, methodically researched information, there was still a significant gap between intention and realization. It shows that the apparently objective representation of the past is actually heavily contingent upon the negotiation of multiple factors, many of which had nothing to do with the historical event itself or with how the creators of the history trail understood it.

8

(En)Countering the cult of the dead
The Langemarck Hall memorial

The most overt confrontation between reason and myth occurs at the western extreme of the Olympic Complex in the structure housing the Langemarck Hall, built as part of the 1936 Reichssportfeld as a national memorial to all German youths who fell in the First World War (Figure 3.9). Its namesake, the Battle of Langemarck, was a brutal encounter in early days of the war and would go on to be seized upon and mythologized by nationalists in Weimar Germany. Central to these myths was the youth of the German troops who had, according to reports, gone to their deaths bravely and willingly with the *Deutschlandlied* on their lips, an image that would be mobilized in the interwar period as a symbol of the spirit of self-sacrifice.[1] Although this claim was challenged by at least one participant who had been there and heard no singing,[2] the National Socialists would go on to hold this up as an image of heroism, honour and self-sacrifice that the younger generation should strive to emulate and the Langemarck Hall memorial has been identified as key site at which this 'cult of the dead' was enacted.[3] The memorial itself provides a strong example of the use of history in the Third Reich and its communication and distortion via abstracted quotations, symbolism and melodramatic effect.

The Langemarck Hall is situated within a large structure which stands across the Maifeld from the Stadium and, because this single entity is comprised of a variety of elements all of which fulfil completely different functions, it defies easy identification and description. The Langemarck Hall itself is located on the first floor of the structure. The external wall forms the Westtribüne (west terraces) – a stand that was built to hold spectators watching events on the Maifeld.[4] Other components are the seventy-six-metre high bell tower with its two-tier viewing platform and, since 2006, the exhibition 'Historic Site: The Olympic Grounds 1909–1936–2006' which occupies much of the ground floor and some of the first. All four of these elements can and do serve as monikers for the construction as a whole, adding to its complex and elusive status. Visually and spatially this structure is very much integrated into the wider Olympic Complex. It was consciously designed so that the tall thin bell tower that stands on top would be directly in line with the opening in the stadium left by the Marathon Gate and thus punctuate the axiality of the whole complex and fulfil a fundamental role in the composition of the site. While the maintenance of this visual axis was a key part of the post-unification renovation of the Olympic Complex, there is also an

Figure 3.9 The structure containing the Langemarck Hall from across the Maifeld, flanked by Wackerle's 'Horse Tamers' (1936). The bell tower and the Westtribüne are visible here.
Photograph: By author.

element of dislocation whereby people who wish to visit the exhibition or to ascend the bell tower cannot cut across the Maifeld but must actually leave the stadium complex and take a ten- to fifteen-minute detour through the wider Olympic Park. A map in a 1937 guidebook indicating footpaths around the Reichssportfeld suggests that was the case in the original iteration of the site as well as now.[5] Both the structure's visual prominence and its physical dislocation have shaped post-unification responses to it, the former providing an impetus to respond to it while the latter simultaneously led to its initial exclusion from the historical commentary which addressed the main body of the site. Exploring post-unification responses to this element of the site demonstrates that just as the attempt to impose order on the history of the former Olympic Stadium was challenged by its complexity, so too is our attempt to provide a commentary on the Berlin Republic's response to its past. The post-unification intervention into the structure housing the Langemarck Hall simultaneously sets up and breaks down a series of binaries that structure our relationship with the National Socialist past thus evading easy categorization and analysis.

In order to reflect the changes and continuities to the site, it is perhaps best to begin with contemporary accounts of the original construction. A 1936 guide to the Olympic site begins its discussion of the structure from outside with a vivid description of the Westtribüne. It outlines how this stand, equipped with pedestals upon which flags could be mounted and a raised podium from which Hitler could deliver speeches, had been specifically designed to complement the 'patriotic rallies' which would take place on the Maifeld. According to the guide, as well as the

250,000 participants that the Maifeld could 'comfortably' hold, the stand itself had the capacity to accommodate 60,000 spectators. Atop the structure is the seventy-six-metre bell tower, which housed the Olympic Bell, embossed with the words 'Ich rufe die Jugend der Welt' (I call the youth of the world). A lift would take visitors to a viewing platform at the very top of the tower from which they could survey the composition of the site in its entirety. The structure itself also contained functional spaces for events coordinators and journalists and, of course, occupying the first floor, the Langemarck Hall memorial.

The layers of symbolism within the memorial are outlined by its architect, Werner March, in a 1936 article about the Olympic Complex. He explains that its decoration is both allegorical and simple (Figure 3.10). Twelve sturdy pillars carry the seventy-six flags of the regiments that took part in the battle, and where the shaft of the bell tower passes through the Hall it is adorned with ten shields, each bearing the names of the divisions and their units. In the western area of the memorial, earth from the cemetery at Langemarck was placed underneath the floorboards, protected by a steel plate emblazoned with the Langemarck Cross.[6] In one of the 1936 guides to the site this shrine, holding earth 'soaked with the blood of German youths' is described as the memorial's 'sacred centre'.[7]

The two shorter walls of the hall carry, in stone lettering, quotations from Walter Flex and Friedrich Hölderlin. On the northern wall is the inscription:

Ihr heiligen grauen Reihen geht unter Wolken des Ruhms und tragt die blutigen Weihen des heimlichen Königtums[8]

Figure 3.10 Inside the Langemarck Hall memorial.
Photograph: By author.

On the southern:

> Lebe droben, O Vaterland, Und zähle nicht die Toten! Dir ist Liebe! Nicht Einer zu viel gefallen[9]

Finally, the view from the Langemarck Hall faces westwards, away from the rest of the Olympic Complex. March considered this incorporation of the German landscape into the memorial would create a connection with *Heimat*.[10]

Hitler consolidated the links between these layers of symbolism and the 1936 Olympics by entering the stadium via this ensemble, having first paused in the memorial, as he went to open the Games.[11] Yet the power of the Langemarck Hall was not to be bound either by the structure that housed it or by the relatively short duration of the Olympics. March explained that situating the memorial beneath the bell tower transformed that tower into a symbol of the German memorial so that its visual prominence across the Reichssportfeld would, in turn, endow the entire Olympic Complex with a consciousness of Langemarck and the structure's valuable contents. This connection would, March anticipated, endure beyond the Olympic Games so that sporting competitions, musical performances at the outdoor theatre and the large demonstrations on the Maifeld would all take place in view of the memorial for the German youth who in 1914 went to their deaths singing for Germany.[12] The memorial's connection with death would go on to be further strengthened when in 1943 Hans von Tschammer und Osten, Imperial Head of Sport and president of the National Socialist Sports League of the German Reich, died and was granted a state funeral. After the ceremony, which was held at the Reich Chancellery and at which Goebbels delivered the eulogy, the urn containing his remains was placed inside the Langemarck Hall on 2 May 1943.[13]

Despite the high-profile of the memorial and it centrality to some of the founding myths of National Socialism, from the absence of references to the Langemarck Hall in *Völkischer Beobachter* articles about the site between 1933 and 1934, Schmidt surmises that the idea of including a memorial hall was not incorporated into the design for the Olympic until the later planning phases. The impetus for its inclusion seems likely to have come from Carl Diem who had fought at the Battle of Langemarck. In a letter to March in 1961 he mentions that it was he who had brought the earth from the graves of his fallen comrades back with him and suggested the name the 'Langemarck Hall'.[14] Once the incorporation of the memorial had been agreed, early plans for its design suggest that March had initially proposed a less monumental structure, with gradually inclining ramps rather than the granite steps at the side of the main entrance and a much smaller forecourt than was eventually constructed. Given that alterations to the plans occurred in 1934–5, just as the designs for the rest of the stadium were being adapted to make it appear more monumental, Schmidt suggests we can presume that these changes were similarly imposed from above.[15] The Langemarck Hall structure can thus be seen as an expression of myriad elements of National Socialist ideology which was at the very least sanctioned by, and very likely heavily shaped by, the National Socialist elite.

Post-unification interventions into the site do not, however, only need to respond to the structure's use in the Third Reich but also to its uncritical reconstruction by its original architect in the 1960s. On 15 February 1947, the demolition of the heavily war-damaged bell tower was one of the first significant post-war interventions into the site undertaken by the British. The Olympic Bell was damaged in the process and was buried in order to prevent it being plundered by metal thieves.[16] At March's impetus, the bell was recovered in 1956 but was found to have been damaged beyond repair.[17] It would remain a feature of the Olympic site, however, and is today to be found displayed at ground level in close proximity to the main stadium. The earth from the Langemarck cemetery has disappeared but it is unknown when or how this happened.[18] By June 1958, responsibility for the area of the site on which the structure stands had passed from the British allies back to the German authorities and plans were already well underway for the reconstruction of the bell tower and the renovation of the Langemarck Hall as well as other elements of the Olympic Complex including the swimming stadium and the Waldbühne. His correspondence with the building authorities in charge of the renovations reveals Werner March was involved in these discussions, providing advice on the reconstruction and materials and even designs.[19] March's early post-war designs show he proposed to rebuild the bell tower to its original height of seventy-six metres and for the tower to perforate the Langemarck Hall for half of its height. As the tower rose through the Langemarck Hall it would be clad in glass.[20] In 1960, March was officially given the contract to rebuild the bell tower and renovate the rest of the structure, including the Langemarck Hall. Schäche and Szymanski posit that the awarding of this particular contract may have been a form of compensation for the 1958 construction of Corbusier's *Unité d'Habitation* in close proximity to the Olympic grounds. Known today as the Corbusierhaus, the building was part of the 1957–8 Interbau exhibition which saw celebrated architects including Walter Gropius and Max Taut invited to design solutions to West Berlin's post-war housing problems. According to Schäche and Szymanski, March had vehemently opposed the construction of Corbusier's seventeen-storey apartment block due to its height and dominance over the surrounding area and his fears it would detract from the compositional strength of the Olympic Complex.[21] Questions over whether or not it was appropriate to simply reconstruct the memorial clearly passed through March's mind. In correspondence between March and Diem, Schmidt finds indications that March was unsure about reinstating the former function of the Langemarck Hall, suggesting that perhaps it could be repurposed as a site dedicated to a new ritual around the Olympic Bell. Diem responded that it would be 'idiotic' not to return the room to its former meaning and advised that March simply proceed with the renovation of the Langemarck Hall quietly and avoid public debate.[22] March's dilemma was presumably averted because, as part of the brief he was given for the renovation, the building authority stipulated that the structure would not be fundamentally altered from its original state, only the Führerkanzel (Hitler's pulpit) would be omitted.[23] As a result, rather than seeking to create critical distance from the National Socialist construction and its links to the ideology of the Third Reich, March sought to simply reconstruct and repair it, conflating the different temporal layers.

This issue was problematized at the time with particular focus on the Hölderlin quotation. In early 1967 Berlin's Special Assets and Building Administration received a letter via the Bundestag Petition Committee from a member of public. He had read in *Deutsches Panorama* magazine that the Hölderlin quote would be restored using state money. First, he asked for confirmation that this was correct. Secondly, if this was correct, would this be an indication that the current authorities agreed with the sentiment in the quotation: Did 'one too many' really not fall in the world wars? With regards to the first question, the response was fairly straightforward; as the inscription had not actually been damaged in the war, it didn't need any repair with Federal funds. In answer to the second, more complex element of the query, the complainant was informed that this issue had in fact already come up, been subject to public discussion and subsequently been addressed. The impetus for this had been a Berlin priest, M. Englebert, who had petitioned for the quotation's removal in June 1965. After some deliberation, the Special Assets and Building Administration had decided that removing the citation would not erase the problems associated with renovating such a structure and had instead added the names of the authors of both quotations and the dates of their births and deaths. The rationale for this was that by adding these details, visitors to the Langemarck Hall could situate the quotations within the context from which they originated. In response to the 1967 complainant, the Special Assets and Building Administration reiterated that removing the quotation would not be 'suitable for the critical confrontation with history which is essential for our times'. For information, he was informed that the names and dates were added in April 1966 with a cost of 375 deutschmarks.[24] In this response we see elements of post-authoritarian governmentality in the Bonn Republic but, given the subtlety of merely adding names and dates, we also see that it was not performed as overtly as it would go on to be in the Berlin Republic. It is unclear whether or not this response was deemed satisfactory at the time but it was not generally considered to be so in post-unification debates around the memorial. The same quotations would go on to be highlighted as part of a wider discussion of the site's National Socialist origins in a booklet produced by one of the citizens' groups campaigning against Berlin's application for the 2000 Olympic Games. The anonymous author points out that the quotations fail to reflect that what is commemorated in the Langemarck Hall was, in fact, part of a war of aggression and that this would go on to be repeated at the same place in 1940.[25] Berlin architectural historians Schäche and Szymanski also highlighted the lack of contextualizing information provided in this part of the site, as late as 2001 commenting on the absence of a detailed explanatory panel.[26]

Determining the post-unification response to the structure

In common with the rest of the Olympic site, despite campaigns from citizens' initiatives and academics, it was not until the prospect of the World Cup loomed on the horizon that the structure began to attract significant attention. A 2004 document detailing the guiding principles for the development of the Olympic Complex produced by the Senate Department for Education, Youth and Sport lamented that although the structure containing the bell tower and the Langemarck Hall was of considerable historic and symbolic significance, this was, until now, largely unknown outside of a circle of interested experts. In particular, the Langemarck Hall was highlighted as an 'unappreciated entity'.[27] But even after this report it was still overlooked. The initial design from Gerkan, Marg and Partners (gmp), the architects awarded the contract for renovating the stadium, concentrated on the stadium area and left out more peripheral elements such as the Sports Forum, the Langemarck Hall and the Maifeld.[28] These elements were due to be incorporated into the history trail in a planned 'second stage'; however, by 2005 the funding for this did not appear to be forthcoming.[29] In this sense, the structure's physical dislocation precluded it from the areas prioritized for engagement. Conversely, however, its visual significance within the site as a whole meant that the bell tower played a key role in determining the overall renovation of the rest of the complex. Despite the complications it created for the planned roofing of the stadium, the preservation of the opening at the Marathon Gate to ensure the maintenance of the visual axis which was punctuated by the bell tower was identified as a key priority in the plans to renovate the stadium before the World Cup. This was a key criterion in the judging of the design competition and led to the awarding of the contract to gmp.[30] Indeed, this axis had formed an integral part of March's original design and the bell tower structure which closed off the entire complex at its western edge was a crucial component of this.[31] Furthermore, it was a key element of the spectacle March sought to create; in 1936 he ruminated on the 'striking impact' that would be created through fire of the Olympic torch against the backdrop of the Marathon Gate and the more distant bell tower.[32] The visual effects of this arrangement were also recognized by the post-unification team. In explaining his firm's designs to a meeting of the House of Representatives Committee for Building, Housing and Transport regarding the practical and financial implications of the renovation of the Olympic Stadium, Dr Menting of gmp explained that the maintenance of the axis through the Marathon Gate was 'essential' for maintaining the distinctiveness of the stadium, and that allowing a media-friendly view out of the stadium towards the bell tower was of great importance.[33] Yet the axis was not only a visual feature. According to March, this connection between the Maifeld and the stadium had been ordered by Hitler,[34] and as architectural historians Werner Durth and Paul Siegel argue, the axis is not just about binding elements of the Olympic Complex spatially and aesthetically but also about cementing the connection between the ideas of *Volksgemeinschaft*, physical training, competition, military comradeship and the veneration of heroes.[35] This point was raised by Dietmar Volk of the Green party in one of several meetings of the Berlin House of Representatives in which the renovation of the site was discussed. Volk acknowledged that the building's listed status demands the maintenance of the visual axis but contended that keeping the view to the bell tower also meant maintaining the view to the Langemarck Hall and thus the former Führer cult. His interjection was countered by the meeting's chair who pointed out that linking the Monument Preservation authorities with the former Führer cult was not appropriate and brought the discussion back to the topic at hand.[36]

On 18 March 2004, the House of Representatives met to discuss funding the transformation of the Langemarck Hall area into an exhibition. Again, the structure's prominence on the axis was a crucial determinant in the discussions as the participants were aware that this made it likely that visitors would have questions about it, especially now that they would be aware of the history of the rest of the site through the history trail. This, combined with the prospect of the impending World Cup, and the associated 'millions of visitors from all over the world' and the 'approximately 6000 journalists who would pass through the Bell Tower complex every day in order to get to their workplace', proved to be a key impetus for the decision to pay for the renovation of the building and for the construction of an Information Centre.[37] Given that Federal funds had already been allocated for the installation of an exhibition within the structure on the condition that the building itself would be renovated, the State of Berlin declared that it was prepared to fund the necessary renovations.[38] The start of the 2006 World Cup was recognized as a hard deadline and, as such, it was deemed imperative that plans should start immediately and that building work should commence by March 2005 at the latest.[39]

There was, however, still some uncertainty and debate about exactly what should be housed within the structure and what its relationship with the rest of the site should be. The 2004 guiding principles set out by the Senate Department for Education, Youth and Sport indicate an intention to integrate the structure more tightly into visitors' experience of the Olympic Complex. The proposals included using the structure as one of the main entrances to the entire complex and turning the ground floor and the Langemarck Hall into a visitors' centre. As well as housing an exhibition about the history of the site, the visitors' centre would also contain a souvenir shop, information about sport in Berlin, a hire station for bikes and roller skates and would be a starting off point for guided tours of the complex. The document also highlighted plans to assess the possibility of including catering facilities. While it was hoped that the federal government might assist with the financing of the exhibition, the Senate anticipated seeking private capital to fund the necessary building works.[40] On 15 February 2005 the issue was discussed in the Berlin Senate where it was mandated that as well as creating a place of remembrance, the alterations should work on two levels: first through engaging with the materiality of the site and secondly by constructing a narrative around its history.[41] The commission for the architectural design was given to gmp who had carried out the renovation of the main Olympic Stadium, and the exhibition was put together by the German Historical Museum. An element of uncertainty which does not seem to have been resolved surrounded the connection between the content and layout of the exhibition and that of the history trail. Reflecting on the process of developing the history trail around the rest of the Olympic Complex, Endlich states that the lack of communication and cooperation on this issue 'casts a significant light on the short-sighted political setting of priorities' which arises due to 'pressure for high profile events to be deemed successful'.[42] The exhibition opened on 4 May 2006, five weeks before the start of the 2006 World Cup. In contrast to the renovation carried out in the early 1960s, the resulting (re)ordering of space/time involves the clear identification of the National Socialist layer of the site and the clear designation of it as 'other'. Yet it simultaneously calls this binary into question. This is both apparent through the materiality of the site and through the narratives constructed there, two elements which are very much intertwined.

Materiality

The simultaneous setting up and breaking down of the National Socialist/not National Socialist binary is reflected in the materiality of the structure. The site still strongly attests to its National Socialist origins through its rigidly symmetrical, stone-clad, columned exterior and on the inside through the columns, extensive use of stone and the dramatic lighting concept which uses fixtures clearly designed to resemble burning torches. Gmp set out to ensure their physical alterations to the structure would be 'deliberately distinct in shape and material from the historic fabric and remain instantly recognisable as modern additions'. These 'simple and robust' additions include 'aluminium stelae and benches', a 'transparent cube [which] serves as the museum shop', a 'multimedia-box [which functions as] a space within a space' and 'large frameless panes of glass'.[43] We have already established that while stone and natural materials were instrumentalized in the Third Reich, so too has glass become symbolically laden in the Federal Republic. Its transparency has frequently been juxtaposed with the opacity of politics in National Socialism; its lightweight delicacy contrasted with the megalomania of solid, bombastic National Socialist stone-clad buildings.[44]

The architects have clearly not sought to reshape the site too dramatically; the 'transparent cube' that was added to serve as a ticket office and museum shop is wholly contained within the structure itself and does not disturb the lines or visual impact of the building's exterior. In passing through this cube, however, the visitor's experience of the site is framed in a particular way. The modernity and transparency of the ticket box presents a marked contrast to the building's stone, columned, symmetrical exterior; it indicates to the entering visitor that this building has been 'dealt with'. This highly visible contrast between new and old sets up a binary which structures the visitor's experience throughout the site. The original, stone, columned entrance/the 'transparent cube'; the lights designed to resemble burning torches in the entrance hall and Langemarck Hall/the spotlights recessed into the ceiling of the exhibition space; the stone staircase/the glass lift. Through these examples, the binary becomes one of surface, of material. It sees the modern and technologically advanced put forward in opposition to the natural, to the time-less but not particularly adaptable. This binary can be interestingly explored by focusing on two, very different visual perspectives that the renovated site offers us: the view from the bell tower and one particular element of the exhibition on the ground floor. From the bell tower the visitor has a view of the stadium from above. From this perspective the tension that characterizes the entire Olympic site is instantly apparent: on the one hand, the scale and axiality of the ensemble as well as the allusions to the antiquity and the solidity of its stone-clad exterior all attest to its National Socialist origins; on the other hand, clearly visible atop the 1936 composition is a modern, lightweight cantilevered roof. Also designed by gmp and constructed in time for the 2006 World Cup this roof has been described as 'an artistic engineering feat'.[45] The gmp design was chosen specifically because of its lack of interference with March's construction; it does not break the axiality by enclosing the stadium completely; neither is it particularly visible from outside the stadium at ground level.[46] While one was designed to complement the other, these elements of the site remain distinct. The solid stone of the 1936 structure contrasts strongly with the light, filigree steel roof that appears to be floating above it. Visually, this continues the binary: the modern stadium/the National Socialist prestige building. This dichotomy is challenged, however, by a perspective offered almost eighty metres below the viewing platform, in the exhibition on the ground floor. Here, rather than 'finished' plaster or brick walls which enclose the majority of the exhibition, we can see through to the frame around which the building was constructed. A small sign attached to a vertical beam tells us that we are seeing a 'view to the sub-structure of the grandstands around the Langemarck Hall and the VIP stand'. A short paragraph of text informs us that what we are looking at is the 'filigree ironwork' of the original construction which in its time represented 'state-of-the-art technology' and that 'in its modernity stands in direct contrast to the outward architectural design of the Maifeld grounds'. It also tells us that 'the use of the most modern means of construction to solve building problems was an on-going principle in National Socialist architecture'. This small, not particularly visible plaque problematizes our experience, not only of this structure but of the whole Olympic Complex. It challenges our perceptions of the spaces we have just walked through by revealing that this dimly lit, shadowy, stone, crypt-like space is, in fact, the product of modernity and technology. The breaking down of this binary challenges the othering of National Socialism, revealing that rather than something wholly alien to liberal democracy it is, in fact, simply a different permutation of modernity; to refer back to Dean, the difference between authoritarian and liberal governmentality is one of aspiration and extent rather than of techniques and strategy.[47]

Exhibition

The National Socialist/non-National Socialist binary is further consolidated and challenged through the relationship between the 1936 memorial to the Battle of Langemarck and the 2006 exhibition installed by the German Historical Museum. The most significant element of the National Socialist historicization of the site, the Langemarck memorial, is still largely in its original state. Corresponding to March's 1936 description, the Langemarck Hall today is still a long, dark, narrow room punctuated by twelve columns arranged in two rows which form a walkway down the centre. A dominant feature in the room, the thick columns indicate the privileging of drama over pragmatism; they both obstruct and obfuscate, hindering movement around the room while making movement necessary in order to see all of the hall's contents. The space is lit by dramatic 'up-lighting' and through the daylight from the tall, thin windows. The black steel shields listing the names of the regiments and divisions involved in the battle still line the eastern wall while the shorter northern and southern walls continue to be dominated by the large, stone letters of the Flex and Hölderlin quotations but these are now supplemented with the names and dates of birth and death of their authors. In contrast to this, the 2006 exhibition is a very brightly lit, ordered, rational space (Figure 3.11). There is a strong uniformity to the information boards, both in terms of how the content is arranged on them and in how they are arranged in the rooms. The material is organized thematically into six sections with overlapping chronologies: Sport, Society and Politics; The Olympic Games 1936; Building History of the Site; The Use of the

Figure 3.11 Part of the exhibition 1909 – 1936 – 2006 Historic Site: The Olympic Grounds. *Photograph:* By author.

Grounds; The History of a Myth; and The Current Use of the stadium. The first board in each section displays a title in block capitals and each subsequent board then has its own subheading. Each section has its own colour scheme which is visible both in the colour of these headings and in the coloured rectangle in the top right-hand corner of each board. The dramatic and symbolic properties of the Langemarck Hall memorial are thus emphasized and countered by the rationality of the exhibition yet the two are continually in dialogue with one other, each challenging and consolidating the other.

The most overt confrontation between the two is found in the part of the exhibition situated on the first floor. Entitled 'The History of a Myth', this section has a dual function. As well as informing visitors about the wider history of the site, it also serves to provide a commentary on the very space within which it is situated. Located in a small anteroom which is passed through on the way into the Langemarck Hall memorial, it outlines the development, appropriation and instrumentalization of the myth of the Battle of Langemarck via text and photographs. It begins by discussing reactions to the First World War at the time, highlighting that despite outward shows of enthusiasm and patriotism there was much anxiety and worry among the young, 'inexperienced' volunteers. The 'genesis of the myth' which saw the deaths of the soldiers at Langemarck linked with ideas of 'youth and sacrifice for the nation' is traced back to the first anniversary of the battle in 1915. We then see the 'metamorphosis' and increasing politicization of the myth through the Weimar years and under National Socialism. As this anteroom is something that must be passed through in order to access the Langemarck Hall itself, it can be seen as having been designed to provide some kind of inoculation against the power of the room itself. It is as though the designers hope that immunity to the possible effects of the Langemarck Hall will be developed here before the visitor is exposed to it. The Langemarck Hall offers a bounded space within which some of the more troubling legacies of dictatorship can be located and subsequently bordered, segregated and controlled. As is apparent here, this allows experience of them to be managed, for the encounter to be framed before it occurs.

Today, however, the Langemarck Hall is not as disordered as it first appears. Among the gloom, columns, torches and shields are the traces of post-unification intervention into the space, attempts to order it through unpicking and 'othering' its individual layers. Information boards trace the veneration and instrumentalization of the site in the Third Reich and inform the reader how Hitler's visit immediately before opening the Olympic Games ensured that the connection between sport and military featured heavily in the narratives around the games. Photographs of this visit and other commemorative events at the hall in the 1930s enable the visitor to see that their surroundings have hardly changed. One key difference is, of course, the information boards that provide the commentary. On individual boards the provenance of the two quotes of the wall is expanded upon. It is demonstrated that one of them, that on the southern wall taken from Hölderlin's 1799 ode *Der Tod fürs Vaterland*, was simply appropriated and distorted by the National Socialists and that it actually 'has nothing to do with the Nazi idea of a "community of fate" characterised by a shared "blood bond"'. Rather, it is explained that Hölderlin was 'inspired by the French Revolution and the human rights they embodied'. The quote on the opposing wall, from Flex's *Das Weihnachtsmärchen des 50sten Regiments*, was first published in 1915 and is described as a 'sentimental tale teeming with Christian and nationalist sentiment'. This contextualization of the two quotations both undermines the value of the words themselves and demonstrates the highly selective appropriation of the regime that put them there.

This emotive, irrational, subjective (ab)use of history is presented in marked contrast to the exhibition downstairs which is referred to as a 'documentation centre' rather than a museum – the difference being, in theory if not always in practice, that the former does not contain artefacts while the latter does.[48] This designation has connotations which posit it as a sober, methodologically researched exhibition which presents objective evidence in the form of primary materials and allows visitors to interpret them as they see fit. Macdonald discusses the significance of this distinction at the former rally grounds in Nuremberg, highlighting the potential impact that 'museumification' could have on any artefacts that might, in theory, be available for display (in this case, elevating their status), and the implications it could have for the building in which the museum is housed, increasing its value or 'perfecting' its space.[49] The installation of a documentation centre instead of a museum in the Langemarck Hall could also be understood in those terms. While artefacts are absent, this particular documentation centre makes prolific use of images which include photographs, reproductions of letters and posters, and maps and diagrams. As we have already seen, however, historical representation is contingent upon multiple factors, some of which are wholly unconnected to the historical events themselves and the way in which curators would like them presented. In this particular case, practical and economic issues played a defining role – in 2005 the Senate made it clear that in this exhibition duplicates would be used rather than original materials 'on security and cost grounds'.[50]

The self-conscious use of the image is most apparent immediately upon entering the exhibition. Directly opposite the entrance, in the section of the site that deals with 'The Olympic Games 1936', is a large triptych. This blown-up photographic image divided into three separate sections shows a packed stadium, from the context we can infer that it was taken in the Berlin Olympic Stadium during the 1936 games. Each third of the photograph is on a board, the same size and style as the ones that make up the rest of the exhibition. Like the other information boards in this category, a yellow/orange rectangle is on the right-hand corner of each board. This is the only colour on the image. The photograph is a strong representation of the capacity of the individual to be subsumed into the crowd. The only individual face that can be clearly made out is that of a man in the lower left-hand corner. The other faces are obscured by the sea of arms and hands raised in Nazi salutes and by the fact they are facing slightly away from the camera. In the centre of the image a swastika flag flies on a pole, accentuated by its stark contrast against the light-coloured sky above the stadium. Within the exhibition this photograph is simultaneously highlighted and problematized. As well as being prominently situated within the exhibition, the single image is awarded the same surface area as three of the boards that contain a combination of text and pictures. Yet the division of the photograph into three seems to be a conscious attempt to detract from the image, as if to preclude the possibility of visitors admiring the visual effect of the choreography of crowds shown in the photograph. There is a strong contrast between this image and other photographs in the exhibition which show individuals, including athletes, who would go on to be persecuted by the Nazis for their political stance or ethnic background. These photographs – a mixture of posed and candid shots, of families, individuals and smiling groups of friends – clearly show their subjects' faces while the captions beside the photographs give the details of their respective fates. This is in keeping with a shift that Niven perceived in the revising of the exhibitions at the Ravensbrück Concentration Camp in the 1990s. By moving away from presenting a 'macronarrative' of Holocaust atrocities towards 'micronarratives', communicated through individuals' biographies, photographs, personal items and interviews, there is a shift from 'anonymous group suffering' towards a 'repersonalization' of the individual victims which both facilitates empathy and highlights the complexities and differences which are elided when individuals are subsumed into categories of victimhood.[51] Unlike the crowd in the large image, the people in these photographs are individualized and therefore humanized.

As well as these photographs, images of day-to-day objects that would have been used and possessed by individuals feature on the display boards and go some way towards providing an insight into the history of everyday life. This balancing of displays about grand events, key dates and the political elite with a more bottom-up perspective has been described as 'very much the orthodoxy in German museums today'.[52] While Paver highlights the distortive effect the display of selected everyday items can have in exhibitions which are specifically about National Socialism by creating a concentration of 'Nazi-coded objects' (uniforms, posters, swastika-emblazoned mugs, tools, toys and so on) that would simply not represent lived experience between 1933 and 1945,⁵³ the use of images of material culture here has a different effect. Here, it helps to unsettle the National Socialist/non-National Socialist binary by situating the everyday items of the Third Reich within a longer historical period and showing continuities across perceived political ruptures. A beer mug from a 1923 gymnastics festival, for example, features the black imperial eagle clutching a red shield which is adorned with what the caption tells us is Jahn's 'gymnastics cross', a white, broken cross-like design, thus showing continuity in symbols and design across 1933. Similarly, the image of a 1924 newspaper page that features a drawing depicting a soldier kneeling in a graveyard underneath the words 'Deutschland, Deutschland über alles' shows that the incorporation of the First World War dead into nationalistic discourse had roots going back beyond 1933. Elsewhere within the text of the exhibition we see further indications of continuity across the Nazi seizure of power including nineteenth-century connections between politics, sport and the military and the longer history of the veneration of the athletic physique.

Throughout this exhibition, the ordering of the Olympic Stadium's layers is different to that elsewhere at the site. While the history trail has primarily focused on the othering of the National Socialist layer, the exhibition serves to integrate it into the other layers that make up the site's history. This is apparent through the three dates in the exhibition's title: 1909, the year of the opening of the Grunewald Racecourse; 1936, the year of the National Socialist Olympic Games for which the area was transformed by Werner March; and 2006, the year in which the Olympic Complex was renovated for Germany's hosting of the World Cup. On the one hand, the sequence of dates situates the site's National Socialist use within a broader historical narrative, indicating that it will not be singled out and othered. On the other hand, the inclusion of a middle date highlights a point of change in the trajectory of the site, a disruption in the continuum from the date of the first building on the site to the date of its most recent renovation. Rather than simply identifying the National Socialist layer and holding it up as 'other', then, this exhibition problematizes a straightforward reading of the site as 'National Socialist'. This in turn unsettles a straightforward reading of responses to the past in the Berlin Republic;ust as we saw in the debates around the statues, there seems to be a clear attempt to demonstrate that in the united Germany, history is not instrumentalized as it was in the Third Reich, to overtly hold the reason, research and rationality of contemporary historicization in opposition to the myth, emotion and drama that underpinned National Socialist representations of the past. this approach has the potential to support and consolidate the self-image of the Federal Republic in the same way that myth and emotion did for the Third Reich. This highlighting of how history was instrumentalized by some 'other' regime is, however, in itself, an instrumentalization of history. As well as providing a commentary on the Third Reich, the exhibition therefore also provides an implicit commentary on the system within which it was itself produced. In this it performs and consolidates the post-authoritarian governmentality of the FRG, indicating that it is a society that defines itself by privileging knowledge and understanding over dramatic effect and the distortion of historical 'truth'.

Yet here, the site is not (just) reduced to its National Socialist origins. That part of its history is located within a much broader narrative and the emphasis on continuity across perceived ruptures de-others the National Socialist period. These connections are not just retrospective, as is apparent in final section of the exhibition. Dedicated to the 'Current Use of The Stadium' and located within the small café on the first floor, this section momentarily frees the Olympic Stadium from its National Socialist past: it is fleetingly de-othered. The site portrayed here could be any other modern stadium. Accompanying the boards which cover the International Stadium Festival (ISAF), football cup finals and Hertha BSC's use of the site are three aerial photographs which show the site in 1928, 1954 and 2004, respectively. The curators have clearly decided not to bookend the exhibition with images that correspond to the three years in the exhibition title. Events that occurred during the Third Reich such as 'the tradition of the ISAF, inaugurated in 1937' and the German Football Association's German Cup Final which took place several times in the Stadium 'until 1943' are mentioned but not problematized. The war and unification are referred to simply in terms of how they have affected sports in Berlin; the ISAF, for example, was 'interrupted during and immediately after the war' and the German Cup Final 'has become one of the city's top sports events, particularly since unification'. Both in terms of its content and its location in the site, this section of the exhibition fulfils a 'normalizing' function. Situating the boards within the café takes away the 'exhibition' feel, the information boards become more like a backdrop for diners to peruse as they await their sandwiches. This fairly casual arrangement reflects how the topics dealt with here are among the least problematic for the site. They simply show the use of a modern sports stadium, the properties that are emphasized are those of the generic stadium within the modern city, rather than the traces of dictatorship within the democratic city.

While the attempted reordering of the Olympic Stadium through the rationality of the history trail constitutes it as a space in which post-authoritarian governmentality is performed, the challenging of the National Socialist/not National Socialist binary seen in the Langemarck Hall and the consequent de-othering of the National Socialist layer, and therefore, the site, make it function as a space within which post-authoritarian governmentality is also being transcended. As will be demonstrated in the next chapter, this tension is even more pronounced at the former Flughafen Tempelhof.

Part 4

Freedom? Transcending post-authoritarian governmentality at the former Tempelhof Airport[1]

Introduction

Cycling along Mehringdam from Kreuzberg, the first encounter with Flughafen Tempelhof (Figure 4.1) is surprisingly underwhelming. In fact, it is highly conceivable that you could pass the first section, which runs along Mehringdam from its corner with Schwiebusser Strasse, without even registering that the building you have just passed is, in fact, part of the vast airport complex. At four storeys, this first section is by no means out of proportion with its neighbours and is dwarfed by the eleven-storey block of flats across the road. The colonnaded arcade that protrudes to the edge of the pavement is uncharacteristic of the area but is not a singular feature in the urban environment of Berlin. Even as you round the corner onto Platz der Luftbrücke, it is not immediately clear that the structures to your left form one single, monumental complex due to the row of trees that both mirrors and detracts from its smooth, sweeping curve, forming a screen that diminishes the uniformity of the composition. The unity of the arrangement is further undermined by the distraction of the traffic, the proliferation of street furniture, the greenery of the central reservation and, above all, by the trees in the centre, circular plaza which largely obscure the bulk of the building.

The first indicator that the site might be somewhat out of the ordinary is the sight of the 'hunger claw', stretching out of the greenery in commemoration of the Berlin Airlift (see Figure 4.4). If this induces passers-by to pause and turn around to reassess their surroundings, they will see the stone relief of an eagle affixed to the side of the building they have just passed. In contrast to the warm hue of the Triassic limestone that clads the front of the Tempelhof Airport complex, the eagle is cast in grey stone, the same shade as the Jurassic limestone that surrounds the windows and cornices. The accentuation of these features alerts the observer to the rigidly uniform fenestration which is repeated across the entire front of the building for as far as can be seen. This draws the gaze along the sweeping curve of the building, enabling the observer to finally recognize the unity of the composition within which they are now situated.

Inside, a distinct 'Marie-Celeste' feeling pervades the former airport (Figure 4.2): rows of check-in desks and a still functioning baggage carousel await luggage that will never come; 'departures' and 'arrivals' boards appear ready to display the names of far-off locations which can no longer be reached through the closed gates; the 'school gym' smell lingers in the basketball court which, still replete with the 'Berlin Braves' insignia, water fountain and scoreboard, feels as though it could spring to life at any moment; the scrupulously clean stainless steel food containers under the hot light in the *Deutsche Kantine* could be moments away from being filled with sustenance for the airport's German workers; downstairs, an illustrated fairy tale written in gothic German script brightens up the walls of a bomb-shelter, onto which hastily scribbled tally charts and improvised scoreboards suggest that American service personnel will return in their

Figure 4.1 The former Flughafen Tempelhof. The head of Lemcke's eagle is in the foreground.

Photograph: By author.

Figure 4.2 Inside the former Flughafen Tempelhof.

Photograph: By author.

next break to resume their games and continue to ignore the plea, handwritten onto a pipe in English: 'Please! Don't be destructive'. At the rear of the airport, the smooth tarmac of the runways stretches across the airfield and signs continue to instruct absent aviation crew to 'hold for FOLLOW ME or RTE instructions' or that there should be 'no vehicles beyond this point without radio-contact with the tower (70.15 MHz)'.

Until the 2008 closure of Tempelhof Airport, the site had a long connection with aviation history. Used as a military parade and exercise ground since 1828, by the late nineteenth-century Tempelhofer Feld was the largest remaining expanse of green space in the growing city and its preservation was seen as key to maintaining health and well-being among Berlin's population.[1] Before the commercial and military development of flight that followed the outbreak of the First World War, aviation was primarily associated with meetings and competitions between enthusiasts who would show off their newest innovations. Crowds would be drawn to these displays which took place across Europe and which in Berlin were held on Tempelhofer Feld.[2] After the war, commercial aviation advanced rapidly in Europe, and by the end of 1919, passengers could fly from Berlin to Weimar, Munich and Hamburg. In 1926, as restrictions in the Treaty of Versailles were lifted, Berlin became an international hub. The development of facilities occurred in tandem with the expansion of air travel. From temporary hangars and workshops, airfields across Europe began to expand their refreshment and waiting facilities to meet the needs of their increasing numbers of passengers. At Tempelhof, the existing temporary structures were extended between 1924 and 1927 and included the first permanent structure, containing hangars and workshops, erected on the site to a design by Heinrich Kosina and Paul Mahlberg. This was soon followed by the first terminal building, designed by Paul and Klaus Engler and completed in 1929.[3] By the early 1930s, Tempelhof Airport was one of the busiest in Europe and, as its passengers increased from 32,000 per year in 1926 to over 200,000 in 1936,[4] it was already functioning almost to capacity.

Having impressed the Nazi elite with his Aviation Ministry building, Ernst Sagebiel was commissioned with the design of a new airport which would not only be visually striking enough to function as the gateway to Hitler and Speer's planned new world capital but which would also have thirty times the capacity of its predecessor and would remain in service until the year 2000. The building's structure was completed in 1937 and the interior was on the way to completion in 1939 when resources were diverted to fighting the war.[5] As a result, it was the 1920s airport which was used throughout the war and Sagebiel's building did not fulfil its original function until afterwards when it was taken over by the US Air Force. Tempelhof Airport would go on to play a key role in the 1948-9 Berlin Airlift when planes would land there every three minutes, bringing in the essentials needed to sustain life in the city. From 1951 the airport was reopened to commercial flights and from 1962 the departure hall was opened to the public. By the 1970s, however, the 1930s runways were proving too short for modern planes and this, combined with complaints from locals about noise and disturbance, led to the opening of Tegel airport in 1975 and the closure of Tempelhof. Yet this was not the end of Tempelhof's use as an airport; following the fall of the Berlin Wall, the Americans returned the airport to the State of Berlin who reopened it for short and medium haul flights.[6] This was a short-term solution, however; and as this section of the book will demonstrate, the building's function has been heavily contested and closely bound up with debates about memory politics, political legitimacy and the negotiation of 'freedom' ever since.

The first chapter in this section will begin by exploring the duality within both Tempelhof's aesthetics and in its discursive construction, unpicking the processes through which this National Socialist prestige building has been discursively constructed as a 'site of freedom'. It will then show how this conception of the site has been invoked, negotiated and reframed by different parties seeking to make their case in the debates around the site's function. The following chapter will go on to explore attempts to challenge this dominant narrative by unpicking and highlighting the multiple layers of Tempelhof's history, in particular seeking to make the National Socialist layer more visible. While this response employs the techniques and rationale seen at the Olympic Stadium and is therefore in keeping with the dominant paradigm through which the past is negotiated within post-authoritarian governmentality, it is accompanied by a commodification of some aspects of the site's history in its marketing materials. The selective emphasis on more positive elements of the site's history and the selling of it through the architectural features associated with National Socialist prestige architecture indicate a move beyond post-authoritarian governmentality towards a state where economic and other issues begin to overtake the politics of the past. This is borne out in the final chapter of this section, and of the book, which conceptualizes Tempelhofer Feld as a heterotopia in order to explore indications that while current debates around the development of Tempelhofer Feld invoke the idea of 'freedom', they do so not, primarily, as a response to the past in the post-authoritarian city but in response to the ordering of the advanced liberal city. As a whole, Tempelhof gives us a slightly different insight into post-authoritarian governmentality to what we have seen elsewhere. Although its construction and functions under National Socialism, incorporation into National Socialist propaganda and bearing of the architectural features commonly associated with National Socialist prestige architecture render it, in theory, as historically burdened as the former Aviation Ministry or the Olympic Stadium, the site's use after the war has strongly re-inscribed it within the urban imaginary. Rather than representing a site of dictatorship, it has been configured as a 'site of freedom', a space from which dictatorship was resisted and thwarted. Post-unification interventions into the site have therefore been primarily framed not as an indication of how the Berlin Republic responds to dictatorship but how it celebrates its overcoming.

9

Closing Tempelhof Airport, Berlin's 'gateway to the world'

Tempelhof's future as an airport was brought into question even before it was opened to non-Allied air traffic upon the official unification of Germany on 3 October 1990; in the January of that year, executives from Lufthansa and Interflug announced their intention to build a major new airport in the Berlin area. By the time the US Air Force held their official farewell ceremony on 28 January 1993, Berlin Brandenburg Holding, the company charged with bringing the new super airport into being, had been founded and begun the search for potential locations for the new airport. In May 1996, Schönefeld-Süd was selected, and in July of that year an agreement was signed by the Berlin Senate, thus laying the way for the concentration of air traffic at the new Berlin Brandenburg International airport (BBI). A corollary of this ruling was that Tempelhof would cease to function as an airport in 2004. This decision polarized Berlin along largely party political lines; the pro-closure SPD was supported by The Left Party, Alliance 90/The Greens and various citizens' initiatives and environmental groups who rejoiced at the prospect of the closure of the city centre airport. They were vehemently opposed by the CDU and FDP, who were supported by other citizens' groups and a campaign in the Springer Press. In 2004 Tempelhof was granted a stay of execution when Berlin's highest administrative court deemed that it should stay open until BBI was up and running. This reprieve enabled the anti-closure lobby to gain momentum; their various campaigning activities culminated in the organization of a petition for a referendum. By the 14 February 2008 deadline, the petition had attracted sufficient signatures to bring about a referendum which would ask the voters whether or not they wished to see Flughafen Tempelhof continue to function as an airport. In order for the airport to be saved, 25 per cent of eligible voters would need to vote in support of it; the final tally fell just short at 21.7 per cent.[1] This meant that the referendum, which would not have been legally binding anyway, failed and Tempelhof's fate was sealed. At midnight on 30 October, two planes took off from Tempelhof as part of the closing ceremony and at that point Tempelhof ceased operating as an airport.

Architectural duality

While all three of the sites studied in this book are characterized by a tension between their modern and neoclassical features, it is at Tempelhof that this duality has featured most strongly in the discourse around it. Designed by Ernst Sagebiel to function as the monumental gateway to Germania, the airport is a truly imposing edifice. Although the way in which the city has grown up around it does detract from its monumentality, this is still apparent at the main entrance to the terminal building that is framed by a courtyard and edged by the arcaded walkways of the parallel 90 metre-long, three-storey wings where shops and the Air Mail Office would have been situated. The entrance wall itself is dominated by a row of elongated corniced windows situated beneath two rows of block windows that echo the fenestration seen across the landside of the building. Beneath the tall windows the main doors are recessed into the square columns which are repeated around the courtyard. In Sagebiel's designs the airport was to serve as a lynchpin in the National Socialist reconfiguration of Berlin by punctuating the planned north-south axis of the structure around which the city was to be reshaped.[2] Had his plans been realized, the airport would be much more striking from afar: the circular plaza immediately in front of the airport's main entrance would have been ringed with office buildings housing various aviation-related bodies to create 'a new urban focus' for the city;[3] and the terminal would have been made even more impressive through the construction of a cascade of water flowing from Schinkel's 1821 monument to the Wars of Liberation, passing through two obelisks and into a tremendous fountain which would have been situated on what is now Platz der Luftbrücke. The significance of Schinkel's monument has been debated. To Schröder, it would have taken on special meaning in the context of the preparations for war in 1936;[4] however, to architectural historian Dittrich, the monument would not necessarily have needed to be this particular one: Sagebiel was not interested in it as a symbol of liberation but as a means through which to achieve optical dominance.[5] However, despite these elements of bombastic neoclassicism, Tempelhof is also considered to be an expression of the 'modern international style of the age'.[6] Dolff-Bonekämper points to the smoothness of the façades of the buildings around the main courtyard, their barely visible joints and the lack of decoration which she asserts indicates a 'sparseness [which] clearly derives from the international style of the early 1930s';[7] the fourteen stair towers which punctuate the building's curve have been considered to have been influenced by Hans Poelzig's 1928–31 I.G Farben offices and the 1927 Tannenbergdenkmal in East Prussia and *Neues Bauen* influences, particularly from Le Corbusier's 1922 Vaucresson villa, have also been identified in the building's airside.[8] The influence of Erich Mendelsohn, the renowned expressionist architect under whom Sagebiel had worked until Mendelsohn fled Germany in 1933, has also been identified in several aspects of Sagebiel's design.[9]

Tempelhof is thus a paradigmatic example of a 1930s city airport and has been celebrated for its use of materials and technological innovations that were cutting edge at the time: the speed of construction, for example, is a result of the 'mastery […] of high quality reinforced concrete which engineers had gained by the mid-1930s';[10] and Jockeit and Wendt comment on how the 'archaic appearance of the building conceals a structure built to the rationalised industrial techniques of the day and using the latest building techniques'.[11] As such, the airport building has been abstracted from the political context within which it was built and incorporated into a literature within which it is considered primarily in terms of its architectural and technical merits.

Innovations such as Sagebiel's system to optimize the flow of movement around the airport through designating different levels for passengers, visitors, luggage and airmail and freight are explained, presented diagrammatically and, where appropriate, praised.[12] Most roundly acclaimed is the cantilevered, steel canopy roof over the gates and hangar which at 12 metre high, at least 380 metres wide and forty-nine metres deep could house even medium-sized modern planes (Figure 4.3).[13] As well as enhancing passenger experience by minimizing exposure to the elements during boarding and disembarkation, the roof also precluded the need to de-ice planes in the winter, thus reducing turn-around times and increasing efficiency. Other much-vaunted technical innovations include moving walkways to facilitate passenger movement around the airport, a cutting-edge irrigation system as well as two heating plants and a water works which made the airport independent from the city water supply.[14] Just as the technical side of Sagebiel's design has attracted praise, it has also been subjected to criticism; the concave form of the airside departure gates, for example, has been used as a negative teaching example as it could lead to delays in times of heavy air traffic, particularly in the post-war period as aeroplanes increased in size.[15] As well as through using for a grass, rather than the hard-surfaced airfield which was becoming the international trend, Sagebiel's design is said to have had a limited lifespan through the lack of scope provided for future modifications and extension in producing an airport that was, rather than 'flexible and extendable', produced in 'a definitive state

Figure 4.3 The highly praised technical back of Flughagen Tempelhof.
Photograph: By author.

[...] wrapped in concrete'.[16] Furthermore, Tempelhof has been considered in relation to other airports of the same era. Drieschner, for example, notes that features such as 'dry boarding' and isolated traffic flows were also seen in entries to the American Lehigh competition and similarities have been observed between Tempelhof and entries to the 1928 Royal Institute for British Architects airport design competition, although Tempelhof is the only full realization of these ideas.[17] Similarly, Dolff-Bonekämper has pointed out that the flanking of the passenger terminal with the hangars and creation of 'an effect of protective arms embracing the open field' has echoes of Hamburg's Fuhlsbüttel airport.[18] Tempelhof, therefore, is not treated solely as 'the Nazi airport', as an aberration or anomaly within its type, but as a high-technology construction which happens to comply with the aesthetic requirements of the client who commissioned it, that is the National Socialist government.

This hybridity between an example of National Socialist prestige architecture and of a modern, technical building features very heavily in the construction of the site's materiality right across the German press. On the one hand, the press coverage of the debates over Tempelhof has been full of references to its 'bombastic', 'severe, overpowering and excessive' architecture that 'overwhelms and intimidates'.[19] In some accounts, the building's National Socialist origins actually seem to enhance its allure by adding a layer of intrigue around it. This sensationalism can be seen in *a Frankfurter Rundschau* article where the author describes their tour through an 'eerie cellar labyrinth whose walls are black and porous, where corridors lead to nowhere and steel beams are grotesquely twisted and the air still smells of ash. No-one knows what was burnt here in early 1945, at 1000 degrees nothing was left'.[20] Other articles are full of evocative descriptions of the 'giant catacombs, vaults and galleries of the Nazi building'.[21] Yet at the same time, the site's modernity and city-centre location are both also widely commented upon and contribute strongly to the narrative that presents Tempelhof as a unique, progressive building which should be valued in Berlin; the *Hamburger Abendblatt* considered it to be just as revolutionary architecturally and for European aviation as it ever was;[22] architect Norman Foster publicly praised its 'modern boldness';[23] and the *Frankfurter Rundschau* also features praise of the 'astoundingly modern airport'.[24] This positivity does not demonstrate an erasure or forgetting of the site's origins, but rather an acceptance that both can be highlighted simultaneously. *Die Welt*, for example, sees the airport building as a 'testament to the mixture between monumentality and modernity' and as a 'symbol of progress, megalomania and freedom'.[25] In *Berliner Zeitung*, the building is conceptualized as a 'symbol of the greatness of Berlin, of the hubris and modernity of the Nazis and for West Berlin's resistance to the communist claim to power'.[26]

There is a clear dissonance here between the treasuring of Tempelhof as an architectural gem which should be celebrated and the begrudging preservation of Sagebiel's other major project, the former Aviation Ministry, through a sense of normative obligation. This is, to a large extent, due to the role that Flughafen Tempelhof played in the years after the war which meant that the memory politics that needed to be negotiated there after unification had a very different dynamic to those at the former Aviation Ministry. The Aviation Ministry's past, dominated by the Third Reich and the GDR, has largely been conceptualized as negative, as something which the Berlin

Republic defined itself against. In contrast, the National Socialist uses of Tempelhof have been strongly overwritten by its post-war functions, particularly the Berlin Airlift which has led to the site's designation as 'symbol of freedom'.

A site of 'freedom'?

Sagebiel's building only actually began to function as an airport after the Second World War ended and the site was established as the headquarters of the United States Air Force in Berlin. Given the geographical isolation of West Berlin, the metaphor of air travel as a 'bridge' connecting West Berlin to the Western world had considerable resonance, predating the airlift through its use in early 1948 when the now-defunct *Der Telegraf* newspaper reported the news that Germans were permitted to fly again with the words 'a bridge is being built from the lonely island of Berlin to the west'.[27] Just months later, Stalin's severing of the overland connections between West Berlin and the rest of the FRG intensified the proliferation of the metaphor of West Berlin as an 'island of democracy' in the sea of Stalinist socialism. Now that the only way to sustain West Berlin was by bringing supplies in by air, Tempelhof became the main hub for the Berlin Airlift with Allied planes, nicknamed the 'raisin bombers', laden with food, building supplies and other necessities landing there at three-minute intervals, cementing Flughafen Tempelhof's status as Berlin's 'Tor zur Welt'.[28] Even after the blockade was lifted in May 1949, air travel was still valued as a means to bypass the East German control points that one would encounter if leaving West Berlin by land.[29] This elimination of the possibility of interference from East German officials meant that, as well as providing a means for refugees from the GDR to flee to the Western world, air travel was the preferred method of conveying West Berlin children for free holidays in the FRG, in what became known as the *Kinderluftbrücke*, and for transporting industrial goods in the so-called *Kommerzielle Luftbrücke* which ran until 1958.[30] To West Berliners and to refugees from the GDR, Tempelhof represented a link outwards to freedom, providing a springboard from which they could access the rest of the Federal Republic as well as the wider Western world. After the Berlin Wall was built in 1961, the flow of refugees from the GDR which had reached around 3,000 per day was, of course, stemmed.[31] This did not, however, turn Tempelhof into a one-way gate outwards to freedom as the airport's geographical proximity to the Eastern bloc meant that it also functioned as a gateway inwards for refugees from the other side of the iron curtain. Between 1963 and 1983 at least thirteen Polish flights were hijacked and diverted to Tempelhof, earning the Polish LOT airline the nickname 'Lands Often at Tempelhof'.[32] The airport's role in facilitating resistance to the dictatorships of the Eastern Bloc came to supersede its National Socialist legacy, inscribing it as Berlin's 'symbol of freedom'.

As well as having been heavily written into the rhetoric around the former airport, Tempelhof's Cold War past is also highly visible at the site itself. Key examples include Eduard Ludwig's 1951 Air Lift Memorial, the remnants of the 1973 celebration of the twenty-fifth anniversary of the airlift and the head of the eagle removed by the Americans from its position on top of the terminal building and returned in 1985.

Figure 4.4 Eduard Ludwig's 'Air Lift Memorial' (1951).
Photograph: By author.

Located on the square outside the building, named Platz der Luftbrücke, or 'Airlift Square' in 1949, the Air Lift Memorial comprises three prongs intended to represent the three air corridors between West Berlin and West Germany on top of a 20 metre high reinforced concrete structure (Figure 4.4).[33] On the base, underneath the inscription

> Sie gaben ihr Leben für die Freiheit Berlins im Dienste der Luftbrücke 1948/9[34]

are the names of the thirty-nine British, thirty-three Americans and five Germans who died assisting with the airlift. The form of the structure is consciously designed to counter the aesthetic of the building behind it and its placement detracts from the axiality of Sagebiel's composition.[35] This was West Berlin's first post-war piece of monumental artwork and, along with the renaming of the square, has been considered to represent Flughafen Tempelhof's transformation into 'the gateway to the free world'.[36] More broadly, the memorial has come to symbolize West Berlin's desire for freedom and incorporation into the political West as well as West Germany's friendship with the United States. Abstracted representations of the structure feature prominently in numerous publications, flyers and even the campaign material for the referendum on Tempelhof's closure.

At the other side of the site and highly visible from Columbiadamm, the road which runs alongside the airfield, are two large signs, each comprising two 'wings' of text, one in German, the other in English, with a centre-piece illustrated with a silhouetted plane flying across a red, white and blue picture of Ludwig's Airlift Memorial. Large capital letters announce the presence of two 'Berlin Airlift Veterans'; a C-54 Skymaster and a C-47 and among contextualizing information about the airlift, the aeroplanes themselves are explicitly referred to within the text: 'this C-54 "Skymaster" actually flew during the airlift' and 'this C-47 is on permanent loan from the Air Force Museum, Wright Patterson AFB, Ohio'. Only the plaques remain, however; the planes themselves are gone, the area is now grassed over, the floodlights in the ground are damaged and the C-47 was taken to the *Deutsches Technikmuseum* in the late 1990s.[37] Yet the signs, the legacy of the celebrations of the twenty-fifth anniversary of the airlift in 1973 which were originally erected to be seen by people passing by the former airport, now serve as a reminder not just of the airlift but of the continued celebration of the airlift at the site.

The eagle, whose head now stands on a low plinth, dates back to the National Socialist use of the building (Figure 4.1). Early architectural drawings show that Sagebiel experimented extensively with different sizes of eagles in a variety of poses in different locations on the building.[38] He finally settled on the 4.5 metre aluminium sculpture made by Walter E. Lemcke which was positioned prominently on the roof of the building, directly above the main entrance. Despite its clear role in contributing to the bombast and monumentality of the site, the eagle survived the post-war denazification of the building and remained in situ until 1962. When it was finally removed, it was due to practical rather than ideological or aesthetic reasons – to make space for radar equipment. The plaque underneath the eagle's head now outlines in both English and German that the head was taken to the museum of the American Military Academy in West Point, New York, but was returned in 1985 'to be shared with the people of Berlin'. The decision to return the eagle's head to the airport met opposition at the time; art historian Hans-Ernst Mittig sought to convince both the US authorities and the Tempelhof mayor not to go ahead with the installation of this 'embarrassing' memorial.[39] The plaque's lack of reflection on the function of the eagle as a symbol of National Socialism has subsequently been criticized and the composition as a whole labelled an 'uncritical' presentation of a relic of the Third Reich.[40] Furthermore, its positioning is ambiguous. On the one hand, it is a significant demotion from the eagle's original rooftop perch where it was highly visible and played a key role in structuring the composition of the site. Yet on the other hand, whereas Ludwig's Airlift Memorial was deliberately designed to counter the monumentality of the airport building, the eagle's new position has been seen as a re-accentuation of the site's axiality and deemed an, albeit unintentional, re-installation of a National Socialist symbol.[41]

Exploring the journey of the eagle's head provides us with an insight into the process behind the re-inscription of this former National Socialist prestige building as a symbol of freedom and democracy. Once part of a symbol of the power of the Third Reich, the head was taken by the Americans 'as a war trophy' following their victory over Germany and has now been reinstated to bear testament to the new relationship between Americans and Germans as 'brothers in arms'.[42] This transformation of the eagle's significance encapsulates that of the airport building as a whole: through its associations with the United States and its liberating actions, it has been converted from a symbol of National Socialism into a symbol of the antidote to totalitarianism.

Invoking 'freedom'

This construction of the site as a symbol of freedom featured prominently in the post-unification debates about the site's functionality, where the Senate's intervention into the fate of the airport was framed as constructing a response not to dictatorship but to 'freedom', broadly understood. The overt assertion that 'Tempelhof is a symbol of freedom' is a performative statement that features heavily in the wider discourse around the site: the proliferation of this claim, seen in numerous books, flyers, and newspaper articles about Tempelhof,[43] continually and actively constructs Tempelhof as this 'symbol of freedom'. The connection between Tempelhof and 'freedom' thus transcends the private memory of the individuals whose lives were directly impacted upon by the airlift and escape route from West Berlin to which the symbolism alludes and becomes part of cultural memory. The extension of this rhetoric is that Tempelhof's function as an airport has continued to be bound up with questions of freedom and of legitimacy. From the outset, the objections to the closure of Tempelhof were couched in terms of freedom, legitimacy and the democratic decision-making process, all concepts which, when challenged, had the potential to strike at the core of post-authoritarian governmentality. The Senate responded by employing the same rhetoric, conceptualizing the closure of the airport as an opening up of the site for the people of Berlin.

The debates around Tempelhof mark a point at which the dominant structuring frameworks of the Berlin Republic were overtly and publicly challenged from a broad support base which drew on both positive and negative aspects of the past in order to make its point. This became particularly apparent during the campaign to 'save' Tempelhof from the threat of closure that followed unification. Those opposed to the closure of the airport explicitly invoked the site's Cold War past to highlight what they perceived to be a democratic deficit in the decision-making process and to demonstrate that the ruling coalition was disregarding the historical significance of the site. CDU campaign material openly accuses the SPD and the Left Party of hindering the democratic operation of the referendum over Tempelhof's future. An undated booklet produced by the CDU states that these parties claim to 'want more citizen participation. Yet this, the first referendum in Berlin, is not what they had in mind and so in some areas there is a very limited possibility for people to cast their vote.' Furthermore, it contends, people who go to sign the petition for a referendum face 'reluctance from some of the administrative staff members and some are even advised not to vote'.[44] The flyer uses these accusations to situate the pro-airport lobby as resisters of, and therefore the opposite to, the undemocratic and thus illegitimate elements of their opponents' campaign; it states that they will not give in to 'fear-mongering', 'administrative tricks' (Verwaltungstricks) or 'threats'. This is underlined through the use of the rhetoric associated with the collapse of the GDR: 'The people are sovereign. We are the people' (**Das Volk ist der Souverän**. Wir sind das Volk).[45] The phrase 'wir sind ein Volk' was also used by the Springer Press to galvanize people into supporting their campaign and going to vote in the referendum.[46] The use of this particular expression goes beyond the deployment of a tool to motivate potential voters; it connects the campaign to maintain flight operations at Tempelhof with the

Monday demonstrations of 1989. The SPD and the Green party are therefore cast in the role of the undemocratic elite seeking to impose their will on the citizens of Berlin while the CDU, FDP and Springer Press take on the mantle of those representing the will of the people in resisting this illegitimate power. That, just as during the Berlin Blockade, Flughafen Tempelhof is the site onto which this contest is projected only serves to give this connection more traction.

Building on this Cold War rhetoric, the legacy of the 'raisin bombers' was frequently deployed as a means of suggesting that those seeking the cessation of flight operations at Tempelhof were disregarding a normative imperative to continue to honour that history.[47] This was particularly the case in the CDU campaign material: 'Thousands of pilots put their lives at stake to save Berlin as they built the air bridge. Dear Berliners, it is not far for you to go and give your signature at the nearest *Bürgeramt!*'[48] In their own campaign material, the SPD countered this by arguing that commemoration of the past at the site should focus on valuing the people involved rather than 'tarmac and cement', and that the stories of these people should be told through an exhibition on the site itself.[49] A newspaper-style flyer produced by the citizens' initiative 'Tempelhof Aufmachen. Für Alle' (Open Tempelhof – for everybody) constituted by members of Alliance 90/The Greens and various other citizens' groups is more blunt in its rejection of the pro-airport campaigners' tendency to draw on what they call the 'romantic memory of Tempelhof as a lifeline for West Berlin'; 'today the Wall is gone and the freedom of Berlin, and of the western world, must no longer be saved by the raisin bombers'. In common with the SPD flyer, it recommends that the history of Tempelhof be commemorated in a museum.[50]

The framing of the debates around Tempelhof's future in terms of legitimacy, of transparency and the (un)representative nature of government is also highly visible in the campaign run in the conservative Springer Press to save the airport. *Bild*, the mass-circulation daily, in particular both reflected and inflamed sentiments that the decision to close Tempelhof had been taken by a political elite 'against the will of 73% of Berliners'.[51] *Bild* firmly inscribed the decision to close Tempelhof as a product of Berlin mayor Klaus Wowereit's 'stubbornness', and his tendency to ignore 'the opinions of Berliners', and all opposition to Tempelhof's closure, 'even that from within his own party'. Key figures were cited complaining about Wowereit's lack of consultation with the public: Martin Lindner, head of Berlin's FDP, accused him of governing 'like a king' against the will of 'three quarters of his subjects'.[52] Headlines such as 'we are keeping Tempelhof alive' and 'majority in favour of keeping Tempelhof Airport' conceptualized the fight to save Tempelhof as a question of 'us' or 'we' (Berliners, normal people) against 'them' (one section of the political elite).[53] The notion of this ever-growing 'we' was consolidated through reports of growing support: 'the entire Berlin FDP faction says yes to Tempelhof';[54] 'one hundred Berliners and their 'yes' to Tempelhof';[55] 'one hundred roofers fighting for Tempelhof';[56] 'sixty-seven bosses for Tempelhof';[57] and by frequent updates on the number of people that had signed the petition for a referendum.[58] The fight was portrayed as going beyond individual interests and being about Berlin as a whole: 'Berlin needs Tempelhof. Berlin wants Tempelhof.'[59] Those who were not part of this 'we' were strongly criticized: dubbed 'Schließungs-Senatorin' (Closure Senator), the Senator for Urban Development Ingeborg Junge-Reyer was accused of 'attacking the friends of Tempelhof' when she announced that those who believed there to be a possibility other than closure are 'wrong and misleading others'.[60] This intensified in the days leading up to the referendum with articles on 'why the legend must not die';[61] 'one hundred reasons to save the airport of hearts';[62] and calls in the imperative such as 'Berliners, save Tempelhof!'[63] The rhetoric invoked in these discussions is indicative of the significance that came to be attached to Tempelhof's function as airport. The idea that far-off destinations should be accessible via that stone-clad building on Platz der Luftbrücke was conceptualized as a cornerstone of the freedom of the Berlin Republic, just as it had been in the Bonn Republic; attempts to curb that access were portrayed as illegitimate attempts to delimit the freedom of Berliners, akin to the actions of the USSR and GDR elites which Tempelhof had played such a key role in thwarting.

The ruling coalition and other parties in favour of terminating Tempelhof's airport function sought to bring about a paradigm shift in the (in)accessibility issues concentrated at the site. Rather than conceptualizing the site as a gateway, as something that could be moved through in order to access another place, they re-inscribed the site as something worthy of access in its own right. They argued that using the site as an airport was, in fact, undemocratic, as it deprived the vast majority of Berliners of the opportunity to access this unique, historically rich site. This becomes apparent through analysis of the anti-airport campaign materials. An image on the front of an SPD flyer is a large landscape photograph showing an aeroplane flying over on the barbed wire security fence around Tempelhofer Feld, behind which a black, yellow and red sign says in German and English 'SECURITY AREA, admittance with permission only'. The message, that the use of Tempelhofer Feld as an airfield means that access is severely restricted, is clear. To make this explicit, the heading on the next page reads: Open Tempelhof – for everybody (Tempelhof aufmachen – für alle). This re-conceptualization of the campaign to 'close' the airport as one to 'open' the site for public use is a clear bid to legitimize this stance by suggesting it is being done on behalf of, rather than in opposition to, the people of Berlin. Within the text, the supporters of maintaining flight operations at the site are accused of being irresponsible and deceitful and of having no clear concept for the future of Tempelhof.[64] Another flyer, this one produced by the citizens' initiative 'Tempelhof Aufmachen. Für Alle' uses slightly different means to convey the same message: its pictures of the vast green space available at Tempelhof are selected to show its potential for public recreational use and its ecological value; a few paragraphs of text take us on an imagined wander through 'Central Park Tempelhofer Feld' on a warm sunny day in 2015, again showing what a wonderful communal and ecological space it could be; and a key theme running through the leaflet is that their campaign is striving to make the site accessible to all, suggesting that government ministries could move into the airport building while the future of Tempelhofer Feld is a matter for the whole of Berlin on which everyone can collaborate, not just the privileged few. These so-called *Tempelhof-Gegner* branded the airport the 'VIP airport' and called for a stop to its 'direct flights to Lichtenstein for tax avoiders'.[65]

It is not possible to say with any certainty to what extent either of these campaigns or, indeed, of memory politics in general, influenced voting behaviour in the 2008 referendum on the fate of the airport. There is, however, a clear distinction between the referendum responses in the districts of Berlin which were in the former GDR and those that were in the former West. First, with an average of 27.35 per cent, turnout was considerably lower in the former Eastern districts compared with the former West's 43.75 per cent. This does not include the figures for the districts of Mitte or Friedrichshain-Kreuzberg, both of which were formed after unification and cross the former border. The turnout there was 30.9 per cent and 30.6 per cent, respectively. There are, of course, myriad potential reasons for the lower turnout in the former East, many of which are unconnected with the specific topic under consideration. However, among those who did vote, the differences in the responses between the two parts of the city is notable. In the former East, an average of 32.53 per cent voted in favour of keeping the airport open whereas in the former West the figure was 73.73 per cent. Again, these figures do not include Mitte (58.4 per cent) or Friedrichshain-Kreuzberg (39.2 per cent).[66] We do, of course, need to be wary of reducing this to the Cold War narratives surrounding the site. While it may well be the case this difference can be at least partially explained by the fact that Tempelhof Airport did not hold the same significance for those who did grow up with the celebration of legacy of the Berlin Airlift or the site's construction as a 'symbol of freedom', there may also be traction in considering that those who grew up under socialism may have been more predisposed to converting something that was portrayed within some of the campaign material as a facility for the elite into a public asset.

The dispute over the future of Tempelhof's airport function situated the site at the centre of a set of high-profile debates which saw each of the opposing sides publicly question the legitimacy of the other. Although there are still occasional voices calling for Tempelhof to be reinstated as a gateway to the wider world, the ruling Senate has generally been successful in reconfiguring the (in)accessibility question at Tempelhof, shifting the focus away from the conceptualization of the site as a portal to other places and towards the idea that the site itself should be accessible to the wider population and that the citizens of Berlin should be able to access and influence the decision-making process of the site's future. The Senate has sought to capitalize on what they conceptualize as the legitimizing function of the cessation of flight operations by highlighting the extent to which they are engaging citizens in the development process. This claim would, however, go on to be undermined by the strong popular resistance to plans to build on the edges of Tempelhofer Feld and to develop the park landscape. The contesting of these ideas, which led to another referendum, fits into wider debates over the trajectory urban development is taking in Berlin and the extent to which it is considered both the cause and product of the dominant market-oriented hegemony which should be challenged and resisted. This will be addressed in the final chapter of this book.

10

The Columbia-Haus concentration camp and the forced labourer barracks

Exposing Tempelhof's 'other' pasts

The former Flughafen Tempelhof presents us with a threshold at which multiple pasts are juxtaposed both with one another and with the present. Underpinning the debates over the site's functionality is the question of how these multiple temporalities should be mediated, of which of the complex layers of this urban palimpsest should most easily accessed and how. As the rhetoric invoked in the debates over the airport's closure indicates, the site's Cold War legacy has long been highly visible and identifiable, yet the entangled layers of its other pasts have remained indistinguishable from one another. Since the site ceased to function as an airport, there has been an increased impetus to unpick, label, order and make visible those hidden traces.

The first and most significant attempt to unpick the layers at Tempelhof was in the report compiled by Alexandra Handrack and Werner Jockeit in 1995 in preparation for the site's designation as a listed building. This can be seen as the first major step towards making the site's multiple temporal layers knowable and manageable. The research, analysis and observations made by the consultants, Jockeit and Handrack, provide the basis for an in-depth understanding of the site's layers: how visible they are and how they interact.[1] The focus of the report was the material constitution of the site rather than how it should be historicized but in their summary the consultants lay the foundations for its future historicization, explaining that to focus purely on function when refurbishing the site would lead to the irretrievable loss of this 'historic witness'.[2] In a later proposed conservation plan for Tempelhof developed with Cornelia Wendt, Jockeit recommends, that 'the legibility of the various phases of use [...] should be conserved as historic traces as long as they do not detract from the original conception and aesthetic relations of the whole'.[3] Post 1945 alterations that Jockeit and Wendt earmark for reversal include the covering up of the undersides of staircases in the former American part and the modified doorways leading to the underground level. In the offices, corridors and meeting rooms of the administrative areas of the site they recommend that the modifications carried out by the US Air Force should be preserved 'for their historical value' but that a 'coherent concept must be defined anew to reveal the basic elements of the original design'. They also suggest that the uncompleted staircases that would have conveyed visitors to the rooftop viewing platforms be left in their current condition, accessible to the public on guided tours.⁴ Despite the level of detail in the report, limited public access to large areas of the site during its use as an airport until 2008 and the question mark over its post-aviation function contributed to the hindering of the development of a coherent, comprehensive narrative about Tempelhof's past. This means that the representation of its multiple temporalities has long been much less apparent there than that which we have seen at the Olympic Stadium and the building itself remains, by and large, in a state of entanglement. However, with the 'opening up' of the airfield as a public park and the building as an event location, Tempelhof has become a popular destination for leisure visitors and part of its development involves the clear, self-conscious attempt to historicize this space.

This overt, public confrontation with the past is understood as a cornerstone of legitimacy in the Berlin Republic, providing a means through which the peaceful democratic Germany is othered by, and thus defined in contrast to, its past. Yet as we have seen in the analyses of the Aviation Ministry and the Olympic Stadium, the negotiation of the politics of the past is only one facet of perceptions of legitimacy in the Berlin Republic where, as in any other capitalist society, economic factors are also of importance. Accordingly, 'assets' such as Tempelhof are not solely considered for their cultural, historical or social significance but must also become financially viable, if not profitable. As will be revealed through this analysis, this has led to two very different and contradictory approaches to Tempelhof's past: one that seeks to deploy rigorous research in order to establish exactly what happened their during its darkest period and to find a means of communicating this to the wider public clearly and effectively and another which needs to construct a positive narrative through which to market the airport and draws on a heavily selective and sanitized version of the site's history in order to do so. Underlying these divergent approaches to historicizing the site's temporality is the persistence of the highly visible legacy of the Cold War framing of the site's history and the resistance to that by those seeking to counter the relative subordination of the site's National Socialist history.

It has already been established that the frequent invocation of Tempelhof's connection with freedom in the high-profile debates around the airport's closure consolidated its status as a 'symbol of freedom', giving it renewed emphasis to younger generations who didn't remember the air lift or even much of the Cold War. The prominence of this link with freedom seemed set to endure when the public park that opened up on the former airfield in 2010 was named *Tempelhofer Freiheit*. As a National Socialist construction, Flughafen Tempelhof, is not, of course, solely a site of freedom and this apparent official legitimization of a highly reductive representation of its complex past has caused great consternation among historians, citizens' initiatives and other campaign groups.⁵ The Senate and representatives from Tempelhof Projekt GmbH, the company contracted by the Senate to manage the site's preservation and development, initially sought to defend the name. They argued that the name was about the site's future rather than its past but finally, as will be discussed below, relented in 2014 and agreed not to use the term anymore.⁶ The protests over the naming of the park were just one strand within a number of campaigns to make the site's use under National Socialism more visible. In particular, citizens' groups, historians and some politicians wanted to increase public awareness of the concentration camp which had stood on the site before the construction of the current building and of the forced labourers who were compelled to work in the airport building during the war and were housed in exceedingly harsh conditions on the airfield.

The concentration camp

Almost immediately after coming to power, the Nazis carried out mass arrests of potential political opponents. Despite official claims that these arrests were legitimate in accordance with the Decree from the Reich President for the Protection of People and State which came into effect following the Reichstag Fire, Wachsmann shows that they were characterized by abuses of power and lack of judicial oversight. With an estimated 200,000 political prisoners detained at one time or another in 1933, the question of where to house them presented a problem. The regime made use of existing prisons and workhouses but, as these proved to be insufficient, the SA and the SS utilized pubs, former restaurants, hotels, castles, sportsgrounds and youth hostels as improvised prisons and early concentration camps. As these buildings had not been designed for these purposes and lacked adequate hygiene, cooking, heating and sleeping facilities, the prisoners lived in dreadful conditions, exacerbated by the harsh brutality of the guards.[7]

One building in which they were incarcerated was a dilapidated former Prussian military prison, the Columbia-Haus, which had been out of use since the 1920s.[8] Built in 1896, this redbrick construction on the Tempelhofer Feld contained 156 cells, a guard room, a court and various administrative offices. In keeping with the improvised nature of prisons at this time and the lack of space available to house those caught up in mass arrests, Schilde argues that we can assume all of these spaces would have been used to house prisoners of the Nazi regime.[9] The first use of the Columbia-Haus under the Third Reich was as a Gestapo prison, used to relieve the strain on the cells in their headquarters at Prinz-Albrecht-Strasse which were already filled beyond capacity. It held political opponents, particularly communists and social democrats, clerics, Jews, homosexuals, intellectuals and, following the Night of the Long Knives, members of the SA Prisoners would be taken from the Columbia-Haus to Prinz-Albrecht-Strasse for interrogation as required.[10] On the 8 January 1935 it was officially brought under the remit of the Concentration Camp Inspectorate and became Berlin's only SS-run concentration camp. As the concentration camp system was rationalized and inmates were taken to larger purpose built concentration camps, such as Sachsenhausen, the Columbia-Haus camp was closed on 5 November 1936 and the prisoners transferred to other camps.[11] The building itself was demolished in 1938 in order to accommodate Sagebiel's plans for the new airport on Tempelhofer Feld. We still do not know exactly how many people were imprisoned in the Columbia-Haus although it is estimated that at least 8,000 were held there throughout the three years of its operation. The conditions were notoriously harsh, there was severe overcrowding and the facilities were woefully inadequate; the prisoners also had to contend with the brutal treatment and abuse from their captors. The commandant of the Columbia-Haus concentration camp, Karl Koch, would use his experience there to shape his career in the Third Reich which saw him going on to become commandant of Buchenwald.[12]

The forced labourers

During the war, Germany became increasingly reliant on foreign workers to make up the labour shortages caused by the conscription of Germans to the army. In May 1940, there were 1.2 million foreign workers, both men and women, working in Germany.[13] By the end of the war this figure was around 7 million.[14] The means by which these workers came to be in Germany and the conditions they faced once they arrived varied considerably and reflected the Nazi racial hierarchy. Some civilians went voluntarily, enticed by adverts promising decent wages and working conditions; others, including civilians, were sent there by force. The tactics for 'recruiting' civilians from the occupied territories in Eastern Europe oscillated between enticement and forcibly taking young, able-bodied men and women from the streets. As the war progressed and Germany's labour shortages intensified, so too did the brutality of this 'recruitment' process. Evans writes of entire villages being burned down to find young men who were suspected of hiding and of increasing numbers being simply seized from the streets.[15] In Germany, housing provided for the foreign workers ranged from private accommodation to hostels and camps. Civilian volunteers from Western European countries occupied by or allied to Germany were offered the same wages and conditions as their German counterparts and their treatment was generally infinitely better than that of prisoners of war or workers from the East who were housed in camps.[16] Even within the camps themselves, there was a distinct differentiation in conditions between the groups of prisoners depending on their place in the Nazi racial hierarchy. This would impact upon the workers' accommodation and washing facilities, pay, treatment by guards and freedom of movement. The harshest conditions were reserved for Jews and Soviet prisoners of war.[17]

Two major users of forced labour at Tempelhof were Weser Flugzeugbau GmbH (Weserflug) and Lufthansa, both of whom housed at least some of their workers on Tempelhofer Feld. Weser Flug started using Sagebiel's building in 1939 for the repair and production of aeroplanes. Perhaps most notable among their activities was the assembly of *Sturzkampfbomber* commonly known as Stuka dive bombers. They began using forced labourers after the outbreak of war and the numbers increased from around 1000 workers in later 1940 to over 4000 by 1944. Many of the early forced labourers were Polish or from other Eastern European countries. Later there would be up to twenty different nationalities, including French and Soviet prisoners of war. Weser Flug housed its foreign labourers in four separate camps on Tempelhofer Feld with prisoners divided according to their status – civilian, prisoner of war, foreign or German.[18] Lufthansa also used Sagebiel's building for aeroplane maintenance and also deployed forced labourers. Theirs came largely from Poland, Ukraine and the Netherlands plus German Jews who were later sent to concentration camps. Between 1942 and 1944, these workers were also housed in wooden barracks on Tempelhofer

Feld, this time to the north of the hangars of the old airport.[19] The Lufthansa camp was damaged during air raids and subsequently demolished.[20]

Increasing the visibility of Tempelhof's darker pasts

Memorial

These elements of Tempelhof's history have long been much less prominent than its post-war usage. Campaigns from citizens' groups and historians for increased awareness of the concentration camp began in the 1980s, but it was not until after unification that these had a significant impact. This is discussed later in this chapter. The experiences of forced labourers in Nazi Germany have been even more marginalized in public memory discourses. In 1993, the Berlin History Workshop launched a project to counter this by uncovering more information about the 'forgotten camps' in Berlin and Brandenburg. They collected and published testimonies and photographs of former forced labourers and have sought to bring them to public attention through exhibitions, publications, tours and the launch of an app.[21] However, memory activists have found the camp at Tempelhof particularly difficult to inscribe into public memory due to the lack of any visible remnants on the airfield and the prominence of the airlift.[22]

The delayed incorporation of the Columbia-Haus concentration camp into the memory landscape is largely in keeping with the fate of Berlin's other improvised prisons, very few of which have been marked by a plaque or memorial. Jordan finds that of 150 such sites in Berlin, only ten have been marked.[23] As a result, this element of these sites' histories has been largely overlooked and forgotten. The Columbia-Haus was much bigger than many of these but even this camp remained unmarked and largely forgotten about until the mid-1980s when two SPD members who had been persecuted by the Nazis, Erwin Beck and Heinz Dreibert, began doing anti-fascist walking tours which incorporated the Columbia-Haus.[24] Academic research into the site's history also began in the late 1980s as historian Kurt Schilde produced a book containing biographical details of the victims of Nazism in the Tempelhof district.[25] In the same year, Schilde and Tuchel published their findings about the Columbia-Haus. Accompanying their own commentary, the book contained copies of primary documents, maps and photographs and extracts from the testimony of former prisoners which combined to give an indication of the true scale and the horror of what occurred in the now-demolished building.[26] Their findings led to the installation of a permanent exhibition about the Columbia-Haus at a local museum and public interest in the site started to gather momentum.[27] It was not, however, until 1994 that a memorial would finally be unveiled.

The memorial, designed by sculptor Georg Steibert, is an abstract representation of the cross-section of an empty building divided into small cells (Figure 4.5). One of the gable ends stands slightly away from the main structure, bearing a distinct similarity to a headstone it is engraved with the words 'Erinnern, Gedenken, Mahnen: Das Columbia-Haus war ab 1933 Gefängnis und vom 8.1.1935 bis 5.11.1936 ein Konzentrationslager der Nationalsozialistischen Machthaber. Hier wurden Menschen

Figure 4.5 Georg Steibert's 'Columbia-Haus Memorial' (1994).
Photograph: By author.

gefangengehalten, entwürdigt, gefoltert, gemordert'.[28] The 'hier' in the inscription is significant. Academics and memorial campaigners have often highlighted the importance of erecting memorial markers on the very spot where the events they commemorate took place. Referred to by Assmann as 'indexicality', this is seen to increase the efficacy of a given marker through the creation of a clear connection between a precise physical point in the site's past and in its present.[29] However, as the airport was still operational at the time of the memorial's design and inauguration, it is not on the site of the Columbia-Haus itself. Rather, it stands across the road rendering the 'hier' somewhat misleading.

Once the airport closed, campaigners were galvanized in their efforts to make this element of the Tempelhof's history more visible and pushed for a memorial to be erected on the site at which the camp had stood. In a flyer produced by Uwe Doering of the Left party, for example, he referred to Steibert's structure as 'the memorial on the wrong side of the road' and pointed out that the reasons for it not being in its 'historically correct place' no longer applied. As a member of the Berlin House of Representatives, he worked with his fellow Left party members Thomas Flierl and Wolfgang Bauer to call on the Senate to ensure that the forthcoming development of Tempelhofer Feld should also include plans for a place of information and commemoration. They suggested that the conceptualization and development of the information and memorial centre should be overseen by the Topography of Terror Foundation and that it should be financed by the funds available for the development of Tempelhofer Feld.[30] The SPD raised the same issue in a motion to the Tempelhof-Schöneberg District Assembly.[31] These calls were welcomed by the citizens' initiative the Association for the Commemoration of Nazi

Crimes around and on Tempelhofer Feld (Förderverein zum Gedenken an die Nazi-Verbrechen um und auf dem Tempelhofer Feld). Also known as THF 1933–45, this organization was formed in 2010 to give coherence to the demands of local citizens, members of the SPD youth wing and former victims of Nazi persecution who had been calling for increased visibility of Tempelhof's use during the Third Reich since the mid-1990s.[32]

As part of an attempt to make Tempelhof's other pasts more visible by increasing the quality, quantity and depth of the coverage of its history, the Berlin Forum for History and Present presented the Senate Department for Urban Development with a plan for the development of a historical commentary in June 2010. The State of Berlin agreed to establish a 'panel of experts' in order to devise a strategy to historicize Tempelhof. The panel met for the first time in August 2010 and decided that rather than focusing solely on the site's use between 1933 and 1945, the historicization should address the longer history of Tempelhofer Feld and, in terms of its execution, should be linked with the provision of information in the wider city of Berlin. The Berlin Forum for History and Present was then officially commissioned by the Senate Department for Urban Development to develop a 'history trail' around Tempelhofer Feld.[33] To build on the work of the panel of experts, a 'round table' comprised of representatives from Berlin museums, memorial sites, various Senate departments, Tempelhof Projekt GmbH and citizens' initiatives including the Berlin Forum for History and Present and the Association for the Commemoration of Nazi Crimes around and on Tempelhofer Feld as well as other interested citizens was organized by the Senate. The first of their quarterly meetings took place on 21 May 2012. A central discussion point was the question of how they should respond to the site's National Socialist history.[34] The round table agreed that the proposed history trail alone would not go far enough in elucidating the National Socialist use of the site and suggested the development of an information centre inside the airport building itself which would provide a clear history of the site with particular focus on the Nazi period. In addition, they suggested outdoor installations on Tempelhofer Feld itself in order to mark the actual points linked to the site's Nazi use. While it was proposed that Tempelhof Projekt and Grün Berlin should take care of the operational issues around the two projects, it was agreed that content development should be overseen by the Topography of Terror Foundation and the German Resistance Memorial Centre.[35]

Excavation

In 2012, excavations of Tempelhofer Feld began. These were led by archaeologists Professor Susan Pollock and Professor Reinhard Bernbeck of the Freie University, Berlin, in conjunction with the Office of Monument Protection of the State of Berlin. The main impetus for the State of Berlin to commission the excavation was that plans were underway for Tempelhofer Feld to host the 2017 International Garden Show which would have entailed considerable intervention into the landscape and German law stipulates that before public land can be developed, any possible cultural remains must be excavated by archaeologists before they are disturbed.[36] The excavation would also tie in with the 'Destroyed Diversity' project, the theme chosen for the Berlin-wide commemoration of the eightieth anniversary of the Nazi seizure of power and the seventy-fifth anniversary of the Night of Broken Glass.[37] The archaeologists identified four areas of study: two parts of the former airfield which had been used to house the forced labourers, the site's first airport and the Columbia-Haus concentration camp. Setting out their goals, Pollock and Bernbeck highlighted the ongoing dearth of information, documentation and personal testimony about the daily life of forced labourers and explained that they sought to mitigate this somewhat by providing some insight into their experiences.[38] The excavation of the former Columbia-Haus concentration camp began in 2013. Much had been destroyed for the construction of Sagebiel's airport and very few items were found, suggesting that the building had been completely emptied before its destruction. The remains of a lampshade and a wall hook were among the only discoveries that could be dated to the Nazi era. Otherwise, the excavation uncovered part of the foundation and a damaged cellar wall was salvaged.[39] Much more was discovered through the excavations of the forced labourers' barracks and Pollack and Bernbeck and their team have been able to use this to shine a light on elements of the prisoners' lives and the conditions in which they were kept.

Through analysing the remains of the structures, they were able to establish that the thin wooden walls would have provided a maximum of eight degrees Celsius difference from the temperature outside, leading to freezing conditions inside the barracks in the winter.[40] The toilet and washing facilities were also completely inadequate for the approximately 200 forced labourers which oral testimony suggests were held in each barracks.[41] Hot water was available, although this is seen by the archaeologists as an indication of the material the labourers were working with and of the German officials' preoccupation with preventing the spread of infectious disease rather than a concern for their workers' comfort.[42] Similarly, air raid shelters were provided but this was also considered to be more about maintaining the work force than concerns about their safety. These seem to have been heavily used and, again, inadequate for the number of workers using them meaning the occupants would have been in extremely cramped conditions for extended periods.[43] The excavation also provides an insight into the level of oversight in the camp, in particular, the external lighting points to a high level of surveillance of the prisoners.[44] The barracks holding the Soviet prisoners of war were separated from the rest of the camp by barbed wire fencing and were found to have been much more heavily fortified than those holding civilians with the barbed wire fencing continuing below ground to preclude the possibility of escaping through digging tunnels.[45]

The excavations of the Weserflug barracks also revealed kitchenware and some personal possessions including rosary beads, simple jewellery and handmade toys such as marbles and dominoes pieces crafted from scrap. The latter tended to be located in the Soviet prisoner of war section. Using hospital records and oral testimony, the archaeologists had been able to establish that children lived in the camp too and one possible explanation given for the presence of the toys is that they may have been made by Soviet prisoners of war to pass to female workers for their children.[46] In contrast, in her analysis of the finds at the Lufthansa camp, Starzmann is struck by the lack of personal items. She explains that whereas personal items recovered from Buchenwald or Sachsenhausen raise the possibility that they may have given hope or comfort to their owner or maker, the majority of the articles recovered at the Lufthansa camp were 'unnervingly neutral' items such as bottles, crockery and building materials.[47] In a later article, she does, however, highlight that this does not necessarily mean that there were no acts of resistance or individuality, rather that traces of them may not remain or we may not know where to look for them.[48] This view supports Peukert's findings on resistance among forced labourers across Germany. He finds that although it is impossible to know whether or not those accused of slowdowns or sabotage were deliberately disrupting production or simply suffering from extreme fatigue, there is evidence of organized resistance among forced workers, particularly Soviet prisoners of war who carried out activities including creating and distributing leaflets, attempting to form resistance networks and preparing for armed struggle.[49] Activities such as these would not necessarily leave traces that would be uncovered in an archaeological excavation. Another limitation to the insights offered by excavations that the archaeologists are keen to emphasize involves pitfalls of attaching narratives to particular finds. One such example is a condom discovered near the Weser Flug barracks. On the one hand, this could be the trace of a consensual romantic relationship between prisoners. Some inmates did have some access to the Black Market so may have had the possibility of acquiring such a thing although the likeliness of their having had the means to actually purchase such a luxury item is rather remote. On the other hand, it could attest to a non-consensual interaction between a guard and a female prisoner. As Pollack and Bernbeck highlight, both such relationships are known to have taken place within forced labourer barracks. A further possibility is that it is neither of these, not least because it is impossible to date the find exactly and it was discovered near, not in, the barracks.[50]

Overall, the excavations led to the recovery of over 20,000 mobile articles, leaving the team with the challenge of determining what exactly to do with them and how best to communicate what they reveal about the forced labourers to the public. In their report to the round table they emphasized the need to find a place for storage and ongoing research and analysis and suggest that the long-term display of the items in an 'archaeological window' would be highly desirable and relatively easy to set up.[51] The other members of the round table were also keen to keep the objects at Tempelhof itself and that the findings of the excavation which should be presented either in the places in which they were found or in the exhibition in the terminal building.[52]

History trail

In the meantime, members of the expert committee had been developing the history trail. This was to be made up of twenty-seven different information boards which would be installed at twenty locations around the site and cover its history from its use by the Knights Templar until the cessation of flight operations in 2008. The trail was designed around key themes which had been identified by the expert committee in March 2011 and agreed upon by the round table in May 2012. Of these, eight were identified as being priorities for particularly in-depth coverage due to their historic significance or singularity, their connection to the Feld or their contemporary relevance. As well as the Columbia-Haus and the forced labourers, these included Tempelhofer Feld's significance in aviation history, the first airport on the Feld, the Islamic Cemetery, the use of the Feld for Nazi rallies, Sagebiel's airport building and its functions under National Socialism and the Berlin blockade and airlift.[53] The intention was for the findings of the excavations to feed into the history trail and for an appropriate way to build on the history trail to be developed once the excavations had finished and the findings processed.[54]

The first three elements of the history trail were unveiled on 4 July 2012, two at the site of the former concentration camp and one at that of the forced labourer barracks (Figure 4.6). The installation of these three boards was intended by the development committee to send a strong signal of the planned expansion and deepening of the coverage of Tempelhof's history and to increase public awareness of these two particular dimensions of that history.[55] Reflecting on the development of the trail, its organizers explain the significance of the boards being installed in the 'authentic places' that is, at the very places where the events under discussion took place. Citing architectural historian Winfried Nerdinger they explain that this was because such places can wield a particular 'power of remembrance'.[56] This is evident in the boards themselves. The text opens in a similar way at each of the two areas of the site: 'During the Second World War, a large forced labour camp stood here'; 'Until 1938, Columbia-Haus stood here'.[57] The simplicity and directness of these two short sentences is extremely effective: first it allows no space for obfuscation or ambiguity; and secondly, the assertion that the structures in question 'stood here' highlights the indexicality that

Figure 4.6 Information boards at the site of the Columbia-Haus concentration camp.
Photograph: By author.

is missing from Steibert's memorial. This is consolidated through several of the images used on the boards: accompanying the text on the forced labourers, for example, are photographs taken of the rows of aeroplanes that they were producing. The distinctive curve of Sagebiel's building is instantly identifiable as the backdrop to these pictures, particularly as it is visible from the point at which the information board is situated. The concentration camp is potentially more difficult for modern visitors to the site to envisage as the configuration of Tempelhofer Feld has changed considerably since then. To mitigate this, however, the images on the board include the reproduction of a picture postcard of the area from 1905 with a caption pointing out the military detention centre, an extract from a 1935–8 city map of Berlin, clearly showing the outline of the new airport building and the Columbia-Haus, and a photograph showing the construction of the new airport with the soon-to-be-demolished Columbia-Haus in the background. Ten more boards would be installed on 10 July 2013 and the final batch would go on to be erected in 2015. In terms of their format, the boards deliberately echo those installed elsewhere in Berlin such as at the History Mile on Wilhelmstrasse and at the Berlin Wall.[58] This helps to forge links between this space that was taken out of public use for a long time and the other parts of the city.

In common with the uncertainty that dominated the development of the history trail at the Olympic Stadium, the reports from the members of the round table suggest a lack of clarity over when each successive stage of the history trail would be installed and inaugurated at Tempelhof. In this respect the historicization of Tempelhof seems to have progressed down a similar path to that trodden at the Olympic Stadium almost a decade earlier. Among other things, the lag is indicative of the extent to which the reordering of temporality of a site is bound up with that site's functionality and increased visibility. At the Olympic Stadium the use of the site for the World Cup ultimately provided the impetus for historicization and at Tempelhof it has been the closure of the airport and the opening up of a public recreational site. Unlike at the stadium, however, there was no impending internationally significant event on the scale of the World Cup at Tempelhof to serve as an immovable deadline; the continued historicization of the site therefore depended upon sustained action by the panel to mitigate the potential for drift as other spending priorities arose. It is perhaps due to the experience at the Olympic Stadium following the insolvency of Walter Bau AG that the members of Tempelhof's round table, several of whom had also worked on the history trail at the Olympic Stadium, had emphasized to the Senate from the outset; that in order to ensure that these projects would be meaningful and lasting, it was vital to have assurance that long-term maintenance costs would be met and that funds would be ringfenced for continued research and development.[59]

Beyond post-authoritarian governmentality?

At both the Aviation Ministry and the Olympic Stadium we have seen how the relationship with the past has been informed by other, more practical considerations – funding, legal frameworks, questions of landownership and so on. Where memory politics do prevail, we have not seen anything other than rational, pedagogical engagement with the past. At Tempelhof, however, we see that the strong political impetus to develop a post-airport function for Tempelhof that makes the site both a well-used, attractive leisure destination for visitors and a financially viable, or even profitable, entity has impacted upon the relationship with the past constructed there. In the period after the airport's closure, the long-drawn-out search for a function for Tempelhof's building produced much public ire. Even as ideas for an alternative role for the building were expressed, they were undermined by a lack of consensus and the increasingly apparent lack of the financial means needed to make the never-completed building fit for purpose. The public became frustrated after months of beginning to engage with one idea only for it to be scrapped and supplanted by another. In the press, much of this frustration was directed towards the 'lack of a clear concept' and the 'vague' plans of the governing bodies who were believed to have misled the public by giving the impression they had a plan for Tempelhof's afterlife in order to 'sweeten the closure'.[60]

Some of the office space has now been rented out to various organizations, and in 2009 the main terminal building, the site's most iconic feature, became available for hire and has since hosted large-scale, high-profile events such as Bread and Butter and the Berlin Festival. The former Tempelhof Airport was marketed as an event location through its website and through a high-quality, image rich brochure entitled *Tempelhofer Freiheit: Unlimited Event Location Tempelhof Airport*. Through both of these media, the marketing strategy was clearly to highlight the site's uniqueness and its flexibility in terms of the space it offers to potential hirers. The building's previous uses and its aesthetics underpin both of these and, in contrast to the detailed, rigorously researched information about these that we see emerging at the site itself, the marketing material relies on the commodification of carefully selected elements of the site's history and interpretations of its aesthetics.

In the brochure, although the site's 'historical significance' is referred to repeatedly, its National Socialist phase is not lingered on – it is noted in the timeline that the site was constructed between 1936 and 1942 but the short text in the 'history' section jumps from when 'pioneers like Orville Wright or Ferdinand von Zeppelin made history' to the post-war period when 'the airport became myth and a symbol of freedom during the time of the Berlin Blockade and the Airlift'.[61] The thematization of aspects of the site's history links to desirable traits one might look for in an 'event location' today. The site is established as a late eighteenth-/early nineteenth-century 'stage for the new' in a double-page spread that celebrates its aviation history, informing potential investors that 'the population of Berlin was always present at such events and thus, from early on, came to see the place as a stage for new inventions'.[62] On the very next page the airport is in its post-war role as 'the symbol of freedom', as illustrated by images and information about the airlift.[63] The site then becomes a glamorous 'gateway to the world' on the next page, with images of Sophia Loren and Cary Grant at Tempelhof Airport in 1959 and 1960, respectively.[64] The only explicit reference to the building's origins is towards the very end of the brochure and echoes the very narrative of the site's history that the expert committee has been working to challenge: 'When the National Socialists built the airport they had in mind a monument made of stone. The Americans, however, turned it into a symbol of freedom after World War Two.'[65]

The 'selling' of the building through the historicization of its materiality is particularly overt on the website. Here, the narratives constructed around the building's historical significance largely focus around its use by the Americans and its former function as an airport: suggested locations for events include the restaurant 'nicknamed "Air Base" by American GIs'; the transit areas 'once used as passenger waiting rooms' now offer 'generous areas for calm lounge areas or exhibitions, press conferences or lectures with extra special flair'; the hangars provide 'a real airport atmosphere without the airport noise'; 'other rooms' available for hire include the GAT area, the former fire station and the roof tower which is 'an exclusive inspiring open location that is perfect for high-end meetings'.[66]

The site's monumentality is celebrated in a double-page spread showing the airport's front-entrance which folds out into a four-page panorama of the airport's 'spectacular entrée' with 'flawlessly working baggage carousel'.[67] Sagebiel's widely acclaimed cantilevered airside roof is noted for its capacity to 'enable elaborate hanging installations' and its negation of the need for 'restrictive post or pillars' which makes the space ideal for 'festive banquets, concerts, film productions, exhibitions and sport events'.[68] What is particularly noteworthy is that the attributes which have been used to condemn other National Socialist buildings are actually used to sell this one: the 'imposing monumental architecture' of the main hall, for example, is presented as providing the 'perfect entrance gateway for your event'.[69] The testimonials from those who have held events in the building also highlight these elements: 'The ample space and neo-classicist architecture are in themselves a unique selling point for any event'; 'here, exhibitors don't need to boast with impressive stalls but can in fact make full use of the formidable visual background of the airport's architecture'.[70] In this way, the very features that have been problematized and deemed to require a clear and coherent response at other sites are used to sell this one. This largely becomes possible through this particular site's post-National Socialist use which is considered to have cleansed it, to have transformed it into the antidote to, rather than the symbol of, totalitarianism. However, perhaps it can also be seen as indicative of a move towards advanced liberal governmentality, where economic and other issues begin to overtake the politics of the past as salient issues. After all, post-authoritarian governmentality must necessarily be a period of transition: no state can continue to define itself so wholly in opposition to its dictatorial past forever. Analysis of all of these sites has demonstrated that memory politics has long had to compete with more practical issues and, at some point a stage must be reached when an adequate and appropriate response to 'the past' will be widely considered to have been formulated and, as such, no longer needs to be continually performed either through political discourse or through the built environment.

Just as the development of Tempelhof itself is still very much in flux, so too are the conceptions of freedom being written onto the site. In 2014 a referendum organized by citizens' initiative '100% Tempelhofer Feld' saw the citizens of Berlin successfully oppose the Senate's proposal to build on the airfield. This process shifted perceptions of the nature of the 'freedom' embodied by Tempelhof towards notions of the freedom to shape the city and the freedom of open space. But this in turn led to a degree of muffling of the exploration of Tempelhof's darker history. The outcome of the referendum required the cessation of all development on the Feld, including the archaeological excavations that were then wound up in June 2014.⁷¹ A year later, the site was written into more contemporary debates about freedom and its limitations as it was used to house refugees fleeing violence in Syria, Iraq, Afghanistan and other places. This brought to the fore further contests about the extent and nature of the 'freedom' offered at the site; the offering of sanctuary was seen, at least by parts of the population, as something to be celebrated but the conditions in which the refugees were housed were deplored.⁷² This also temporarily limited the capacity of the airport building to host events and has curtailed the marketing of this element of the site. The current marketing of the much smaller spaces still available to hire is now much more muted with only vague references to the venue's 'historical significance' and unique atmosphere.⁷³

In the meantime, the site's National Socialist history has certainly become more visible. In their report to 2014 round table, Tempelhof Projekt acknowledged the objections from some participants to the name 'Tempelhofer Freiheit' and committed to following the Senate's lead in ceasing to use that term. From that point on they determined they would use 'Tempelhofer Feld' to refer to the former airfield and 'Flughafen Tempelhof' to market the building. The question of whether a new name was required to refer to the site as a whole was still under discussion.⁷⁴ Furthermore, the development of the history trail continued to completion in December 2015 and now comprises twenty-seven boards in twenty locations around the site, and tours of the building are now offered which tell visitors about the multiple facets of Tempelhof's past. On 4 September 2018, a temporary exhibition was unveiled in the airport building covering the many different dimensions of the site's former uses. In her inauguration speech, Member of the Bundestag and Representative for Culture and Media Professor Monika Grütters celebrated the fact that the exhibition covered the multiple histories of the airport building and thanked the team who had worked to uncover its many layers, particularly that of the forced labourers which, she acknowledged, was still insufficiently researched.⁷⁵ It is telling that although the exhibition also contained displays relating to the aspects of Tempelhof's history which had previously dominated its representation, such as the early days of flight and the Berlin Airlift, coverage of the exhibition's opening in *Der Tagesspiegel* foregrounded information about the Columbia-Haus and the conduct of its commandant Karl Koch.⁷⁶ These elements of Tempelhof's past also featured prominently in other press reports of the exhibition's opening.⁷⁷ However, not all parties consider the appropriate historicization of the site to have been fully achieved. Even after the completion of the history trail, the SPD continued to campaign for further engagement with the past including the launching of an artistic competition to design a place of reflection dedicated to the forced labourers which would incorporate the findings of the excavations and for the identification of a site for a permanent information centre.⁷⁸ The citizens' initiative Verein THF 1933–45 has also declared its intention to continue its own research and public relations activities independently of the round table.⁷⁹

The Senate has promised that Flughafen Tempelhof's remaining refugees will be settled elsewhere by the end of June 2019.⁸⁰ Furthermore, Tempelhof Projekt has announced that modifications will be made to the building in 2019 in order for it to be authorized as a 'permanent place of assembly' under German law. This will involve changes to fire safety, accessibility and operational safety, which will make things easier for event organizers who had previously needed to seek authorization for each individual hire period. It is expected that this will make Flughafen Tempelhof an even more attractive venue.[81] Given that the historicization of the site is now more coherent and public awareness of the multiple dimensions of Tempelhof's history has been heightened, it will be interesting to see if, once renewed marketing efforts begin in earnest, they are more in line with the more nuanced approach to the site's history that has become increasingly established.

11

Contesting freedom

The proposed development of the heterotopia of Tempelhofer Feld

A key element of the official discourse around the closure of the airport was that it would bring a unique asset back into public use: a 270-hectare area of open space which would now be accessible to all (Figure 4.7). Although it had been subjected to the very particular ordering processes required of its previous functions, Tempelhofer Feld's use as a military exercise and parade ground and then as an airfield had preserved the vast green area. As such, Tempelhofer Feld offers a tranche of open space which, through historical circumstance, has persisted within the urban area. So huge is this area that it offers genuine respite from the sights and sounds of the city and has become a vital habitat for scores of species. Since the cessation of flight operations it has, however, been exposed to the forces acting on the twenty-first-century Western European city and is now the subject of a continual struggle between multiple political, economic, environmental and social actors seeking to bring to fruition their own, often opposing ideas about what the site should be. In May 2010, the former airfield opened as a city park and rapidly became one of the most popular recreational sites in Berlin and, as its future development was debated, simultaneously one of the most contested. These contests were underlined by original name of the park, 'Tempelhofer Freiheit', which simultaneously both strengthens and reframes the dominant narrative around the site: on the one hand drawing on and consolidating the discursive connection between Tempelhof and freedom which was engendered during the Cold War as discussed in the last chapter; on the other hand, reconfiguring the former airport as a 'site of freedom' in itself, rather than simply a portal through which other sites of 'freedom' can be accessed. The focus of this chapter will be on this latter understanding of the name 'Tempelhofer Freiheit', that which sees it as a reference to the site's current function within the urban environment of Berlin, that of providing access to fresh air and nature and existing as a space of 'freedom' from the rigorous ordering that prevails across the city. Indeed, this is the conception of freedom that dominates the marketing and visitor information material about the park where images of its huge open sky, vast horizons and expansive, relatively unstructured terrain abound as do written references to 'free space', 'openness' and 'large meadows'.[1]

Figure 4.7 Tempelhofer Feld.
Photograph: By author.

Heterotopia

In many ways, Tempelhofer Feld is a heterotopia. Constituted by its relationship with the rest of space, Foucault's heterotopia is a place of difference in which the power relations that prevail elsewhere operate somewhat differently, thus creating a rupture which simultaneously represents, contests and inverts those power relations. Unlike perfected but unreal utopia, heterotopia are real sites, actual spaces and places through which all others are challenged and contested.[2] The rupture presented by heterotopia creates gaps through which the power relations which are so naturalized elsewhere become apparent. Through probing these gaps we can therefore gain an insight into these power relations and into the governmentality that they constitute.

Having appropriated the word 'heterotopia', literally meaning 'another place', from the medical term for tissue that is growing where it should not, Foucault first used the term in his preface to 'The Order of Things'. In explaining how his initial amusement at the bizarre categorization of animals that Borges reports finding in a Chinese encyclopaedia gave way to unease, he reflects on how this evidence of an entirely different system of thought revealed the limitations of our own and the impossibility of thinking certain things. Intrigued and perplexed by the juxtapositions the encyclopaedia presented him with, he conceptualized it as a 'heterotopia', explaining that heterotopias 'are disturbing, probably because they secretly undermine language, because they make it impossible to name this and that, because they shatter or tangle common names, because they destroy "syntax" in advance, and not only the syntax with which we construct sentences but also that less apparent syntax which causes words and things (next to and also opposite one another) to "hold together".[3] He first applied the concept to physical, material space in a lecture given to architects in 1967. After his death, the notes for this lecture were published in French as *'Des espaces autres'* in 1984 and translated into English as 'Of Other Spaces' in 1986. Although Foucault did not personally review the notes for publication, he did allow the manuscript to be released into the public domain at an exhibition in Berlin not long before his death.[4]

In the lecture, Foucault advocates the undertaking of a 'systematic description' or a 'heterotopology' of these 'other sites' and outlines the principles around which it could/should be structured. The first principle is that the constitution of heterotopia is common to all cultures around the world and that while there is no single, uniform form of heterotopia, there are two main categories into which they can be classified: first, heterotopia of crisis. Prevalent in 'primitive societies' but disappearing today, heterotopia of crisis are those spaces used for events such as the honeymoon trip that are supposed to take place 'elsewhere'; and secondly, heterotopia of deviation are places such as prisons and psychiatric hospitals in which those considered to be 'deviant in relation to the required mean or norm' are placed.[5] The second principle is that due to the relational constitution of the heterotopia, the function of a particular heterotopia can change over time in accordance with shifts in social relations. Foucault provides the example of the cemetery here, tracing its move from the centre of the city to the periphery as ideas about death and illness began to change in the early nineteenth century. The third principle is the capacity of the heterotopia to juxtapose 'in a real place several spaces, several sites that are in themselves incompatible'. One example he provides is that of the theatre, upon the stage of which we experience 'a whole series of places, all of which are foreign to one another'.[6] The fourth principle is concerned with temporality at heterotopia, which tends to represent an 'absolute break with traditional time' which can come about either through the 'indefinitely accumulating' time of the library or the museum or through the 'fleeting, transitory, precarious' time seen at the fairground which lies empty for most of the year only to teem with activity at specified periods.[7] The fifth principle is that heterotopia are characterized by 'a system of opening and closing that both isolates them and makes them penetrable'.[8] This system could be founded upon compulsory entry to the site in question, as is the case with the prison, or it could involve the processes which the individual needs to undergo in order to gain admittance. The final principle is that heterotopia 'have a function in relation to all space that remains' in providing either a space of illusion or a space of compensation.[9]

Despite the apparently didactic quality of laying out six numbered principles as a framework that the reader can, apparently, apply in order to carry out their own heterotopology of a given space, 'Of Other Spaces' does not provide us with a coherent, straightforward checklist. Although they are given the same status in the text, principles three and six seem to be more overarching qualities within which the others would be sub-points. Accordingly, there is a considerable fluidity in how they have subsequently been applied with users of the concept tending to focus on one or two of the principles to carry out their analysis. Guillot, for example, focuses on the heterochronia outlined in principle four in his study of luxury condominiums in Singapore, and Collins and Opie use the same to explore the presence of the past at the roadside shrine.[10]

The imprecise nature of Foucault's heterotopia has generated considerable exasperation, even from the scholars who employ the concept in their work: to Soja it is 'frustratingly incomplete, inconsistent, incoherent';[11] to Dehaene and De Cauter 'one gets the feeling that it lacks definition and is perhaps too encompassing';[12] whereas to Johnson it is 'briefly sketched and somewhat confusing';[13] and to Topinka it is 'unwieldy'.[14] This fluidity and ambiguity serves to both consolidate and undermine it as an analytical tool. On the one hand, it means that it can be, and has been, deployed within a range of contexts. A significant literature exists which has followed Foucault's earlier use of the term, applying the concept to film, literature and to language.[15] The later use of the concept has also been used to unlock a vast range of real, physical sites: the *Palais Royal* in Paris, the stonemason's lodge and the factory,[16] the public park;[17] the shopping mall,[18] the gated community,[19] the cathedral,[20] sports grounds,[21] fascist-era Sicilian *borghi*,[22] Las Vegas,[23] Los Angeles[24] and areas of cities.[25] The proliferation of its use has led the concept to become increasingly established in Anglophone, and to an extent German, scholarship.[26] On the other hand, not all of these uses can be said to lead to a coherent, conceptual definition of the term. In some cases, the concept is under-theorized, thus supporting the argument that too many of its proponents 'simply [call] up the heterotopia as some theoretical *deus ex machina*'.[27] Even one of the term's most celebrated proponents, Edward Soja, has been accused of only providing a brief outline of the concept before using it in his work.[28] Soja does rectify this in his later work where he prefixes a revised and expanded version of his heterotopology of LA with more engagement with the concept itself. Here, he too laments the uncritical use of the term, citing 'many in most spatial disciplines' as well as social theorists, historians, anthropologists and others who use the concept 'for intellectual, philosophical, and political legitimization of their new-found and longstanding spatial perspectives'. While this has played a key role in the re-establishment of a critical spatial perspective, he argues that such works 'have missed the central point' which is to recognize and attempt to 'detonate' the discursive limitations to conventional thinking about space.[29]

Perhaps as a consequence of the prevalence of the under-theorized use of the concept, two key criticisms have been prominently levelled at it. The first is that the concept is too broad to actually be useful. Not only has Foucault himself provided a wide range of examples of heterotopic sites – the theatre, the garden, the cemetery, the brothel, the ship but his work has, in turn, generated a substantial literature around the vast range of sites labelled 'heterotopia' which is listed above. This has led scholars to comment that one would be hard pressed to identify a site which could not be said to constitute a heterotopia.[30] Saldanha remarks that 'one wonders where there is still space left for mainstream society,'[31] while Harvey points out the 'banality' of a concept within which 'anything "different" — however defined' might be included.[32] The second charge is that Foucault's conception of the heterotopia indicates a structuralist tendency in his approach to space, that in setting up this opposition between 'other' space and 'the rest' of space, Foucault is suggesting a flat, homogenous 'rest' of space. His attempt to capture spatial differentiation therefore actually has a totalizing effect.[33] Along these lines, Harvey rejects what he considers Foucault's 'Kantian (Newtonian)' approach to space and considers his heterotopia as 'a very undialectical rendering of what space is and can be about'.[34] It does not, however, take much of a conceptual leap to see how these arguments can cancel each other out. Rather than conceiving of homogenous, flat space to which a particular space is 'other', we can seize on the ubiquity of the heterotopia to see how space is, in fact, populated by multiple heterotopia, all heterotopic in different ways, through creating different ruptures and unsettling different combinations of the power relations. Even if a site disrupts and challenges the hegemonic narrative over, say, a nation's past, it may still perpetuate the dominant relations in respect to, for example, gender, sexuality or race. So, the fact that so many types of space could be, and are, considered heterotopic does not diminish the relevance of the heterotopia. On the contrary, it heightens it, as it is this plurality that places the concept at the heart of considerations of spatial altereity and heterogeneity and which highlights the productive potential of space. Furthermore, to see the heterotopia as indicative of an 'undialectial' understanding of space overlooks or ignores the contingent and relational properties of the heterotopia, its constitution through juxtapositions and the productive potential of the clashes that those juxtapositions bring about. The relations that cause the ruptures are not static, they are contingent and there is, in fact, a continual dialectic between the dominant ordering and the heterotopic as each both shapes, and is shaped by, the other – the prevailing dominant order responds to the heterotopia in its midst and the heterotopia is altered – whether it absorbs or resists that response. The productive potential of the heterotopia is recognized by Topinka who combines Foucault's definition of heterotopia in 'The Order of Things' with that in 'Of Other Spaces' to highlight how the ruptures that occur at both the discursive and the spatial heterotopia give birth to new ways of knowing. In demonstrating how both of Foucault's conceptualizations of the heterotopia function as sites at which ordering processes become legible, he reveals the potential for heterotopia to contest received knowledge and problematize order and space concluding that it is through the clashes between the dominant order and alternative ordering of the heterotopia that new forms of knowledge emerge.[35]

Tempelhofer Feld – between heterotopia of illusion and of compensation

In keeping with the proclivity of users of the concept to focus primarily on just one of Foucault's six principles, as mentioned earlier, the analysis of Tempelhofer Feld will largely draw on that outlined as number six. This says that the rupture created by heterotopic spaces takes place between two poles, between that of 'illusion' and that of 'compensation'. While spaces that constitute 'heterotopia of illusion' are exemplified by the brothel and serve as sites of disorder which expose the illusory nature of order elsewhere, the so-called 'heterotopia of compensation' function as sites of extreme regulation which highlight the messiness elsewhere as can be seen with the Jesuit colonies in South America.[36] While the wider literature has tended to identify particular sites as either heterotopia of illusion or of compensation, the analysis in this chapter will follow scholars such as Philpotts who have shown that the same site can simultaneously function as both.[37] First, the relationship between the heterotopia of illusion and of compensation is scalar, not binary and any site which is not situated at either extremes of the scale will therefore exhibit both compensatory and illusory characteristics. At one extreme, the ideal heterotopia of compensation is a space of order, of regulation, of a level of control that cannot be extended beyond a bounded, limited area. A prime example of this would be a perfect realization of Bentham's panopticon, the disciplinary device conceived of by Foucault as creating the possibility 'to induce in the inmate a state of conscious and permanent visibility that assures the automatic functioning of power'.[38] While we must own that the construction of a 'perfect' panopticon, and therefore an ultimate heterotopia of compensation, is theoretically possible, the absence of any margin for error in its construction or operation drastically diminishes the likelihood of its perfect realization and optimal operation; the 'slightest noise, a gleam of light, a brightness in a half-opened door would betray the presence of the guardian'.[39] Wherever the level of total order of the perfectly operating panopticon cannot be fully realized, where there exists the smallest corner which has not been pervaded by the dominant power relations, the tiniest space within which the individual can escape for even a moment, illusory elements begin to feature within the heterotopia of compensation. At the other end of the scale, the heterotopia of illusion is posited as a site of disorder, a site which, through the absence of certain norms or structures, reveals the contingency and construction of those norms or structures when they are present elsewhere. Yet even within the heterotopia of illusion certain ordering is present, without it relationships and interactions cannot take place. The example of the brothel that Foucault provides is a case in point; there are power relations between all the individuals within that space – sex workers, clients and madams. The social structures may be distinct from those outside the confines of the brothel but are structures, nonetheless. Just like the most realizable heterotopia of compensation, the heterotopia of illusion is not a break from ordering, it is, as Hetherington suggests, a space of alternate ordering.[40] Secondly, to move beyond the binary constructed between 'spaces of domination/spaces of resistance' we need to recognize that both the illusory and compensatory properties of a heterotopia have the power to consolidate and challenge dominant power relations. In addition to confirming hegemonic power relations by showing their full realization, the qualities of the heterotopia of compensation simultaneously have the potential to destabilize them through the contrast it provides with the outside world. The juxtaposition is so great that the contingency of the ordering structures becomes apparent and thus liable to be called into question. Similarly, rather than solely undermining the dominant power relations by appearing to subvert them, the properties of the heterotopia of illusion diminish the risk of their being challenged by locating that challenge, within an identifiable, bordered and segregable space; it provides a time-space within which such activities and interactions which would be considered to contravene social norms can be contained.

Today, the park at Tempelhofer Feld appears at first glance to constitute a heterotopia of illusion. It is predominantly characterized by the traces of its former use; the runways and the signs with instructions for pilots remain in place and were quickly appropriated by users of the park for their own, diverse recreational purposes. It is the combination of the juxtaposition between the traces of its former, highly defined function and the countless possibilities for contemporary use and the lack of overarching design and development that give Tempelhof its appeal and its appearance of constituting what Ward Thompson would describe as a 'loose-fit environment'.[41] The park's status as a heterotopia of illusion is consolidated by the sense of anonymity, of respite from the regulatory gaze of both authority figures and of other subjects which derives from its vastness, while its relative lack of internal structuring gives relief from the material arrangements that shape our movement and behaviour as we move through the city. Yet there is a tension between the claims made of 'Tempelhofer Freiheit', in terms of the freedom it offers, and the very fact that the site is subject to such claims, that it has been incorporated into a marketing strategy which seeks to shape public understanding of the site and delimit the potential ways in which individuals can respond to and engage with it. This tension is also present in the heavily contested discussions about the development of the materiality of the park; the expressed intention is to provide an infrastructure and facilities which will optimize the extent to which people can enjoy the freedom offered by the park.[42] Yet as the park landscape becomes increasingly consciously shaped, so too will the ways in which people go on to use and engage with it, as the possibilities for use become increasingly defined and delimited by the surroundings they are presented with. What is perceived as heterotopia of illusion is undergoing a compensatory (re)ordering.

While the transition from the functional to the recreational, from the highly regulated to the virtually anonymous does, indeed, mark the former airfield as a leftover space recovered and reappropriated by the people of Berlin, even without further intervention Tempelhofer Feld is far from functioning as an extreme example of a heterotopia of illusion. Since it opened, the park has been a delimited, contained area with designated entry points, each with information about park opening and closing times and a list of rules for conduct within the park. Contrary to the impressions created by its vast openness and reappropriated airport equipment, Tempelhofer Feld is a governable, knowable site upon which hegemonic ordering processes can be, and are, enacted. Plans to develop the park further, and thus to intervene even more into its landscape have proven a catalyst in igniting debates over how the Feld should be constituted and who has the right to make that decision. Despite the Senate's claims that they 'are not about to build a park in the traditional sense at Tempelhof',[43] not long after the former airfield opened for public use, various activists and citizens' groups expressed their concerns at what they saw as Tempelhofer Feld's imminent transformation from 'anti-park' to 'designer park'.[44] This designation of 'anti-park' alludes to the notion that, as an appropriation of left-over space, Tempelhofer Freiheit was not (yet) the product of an overarching 'park design' process and consequently did not subject the user to the ordering processes active in the traditional park. The ordering of an ostensibly unordered space is a key issue in public park design; as a generic type the public park has long functioned as a site in which a particular society's notions of 'freedom' are continually expressed, challenged, reconfigured and resisted. The very materiality of the park is incorporated into this negotiation process right from the shaping of the landscape that actually constitutes the park to the strategic positioning of various features upon it and culminating in the impact of these ordering processes upon the subjectivity of its users. The public park can therefore be conceptualized as a hybrid site, one of simultaneous freedom and regulation. This is particularly visible in the processes behind the development of the nineteenth-century public park. On the one hand, the increased provision of access to green space to the masses can be seen as indicative of a gradually democratizing, equalizing society, one in which outdoor recreation is not considered purely the preserve of the elite.[45] On the other, it is tightly bound with questions of subjectivity and the constitution of the 'right' kind of citizen. As architect and sociologist Cranz explains, this derives from nineteenth-century ideas that attunement, with contemplation of and immersion in nature, was beneficial to the mind, body and spirit of the citizen and therefore something that should be encouraged among the working class. As a place of respite from the pollution, crowding, indoor work and constant exposure to the artificial and to the commercial of the city, the public park was seen as providing an antidote to the urban environment which could 'stimulate and exercise the unused part' of the worker's mind.[46] Underpinning these ideas was the notion that if the public park could be effectively shaped, so too could the subject that used it. The development trajectory originally proposed for the former airfield was seen by protest groups as an extension of attempts to manage its wilderness, to limit access to it, to shape how it is to be used and experienced and, most significantly, to repackage parts of it as a commodity. As aspects of these ordering processes were identified, challenged and resisted by various different groups and individuals, multiple, continually shifting thresholds developed at which the nature of 'freedom', the balance between illusion and compensation, at Tempelhof was, and still is, constantly (re)asserted (re)contested and (re)negotiated.

In January 2011, Tempelhof Projekt GmbH became responsible for the management of the former airport building and the airfield. Their publicized goal is 'the long-term integration of Tempelhofer Freiheit into the social, cultural and economic environment of the city'.[47] The corporate, market-oriented construction of the site became increasingly apparent in early 2011 with the inception of the brand 'Tempelhofer Freiheit' and the launch of a strategic brand management campaign carried out by a professional marketing company.[48] The 'Freiheit' Tempelhof has historically represented is a very specific type of freedom; that propagated by Cold War US foreign policy, that is, that of a Western, capitalist ideology. It is perhaps appropriate then to see Tempelhof become a site where that ideology is both enacted and contested. In discussions around the development of the site the argument is often made by politicians and by the site's corporate managers that, in a bankrupt city, Tempelhof needs to become economically viable – a notion challenged by those who wish to see the vast space embraced as a unique asset for reasons not connected to its financial worth. The next section of this chapter will look at the proposed development of spatial governance at Tempelhofer Feld and reactions to the prospect of increasing intervention into its landscape. The final section will consider the 'Pioneer Projects' at the site in context with Berlin's wider culture of the short-to-medium term, grass-roots appropriation of left-over spaces, considering the implications of the State of Berlin's publicized goal of incorporating 'informal and interim uses of space into the formal planning process for the first time'.[49]

Shaping (Tempelhofer) Freiheit

The question of (in)accessibility has featured heavily in the negotiation of 'freedom' at Tempelhofer Feld, primarily in the consolidation of the rhetoric which configured the closure of the airport as a transformation of an inaccessible site to an accessible one. Senator Junge-Reyer announced in 2009, for example, that 'Tempelhofer Feld will be open to all'.[50] Several of the mainstream papers also conveyed this message: the idea of the citizens of Berlin 'conquering' or 'recapturing' the Feld through the opening of the park featured in *Berliner Zeitung* and the *Berliner Morgenpost*.[51] The *Taggesspiegel* pointed out that 'now the former airfield which has been inaccessible for about eighty years belongs to Berliners'.[52] Perhaps as a response to the claims that the closure of the airport was indicative of a democratic deficit, the official narratives around the site have not only focused on increased physical access to the site but also focused on the accessibility of the decision-making process around the site's development and, by extension, on the transparent, participatory, democratic nature of decision-making in Berlin. To ensure the dissemination of this message it has been communicated through various media, most notably on the park's official website where the user can read through the 'planning history' of the site and become aware of the various workshops and consultation periods that have occurred since alternative use for the site started being discussed in 1994. The 2007 'Online-Dialog Tempelhof' provided the first official channel through which the general public could share their ideas for Tempelhof. This well publicized consultation exercise was overtly incorporated into the idea that Tempelhof was about to become available for the 'disposal of the whole city' following the imminent closure of the airport.[53] The image of this exercise as an accessible, democratic, modern process is consolidated through a variety of YouTube videos of the consultation process, one of which shows a montage of the series of events that accompanied the consultation such as bus tours of the site, exhibitions and lectures as well as workshops at the site itself to aid participation in the online discussion.[54]

The first phase of the online dialogue took place between May and July 2007 and asked participants: 'What does Berlin need in this location?' The submitted suggestions were then grouped into categories such as 'creation of green space'. The second phase took place between October and November 2007 and involved a moderated discussion of the ideas suggested in the first phase. An exhibition showing how these ideas might be realized was set up in the airport building and visitors could comment on or rate each idea. The consultation process attracted widespread attention and the Senate proclaimed it 'the most used online dialogue for urban development in Berlin'.[55] Beyond the particulars of specific ideas, the planning authorities were able to use the public input into the dialogue to legitimize the plans for the development of the park. Through abstracting from, for example, the 342 individual ideas which involved some reference to the incorporation of an element of open space it was possible to generate evidence of a popular mandate for a park. It is then, perhaps not surprising that 'the overall result of this planning phase was to confirm the central idea of the 1999 master plan': a central open space and three building sites situated in relation to the surrounding city.[56] There is considerable information about this consultation on the official website and a PDF of a detailed presentation of the results is freely available to download from the website of the Senate Department for Urban Development.[57] Before a design for the park was chosen, citizens were invited to give feedback on the six shortlisted designs which were exhibited in the former airport building. As the official mouthpiece for the site, the website was used to emphasize the transparency of this process and the level of this engagement with the people of Berlin: 'Citizens were involved in the planning process from the beginning, participating in discussions, surveys and visitor monitoring. The project will retain this participatory character as it goes on.'[58] This repeated emphasis on the level of public engagement involved in the development of Tempelhofer Feld has, however, been challenged by interest groups such as Tempelhof Für Alle who campaigned against the planned development and privatization of Tempelhofer Feld before becoming subsumed into other citizens' initiatives such as Stadtteilinitiative Schillerkiez and Initiative 100% Tempelhofer Feld.[59] On their legacy website, which remains 'as an archive of the protests around the opening of Tempelhofer Feld', they argue that although the Senate Department for Urban Development is fond of talking about citizen participation and dialogue, in reality there is only scope for this participation to take place within the framework of the plans and concepts 'already decided from above'; ideas that do not fit into this are 'unwanted'.[60] Indeed, there is no space for this dialogue to take place on Tempelhof's official website, despite it having been billed as the 'central communication instrument' for Tempelhofer Freiheit.[61] Although officially organized public meetings are advertised there is no online public forum or chat facility, neither are there links to the websites of the many initiatives who have taken an active interest in Tempelhof's future. That the site's development is contested can, however, be inferred from the sheer volume of material devoted to informing the public about it. This both demonstrates the transparency of the decision-making process and provides a platform from which decisions can be legitimized but not contested by the site's users. The downloadable PDF of a report about the economic consequences of 'not building' on Tempelhofer Feld is a case in point.[62]

Scottish landscape architects GROSS.MAX were awarded the contract to design the park and on 6 March 2013 a 'masterplan' for the future of Flughafen Tempelhof was unveiled at a public meeting in the former airport building.[63] The plans confirmed the intention to 'develop' the former airfield in two senses of the word: to build new 'city quarters' on the field's edges and to alter its internal structure.[64] Through the proposed construction of 4,700 new apartments, commercial spaces and a new public library on edges of the airfield and the reshaping of the remainder, the Senate Department for Urban Development stated that they were meeting demands for increased housing in Berlin as well as calls for improved facilities at the park.[65] However, both elements of this proposed reconfiguration of Tempelhofer Feld met with resistance: citizens' initiatives such as 100% Tempelhofer Feld led the campaign against the proposal to build on the former airfield. They organized a petition for a referendum with the support of Green and Left Party politicians who submitted a motion to the Berlin House of Representatives for a halt to the planning process while this petition was still running.[66] The reaction was not only against the proposal to build on the site but also about the plan to reshape the 230 hectares that would have remained as parkland.

The 2013 'masterplan' made clear that significant intervention into the remaining park landscape was envisaged.[67] This was the outcome of a deliberation over the extent to which green spaces should be contained, controlled and manipulated which is a characteristic of park design and one that goes a considerable way to determining the extent to which the site becomes a heterotopia of compensation. In the gardens of the baroque or Renaissance period, for example, the taming and dominating of nature was celebrated in features such as fountains which provided a showcase of the mastery of the movement of water through hydraulics.[68] Elements of this shaping of nature persisted throughout the nineteenth century: Cranz outlines how allegorical flower displays were prevalent in several American parks and the German landscape gardener Kanst was renowned for arranging and manipulating plants and flowers to replicate recognizable forms.[69] Landscape architect Jirku explains that in the twenty-first century, however, we are generally so confident in our mastery of nature that we are often glad when it reasserts itself. Drawing on Simmel, she considered this to be heightened when the object that is being reclaimed was originally constructed for a highly functional purpose, the factory, the railway or the airport. In their ruined, overgrown forms, 'the work of man is finally experienced as nature'.[70] Part of the allure of Tempelhofer Freiheit is the manifestation of the capacity of nature to reclaim and reassert itself, to resist and counter the ordering that has been imposed on the site in the past: the instructional signs which were installed to regulate movement and activity within the site are now meaningful only for their novelty value and are being gradually subsumed into the greenery that is growing up them; areas of hard-standing, put down to counter the irregularities of the ground are becoming increasingly dominated by the resurgence of nature. Conversely, the proposed water feature at Tempelhofer Feld which would have consisted of a four-hectare water basin to collect rainwater from the building attests to a paradigm shift in how water and other natural resources are understood today. Rather than showcasing human dominance over nature, the planned collection and redistribution of rainwater is a demonstration of a twenty-first century normative imperative to actively assist nature.

Other elements of the masterplan suggest a will to govern and structure the space but to do so in subtle, seemingly organic ways. This was a challenge faced by celebrated nineteenth-century public park designer Olmsted and his contemporaries who, in wishing to create as strong a juxtaposition between the park and the city as possible, sought to diminish or disguise the artificiality of the park landscape. Olmsted considered 'pure wilderness' to constitute the ideal urban green space. Recognizing the impossibility of recreating this, however, he compromised with the construction of a 'pastoral middle landscape'. Features of nature such as trees and meadows which could be 'transplanted or duplicated by human ingenuity' were widely celebrated and formed the basis for the development of park design.[71] Trees and meadows (Wiesen) were, indeed, key elements of GROSS.MAX's plan for Tempelhof's development, yet in this instance they were to be used to break up the wilderness, rather than recreate it. Joyce explains that the nineteenth-century public park was characterized by the variation of the (in)finitude of space, achieved through the strategic planting of trees to open and close the panorama.[72] The vast emptiness of Tempelhof's horizon marks a significant divergence from this but the map which accompanies the 'masterplan' indicates plans to plant a considerable number of trees around the edges of the park which would realize the importance attributed to 'the creation of shaded leisure areas' in an earlier leaflet.[73] The positioning of these trees suggests they would also fulfil another function; screening the new city quarters which were to be controversially built at the park's edges. Despite the expressed plans to maintain the 'unique, vast view of the sky',[74] this contraction of the site's perimeter would have diminished the empty horizons for which the Feld's panorama is currently renowned.

However, the most significant intervention into Tempelhof's landscape, the element of GROSS.MAX's design which would have most significantly reconfigured both the Feld itself and how it is used is the system of pathways they devised. Taking on the form of the curve of the airport building, these paths were to follow the lines of that quarter-circle to create several complete, overlapping circles of varying sizes. Where the circles overlapped, they were intended to create new areas which, the masterplan explains, would have been used for 'sports, games, relaxation and refreshments'. The idea was that activity would be concentrated in the areas where several paths intersect one another while few paths would reach into the greater expanse of the area. This shaping of the use of the space through the design of the space itself carries echoes of nineteenth-century ideas of park design. Drawing on Olmsted, Joyce examines the governance of bodily conduct through the careful design of movement around the park where 'graceful contours' and 'simple' variety were introduced to encourage walking.[75] While the techniques for shaping movement and use of the space are similar, the objectives diverge considerably. The nineteenth-century park was to be a space of assimilation, a place where the working class would be exposed to and, it was hoped, seek to emulate the comportment of their 'betters'.[76] The twenty-first century park designed by GROSS.MAX, however, encourages plurality and heterogeneity of use. In consciously designing the space so that it would 'create livelier and quieter areas',[77] the masterplan seeks to accommodate a range of uses of the park by making it less likely that noisier, livelier users would detract from the peace and solitude that others might be seeking. Conversely, however, it is in the very act of shaping the park to allow and facilitate this heterogeneity that the possibilities of use are delimited.

In other ways, the ordering processes that Joyce identified in the nineteenth-century public park have been active at Tempelhofer Feld since its opening. There is, of course, considerable relaxation in the idea of what is 'appropriate' for a public park; swearing and dirty clothes are not explicitly banned, for example, yet boards at Tempelhof's entrances and the 'visitor information' flyer list sixteen 'terms of use' that 'every visitor is required to comply with' (Figure 4.8).[78] This specifies behaviours and activities such as peddling, camping, graffitiing and using motor vehicles that are to be excluded from the park as well as those such as barbecuing and letting dogs run free which are permissible only in designated areas. It is rule number one that proved most controversial: 'Visiting Tempelhof Park is permitted only during opening hours [...] the entrance gates will be locked [at closing time ...]. The security service is authorized to exercise the property rights'. As established earlier in this chapter, the question of (in)accessibility has featured heavily in the discourse around Tempelhof, so when it became clear that the new site of 'freedom' would have a perimeter fence and security guards to enforce set opening and closing hours, the issue attracted a lot of attention

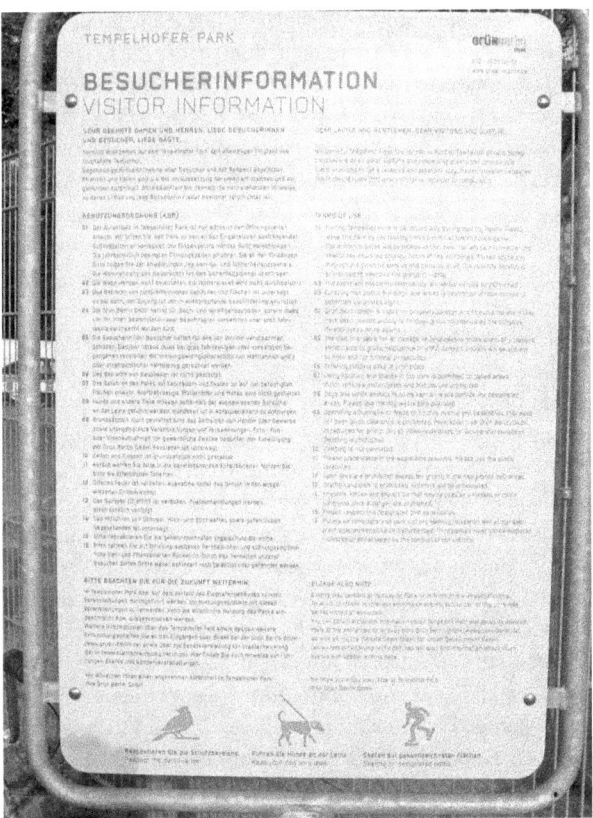

Figure 4.8 Tempelhofer Feld 'terms of use'.
Photograph: By author.

and it was remarked that the new park would 'not be like any other in Berlin'.[79] The idea that the space would function as 'a people's park – until the sun goes down' – was considered particularly problematic by a group who came to be known as the *Zaungegner*.[80] The contentious issue of the fence surrounding the park was highlighted in the *Tageszeitung* which explained that 'for many the fence is a symbol of politics from above, against the will of the people'.[81] The more active *Zaungegner* united under the banner of 'Reclaim Tempelhof', forming a group which opposed the 'neoliberal plans of the Senate' regarding the future of the park: 'instead of a real autonomous space the Senate wants to establish a park which is surrounded by barbed wire and a security fence'. Reclaim Tempelhof objected to the limiting of access to five entrance gates which made 'the park controllable and manageable' and to the impending construction of private, luxury houses around the edge of the Feld which would lead to the increase in rents and thus to the 'displacement of people'.[82]

Reclaim Tempelhof's reaction against the idea that through the designated entry points and the non-porous boundaries of Tempelhof, the park and its visitors become countable, knowable and therefore manageable feeds into a wider theme which is particularly salient in contemporary Berlin: resistance to the homogenization both of space and of the individuals that inhabit that space. In its current configuration Tempelhofer Feld is demarcated as a 'place' wherein particular norms of behaviour are expected and, to an extent, enforced. This is consolidated by the fact that an extension of the rule that visitors to the park need to leave before dusk is that the public can only use the park during daylight hours, that is when they are visible. This suggests that when they cannot be seen, and thus monitored, the 'general public' may choose not to conduct themselves 'appropriately'. As well as negating the issue of (in)accessibility, the removal of the fence would reframe the site as a left-over 'space' where users would be more at liberty to define their own norms of behaviour. The very question of Tempelhof's (in)accessibility undermines the construction of the site as a shared, common asset due to its invocation, and consolidation, of a power structure which sees a designated group given the right to limit the access of others. Yet within just a few years, the fence and the park's opening and closing times had largely been accepted as part of the park. Active citizens' groups continue to decry their presence but even their focus shifted to the plans to reorder Tempelhof in other ways. In the wider discourses around the site, the fence and opening hours became naturalized and hardly visible; at that particular point the dominant power relations had been successfully asserted and normalized and those seeking to counter them were compelled to reconfigure their resistance, finding another threshold at which they contest these ordering processes. That threshold was then relocated to the proposals put forward on the masterplan; with support from other local and community groups, the citizens' initiative 100% Tempelhofer Feld arranged demonstrations, disseminated information and sought to drum up support for the petition for a referendum in order to stop the plans to build around the edges of Tempelhofer Park and to configure the rest as a 'designer park'.[83] The petition succeeded and the referendum, which was held in May 2014, saw 65 per cent Berliners vote against the development of Tempelhofer Feld.[84] The success of the citizens' initiative's campaign brought development of Tempelhofer Feld to a halt. This has not, however, brought their campaigning to an end. The citizens' initiative 100% Tempelhofer Feld is still active and continues to monitor any intervention into the Feld and any proposals for its future while maintaining pressure on the authorities in order to ensure that the spirit of the referendum vote is upheld.[85]

Spontaneous spaces?

While the coverage of these debates in the mainstream press challenges the narratives of dialogue, engagement and transparency which have been constructed around the development of the former airport, when one is actually at the site a distinct impression of grass-roots driven, spontaneous use of the Feld is created by the presence of 'pioneer' projects. When the visitor stumbles upon these projects their haphazard layout, makeshift signage and lack of corporate branding create the idea of an innovative, creative appropriation of space (Figure 4.9). This appearance, however, belies their more compensatory properties and their origins within a conscious urban development strategy that fits into a much wider project that addresses the

Figure 4.9 Pioneer projects at Tempelhofer Feld.
Photograph: By author.

interim use of space and seeks to incorporate it into both an economic and regulatory mainstream. It is through the official website that citizens are invited to apply to develop intermediate or 'pioneer' projects. Intended to foster the creative, innovative use of the vast space offered by the Feld, Tempelhof's 'pioneers' are encouraged to launch small-scale enterprises which will become 'economically independent, work with existing local resources and contribute to increasing the value and quality of the location'. The projects which are already in operation highlight the diversity of potential projects: they range from a unicycle school to Segway rental; from a mini art golf course to community gardening and educational initiatives. The website highlights that these projects are expected to develop in parallel with the overall site: while they allow their instigators to make a profit from them and to add value to the site, they must expect to have to make way as the wider space develops. Stating that 'the spontaneous, informal use of undeveloped spaces is characteristic of Berlin' it explains that the State of Berlin is trying to 'incorporate these informal and interim uses of space into the formal planning process for the first time'.[86]

It is, indeed, the case that Berlin is a city comprised of surfaces and spaces highly prone to re-appropriation and re-inscription: from the graffiti that adorns many of its walls to the projecting of films onto the sides of the buildings beside the vacant plots of buildings destroyed in the war; from the installation of ateliers and galleries in a former department store (Tacheles) to the setting up of what would become world-famous techno clubs in the vault of another former department store (Tresor) or power station (Berghain). Till suggests we understand such sites as 'interim spaces', a term that recognizes the spatial fluidity of the projects which inhabit them (i.e. they are not necessarily contained by the boundaries of previously designated 'place') and that 'allows for the dynamic and open-ended sense of in-betweenness, interventions and unexpected possibilities'.[87] While the number of derelict sites caused by de-industrialization, abundance of infrastructure and political faults across Europe means that the appropriation of disused space is not a Berlin-specific phenomenon,[88] a combination of factors has generated the conditions needed for a culture of re-appropriation to flourish particularly well in Berlin: the low rents and lack of conscription that attracted creative, bohemian young people to the 'island' city of West Berlin; the lack of clear property ownership and low rents that characterized the former East Berlin in the aftermath of unification; high unemployment and the associated feelings of alienation from the commercial mainstream; and an abundance of empty buildings and spaces in poor condition.

In the early to mid-nineties the clubs and bars, music and vintage clothes shops, art galleries, theatres and other creative initiatives that developed and multiplied in these spaces were noticed but largely ignored by the municipal authorities. In the late nineties, however, increasingly market-oriented ideas became a key element of urban planning and the city authorities sought to integrate the majority of these interim projects into wider urban development practices.[89] The informal economies that have grown up around many of the temporary projects, as well as their positive transformative effects upon their localities, have not gone unnoticed by either the owners of many of the buildings or the city authorities. Although many landowners were initially reluctant to allow the *Zwischennutzung* (interim use) of their properties, the precedent set at places like the Hackesche Höfe has made them more enthusiastic: Louekari outlines how, before ownership of the derelict courtyard complex could be established after the fall of the wall, students, artists and young designers established a variety of creative initiatives there which proved extremely popular, transforming the area into a vibrant, bustling part of the city. This popularity meant that once ownership was determined the rents were set so high that the original users could no longer stay.[90] This process has been seen across many of the gentrifying/gentrified areas of Berlin, largely in Prenzlauer Berg, Friedrichshain and Kreuzberg.

Recognizing that such cultural initiatives enabled Berlin to differentiate itself from other European cities in the heavily saturated but potentially highly lucrative culture industry and pushed by the loss of two thirds of the city's industrial jobs in the early 1990s,[91] the city authorities sought to develop Berlin as a 'brand' which could attract both tourists and the creative industries.[92] Lange outlines how the web, fashion and multimedia designers he describes as 'culturepeneurs' became Berlin's new 'export good', used by Berlin's PR agency Partner für Berlin as ambassadors to represent the young, trendy 'new' Berlin abroad.[93] Meanwhile, as Colomb demonstrates, place marketing campaigns designed to bring in tourists moved from the more conventional approach of highlighting famous sights such as the Reichstag, the Brandenburg Gate and the Sony Centre to depicting some of the city's more improvised spaces such as the urban beaches and the *Badeschiff*. She finds that although more radical projects are not featured in official marketing material , they tend to attract the attention of the international media and thus also contribute to the allure which draws in tourists.⁹⁴ This awareness of the benefits of interim projects in temporary spaces also led to the commissioning of two complementary projects: Urban Catalysts, an interdisciplinary European Commission-funded project led by architects Philip Oswalt and Klaus Overmeyer and running between 2001 and 2003, which explored temporary use of spaces in five different European cities, including Berlin; and the Space Pioneers project, led by Klaus Overmeyer, which ran from 2004 to 2005 to assess the potential of *Zwischennutzungen* in Berlin to shape urban development. These projects mapped the characteristics of the 'space pioneers' and their temporary projects, charting the reasoning behind the selection of particular sites, priorities and obstacles, financial operations and the relationships between the 'space pioneers' and other stake holders (site owners, agents, consumers and the local authorities). These project reports also highlighted the positive long-term effects on a city that spontaneous, temporary uses can have and suggested ways in which these temporary uses could be successfully incorporated into the planning and management of cities. As such the temporary users were discursively, and, in some cases, actually, transformed from unknowable subcultures to 'urban players that act deliberately and follow certain visions'.⁹⁵ Tempelhofer Feld has become a microcosm of this. Diverse projects are actively encouraged and the seemingly haphazard way they are placed on the field certainly appears to be in keeping with Berlin's cultures of the spontaneous use of space. This belies the fact that the initiators of each project have gone through a two-step application process and demonstrated their adherence to 'at least one or more [...] guiding themes' in order to establish themselves on the Feld.⁹⁶ Through the mapping of the projects and the key actors they became knowable and therefore governable. They could be brought into the mainstream infrastructure of urban governance, regulated and potentially incorporated into the commodification of subcultures that contributes to 'brand Berlin' and brand 'Tempelhofer Freiheit'. Berlin's heterotopia of illusion have thus become increasingly compensatory.

While the narratives around the former Aviation Ministry and the Olympic Stadium have become increasingly settled, Tempelhof is still a heavily contested site. Just as we saw at the other two sites, the debates around Tempelhof are underpinned by a negotiation of the relationship between illusion and compensation, between order and disorder and freedom and control. Unlike at the other sites though, these debates are not primarily framed by the politics of the past, the tension currently being negotiated at Tempelhof between dominant power relations and the various groups and individuals who challenge and resist them does not necessarily give us an insight into post-authoritarian governmentality but rather into the politics of the advanced liberal city.

Conclusion

In this book I have used post-unification responses to the former Aviation Ministry, the Olympic Stadium and the former Tempelhof Airport in order to explore some of the ways in which the Berlin Republic overtly differentiates itself from its predecessors; references to various forms of plurality which indicate that heterogeneity is not merely tolerated but is embraced and allowed to flourish; the depth of content and the pedagogical tone that suggests a valorization of rational, objective knowledge; and multiple references to 'freedom' which emphasize how it is celebrated in the Berlin Republic. In doing so I have attempted to identify some of the myriad technologies that not only foster this plurality, knowledge and freedom but also simultaneously structure and delimit them. The analysis of the former Aviation Ministry, for example, revealed the gap between the official narrative, which foregrounded an intention to preserve the multiple layers of the site, and the actual outcome of the renovation process, which saw many traces of the GDR dismissed as worthless and discarded; it exposed the discursive and regulatory frameworks that structure the output of the parties seeking to write their version of history on to the fabric of the building; and it showed how, despite a range of strategies deployed to demonstrate that the political institutions and the political processes of the Berlin Republic are considerably more accessible than those of the Third Reich or the GDR, this access is still strongly delimited, and that while contemporary technologies of exclusion may be more subtle, they are still in operation. The analysis of the Olympic Stadium revealed the processes by which reasoned historical commentary became the dominant paradigm through which the legacies of National Socialism would be confronted, showing that this was not inevitable as there were other ideas about how the past should be responded to. These, however, were silenced and marginalized. It also highlights the very conscious juxtaposition between this rational approach to the past and the dramatized, selective, emotive use of history under the Third Reich, showing how the National Socialist instrumentalization of history is, in turn, instrumentalized in post-unification Germany. At the former Tempelhof Airport, we saw that while 'freedom' was frequently invoked in the discourse around the site, its meaning is highly contingent and liable to be reframed to suit particular aims.

As highlighted in the introduction, however, there is no power without resistance. All of these power relations are in continuous conversation with numerous other forces that resist, challenge, subvert and undermine them. This became apparent in all of the case studies where we saw how citizens' initiatives, veterans' groups, memorial entrepreneurs and others continually challenge these structuring frameworks and how the materiality of the sites and issues such as funding defy attempts to impose order on them so that the position of the boundaries around the field of possibilities is continually being renegotiated. This reveals not a binary of power/resistance but an insight into how dominant power relations are simultaneously challenged and consolidated. As messy, jumbled legacies of dictatorship, all three sites have the potential to undermine the democratic credentials of the Berlin Republic's capital city but all can also be presented as containers within which the traces of the past can be enclosed and, through post-unification intervention, ordered, regulated and managed. Yet this in turn continually opens up new scope for resistance and challenge: we see this in the memorial entrepreneurs at the former Aviation Ministry who continually push at the boundaries which structure memorialization at the site, forcing (re)negotiation and compromise; we see it at the Olympic Stadium where the materiality of the site resists and subverts attempts to reorder it; and we see it at Tempelhof where many of the frameworks developed to structure freedom at the site have been overtly identified and challenged by different interest groups. These sites all provide a platform for the performance of post-authoritarian governmentality but they also function as spaces where its techniques of conducting conduct are continually resisted, (re)asserted and (re)negotiated.

This book has argued that these tensions all underline a specifically post-authoritarian governmentality that has operated in Germany in the years following unification. Surely though, these tensions and the techniques used to negotiate them are those that underpin existing conceptions of liberal governmentality? After all, the tension between managing and embracing heterogeneity, of valorizing an 'objective' knowledge and negotiating the balance between freedom and control are hardly unique to post-unification Germany. As we established in Chapter 1, however, the distinction between different forms of governmentality does not come down to their techniques or strategies of rule but to the aspirations that inform them and the extremes to which they are taken. To a much greater extent than the nineteenth-century liberal state or twentieth-century advanced liberal democracies, the Berlin Republic needs to demonstrate its democratic credentials. Unlike these other states, the Berlin Republic needs to re-encode technologies of governance that were used for decidedly illiberal rule and, further unlike these other states, governance in the Berlin Republic takes place within a wider political, social and cultural landscape that is heavily informed by past dictatorship. Furthermore, as the analysis in this book has shown, the politics of the past do not only impact upon how its traces themselves are responded to but also impact the processes by which the decisions about what to do with the traces are made and communicated. The extremely high level of sensitivity with which these tensions must be negotiated is what creates the need to identify a specifically post-authoritarian governmentality.

However, as I add the finishing touches to this book in early 2019, the world seems a very different place to that of late 2010 when the ideas for this project were beginning to take shape. The rise in populist politics across Europe and the United States has seen a resurgence of the language and symbols of Nazism which had seemed long-since reduced to the preserve of a minority; far-right nationalist political parties who publicly express anti-immigration and anti-Islamic views are enjoying new levels of support at the ballot box, while verbal and physical attacks on minorities are on the rise; academic experts on the Third Reich have found themselves engaged in discussions of the extent to which recent shifts in policy and political discourse do or do not echo that of Germany in the 1930s;[1] and the growing rejection of expert views on topics ranging from vaccinations to climate change attest to challenges to the forms of knowledge acquired through rigorous research and peer review. In Germany, the most prominent manifestation of this is the Alternative for Germany Party (AfD) whose gain of 12.6 per cent of the vote in the 2017 federal elections saw a radical right party take seats, ninety-four of them, in the Bundestag for the first time since the war. Attributing this primarily to the Euro Crisis and to Merkel's policies on immigration, political scientists question whether or not this represents the end of Germany's successful 'containment' of the far right which has seen previous far-right parties (the National Democratic Party, the Republikaner, the German People's Union and the Schill Party) fail to gain any significant traction.[2] In keeping with right-wing parties elsewhere, the AfD challenges the narratives and veracity of the established media, which they dismiss as *Lügenpresse* (lying media) and centre their campaigns around Euroscepticism, immigration and asylum seekers and traditional values and gender politics.[3] Yet they have also invoked the politics of the German past; in 2017 Björn Höcke challenged Weizsäcker's 1985 speech and condemned the erection of Berlin's Memorial to the Murdered Jews of Europe, arguing that 'these stupid politics of coming to grips with the past cripple us, we need nothing other than a 180-degree reversal on the politics of remembrance'[4] and Frauke Petry, who has since left the party, has been criticized for using the language of National Socialism such as the word *Volk*.[5]

So, is it still appropriate to talk of a post-authoritarian governmentality in operation in Germany? While the increased traction of right-wing politics and rhetoric does seem to fly in the face of a political culture defined in direct opposition to its authoritarian past, it is important to note that these views are those of a minority, and that they are invariably met by horror, consternation and outrage by the majority of ordinary Germans and mainstream political parties. The reactions against right-wing populism have manifested themselves in a range of ways: the language of the AfD has been publicly condemned by other politicians;[6] an art collective, the Centre for Political Beauty, outraged at Höcke's comments on the Berlin Holocaust memorial erected a replica of it in his hometown;[7] and popular protests against the AfD have seen thousands of people take to the streets in cities across Germany, far outnumbering those turning out for pro-AfD demonstrations.[8] Among academics, political scientist David Art has pointed out that the very fact that Merkel was able to accept such a large number of refugees and agree to a German bailout of the Eurozone in the first place indicates a lack of a strong and well-established radical right;[9] and historian of modern Germany, Richard Evans, argues that the vocal far right has been unable to disturb the German consensus on its Nazi past and that, conversely, 'all the other main political parties … are even more committed to the dominant German culture of memory'.[10]

Even before the AfD's challenge to the importance of *Vergangenheitsbewältigung*, questions over the possibility of Germany's 'normalization' had concerned academics, cultural commentators and others for decades, and this intensified after unification. Cultural historian Gay is somewhat pessimistic about Germany's prospects for 'normality'. She considers the Berlin Republic to be caught up in a 'dialectic of normality' whereby Germany compares itself with other, 'normal' nations but in doing so only serves to highlight the 'absolute abnormality' of its National Socialist past.[11] Elsewhere, a distinct shift has been identified as occurring in the late 1990s when normalization came instead to be associated with contemporary Germany's core values, with its democratic stability, Westernization and Europeanization.[12] Indeed, what seems to be a common thread through the literature around this is an understanding that any 'normality' in Germany will be achieved through a de-centring of the national; through the transnationalization of German historiography;[13] through Germany's involvement in supranational organizations and actions;[14] and through its successful self-representation by internationally consumed cultural products.[15] However, if there is such a thing as a 'normal' nation, surely, this highly considered, self-conscious focus on whether or not a particular nation will ever fit that norm only serves to other that country further. Perhaps a more valuable question is this one: Will 'advanced liberalism' ever be an adequate paradigm through which to explore governmentality in Germany?

Through the analysis of the buildings in this book we have seen some indications that this might be the case. At Tempelhof in particular, while some actors, such as those campaigning for the construction of a memorial on the site of the former concentration camp, strive to ensure that its past is made more visible, the issues around the site's ordering are being increasingly understood in relation to advanced liberal democracy. To a lesser extent, the incorporation of the Olympic Stadium into the longer narratives of history, as seen in the exhibition there, could be seen as rendering its National Socialist layer less pertinent. At the former Aviation Ministry, however, the politics of the past continue to frame the representation of, and responses to, the site. The differences can, of course, in part be attributed to the sites' functions. Housing a government ministry, the former Aviation Ministry is much more tightly bound into the performance of legitimacy in the Berlin Republic than the other sites. The Olympic Stadium, in functioning as a stage on which Germany presents itself to the outside world, is also liable to be caught up in this performance of legitimacy through providing a demonstration of how Germany responds to its past. Its construction in the urban imaginary is also strongly shaped by its role as the home ground of local football team, Hertha Berlin. The emotions that this excites from some quarters overshadow the site's National Socialist otherness. At Tempelhof, the politics of the past featured heavily in the earlier debates around the future of the site and can be seen as the reason that it attracted so much public interest. It has now, however, been incorporated into other narratives, particularly those which see Berliners striving to defend 'their' public assets and spaces against developers and the market forces of advanced liberalism. While various different actors continue to invoke the idea of 'freedom' to make their case about Tempelhof's future, they do so not, primarily, as a response to the politics of the past but in response to the ordering of the advanced liberal city.

Essentially, what this reveals is unevenness: while some evidence suggests that Germany is indeed moving beyond post-authoritarian governmentality, other evidence indicates that it is not. Fortunately, the study of governmentality does not just allow for recognition of unevenness, of contingency, of plurality and of being unable to come up with a single answer but encourages it. As was established in Chapter 1, different variants of governmentality do not seamlessly segue into one another, and even across apparent ruptures there are elements of continuity. Like the built environment, a particular governmentality is always informed to some degree by what went before it and so, in this sense, there will always be an element of 'post-authoritarianness' in German governance; Germany's technologies of government will always bear traces of having been re-encoded, reshaped and adapted from a period of authoritarian rule. Our understanding of a particular governmentality is, however, primarily determined by its dominant characteristics. The issue at stake is the question of whether or not the politics of the past will continue to play a key role in shaping the operation of advanced liberalism in Germany. Indications are that this is beginning to wane. Recent studies that show a reduction of historical awareness among young Germans[16] and the increasing significance of issues such as immigration, globalization, educational reform and economic growth seem to bear this out.[17] As the number of people with first-hand memory of National Socialism diminishes and a new generation of voters with no living memory of either the Third Reich or the GDR emerges, it is perhaps inevitable that the politics of the past will be superseded by other issues. However, given the current political climate, the work being done by memory activists, citizens' initiatives, historians, archaeologists and architects such as those highlighted in this book is even more important now than ever. Using evidence to establish exactly what happened under the Third Reich and finding the means to communicate that to the wider public; developing ways to challenge the built legacies of the regime, from its bombastic architecture to its sculptures venerating the cult of the body; and campaigning for memorials to ensure that the extent of the atrocities committed under the Third Reich is written on to the urban fabric are all vital ways of countering any distortion or forgetting of the nature of National Socialism.

Notes

Introduction

1. The site of the *Führerbunker* fell just inside the borders of the GDR, the government of which sought to keep its location a secret from its citizens. See Brian Ladd, *The Ghosts of Berlin: Confronting German History in the Urban Landscape* (London: University of Chicago Press, 1997), 127–8.
2. See, for example, Jennifer Jordan, *Structures of Memory: Understanding Urban Change in Berlin and Beyond* (Stanford, CA: Stanford University Press, 2006), 189–90; Lutz Kaelber, 'New Analyses of Trauma, Memory, and Place in Berlin and Beyond: A Review Essay', *Canadian Journal of Sociology Online* (May–June 2007), 1–10.
3. Christopher Stoltzenberg, 'Debunking Hitler: Marking the Site of the Führer's Bunker', *Spiegel Online International*, 9 June 2006, http://www.spiegel.de/international/debunking-hitler-marking-the-site-of-the-fuehrer-s-bunker-a-420483.html.
4. See, for example, Claire Colomb, 'Requiem for a Lost *Palast*: "Revanchist Urban Planning" and "'Burdened Landscapes" of the German Democratic Republic in the New Berlin', *Planning Perspectives*, 22 (2007), 283–323; kla, 'Luxury Project Suspended: Protests in Berlin Save the Wall for Now', *Spiegel International Online*, 4 March 2013, http://www.spiegel.de/international/germany/investor-seeks-compromise-in-controversial-berlin-wall-a-886714.html [last accessed 24 July 2014]; Lutz Koepnick, 'Redeeming History? Foster's Dome and the Political Aesthetics of the Berlin Republic', *German Studies Review*, 24 (2001), 303–23.
5. Manfred Görtemaker, Michael Bienert and Marko Leps, *Orte der Demokratie in Berlin: Ein Historisch-Politischer Wegweiser* (Bonn: BpB, 2004), 221.
6. Robert R. Taylor, *The Word in Stone: The Role of Architecture in the National Socialist Ideology* (London: University of California Press, 1974), 196.
7. Volker Kluge, *Olympiastadion Berlin: Steine Beginnen zu Reden* (Berlin: Parthas Verlag, 1999), 15.
8. Wolfgang Schäche and Norbert Szymanski, *Das Reichssportfeld: Architektur im Spannungsfeld von Sport und Macht* (Berlin: be.bra-Verlag, 2001), 58.
9. H. Nienhoff, 'Faszination Des Raumes', *architektur + bauphysik*, 7 (2006), 18.
10. Hans Pfundtner, 'Die Gesamtleitung der Errichtung des Reichssportfeldes', in *Das Reichssportfeld: Eine Schöpfung des Dritten Reiches für die Olympischen Spiele und die deutschen Leibesuebungen*, ed. Reichsministerium des Innern (Berlin: Reichspartei Verlag, 1936), 11.
11. Hans-Ernst Mittig, 'Kunst und Propaganda im NS-System', in *Moderne Kunst 2: Das Funkkolleg zum Verständnis der Gegenwartskunst*, ed. Monika Wagner (Hamburg: Rowohlt Taschenbuch Verlag GmbH, 1991), 455.
12. Matthias Donath, *Garden Guide: The Olympic Grounds – Former Reichssportfeld* (Berlin: Landesdenkmalamt (Berlin) and Museumspädagogischer Dienst (Berlin), 2001), 9.

13 Arbeitsgemeinschaft Reinald Eckert und Wolfgang Schäche, 'Das Ehemalige Reichssportfeld, Geschichte und Bestand', in *Kooperatives Gutachterverfahren Olympisches Dorf und Olympiagelände*, ed. Thies Schröder, Senatsverwaltung für Stadtentwicklung und Umweltschutz (Berlin: Kulturbuchverlag, 1993), 33.
14 Philipp Meuser, *Vom Fliegerfeld zum Wiesenmeer: Geschichte und Zukunft des Flughafens Tempelhof* (Berlin: Quintessenz Verlags GmbH, 2000), 31.
15 Axel Drieschner, 'Ernst Sagebiel's Tempelhof Airport: Typology, Iconography and Politics', in *Historic Airports: Proceedings of the International L'Europe de L'Air Conferences on Aviation Architecture Liverpool (1999), Berlin (2000), Paris (2001)*, ed. Bob Hawkins, Gabriele Lechner and Paul Smith (London: English Heritage, 2005), 100; Meuser, *Vom Fliegerfeld zum Wiesenmeer*, 31–3.
16 Gabi Dolff-Bonekämper, 'Berlin-Tempelhof', in *Berlin Tempelhof, Liverpool Speke, Paris Le Bourget: Airport Architecture of the Thirties*, ed. Paul Smith and Bernard Toulier (Paris: Editions du Patrimoine, 2000), 52.
17 Ibid., 57; Drieschner, 'Ernst Sagebiel's Tempelhof Airport', 100–111; Manfred Hecker, 'Berlin-Tempelhof: A City Airport of the 1930s', in *Historic Airports: Proceedings of the International L'Europe de L'Air Conferences on Aviation Architecture Liverpool (1999), Berlin (2000), Paris (2001)*, ed. Bob Hawkins, Gabriele Lechner and Paul Smith (London: English Heritage, 2005), 92–4.
18 Frank Schmitz, *Flughafen Tempelhof – Berlins Tor zur Welt* (Berlin: be.bra, 1997), 105.
19 Mitchell Dean, *Governmentality: Power and Rule in Modern Society* (London: Sage, 2010), 23.
20 John Czaplicka, 'History, Aesthetics and Contemporary Commemorative Practice in Berlin', *New German Critique*, 65 (1995), 155–87; Jordan, *Structures of Memory*; Sharon Macdonald, 'Undesirable Heritage: Fascist Material Culture and Historical Consciousness in Nuremberg', *International Journal of Heritage Studies*, 12 (2006), 9–28; and Karen Till, 'Interim Use at a Former Death Strip? Art, Politics and Urbanism at *Skulpturenpark Berlin_Zentrum*', in *The German Wall: Fallout in Europe*, ed. Marc Silberman (New York: Palgrave Macmillan, 2011).
21 Unless otherwise stated, all references to the materiality of the sites draw on their condition in summer 2012.
22 Patrick Joyce, *The Rule of Freedom: Liberalism and the Modern City* (London: Verso, 2003); Maiken Umbach, *German Cities and Bourgeois Modernism, 1890-1924* (Oxford: Oxford University Press, 2009).

Chapter 1

1 Michel Foucault, Lecture, 1 February 1978, printed in *Security Territory, Population: Lectures at the Collège de France 1977–1978*, ed. Michel Senellart, F. Ewald, Francois Fontana and Arnold I. Davidson, trans by Graham Burchell (New York: Palgrave Macmillan, 2009), 88–9.
2 Michel Foucault, Lecture, 1 February 1978, printed in *Security Territory, Population*, 95; On the emergence of 'population' as an economic and political problem see also Michel Foucault, *The History of Sexuality Volume One: An Introduction*, trans. Robert Hurley (New York: Pantheon Books, 1978), 25.
3 Michel Foucault, 'Space, Knowledge, and Power', in *The Foucault Reader*, ed. Paul Rabinow (London: Penguin, 1991), 242.

4 Dean, *Governmentality*, 17.
5 See, for example, Michel Foucault, *Discipline and Punish: The Birth of the Modern Prison* (London: Penguin, 1991).
6 Michel Foucault, Lecture, 8 February 1978, printed in *Security Territory, Population*, 119–20 (footnote).
7 Thomas Lemke, '"The Birth of Bio-Politics": Michel Foucault's Lecture at The Collège de France on Neo-liberal Governmentality', *Economy and Society*, 30 (2001), 190–207, 191.
8 Among many examples, see David Garland, '"Governmentality" and the Problem of Crime: Foucault, Criminology, Sociology', *Theoretical Criminology*, 1 (2) (1997), 173–214 ; Donald Gillies, 'Developing Governmentality: Conduct and Education Policy', *Journal of Education Policy*, 23 (4) (2008), 415–27; Anita Harris, 'Discourses of Desire as Governmentality: Young Women, Sexuality and the Significance of Safe Spaces', *Feminism & Psychology*, 15 (1) (2005), 39–43; Wendy Larner and William Walters, eds. *Global Governmentality: Governing International Spaces* (London: Routledge, 2004); Anna Pratt and Sara K. Thompson, 'Chivalry, "Race" and Discretion at the Canadian Border', *The British Journal of Criminology*, 48 (5) (2008), 620–40.
9 See, for example, Derek Kerr, 'Beheading the King and Enthroning the Market: A Critique of Foucauldian Governmentality', *Science and Society*, 63, no. 2 (1999), 173–202.
10 Stephen Legg, 'Subjects of Truth: Resisting Governmentality in Foucault's 1980s', *Environment and Planning D: Society and Space* 31, no. 1 (2019), 27–45, 28.
11 For a detailed discussion of this criticism and response to it, see Bob Jessop, 'From Micro-Powers to Governmentality: Foucault's Work on Statehood, State Formation, Statecraft and State Power', *Political Geography*, 26, (2007), 34–40.
12 Kim McKee, 'Post-Foucauldian Governmentality: What Does It Offer Critical Social Policy Analysis?' *Critical Social Policy* 29 (3) (2009), 465–86, 476.
13 Ulrich Bröckling, Susanne Krasmann and Thomas Lemke, eds. *Governmentality: Current Issues and Future Challenges* (London: Routledge, 2010), 20.
14 Pat O'Malley, Lorna Weir and Clifford Shearing, 'Governmentality, Criticism, Politics', *Economy and Society*, 26 (4) (1997), 501–17, 509.
15 Ibid., 514.
16 Thomas Lemke, 'Foucault, Governmentality and Critique', *Rethinking Marxism*, 14 (3) (2002), 46–64, 54. For a fuller and updated discussion, see Thomas Lemke, *Foucault, Governmentality and Critique* (London: Routledge, 2015).
17 For an excellent overview of different forms of governmentality, see Dean, *Governmentality*.
18 Ibid., 131.
19 Joyce, *The Rule of Freedom*, 4.
20 Michel Foucault, *Power/ Knowledge: Selected Interviews and Other Writings 1972–1977*, ed. Colin Gordon (New York: Pantheon Books, 1980), 194.
21 Michel Foucault, Lecture, 11 January 1978, printed in *Security Territory, Population*, 1, see also Michel Foucault, *The History of Sexuality Volume 1: An Introduction*, trans. Robert Hurley (New York: Pantheon Books: 1978).
22 Michel Foucault, Lecture 11, 17 March 1976, printed in *Society Must Be Defended: Lectures at the Collège de France 1975 -1976*, ed. Ewald Bertani, Fontana and Davidson and trans. David Macey (New York: Picador, 2003), 243–6.
23 See, for example, Matthew G. Hannah, *Governmentality and the Mastery of Territory in Nineteenth-Century America*,(Cambridge: Cambridge University Press, 2000);

Stephen Legg, 'Foucault's Population Geographies: Classifications, Biopolitics and Governmental Spaces', in *Population, Space and Place*, 11 (2005), 137–56; Umbach, *German Cities and Bourgeois Modernism, 1890-1924*; Paul Rabinow, *French Modern: Norms and Forms of the Social Environment* (London: The MIT Press, 1989).

24 Nikolas Rose, 'Government, Authority and Expertise in Advanced Liberalism', *Economy and Society*, 22 (1993), 283–99, 283.

25 See, for example, John L. Campbell and Ove Kaj Pedersen, *The Rise of Neo-Liberalism and Institutional Analysis* (Oxford: Princeton University Press, 2001); Henk Overbeek, *Restructuring Hegemony in the Global Political Economy: The Rise of Transnational Neo-Liberalism in the 1980s* (London: Routledge, 1993); and Susanne Soederberg, Georg Menz and Philip G. Cerny, *Internalizing Globalization: The Rise of Neo-liberalism and the Decline of National Varieties of Capitalism* (Basingstoke: Palgrave Macmillan, 2005).

26 Dean, *Governmentality*, 175–6.

27 Rose, 'Government, Authority and Expertise in Advanced Liberalism', 298.

28 Nikolas Rose, *Powers of Freedom: Reframing Political Thought* (Cambridge: Cambridge University Press, 1999), 142.

29 Dean, *Governmentality*, 197–8.

30 Rose, *Powers of Freedom: Reframing Political Thought*, 147–55.

31 Dean, *Governmentality*, 194–5.

32 Ibid., 196–7.

33 D. Cowan and A. Marsh, 'From Need to Choice, Welfarism to Advanced Liberalism? Problematics of Social Housing Allocation', *Legal Studies*, 25 (2005), 22–48; Catherine McDonald and Greg Marson, 'Workfare as Welfare: Governing Unemployment in the Advanced Liberal State', *Critical Social Policy*, 25 (2005), 374–401.

34 Vaughan Higgins, 'Calculating Climate: "Advanced Liberalism" and the Governing of Risk in Australian Drought Policy', *Journal of Sociology*, 37 (2001), 299–316; Nigel Parton, 'Risk, Advanced Liberalism and Child Welfare: The Need to Rediscover Uncertainty and Ambiguity ', *British Journal of Social Work*, 28 (1998), 5–27.

35 Joan Pujolar, 'African Women in Catalan Language Courses: Struggles over Class, Gender and Ethnicity in Advanced Liberalism', in *Words, Worlds, and Material Girls: Language, Gender, Globalization*, ed. Bonnie McElhinny (Berlin: Walter de Gruyter GmbH, 2007); Virginia Watson, 'Liberalism and Advanced Liberalism in Australian Indigenous Affairs', *Alternatives: Global, Local, Political*, 29 (2004), 577–98.

36 Michel Foucault, Lecture, 11, 17 March 1976, printed in *Society Must Be Defended*, 259–60.

37 Michel Foucault, Lecture, 7 March 1979, printed in *The Birth of Biopolitics*, 190–1.

38 See, for example, Michael Geyer and Sheila Fitzpatrick, *Beyond Totalitarianism: Stalinism and Nazism Compared*, (Cambridge: Cambridge University Press, 2009).

39 Dean, *Governmentality*, 155.

40 Ibid., 163–9.

41 Legg, 'Foucault's Population Geographies', 145.

42 Dean, *Governmentality*, 163–9.

43 Rose, *Powers of Freedom: Reframing Political Thought*, 23; also Dean, *Governmentality*, 23.

44 On British governance of space in India, see Thomas Osborne, 'Bureaucracy as a Vocation: Governmentality and Administration in Nineteenth-Century Britain', *Journal of Historical Sociology*, 7 (1994), 289–313; On National Socialist interventions

into space in the East see Robert-Jan van Pelt, 'Auschwitz: From Architect's Promise to Inmate's Perdition', *Modernism/ Modernity*, 1 (1994), 80–120 especially 87–8.
45 On the prevalence of authoritarian governmentality within neoliberal rationalities of rule in Egypt, see Ismail Salwa, 'Authoritarian Government, Neoliberalism and Everyday Civilities in Egypt', *Third World Quarterly*, 32 (2011), 845–62; On the Chinese party-state see Gary Sigley, 'Chinese Governmentalities: Government, Governance and the Socialist Market Economy', *Economy and Society*, 35 (2006), 487–508.
46 Dean cites Bauman's highly influential work Zygmunt Bauman, *Modernity and the Holocaust* (Cambridge: Polity, 1989); See also S. N. Eisenstadt, 'Multiple Modernities', *Daedalus*, 129 (Winter 2000), 1–29; Roger Griffin, 'Modernity, Modernism, and Fascism. A "Mazeway Resynthesis"', *Modernism/ modernity*, 15 (January 2008), 9–24.
47 For an excellent discussion of how these factors have impacted upon right-wing extremism in post-war Germany, see Lee McGowan, *The Radical Right in Germany 1870 to the Present* (London: Routledge, 2014).
48 Michel Foucault, Lecture, 31. January 1979, printed in *The Birth of Biopolitics*, 94.
49 Ibid., 81–6.
50 Ibid., 93–5.
51 Ibid., 75–6. For more on 'state-phobia' and Foucault's views on the West German state, see Matthew Hannah, 'State Knowledge and Recurring Patterns of State Phobia: From Fascism to Post-politics', in *Progress in Human Geography*, 40 (4) (2016), 476–94.
52 Michel Foucault, Lectures from 31 January to 21 February 1979, printed in *The Birth of Biopolitics*, 75–184.
53 Michel Foucault, Lecture, 31 January 1979, printed in *The Birth of Biopolitics*, 86.
54 Michel Foucault, Lecture, 7 March 1979, printed in *The Birth of Biopolitics*, 186.
55 Stefan Lanz, 'Be Berlin! Governing the City through Freedom', *International Journal of Urban and Regional Research*, 37 (2013), 1305–24.
56 Nadine Marquardt and others, 'Shaping the Urban Renaissance: New-Build Luxury Developments in Berlin', *Urban Studies*, 50 (2013), 1540–56, 1545.
57 Neil Gregor, *Haunted City: Nuremberg and the Nazi Past* (London: Yale University Press, 2008), 4.
58 Robert Moeller, 'The Politics of the Past in the 1950s: Rhetorics of Victimisation in East and West Germany', in *Germans as Victims: Remembering the Past in Contemporary Germany*, ed. Bill Niven (Basingstoke: Palgrave Macmillan, 2006), 29.
59 Mary Fulbrook, *Reckonings: Legacies of Nazi Persecution and the Quest for Justice* (Oxford: Oxford University Press, 2018), 212–19.
60 Konrad H. Jarausch, *After Hitler: Recivilizing Germans, 1945-1995* (Oxford: Oxford University Press, 2008), 54.
61 Fulbrook, *Reckonings*, 210–11.
62 Herf, Jeffrey. *Divided Memory* (London: Harvard University Press, 1997), 267–8.
63 See, for example, Fulbrook, *Reckonings*, 239–40.
64 Jarausch, *After Hitler*, 55.
65 Bill Niven, *Facing the Nazi Past: United Germany and the Legacy of the Third Reich* (London: Routledge, 2003), 2.
66 Herf, *Divided Memory*, 283–5; Niven, *Facing the Nazi Past*, 3.
67 Moeller, 'The Politics of the Past in the 1950s', 39.
68 See David Cesarani, *After Eichmann: Collective Memory and Holocaust Since 1961* (London: Routledge, 2013); Philipp Gassert and Alan E. Steinweis, eds. *Coping with*

the Nazi Past: West German Debates on Nazism and Generational Conflict, 1955-1975. (Oxford: Berghahn Books, 2007); Devin O. Pendas, *The Frankfurt Auschwitz Trial, 1963-1965: Genocide, History, and the Limits of the Law* (Cambridge: Cambridge University Press, 2006).
69 Herf, *Divided Memory*, 353–8.
70 Rudy Koshar, *From Monuments to Traces: Artefacts of German Memory, 1870-1990*, (London: University of California Press, 2000), 226–39.
71 McGowen, *The Radical Right in Germany*, 156–8.
72 Cited in Anna Saunders, 'Challenging or Concretising Cold War Narratives? Berlin's Memorial to the Victims of 17 June 1953', in *Memorialisation in Germany since 1945*, ed. Bill Niven and Chloe Paver (Basingstoke, Hampshire: Palgrave Macmillan, 2010), 298.
73 Maja Zehfuss, *Wounds of Memory: The Politics of War in Germany* (Cambridge: Cambridge University Press, 2007), 32–3.
74 See Niven, *Facing the Nazi Past*, 140–69 and 194–232.
75 Cited in Bill Niven and Chloe Paver, 'Introduction', in *Memorialisation in Germany since 1945*, ed. Bill Niven and Chloe Paver (Basingstoke: Palgrave Macmillan, 2010), 1.
76 For excellent discussions of these debates, see Stefan Berger, *The Search for Normality: National Identity and Historical Consciousness in Germany since 1800* (Oxford: Berghahn Books, 1997), ch. 7; Konrad H. Jarausch and Michael Geyer, *Shattered Past: Reconstructing German Histories* (Oxford: Princeton University Press, 2009), ch. 2.
77 Jorg Roesler, 'Privatisation in Eastern Germany: Experience with the Treuhand', *Europe-Asia Studies*, 14 (3),(1994), 505–17, 509.
78 Peter C. Caldwell and Karrin Hanshew, *Germany since 1945: Politics, Culture and Society* (London: Bloomsbury, 2018); Paul Cooke, *Representing East Germany since Unification: From Colonisation to Nostalgia* (Oxford: Berg, 2005); Justinian Jampol, 'Problematic Things: East German Materials after 1989', in *Divided Dreamworlds? The Cultural Cold War in East and West*, ed. Peter Romijn, Giles Scott-Smith and Joes Segal (Amsterdam: Amsterdam University Press, 2012).
79 Koshar, *From Monuments to Traces*, 4.
80 The term 'long 1960s' is used here to denote recent moves away from locating West Germany's confrontation with the Nazi past specifically in 1968 or even in the 1960s as a whole. The term is borrowed from Habbo Koch, 'The Return of the Images: Photographs of Nazi Crimes and the West German Public in The "Long 1960s"', in *Coping with the Nazi Past: West German Debates on Nazism and Generational Conflict 1955-1975*, ed. P Gassert and A. Steinweis (Oxford: Berghahn Books, 2006). This volume provides an excellent overview of the debates around this issue. On the impact of shifts in memory culture in the 1960s on the built environment, see Neil Gregor, *Haunted City*.
81 Michel Foucault, Lecture 7 March 1979, printed in *The Birth of Biopolitics*, 185–214.
82 Henry Rousso and Arthur Goldhammer, *The Vichy Syndrome: History and Memory in France since 1944* (Cambridge, MA: Harvard University Press, 1994); Caroline Alice Wiedmer, *The Claims of Memory: Representations of the Holocaust in Contemporary Germany and France* (London: Cornell University Press, 1999).
83 See, for example, Richard J. Evans, 'From Nazism to Never Again: How Germany Came to Terms with Its Past', *Foreign Affairs*, 97 (2018), 8–15, 9; Gavriel D. Rosenfeld and Paul B. Jaskot, 'Introduction', in *Beyond Berlin: Twelve German Cities Confront*

the Nazi Past, ed. Gavriel D. Rosenfeld and Paul B. Jaskot (Ann Arbour: University of Michigan Press, 2008), 11.

84 *Der Spiegel*, 'Gauland provoziert mit Rede zu Deutschlands Nazi-Vergangenheit', 14 September 2017 https://www.spiegel.de/politik/deutschland/alexander-gauland-provoziert-mit-rede-zu-deutschlands-nazi-vergangenheit-a-1167750.html; *Der Tagespiegel*, 'Oppermann über Gauland: "Geschmacklose Geschichtsklitterung"', 15 September 2017, https://www.tagesspiegel.de/politik/rede-des-afd-spitzenkandidaten-oppermann-ueber-gauland-geschmacklose-geschichtsklitterung/20332986.html; *DW* 'Gauland bezeichnet NS-Zeit als "Vogelschiss in der Geschichte"', 2. June 2018, https://www.dw.com/de/gauland-bezeichnet-ns-zeit-als-vogelschiss-in-der-geschichte/a-44054219

85 Niven and Paver, 'Introduction', in *Memorialisation in Germany since* 1945, 1.

86 On debates around Germany's involvement in military activity, see Zehfuss, *Wounds of Memory*, especially 1–20. On how politics of the past informs contemporary debates over surveillance, privacy and personal data, see Lauren Rakower, 'Blurred Lines: Zooming in on Google Street View and the Global Right to Privacy', *Brooklyn Journal of International Law*, 37 (2011), 317–47.

87 Joyce, *Rule of Freedom*, 162–3.

88 Ibid., 30–1.

89 Michel Foucault, Lecture 10 January 1979, printed in *The Birth of Biopolitics*, 10–12.

90 Michel Foucault, Lecture 11, 17 March 1976, printed in *Society Must Be Defended*, 251.

91 Margo Huxley, 'Geographies of Governmentality', in *Space, Knowledge and Power: Foucault and Geography*, ed. Jeremy Crampton and Stuart Elden (Oxon: Routledge, 2016), 190–1.

92 See, for example, Jeremy W. Crampton and Stuart Elden, 'Introduction: Space, Knowledge and Power: Foucault and Geography', in *Space, Knowledge and Power: Foucault and Geography,* ed. Jeremy W. Crampton and Stuart Elden (Oxon: Routledge, 2016); Kevin Hetherington, *The Badlands of Modernity: Heterotopia and Social Ordering* (London: Routledge, 1997), 42; Margo Huxley, 'Space and Government: Governmentality and Geography', *Geography Compass,* 2 (5) (2008), 1635–58.

93 Stuart Elden, 'Governmentality, Calculation, Territory', *Environment and Planning D: Society and Space*, 25 (3) (2007), 562–80; Hannah, *Governmentality and the Mastery of Territory*.

94 Thomas Osborne and Nikolas Rose, 'Governing Cities: Notes on the Spatialisation of Virtue', *Environment and Planning D: Society and Space,* 17 (1999), 737–60 735–9.

95 Alan J. Kidd and Kenneth W. Roberts, *City, Class and Culture: Studies of Social Policy and Cultural Production in Victorian Manchester* (Manchester: Manchester University Press, 1985), 31.

96 Ibid., 38–56.

97 Osborne and Rose, 'Governing Cities: Notes on the Spatialisation of Virtue', 735.

98 Mary Poovey, *Making a Social Body: British Cultural Formation, 1830-1864* (London: University of Chicago Press, 1995), 37–45.

99 See, for example, Simon Gunn, *The Public Culture of the Victorian Middle Class: Ritual and Authority and the English Industrial City, 1840-1914* (Manchester: Manchester University Press, 2000); Joyce, *The Rule of Freedom*; Kidd and Roberts, *City, Class and Culture: Studies of Social Policy and Cultural Production in Victorian Manchester*; R. J. Morris, 'The Middle Class and British Towns and Cities of the

Industrial Revolution, 1780-1870', in *Pursuit of Urban History*, ed. Derek Fraser and Anthony Sutcliffe (London: Edward Arnold, 1983), 286–306; Chris Otter, 'Making Liberalism Durable: Vision and Civility in the Late-Victorian City', *Social History*, 27 (2002), 1–15; Rabinow, *French Modern*; Umbach, *German Cities and Bourgeois Modernism, 1890-1924*.

100 Margo Huxley, 'Geographies of Governmentality', 196.
101 Katherine Beckett and Steve Herbert, 'Dealing with Disorder: Social Control in the Post-industrial City', *Theoretical Criminology*, 12 (1) (2008), 5–30.
102 Gail M. Zuckerwise, 'Governmentality in Amsterdam's Red Light District', *City*, 16 (1–2) (2012), 146–57.
103 Alberto Vanolo, '"Smartmentality": The Smart City as Disciplinary Strategy', *Urban Studies*, 51 (5) (2014), 883–98.
104 Otter, 'Making Liberalism Durable', 5.
105 Joyce, *The Rule of Freedom*; Otter, 'Making Liberalism Durable'.
106 Vanolo, '"Smartmentality"': 883–98.
107 Marco Cicchini, 'A New "Inquisition"? Police Reform, Urban Transparency and House Numbering in Eighteenth-Century Geneva', *Urban History*, 39 (4) (2012), 614–23.
108 Stephen Legg, 'Governmentality, Congestion and Calculation in Colonial Delhi', *Social and Cultural Geography*, 7 (5) (2006), 709–29.
109 Marit Rosol, 'On Resistance in the Post-political City: Conduct and Counter-Conduct in Vancouver', *Space and Polity*, 18 (1) (2014), 70–84.
110 Foucault, Security, Territory and Population, lecture, 1 March 1978, 191–226.
111 Michel Foucault, 'Society Must Be Defended', in *Lectures at the College De France 1975-76*, ed. M. Bertani, F. Ewald and A. Fontana (London: Penguin, 2005), 26–9.
112 Michel Foucault, '"Truth and Power" Interview with Alessandro Fontana and Pasquale Pasquino', in *Power/ Knowledge*, ed. Colin Gordon (New York: Pantheon, 1980), 118–19.

Chapter 2

1 Jennifer Jordan, 'A Matter of Time: Examining Collective Memory in Historical Perspective in Postwar Berlin', *Journal of Historical Sociology*, 18 (2005), 37–71, 42.
2 Andreas Huyssen, *Present Pasts: Urban Palimpsests and the Politics of Memory* (Stanford: Stanford University Press, 2003), 81.
3 M. Crang, 'Envisioning Urban Histories: Bristol as Palimpsest, Postcards and Snapshots', *Environment and Planning A*, 28 (1996), 429–52; Kimberly Powell, 'Remapping the City: Palimpsest, Place, and Identity in Art Education Research', *Studies in Art Education*, 50 (2008), 6–21.
4 For a fuller discussion of the Aviation Ministry, Olympic Stadium and Tempelhof Airport as palimpsests see Clare Copley, '"Stones do not Speak for Themselves": Disentangling Berlin's Palimpsest', *Fascism*, 8(2) (2019), 219–49.
5 Hans Pfundtner, 'Die Gesamtleitung der Errichtung des Reichssportfeldes'; Ernst Sagebiel, 'Vom Bau des Reichsluftfahrtministeriums', *Monatshefte für Baukunst und Staedtebau*, 20 (1936), 81–92; Anon., 'Zur Neugestaltung der Reichshauptstadt', *Bauen-Siedeln-Wohnen*, 18 (1938), 246.

6 Bernd Nicolai, 'The Berlin Olympic Stadium: How to Deal with the First "Gesamtkunstwerk" of the Third Reich Today?', in *Sport Stätten Kultur / Sport Sites Culture*, ed. Fiona Laudamus, Michael Petzet and John Ziesemer (Munich: ICOMOS Nationalkomitee der Bundesrepublik Deutschland, 2002), 37.
7 Matthew Philpotts, 'Cultural-Political Palimpsests: The Reich Aviation Ministry and the Multiple Temporalities of Dictatorship', *New German Critique*, 39 (117) (2012), 207–30, 212–13.
8 Bernd Hettlage and Wolfgang Reiher, *Olympiastadion Berlin: Die Neuen Architekturführer* (Berlin: Stadtwandel, 2006), 9.
9 Matthias Donath, 'Konservieren und kommentieren – Denkmalvermittlung für das Olympiagelände', in *Sport Stätten Kultur / Sport Sites Culture*, ed. Fiona Laudamus, Michael Petzet and John Ziesemer (Munich: ICOMOS Nationalkomitee der Bundesrepublik Deutschland, 2002), 81.
10 Matthias Donath, 'Konservieren und kommentieren – Denkmalvermittlung für das Olympiagelände', 83.
11 Hecker, 'Berlin-Tempelhof: A City Airport of the 1930s', 93.
12 Thomas Schmidt, *Das Berliner Olympia Stadion und seine Geschichte* (Berlin: Express Edition, 1983), 19–21.
13 Stefanie Endlich and Beate Rossié, 'Zum Umgang mit den Skulpturen von Breker, Thorak und anderen Bildhauern auf dem Berliner Olympiagelände', in *Zeitgeschichte-online, Thema: Wohin mit Breker? Zum Umgang mit NS-Kunst in Museen und im öffentlichen Raum*, hrsg. von Jan-Holger Kirsch, Dezember 2006, http://www.zeitgesch ichte-online.de/portals/_rainbow/documents/pdf/endlich_rossie_breker.pdf [accessed 1 March 2018].
14 Sharon Macdonald, 'Words in Stone? Agency and Identity in a Nazi Landscape', *Journal of Material Culture*, 11 (1–2) (2006), 105–26, 109.
15 Robert R. Taylor, *The Word in Stone: The Role of Architecture in the National Socialist Ideology* (Berkeley and London: University of California Press, 1974), 17.
16 Taylor, *The Word in Stone*, 23–4.
17 See, for example, Jonathan Petropoulos, *Art as Politics in the Third Reich* (London: University of North Carolina Press Books, 1999) especially 51–74.
18 Barbara Miller Lane, *Architecture and Politics in Germany 1918-1945* (Cambridge, MA: Harvard University Press, 1968), 3–9; See also Jonathan Petropoulos, *Artists Under Hitler: Collaboration and Survival in Nazi Germany* (London: Yale University Press, 2014) especially 49–176.
19 Nicolai, 'The Berlin Olympic Stadium', 38.
20 On the 'eclecticism' of architecture in the Third Reich, see, for example, Barbara Miller Lane, *Architecture and Politics in Germany 1918-1945*; Wolfgang Pehnt, *Deutsche Architektur seit 1900* (Munich: Deutsche Verlags-Anstalt, 2005), 197–202; Taylor, *The Word in Stone*.
21 Donath, 'Konservieren und kommentieren', 84.
22 Jakob Straub and Andreas Fecht, *Schatten der Macht: Architektur des Nationalsozialismus in Berlin* (Berlin: Jovis Verlag, 2006), 12.
23 Taylor, *The Word in Stone*, 219–20; See also Kathleen James-Chakraborty, *German Architecture for a Mass Audience* (New York: Routledge, 2000), 90–1; Ladd, *The Ghosts of Berlin*, 135.
24 Linda Schulte-Sasse, 'Retrieving the City as Heimat: Berlin in Nazi Cinema', in *Berlin: Culture and Metropolis*, ed. Charles Haxthausen and Heidrun Suhr (Oxford: University of Minnesota Press, 1990), 166.

25 Ladd, *The Ghosts of Berlin*, 135; Taylor, *The Word in Stone* 20.
26 Joyce, *The Rule of Freedom*, 148–50; Rabinow *French Modern*, 76–78.
27 On Germania, see Ladd, *The Ghosts of Berlin*, 134–41.
28 Taylor, *The Word in Stone*, 20.
29 Andrew Webber, *Berlin in the Twentieth Century: A Cultural Topography* (Cambridge: Cambridge University Press, 2008), 22.
30 Ladd, *The Ghosts of Berlin*, 139.
31 Paul B. Jaskot, *The Architecture of Oppression: The SS, Forced Labour and the Nazi Building Economy* (London: Routledge, 2000).
32 On traces of Germania, see, for example, Tilmann Buddensieg, *Berliner Labyrinth: Preußische Raster; vom Lustgarten zum Alexanderplatz, vom Reichstag ins Reichssportfeld, von Moabit nach Britz, vom Kemperplatz zum Waldsängerpfad – 'Ich sehe keinen Ausweg aus diesem Labyrinth' (Schinkel, 1829)* (Berlin: Wagenbach, 1993).
33 On Stalinallee, see Greg Castillo, 'The Nylon Curtain: Architectural Unification in Divided Berlin', in *Berlin: Divided City 1945-1989*, ed. Philip Broadbent and Sabine Hake (Oxford: Berghahn Books, 2010); On the television tower, see Heather Gumbert, 'Constructing a Socialist Landmark: The Berlin Television Tower', in *Berlin: Divided City 1945-1989*, ed. P. Broadbent and S. Hake (Oxford: Berghahn Books, 2010), 89–99; On the Palace of the Republic), see Colomb, 'Requiem for a Lost *Palast*'.
34 Ladd, *The Ghosts of Berlin*, 182.
35 Ibid., 188. See also Castillo, 'The Nylon Curtain', 46–55.
36 Deborah Ascher Barnstone, *The Transparent State: Architecture and Politics in Postwar Germany* (London: Routledge, 2005).
37 For excellent overviews of this, see Gavriel Rosenfeld, '"The Architects" Debate: Architectural Discourse and the Memory of Nazism', *History and Memory*, 9 (1997), 189–225; or Kathleen James-Chakraborty, 'Memory and the Cityscape: The German Architectural Debate about Post-Modernism', *German Politics and Society*, 17 (1999), 71–83.
38 See, for example, Eric Jaroskinski, 'Building on a Metaphor: Democracy, Transparency and the Berlin Reichstag', in *Berlin: The Symphony Continues: Orchestrating Architectural, Social and Artistic Change in Germany's New Capital*, ed. C. Costabile-Henning, R. Halverson and K. Foell (Berlin: Walter de Gruyter GmbH, 2004); Koepnick, 'Redeeming History? Foster's Dome and the Political Aesthetics of the Berlin Republic'; Wise, *Capital Dilemma*.
39 Monica Riera, 'How Should We Build? Architecture, History and the Post-Cold War Context in Germany', *National Identities*, 8 (2006), 388.
40 Barnstone, *The Transparent State*, 104–6.
41 Florian Urban, *Neo-Historical East Berlin: Architecture and Urban Design in the German Democratic Republic 1970-1990* (Farnham: Ashgate, 2009), especially chapter 4.
42 Sharon Macdonald, *Difficult Heritage: Negotiating the Nazi Past in Nuremberg and Beyond* (London: Routledge, 2010), 1–7.
43 Ibid., 8.
44 See, for example, Paul Jaskot, 'The Reich Party Rally Grounds Revisited', in *Beyond Berlin*, ed. Rosenfeld and Jaskot; Susanne C. Knittel, 'Remembering Euthanasia, Grafeneck in the Past, Present, and Future', in *Memorialisation in Germany since 1945*, ed. Bill Niven and Chloe Paver (Basingstoke: Palgrave Macmillan, 2010), 124–33; Hilary Potter, 'Rosenstraße: A Complex Site of German-Jewish Memory', *Memorialization in Germany since 1945*; Harold Marcuse, *Legacies of Dachau: The*

Uses and Abuses of a Concentration Camp, 1933-2001 (Cambridge: Cambridge University Press, 2001).
45 Gregor, *Haunted City*; Gavriel D. Rosenfeld, *Munich and Memory: Architecture, Monuments, and the Legacy of the Third Reich* (London: University of California Press, 2000); Macdonald, *Difficult Heritage*.
46 Gavriel D. Rosenfeld and Paul B. Jaskot, 'Introduction', in *Beyond Berlin*, ed. Rosenfeld and Jaskot, 14–18.
47 Ibid., 11.
48 Jürgen Faulenbach and Carola Schüller, *Informationen zur Politischen Bildung: Hauptstadt Berlin* (Bonn: Bundeszentrale für Politische Bildung, 1993), 32.
49 Norbert Blüm, 'Die Hauptstadt-Debatte des Deutschen Bundestages vom 20. Juni 1991', in *Broschüre: Dokumente zur Bundeshauptstadt Berlin,* ed. Presse- und Informationsamt des Landes Berlin (Berlin: Presse- und Informationsamt des Landes Berlin, 1994), 12.
50 Eva Schweitzer, *Großbaustelle Berlin: Wie Die Hauptstadt Verplant Wird* (Berlin: Nicolai, 1996), 15.
51 Jürgen Faulenbach and Carola Schüller, *Informationen zur Politischen Bildung: Hauptstadt Berlin*; Peter Zlonicky, 'Ein Zwischen-Resümee', in *Hauptstadt Berlin: Festung, Schloss, Demokratischer Regierungssitz. Städtbau und Architektur Bericht 10,* ed. Hans Stimmann (Berlin: Senatsverwaltung für Bau-und Wohnungswesen, 1992), 17.
52 Peter Conradi, 'Gastvortrag: Parlaments- und Regierungsbauten in Bonn und Berlin', in *Machtarchitekturen: Beiträge zur Diskussion Politischer Bauten u.a. von Bruno Flierl, Peter Conradi, Werner Sewing, Axel Schultes und Charlotte Frank,* ed. Florian Dreher and Klaus-Tilman Fritzsche (Berlin: Universität der Künste, 2004), 71.
53 Maurice Halbwachs and Lewis A. Coser, *On Collective Memory* (Chicago: University of Chicago Press, 1992), 43.
54 Jan Assmann, 'Collective Memory and Cultural Identity', *New German Critique,* 65 (1995), 123–33, especially 126–30. Other scholars dispute the possibility for memory to transcend individual experience. See, for example, Susan Sontag, *Regarding the Pain of Others* (New York: Farrar, Straus and Giroux, 2003), 85; Noa Gedi and Yigal Elam, 'Collective Memory – What Is It?', *History and Memory,* 8 (1996), 30–50, 40; Sarah Foot, 'Remembering, Forgetting and Inventing: Attitudes to the Past at the End of the First Viking Age', *Transactions of the Royal Historical Society (Sixth Series),* 9 (1999), 185–200, especially 187–8.
55 Pierre Nora, 'Between Memory and History: Les *Lieux de Mémoire*', in *Representations,* 26 (7) (1989), 7–24.
56 Pierre Nora, *Realms of Memory, vol. 1: Conflicts and Divisions* (New York: Columbia University Press, 1996), 7–8.
57 Ibid.
58 Etienne François and Hagen Schultze, *Deutsche Erinnerungsorte Band 1* (Munich: Verlag C. H. Beck, 2002). 10.
59 Etienne François and Hagen Schultze, *Deutsche Erinnerungsorte Bände 1-3* (Munich: Verlag C. H. Beck, 2002, 2003 and 2009 respectively).
60 Jordan, 'A Matter of Time: Examining Collective Memory in Historical Perspective in Postwar Berlin'; Jordan, *Structures of Memory*; Rudy Koshar, *Germany's Transient Pasts: Preservation and National Memory in the Twentieth Century* (London: University of North Carolina Press, 1998), 11–14; See also Koshar, *From Monuments to Traces*.

61 John Czaplicka, 'History, Aesthetics and Contemporary Commemorative Practice in Berlin', *New German Critique,* 65 (1995), 155–87; Anna Saunders, 'Remembering Cold War Division: Wall Remnants and Border Monuments in Berlin', *Journal of Contemporary European Studies,* 17 (2009), 1–19; James Young, 'The Counter Monument: Memory against itself in Germany', *Critical Inquiry,* 18 (1992) 267–96.

62 Maoz Azharyu, 'German Reunification and the Politics of Street Names: The Case of East Berlin', *Political Geography,* 16 (1997), 479–93; Colomb, 'Requiem for a Lost *Palast*: "Revanchist Urban Planning" and "Burdened Landscapes" of the German Democratic Republic in the New Berlin'; Thomas Flierl, 'Government Buildings of the GDR: On Dealing with Their History and Architecture', in *Bau und Raum Jahrbuch / Building and Regions Annual,* ed. Annegret Burg (Tübingen: Ernst Wasmuth Verlag GmbH & Co, 2001/2002), 91–3.

63 Barnstone, *The Transparent State*; Flierl, 'Government Buildings of the GDR: On Dealing with Their History and Architecture'; Florian Dreher and Klaus-Tilman Fritzsche, 'Vorwort: Architektur und Repräsentation – Demokratie als Bauaufgabe', in *Machtarchitekturen: Beiträge zur Diskussion Politischer Bauten u.a von Bruno Flierl, Peter Conradi, Werner Sewing, Axel Schultes und Charlotte Frank,* ed. Florian Dreher and Klaus-Tilman Fritzsche (Berlin: Universität der Künste, 2004), 6–7; Ulf Meyer, *Bundeshauptstadt Berlin / Capital City Berlin* (Berlin: Jovis Verlag, 1999); Wolfgang Pehnt, 'Der Wunsch, zu sein wie Andere auch: Zur Architektur der Deutschen Hauptstadt', in *Ein Neues Deutschland? Zur Physiognomie Der Berliner Republik,* ed. Karl Heinz Bohrer and Kurt Scheel (Berlin: Klett-Cotta, 2006), 758–70; Michael Z. Wise, *Capital Dilemma: Germany's Search for a New Architecture of Democracy* (New York: Princeton Architectural Press, 1998); Koepnick, 'Redeeming History? Foster's Dome and the Political Aesthetics of the Berlin Republic'; Jaroskinski, 'Building on a Metaphor'.

64 Elke Heckner, 'Berlin Remake: Building Memory and the Politics of Capital Identity', *The Germanic Review: Literature, Culture, Theory,* 77 (2002), 304–25, 305. On how Critical Reconstruction responds to economic and environmental needs rather than an appeal for nostalgia, see Michael Hebbert, 'The Street as Locus of Collective Memory', *Environment and Planning D,* 23 (2005), 581–96. For an overview of the debate around Critical Reconstruction among urban designers and architects, see Annegret Burg and Senatsverwaltung für Bau- und Wohnungswesen, *Neue Berlinische Architektur: Eine Debatte* (Berlin: Birkhäuser Verlag, 1994).

65 Buddensieg, *Berliner Labyrinth*; Ladd, *The Ghosts of Berlin*; Pehnt and Wüstenrot Stiftung, *Deutsche Architektur Seit 1900*; Schäche, *Architektur und Städtebau in Berlin zwischen 1933 und 1945: Planen und Bauen unter der Ägide der Stadtverwaltung* (Berlin: Gerbr. Mann Verlag, 1992).

66 Harald, Bodenschatz, Friedhelm Fischer and Engelbert Luetke-Daldrup. 'Berlin: Hauptstadt mit Vergangenheit - zur Geschichte der Standorte für Regierungsfunktionen', in *Architektur in Berlin – Jahrbuch,* ed. Lothar Juckel for the Architektenkammer Berlin (Hamburg: Junius Verlag GmbH, 1992); Helmut Engel and Wolfgang Reuß, *Berlin – Woher Wohin? Oder: Dicht daneben ist auch vorbei!* (Berlin: Mann, 1995); Bruno Flierl, *Berlin baut um – wessen Stadt wird die Stadt?: Kritische Reflexionen 1990-1997* (Berlin: Verlag für Bauwesen, 1998); Schweitzer, *Großbaustelle Berlin*.

67 Peter Marcuse, 'Reflections on Berlin: The Meaning of Construction and the Construction of Meaning', *International Journal of Urban and Regional Research,* 22 (1998), 331–8.

68 Berlin mayor Wowereit described Berlin as 'poor, but sexy' (arm, aber sexy) in an interview with *Focus Money* magazine in 2003. The phrase went on to function as an unofficial slogan for Berlin as explained in Claire Colomb, *Staging the New Berlin: Place Marketing and the Politics of Urban Reinvention Post-1989* (London: Routledge, 2012), 259.
69 Bastian Lange, 'From Cool Britannia to Generation Berlin? Geographies of Culturepreneurs and Their Creative Milieus in Berlin', in *Cultural Industries: The British Experience in International Perspective*, ed. C. Eisenberg, R. Gerlach, and C. Handke (Online: Humboldt University Berlin Edoc- Server, 2006) http://edoc.hu-berli n.de/conferences/culturalindustries/lange-bastian/PDF/lange.pdf [accessed 20 March 2013]; Meri Louekari, 'The Creative Potential of Berlin: Creating Alternative Models of Social, Economic and Cultural Organisation in the Form of Network Forming and Open-Source Communities', *Planning Practice and Research*, 21 (2006); Till, 'Interim Use at a Former Death Strip?', 463–81.

Introduction to Part 2

1 Sagebiel, 'Vom Bau des Reichsluftfahrtministeriums', 81.
2 Ibid.
3 For an excellent analysis of this, see Elke Dittrich, *Ernst Sagebiel: Leben und Werk (1892-1970)* (Berlin: Lukas Verlag, 2005), 41–152.
4 Bundesministerium der Finanzen, *The Detlev Rohwedder Building – German History Reflected* ed. D. Hansen and M. Jachmann (Berlin: Bundesministerium der Finanzen, 2008), 10–13.
5 Order from Soviet Major General Major Barinow to Oberbürgermeister der Stadt Berlin, Dr Werner, 27 June 1945, LAB C Rep 101 Nr 13.
6 Order from Soviet Major General Major Barinow to Oberbürgermeister der Stadt Berlin, Dr Werner, 11 August 1945, LAB C Rep 101 Nr 13.
7 Eric Weitz, *Creating German Communism 1890-1990* (Princeton, NJ: Princeton University Press, 1997), 350.
8 Roesler, 'Privatisation in Eastern Germany', 209.
9 Heather M. Stack, 'The "Colonization" of East Germany? A Comparative Analysis of German Privatization', *Duke Law Journal*, 46 (5) (1997), 1211–53. See also Caldwell and Hanshew, *Germany since 1945*; Roesler, 'Privatisation in Eastern Germany'.

Chapter 3

1 Dörte Hansen and Maika Jachman, *Das Detlev-Rohwedder-Haus: Spiegel der deutschen Geschichte* (Berlin: Bundesministerium der Finanzen, 2015).
2 Visitor Book of the German Finance Ministry, 2005. Many thanks to Herr Pakull for giving me access to them and such detailed information about the building.
3 Schweitzer, *Großbaustelle Berlin*, 19.
4 Laurenz Demps, Eberhard Schultz and Klaus Wettig, *Das Bundesfinanzministerium: Ein Belasteter Ort?* (Berlin: Parthas, 2001), 46.
5 D. Hansen and M. Jachmann, *The Detlev Rohwedder Building – German History Reflected* (Berlin: Bundesministerium der Finanzen, 2008), 82.

6   Görtemaker, Bienert and Leps, *Orte der Demokratie in Berlin: Ein Historisch-Politischer Wegweiser*, 223; see also M. Lambrecht, 'Rexrodt Mag den Treuhand-Sitz', *Berliner Zeitung*, 30 January 1993, 17.
7   *Der Spiegel*, 'Ein Kapitaler Selbstbetrug', 5/1993, 49–51.
8   *Berliner Zeitung*, 'Ein Bau so dunkel wie das Nazi Reich', 23 May 1997. Unless otherwise indicated (through provision of page numbers or other URLs), all newspaper articles were accessed via LexisNexis Academic.
9   Harald Bodenschatz, Johannes Geisenhof and Dorothea Tscheschner, Report, 'Gutachten zur Bau-, Stadtbau- und Nutzungsgeschichtlichen Bedeutung des "Hauses der Parlementarier" (ehem. Reichsbankgebäude bzw. Zk-Gebäude der SED), des Treuhandgebäudes (Detlev-Rohwedder-Haus, ehem. Gebäude des Reichsluftfahrtministerium bzw. Haus Der Ministerien) und des ehemaligen Staatsratsgebäudes' (Berlin: Planungsbüro Gruppe DASS, 1993), 96. Many thanks to Professor Dr. Bodenschatz for giving me a copy of this from his personal papers.
10 Ibid., 94–5.
11 Ibid., 94.
12 Frank Pieter Hesse, 'Die Standorte von Parlament und Regierung. Wege der Denkmalpflege', in *Hauptstadt Berlin: Denkmalpflege für Parlament, Regierung und Diplomatie 1900-2000. Beiträge zur Denkmalpflege in Berlin,* ed. Frank Pieter Hesse and Jürgen Tietz (Berlin: Verlag Bauwesen for the Landesdenkmalamt Berlin, 2000), 15; also on Töpfer's 'praiseworthy pragmatism', see Dieter Hoffmann-Axthelm, 'Former Government Buildings in Berlin and their Future', in *Bau und Raum Jahrbuch / Building and Regions Annual,* ed. Annegret Burg (Tübingen: Ernst Wasmuth Verlag GmbH & Co, 2001/2002), 89.
13 Wise, *Capital Dilemma*, 91.
14 Report, Pitz and Hoh Werkstatt für Arckitektur und Denkmalpflege GMBH. 6. February 1997. LDA BMF 973533.10/I.
15 See, for example, LDA D-R-H Betreuung Baudenkmal – Schriftverkehr 003533.2/I.
16 Report Pitz and Hoh Werkstatt für Arckitektur und Denkmalpflege GMBH. 6. February 1997. LDA BMF 973533.10/I.
17 On this see, for example, Macdonald, 'Undesirable Heritage', 9–28 (20).
18 Hesse, 'Die Standorte von Parlament und Regierung', 17.
19 Jörg Haspel, 'Vorwort: Architekturzeugnisse der NS-Zeit Erhalten, um zu Erinnern', in *Architektur in Berlin 1933-1945 – Ein Stadtführer,* ed. Matthias Donath (Berlin: Lukas Verlag for the Landesdenkmalamt Berlin, 2004), 9.
20 Philpotts, 'Cultural-Political Palimpsests', especially 209–10.
21 Christine Hoh-Slodczyk, 'Original- Veränderung-Bestand', in *Das Detlev-Rohwedder-Haus: Architektur und Nutzung,* ed. Hans-Joachim Henzgen and Andrea Ulrich for the Bundesministerium der Finanzen Referat Presse und Information (Berlin: Bundesbauamt III, 1999), 13.
22 Hansen and Jachmann, *The Detlev Rohwedder Building*, 55.
23 Ibid., 40.
24 HPP International, 'Der Kleine Saal', in *Das Detlev-Rohwedder-Haus: Architektur und Nutzung,* 35.
25 Hansen and Jachmann, *The Detlev Rohwedder Building*, 55.
26 Hans Wolfgang Hoffmann, 'Licht ins Dunkel: Ein sperriges Erbstück für den Finanzminister', *Stadtforum,* 25 (1997), 24–5, 25.
27 Hansen and Jachmann, *The Detlev Rohwedder Building*, 40–1.
28 Hoffmann, 'Licht ins Dunkel', 25.

29 Visitor Book of the German Finance Ministry, 2012.
30 Maoz Azharyu, 'German Reunification and the Politics of Street Names: The Case of East Berlin', *Political Geography*, 16 (1997), 479-93; Caldwell and Hanshew, *Germany since 1945*, 268-9; Colomb, 'Requiem for a Lost *Palast*'; Flierl, 'Government Buildings of the GDR', 91-3.
31 Jampol, 'Problematic Things', 201-2.
32 Bodenschatz, Geisenhof and Tscheschner, 'Gutachten zur Bau-, Stadtbau- und Nutzungsgeschichtlichen Bedeutung', 53.
33 Philpotts, 'Cultural-Political Palimpsests', 223-25.
34 See, for example, meeting minutes, 23 June 1999. LDA 003533.9/I.
35 Stefan Damm, Klaus Siebenhaar and Stefan Zang. *Schauplatz Berlin 1933. 1945. 1961. Heute* (Berlin: Bostelmann and Siebenhaar, 2005), 40-1.
36 Hansen and Jachmann, *The Detlev-Rohwedder Building*; Henzgen and Ulrich (eds), *Das Detlev-Rohwedder-Haus: Architektur und Nutzung*.
37 Bundesfinanzministerium, 'Virtueller Besuch im BMF' (undated webpage). http://www.bundesfinanzministerium.de/Web/DE/Ministerium/Virtueller_Besuch/virtueller_besuch.html [accessed 17 November 2013].
38 Haspel, 'Vorwort: Architekturzeugnisse der NS-Zeit erhalten, um zu erinnern', 9-11.
39 Matthias Donath, *Architektur in Berlin 1933-1945 – Ein Stadtführer* (Berlin: Lukas Verlag for the Landesdenkmalamt Berlin, 2004), 45.
40 Hoffmann-Axthelm, 'Former Government Buildings in Berlin and their Future', 91.
41 Günter Schlusche, 'Die Parlaments- und Regierungsbauten des Bundes im Kontext der Berliner Stadtentwicklung', *Aus Politik und Zeitgeschichte,* B 34-35 (2001), 16-24, 20.
42 Ibid., 20.
43 Atelier für Lichtplanung Kress und Adams, 'Das Lichtkonzept', in *Das Detlev-Rohwedder-Haus: Architektur und Nutzung*, 23.
44 Poly, 'Die Aussenanlagen', in *Das Detlev-Rohwedder-Haus: Architektur und Nutzung*, 18.

Chapter 4

1 Hans Coppi, *Dieser Tod paßt zu mir: Harro Schulze-Boysen, Grenzgänger im Widerstand, Briefe 1915 – 1942* (Berlin: Aufbau-Verlag, 1999), 316-18.
2 Catherine A. Epstein, *Nazi Germany: Confronting the Myths* (Chichester: John Wiley & Sons, 2015), 192-3.
3 David Childs, *The GDR: Moscow's German Ally* (Oxon: Routledge, 2015), 31-3.
4 Anna Saunders, *Memorializing the GDR: Monuments and Memory after 1989* (Oxford: Berghahn Books, 2018), 159.
5 Beth Lord, 'Foucault's Museum: Difference, Representation, and Genealogy', *Museum and Society,* 4 (March 2006), 1-14, 7.
6 Hans Maur, *Traditionstätte der Arbeiterbewegung in Zentrum Berlins, der Hauptstadt der Deutsche Demokratischen Republik* (Berlin: Museum für Deutsche Geschichte, 1971), 18.
7 Dagmar Girra, *Gedenktafeln in Mitte, Tiergarten und Wedding: Band 1* (Berlin: Edition Luisenstadt, 2000) 320; Ibid., 17.
8 Bill Niven, *Facing the Nazi Past: United Germany and the Legacy of the Third Reich* (Hoboken, NJ: Taylor and Francis, 4th edn (online access), 2001), 70.
9 Saunders, *Memorializing the GDR*, 160.

10 Mary Fulbrook, *Anatomy of a Dictatorship: Inside the GDR 1949-1989* (Oxford: Oxford University Press, 1995), 177–8.
11 Wolfgang Schäche, *Architektur und Städtebau in Berlin zwischen 1933 und 1945: Planen und Bauen unter der Ägide der Stadtverwaltung* (Berlin: Gerbr. Mann Verlag, 1992), 219–20.
12 Dagmar Girra, *Gedenktafeln in Mitte, Tiergarten und Wedding: Band 2* (Berlin: Edition Luisenstadt, 2000), 652.
13 Although the construction workers on Stalinallee are understood to have started the demonstration, it is generally recognized that other workers joined them as they marched towards the ministry buildings – for example, Allinson finds that they were joined by 'thousands' of other workers, Mark Allinson, *Politics and Popular Opinion in East Germany, 1945-1968* (Manchester: Manchester University Press, 2000), 55; and Fulbrook says they 'joined forces with workers from a hospital building site in Friedrichshain' (Fulbrook, *Anatomy of a Dictatorship*, 182).
14 Saunders, *Memorializing the* GDR, 161.
15 Publicity Postcard, International Society for Human Rights, German Section *Mahnmal 17. Juni 1953*. LAB: D Rep 001 Nr 4519.
16 Letter, Erhard Goehl, Steering Committee, International Society for Human Rights, German Section, to Berlin House of Representatives, Cultural Affairs Committee, 23 April 1994. LAB: D Rep 001 Nr 4519.
17 Letter, Erhard Goehl, International Society for Human Rights, German Section, to Berlin House of Representatives, Cultural Affairs Committee, 23 April 1994. LAB D Rep 001 Nr 4519.
18 Letter, Klaus Pankau, Chairman of Industriewerkschaft Bau-Steine-Erden to the House of Representatives Committee of Cultural Affairs, 24 April 1994. LAB: D Rep 001 Nr 4519.
19 Meeting Minutes, Berlin House of Representatives, Cultural Affairs Committee, Antrag 12/2013 7 March 1994, LAB D Rep Nr 4519.
20 Letter, Dieter Biewald, Berlin House of Representatives, Cultural Affairs Committee to Theodor Waigel 22 September 1994. LAB: D Rep 001 Nr 4519.
21 Letter, Waigel to Biewald, 7 October 1994. LAB: D Rep 001 Nr 4519.
22 See correspondence between the Federal Finance Ministry, the Berlin House of Representatives Cultural Affairs Committee and the Museum Haus am Checkpoint Charlie LAB: D Rep 001 Nr 4519.
23 Berliner Forum für Geschichte und Gegenwart, 'Denkmal für die Ereignisse des 17. Juni 1953' (undated webpage), http://www.bfgg.de/projekte/denkmal-17-juni-1953.html [accessed 29 August 2013].
24 Saunders, *Memorializing the* GDR, 164–9.
25 Hans Eichel, 'Zur Austellungseröffnung "Max Lingner-Berliner Waldbild" (speech delivered at the Federal Finance Ministry, Berlin, 16 January 2002), www.bundesfinanzministerium.de/Akturelles/Reden-394.9937.htlm [accessed 18 June 2003].
26 Hansen and Jachmann, *The Detlev Rohewedder Building*, 33.
27 Saunders, *Memorializing the* GDR, 172.
28 Corina Petrescu, *Against All Odds: Models of Subversive Space in National Socialist Germany* (Bern: Peter Lang, 2010), 170 and 177.
29 Holger Hübner with the Gedenkstätte Deutscher Widerstand, 'Gedenktafeln in Berlin' (undated website), http://www.gedenktafeln-in-berlin.de/nc/gedenktafeln/gedenktafel-anzeige/tid/harro-schulze-boysen [accessed 13 June 2013].
30 Saunders, 'Challenging or Concretising Cold War Narratives?', 304.

31 Stefanie Endlich, 'Berlin', in *Gedenkstätten für die Opfer des Nationalsozialismus. Eine Dokumentation. Band II: Bundesländer Berlin, Brandenburg, Mecklenburg-Vorpommern, Sachsen-Anhalt, Sachsen, Thüringen*, ed. Ulrike Puvogel (Bonn: Bundeszentrale für politische Bildung, 2000), 119.
32 Christiane Hoss and Martin Schönfeld, *Gedenktafeln in Berlin: Orte der Erinnerung an Verfolgte des Nationalsozialismus 1991-2001. Schriftenreihe Band 9* (Berlin: Verein Aktives Museum und Widerstand in Berlin, 2002), 139; 'Widerstandsgruppe Rote Kapelle geehrt', *Berliner Zeitung*, 21 November 1994, http://www.berliner-zeitung.de/archiv/widerstandsgruppe-rote-kapelle-geehrt,10810590,8886012.html [accessed 14 July 2013].
33 Press release from the *Berliner Brücke, Wiederanbringen derGedenktafel für Harro Schulze-Boysen am 26, Juli 1994* LAB: B Rep 232–33 Nr 50.
34 Letter from Berliner Brücke to Frau Hoss of the Aktives Museum, (undated) LAB: B Rep 232–33 Nr 50.
35 Ibid.
36 Invitation from the *Berliner Brücke* to the re-installation of the memorial and the renaming of the chapel. LAB: B Rep 232–33 50.
37 Hoss and Schönfeld, *Gedenktafeln in Berlin*, 139.
38 Anon., 'Gedenktafel zur Diamantenen Hochzeit', *Berliner Zeitung*, 27 July 1997, http://www.berliner-zeitung.de/archiv/gedenktafel-zur-diamantenen-hochzeit,10810590,9158320.html [accessed 14 July 3013].
39 The inscription read: Zu gehn bis an des Dunkels Rand /Dahinter liegt, gleich neuem Land, /Des Daseins ganze Fülle!/ Libertas Schulze-Boysen / 20 November 1913–22 December 1942 / Erzähl allen, allen von mir./ Unser Tod muß ein Fanal sein. In Endlich, 'Berlin', in *Gedenkstätten für die Opfer des Nationalsozialismus*, 297.
40 B.Z. 'Finanzministerium Klagt gegen Arbeitsgemeinschaft 13. August', 9 September 2004.
41 Annette Kaminsky, 'Gedenkzeichen, Gedenkstätten und Museen zur Diktator in SBZ und DDR: Berlin', in *Orte Des Erinnerns: Gedenkzeichen, Gedenkstätten und Museen Zur Diktatur in SBZ und DDR*, ed. Annette Kaminsky (Berlin: Ch. Links Verlag, 2007), 85.
42 Antje Lang-Lendorff, 'Bis die Fotos Wieder Hängen', *Berliner Zeitung*, 23 June 2005.
43 Vereinigung 17 Juni 1953, 'Endlich: "Platz des Volksaufstandes von 1953"' (29 March 2013), http://17juni1953.wordpress.com/2013/03/29/endlich-platz-des-volksaufstandes-von-1953 [accessed 1 October 2013].
44 Bundesstiftung Aufarbeitung, 'Plakatausstellung "Wir wollen freie Menschen sein! Der DDR-Volksaufstand vom 17. Juni 1953"', 16 January 2013, http://www.bundesstiftung-aufarbeitung.de/uploads/2013-pdf/17Juni-ausstellung-stadt gemeinde.pdf [accessed 20 February 2013].
45 Bundesfinanzministerium, '"Platz des Volksaufstandes von 1953" – Bezirksamt Mitte befürwortet Benennungsvorschlag des BMF', 3 April 2013, http://www.bundesfinanzministerium.de/Content/DE/Standardartikel/Ministerium/20130303-Platzbenennung.html [accessed 2 October 2013].

Chapter 5

1 Bodenschatz, Fischer and Luetke-Daldrup, 'Berlin: Hauptstadt mit Vergangenheit – zur Geschichte der Standorte für Regierungsfunktionen', 25.
2 Cited in Macdonald, 'Undesirable Heritage', 20.

3 Hans Wilderotter, *Das Haus am Werderschen Markt: Von der Reichsbank zum Auswärtigen Amt / The History of the New Premises of the Federal Foreign Office* (Berlin: Jovis, 1999), 17.
4 Wise, *Capital Dilemma*, 98.
5 Schlusche, 'Die Parlaments- und Regierungsbauten des Bundes im Kontext der Berliner Stadtentwicklung', 21.
6 Petra Hübinger and Joachim G. Jacobs, 'Die Steinernen Innenhöfe als Inszenierung der Macht', in *Das Detlev-Rohwedder-Haus: Architektur und Nutzung*, ed. Hans-Joachim Henzgen and Andrea Ulrich for the Bundesministerium der Finanzen Referat Presse und Information (Berlin: Bundesbauamt III, 1999), 11.
7 Joyce, *The Rule of Freedom*, 160.
8 Ibid., 160–1.
9 Joachim Petsch, *Baukunst und Stadtplanung im Dritten Reich* (Munich: Hanser, 1976), 100.
10 Joyce, *The Rule of Freedom*, 161.
11 Donath, *Architektur in Berlin 1933-1945 – Ein Stadtführer*, 54.
12 Eberhard Schultz, 'Abriss oder Sanierung? Umgang mit einem Historischen Ort / Demolition or Renovation: Handling an Historic Site', in *Das Bundesfinanzministerium: Ein Belasteter Ort?*, ed. Laurenz Demps, Eberhard Schultz and Klaus Wettig (Berlin: Parthas, 2001), 63.
13 Joyce, *The Rule of Freedom*, 161.
14 Petsch, *Baukunst und Stadtplanung im Dritten Reich: Herleitung, Bestandsaufnahme, Entwicklung, Nachfolge*, 100.
15 Donath, *Architektur in Berlin 1933-1945 – ein Stadtführer*, 54.
16 Bodenschatz, Geisenhof and Tscheschner, 'Gutachten zur Bau-, Stadtbau- und Nutzungsgeschichtlichen Bedeutung', 64.
17 Schultz, 'Abriss oder Sanierung? Umgang mit einem Historischen Ort / Demolition or Renovation: Handling an Historic Site', 56.
18 Meeting Minutes. HPP International Planungsgesellschaft GmbH. 12. September 1996. LDA D-R-H 003533.3I.
19 Atelier für Lichtplanung Kress und Adams, 'Das Lichtkonzept', in *Das Detlev-Rohwedder-Haus: Architektur und Nutzung*, 22–3.
20 Regina Poly, 'Die Außenanlagen', 38–9 (18).
21 Fax. Büro Poly to Pitz and Hoh. 29 April 1996. LDA D-R-H 003533.3/I.
22 Meeting Minutes. 10 September 1997. LDA D-R-H 003533.2/I.
23 Hoffmann, 'Licht ins Dunkel: Ein Sperriges Erbstück für den Finanzminister', 25.
24 Joyce, *The Rule of Freedom*, 161–2.
25 HPP International, 'Der Eingang Wilhelmstrasse', in *Das Detlev-Rohwedder-Haus: Architektur und Nutzung*, 27.
26 Joachim Gerz, 'Das Geld, die Liebe, der Tod, die Freiheit – was Zählt am Ende?', in *Das Detlev-Rohwedder-Haus: Architektur und Nutzung*, 45.
27 Hansen and Jachmann, *The Detlev Rohwedder Building*, 69.
28 Bundesfinanzministerium, 'Blick hinter die Kulissen', 7 March 2011, http://www.bundesfinanzministerium.de/Content/DE/Video/2011-03-07-blick-hinter-die-kulissen-textfassung.htm [accessed on 21 September 2013].
29 Bundesregierung, 'Einladung zum Staatsbesuch: 150.000 beim Tag der offenen Tür' (undated webpage), http://www.bundesregierung.de/Webs/Breg/DE/Themen/Tag_der_offenen_Tuer/_node.html [accessed 22 September 2013].
30 Michel Foucault, 'Of Other Spaces', *Diacritics*, 16 (1986), 22–7, 26.

Introduction to Part 3

1 Mittig, 'Kunst und Propaganda im NS-System', 444–5.
2 Thomas Schmidt, *Werner March: Architekt des Olympia-Stadions 1894-1976* (Berlin: Birkhäuser Verlag, 1992), 20.
3 Ibid., 24.
4 Schäche and Szymanski, *Das Reichssportfeld*, 53–9.
5 Wilhelm Frick, 'Gleichwort', in *Das Reichssportfeld: Eine Schöpfung des Dritten Reiches für die Olympischen Spiele und die Deutschen Leibesübungen*, Hrsg Reichsministerium des Innern (Berlin: Reichsparteiverlag, 1936), 1.
6 Albert Speer, *Inside the Third Reich* (London: Phoenix, 2003), 129.
7 Hans-Ernst Mittig interviewed by Gerd Nowakowski published as 'Ein Ort des militanten Totenkults', *Die Tageszeitung* 17, 23 January 1994.
8 Volkwin Marg, *Choreography of the Masses: In Sport. In the Stadium. In a Frenzy* (Berlin: Jovis and the Akademie der Künste, 2012), 80.
9 Diary of Arthur Willoughby Barton, entry dated Saturday 1 August 1936 (unpaginated) NFMA E.1422.
10 Marg, *Choreography of the Masses*, 81–2.
11 Diary of Arthur Willoughby Barton, entry dated Saturday 1 August 1936 (unpaginated) NFMA E.1422.
12 Thomas Schmidt, *Das Berliner Olympia Stadion und seine Geschichte* (Berlin: Express Edition, 1983), 19–22.
13 Letter from Senator for Bau-und Wohnungswesen to Senator für Volksbildung, Berlin Wilmersdorf 26. January 1952; and Completion Certificate from Sager and Wörner Hoch – u. Tiefbau, *Blaupunktbunker Olympiastadion* 4 April 1952 both LAB: B Re 2007-01 Nr 1298.
14 Thomas Schmidt, *Das Berliner Olympia Stadion und seine Geschichte*, 19–22.
15 Ibid., 21.
16 Ibid., 24.
17 Contract between der Bundesschatzminister and the Senator der Finanzen (Berlin), Verwaltung – Vereinbarung June 1963 BARch (Koblenz) B157 6609.
18 Matthias Donath, 'Konservieren und kommentieren', 83.
19 Letter, Werner March to Ministerialdirektor Rossig, Bundesschatzministerium, 27 January 1969, BArch (Koblenz) B157 6609.
20 See letters in BArch (Koblenz) B157 6609.
21 Letter Oberfinanzdirektion to Ministerialrat Müller, Bundesschatzministerium 7 October 1969 BArch (Koblenz) B157 6609.
22 Internal letter at the Bundesministerium der Finanzen, from Referat III B1 to Referat III A1 Bonn-Bad Godesberg 13 October 1969 BArch (Koblenz) B157 6609.
23 Bundesministerium der Finanzen, Internal letter Referat VII A1 to Referat II C/3 Bonn-Bad Godesberg, 21 November 1969.
24 Anon., '"Reichstagslösung" für das Berliner Olympiastadion? – Senat bringt neue Umbauvariante ins Gespräch', *BauNetz*, 24 November 1997, http://www.baunetz.de/meldungen/Meldungen_Senat_bringt_neue_Umbauvariante_ins_Gespraech_2757.html [accessed 13 November 2013].
25 See, for example, Ibid.; and Anna Maria Odenthal, 'Denkmalpflege: Die Geschichtswahrende Modernisierung des Olympiastadions', *architektur + bauphysik,* 7 (2006), 2–8, 3.
26 Nicolai, 'The Berlin Olympic Stadium', 38.

Chapter 6

1. Hilmar Hoffmann, *Mythos Olympia: Autonomie und Unterwerfung von Sport und Kultur: Hitlers Olympiade, Olympische Kultur, Riefenstahls Olympia-Film*, 1st edn (Berlin: Aufbau-Verlag, 1993), 9.
2. Werner March, 'Das Reichssportfeld', *Monatshefte für Baukunst und Städtebau* No. 20, 1936, 276c.
3. Werner March, 'Die baukünstlerische Gestaltung des Reichssportfeldes', in *Das Reichssportfeld: Eine Schöpfung des Drittes Reiches für die Olympischen Spiele und die Deutsche Leibesübungen*, ed. Reichsministerien des Innern (Berlin: Reichssportverlag, 1936), 51.
4. Arbeitsgemeinschaft Reinald Eckert und Wolfgang Schäche, 'Das Ehemalige Reichssportfeld, Geschichte und Bestand', in *Kooperatives Gutachterverfahren Olympisches Dorf Und Olympiagelände,* ed. Schröder, Senatsverwaltung für Stadtentwicklung und Umweltschutz, 43.
5. March, 'Das Reichssportfeld', 276c.
6. Bettina Güldner and Wolfgang Schuster, 'Das Reichssportfeld', in *Skulptur und Macht Figurative Plastik in Deutschland der 30er und 40er Jahre – Eine Ausstellung im Rahmen des Gesamtprojektes der Akademie der Künste 'Das war ein Beispiel nur...' vom 8. Mai bis 3. Juli 1983* (Berlin: Fröhlich and Kaufmann GMBG, 1983), 43.
7. March, 'Die baukünstlerische Gestaltung des Reichssportfeldes', 51–3.
8. Magdalena Bushart, 'Dem Bildwerke auf dem Reichssportfeld in Berlin', in *Das Kunstwerk als Geschichtsdokument: Festschrift für Hans-Ernst Mittig*, ed. Annette Tietenberg (Munich: Klinkhardt und Biermann, 1999), 130.
9. Ibid., 138–9.
10. Güldner and Schuster, 'Das Reichssportfeld', 42.
11. Ibid., 43.
12. Ibid., 42. Arbeitsgemeinschaft Reinald Eckert und Wolfgang Schäche, 'Das Ehemalige Reichssportfeld, Geschichte und Bestand', 43.
13. Stefanie Endlich and Beate Rossié, 'Zum Umgang mit den Skulpturen von Breker, Thorak und anderen Bildhauern auf dem Berliner Olympiagelände', in *Zeitgeschichte-online, Thema: Wohin mit Breker? Zum Umgang mit NS-Kunst in Museen und im öffentlichen Raum*, hrsg. von Jan-Holger Kirsch, Dezember 2006, http://www.zeit geschichte-online.de/portals/_rainbow/documents/pdf/endlich_rossie_breker.pdf [accessed 1 March 2018], 4.
14. Stefanie Endlich and Beate Rossié, 'Zum Umgang mit den Skulpturen von Breker, Thorak und anderen Bildhauern auf dem Berliner Olympiagelände', 3–4.
15. Bushart, 'Dem Bildwerke auf dem Reichssportfeld in Berlin', 129.
16. Wolfgang Ruppert, 'In Stein gehauener Rassenwahn', *Die Zeit*, 17 September 1993.
17. Mittig, 'Kunst und Propaganda im NS-System', 453.
18. Schäche and Szymanski, *Das Reichssportfeld: Architektur im Spannungsfeld von Sport und Macht*, 102.
19. Bushart, 'Dem Bildwerke auf dem Reichssportfeld in Berlin', 139.
20. Arbeitsgemeinschaft Eckert und Schäche, 'Das ehemalige Reichssportfeld, Geschichte und Bestand', 43–4.
21. See, for example, Laragh Larsen, 'Re-placing Imperial Landscapes: Colonial Monuments and the Transition to Independence in Kenya', *Journal of Historical Geography*, 38 (1) (2012), 45–56; Duncan Light, 'Gazing on Communism: Heritage

Tourism and Post-Communist Identities in Germany, Hungary and Romania', *Tourism Geographies*, 2 (2) (2000), 157–76; Paul M. McGarr, '"The Viceroys Are Disappearing from the Roundabouts in Delhi": British Symbols of Power in Post-colonial India', *Modern Asian Studies*, 49 (3) (2015), 787–831; John Newsinger, 'Why Rhodes Must Fall', *Race & Class*, 58 (2) (2016), 70–8.

22 'In Stein gehauener Rassenwahn', *Die Zeit*, 17 September 1993.
23 Hoffmann, *Mythos Olympia*, 9.
24 Ibid., 9.
25 Ibid.
26 Ibid., 188.
27 Hoffmann, 'Kultur als Signal der Völkerverständigung', in *Berlin 2000: Das Olympia Magazin*, May 1992, 15.
28 Hoffmann, *Mythos Olympia*, 188.
29 Ibid., 188–207.
30 'In Stein gehauener Rassenwahn', *Die Zeit*, 17 September 1993.
31 'Herrenmenschen in Cellophan', *Der Spiegel*, 14/1993 (April), 62–70, 68.
32 Hans-Hermann Kotte and Hans Monath, 'Künstlerische Entnazifizierungsversuche zur Rettung der "Jahrtausendspiele"', *Die Tageszeitung*, 27 January 1993.
33 'Herrenmenschen in Cellophan', 65.
34 Vera Fischer, '"Maskenball" für Sportler-Kolosse?', *Berliner Morgenpost*, 7 March 1993.
35 'Herrenmenschen in Cellophan', 68.
36 Kotte and Monath, 'Künstlerische Entnazifizierungsversuche Zur Rettung Der "Jahrtausendspiele"'.
37 Fischer, '"Maskenball" für Sportler-Kolosse?'.
38 In August 1992 after far-right extremists set fire to an asylum-seekers' hostel in Rostock it was reported that 'several thousand people stood by and applauded the attackers' ('In East Germany the Neo-Nazis are Winning', *Spiegel Online International*, 21 August 2002, http://www.spiegel.de/international/germany/press-review-on-the-german-far-right-20-years-after-the-rostock-riots-a-851193.html [accessed 24 August 2013]).
39 Kotte and Monath, 'Künstlerische Entnazifizierungsversuche zur Rettung der "Jahrtausendspiele"'.
40 Tilmann Buddensieg, 'Olympia 1936-Olympia 2000: Anmerkungen zum Reichssportfeld/ auf dem Wege zum Metropole (12) Berlin-Krisen, Kräfte und Konzepte', *Der Tagesspiegel*, 13 December 1992.
41 Ursel Berger, 'Die Athleten Von Olympia-Berlin', *Der Tagesspiegel*, 19 February 1993.
42 Wolf Jobst Siedler, 'Anstössige Athleten. Überflüssige Diskussion: Die Skulpturen des Olympiageländes', *Frankfurter Allgemeine Zeitung*, 12 January 1993.
43 Tilmann Buddensieg, 'Hierzulande ein Stildiktat', *Frankfurter Allgemeine Zeitung*, 23 January 1993.
44 Hans Borgelt, 'Olympia 2000 - eine Ideenfabrik', *Der Tagesspiegel*, 25 October 1992.
45 Dieter Prelinger, 'Olympiadenkmale von 1936', *Der Tagesspiegel*, 8 November 1992.
46 All text from the information boards of the *Historische Kommentierung des Berliner Olympiageländes* is attributable to Stefanie Endlich, Monica Geyler-von Bernus and Beate Rossié, translated by Robin Benson and Don Mac Coitir (Berlin, 2006).
47 'Sollen die Nazi-Skulpturen am Olympia-Stadion verhüllt werden?', *B.Z*, 30 May 2006.

48 Nikolaus Bernau, 'Bildersturm am Olympiastadion', *Berliner Zeitung,* 31 May 2006.
49 Hans-Jörg Vehlewald, 'Riesenstreit um Figuren am Berlin WM-Stadion: Ist das Nazi-Kunst?', *Bild,* 31 May 2006. Similar representations can be seen in Bernau, 'Bildersturm am Olympiastadion'; Rolf Lautenschläger, 'Lea Rosh mag keine Nackten Nazis', *Die Tageszeitung,* 31 May 2006.
50 Nikolaus Bernau, 'Bildersturm am Olympiastadion', *Berliner Zeitung,* 31 May 2006.
51 Lautenschläger, 'Lea Rosh Mag Keine Nackten Nazis'.
52 Haubrich, 'Bulldozer Gegen Breker'.
53 Bernau, 'Bildersturm Am Olympiastadion'.
54 'Sollen die Nazi-Skulpturen am Olympia-Stadion Verhüllt werden?'.
55 Vehlewald, 'Riesenstreit um Figuren am Berlin WM-Stadion: Ist das Nazi-Kunst?'.
56 Richard Herzinger, 'Sollen Nazi-Skulpturen verhüllt werden?', *Welt am Sonntag,* 5 June 2006.
57 Haubrich, 'Bulldozer gegen Breker'.
58 Stefanie Endlich, '"Historische-Kommentierung" des Olympiageländes Berlin', *Gedenkstättenrundbrief* 132 (2006), 3–9, https://www.gedenkstaettenforum.de/nc/gedenkstaettenrundbrief/rundbrief/news/historische_kommentierung_des_olympiagelaendes_berlin/ [accessed 11 April 2018].
59 Lautenschläger, 'Lea Rosh mag keine nackten Nazis'.
60 Vehlewald, 'Riesenstreit um Figuren am Berlin WM-Stadion: Ist das Nazi-Kunst?'.
61 Buchholz, 'Entfernen hilft auch nichts', 29.
62 'Sollen die Nazi-Skulpturen am Olympia-Stadion Verhüllt werden?'.
63 Stefanie Endlich and Beate Rossié, 'Zum Umgang mit den Skulpturen von Breker, Thorak und anderen Bildhauern auf dem Berliner Olympiagelände', 4.

Chapter 7

1 Hans-Ernst Mittig, 'Kunst und Propaganda im NS-System', 450.
2 Ibid., 461.
3 See, for example, Matthias Donath, 'Konservieren und Kommentieren, 85; Stefanie Endlich, '"Historische Kommentierung" am Berliner Olympiastadion', *Verein Aktives Museum: Mitgliederrundbrief 53* (Berlin, June 2005), 12–16; Stefanie Endlich, 'Open-Air-Installation im Olympiastadion "Historische Kommentierung" endlich realisiert', in *Stadtkunst Kunststadt: Informationsdienst der Kulturwerk des BBK Berlins GmbH* 53, 2006, 22.
4 Nicolai, 'The Berlin Olympic Stadium', 38.
5 Stefanie Endlich, '"Historische Kommentierung" am Olympistadion', *Verein Aktives Museum Mitglieder Rundbrief* 53, June 2005, 13.
6 Presse - Und Informationsamt des Landes Berlin, *Leitkonzept für das Olympiagelände Berlin: Pressemitteilung vom 29 June 2004,* https://Www.Berlin.De/Rbmskzl/Aktuelles/Pressemitteilungen/2004/Pressemitteilung.47994.Php [accessed 2 November 2017].
7 Minutes from Abgeordnetenhaus Berlin, Ausschuss für Bauen, Wohnen und Verkehr, 14. Wahlperiode, 6. Sitzung 10 May 2000, http://pardok.parlament-berlin.de/starweb/adis/citat/VT/14/AusschussPr/bwv/bwv14006.i.pdf [accessed 12 October 2018].
8 Endlich, '"Historische Kommentierung" am Olympistadion', 3–4.
9 Ibid., 15.
10 Ibid., 15–16.

11 Olympiasstadion Berlin: Konzeption für die historische Kommentierung und einen Ort der Information. Tischvorlage für die Sitzung der Expertenkommission am 18 September 2003, 4–22 (HEM: Uncatalogued personal papers).
12 Projekt Historische Kommentierung des Olympiastadions: 2. Sitzung des Wissenschaftliches Beirats. Protokoll, minutes of meeting on 25 November 2003 (2 December 2003), 5 (HEM: Uncatalogued personal papers).
13 Olympiastadion Berlin Konzeption für die Historische Kommentierung und einen Ort der Information: Ergänzung (November 2003), 9. See also, Projekt Historische Kommentierung des Olympiastadions: 1. Sitzung der Expertenkommission. Protokoll, minutes of meeting on 18 September 2003 (29 September 2003), 6. (both HEM: Uncatalogued personal papers).
14 Olympiastadion Berlin Konzeption für die Historische Kommentierung und einen Ort der Information: Ergänzung (November 2003), 4.
15 On the Podbielski Oak, see Kluge, *Olympiastadion Berlin: Steine Beginnen zu Reden*, 128.
16 Projekt Historische Kommentierung des Olympiastadions. 2. Sitzung des Wissenschaftliches Beirats. Protokoll, 7 (HEM: Uncatalogued personal papers).
17 For a frank discussion of this see Stefanie Endlich, '"Historische Kommentierung" Am Berliner Olympiastadion', *Verein Aktives Museum: Mitgliederrundbrief* (Berlin, June 2005), 12–16.
18 Projekt Historische Kommentierung des Olympiastadions: 1. Sitzung der Expertenkommission. Protokoll, 5; Projekt Historische Kommentierung des Olympiastadions: 2. Sitzung des Wissenschaftliches Beirats. Protokoll, 4–5 (both HEM: Uncatalogued personal papers).
19 Projekt Historische Kommentierung des Olympiastadions: 2. Sitzung des Wissenschaftliches Beirats. Protokoll, 7 (HEM: Uncatalogued personal papers).
20 Projekt Historische Kommentierung des Olympiastadions, Olympiastadion Berlin Konzeption für die Historische Kommentierung und einen Ort Der Information: Ergänzung, 19 (HEM: Uncatalogued personal papers).
21 Ibid., 20.
22 Projekt Historische Kommentierung des Olympiastadions: 2. Sitzung des Wissenschaftliches Beirats. Protokoll, 6 (HEM: Uncatalogued personal papers).
23 Mona Baker, *Translation and Conflict: A Narrative Account* (London: Routledge, 2006), 114.
24 Kluge, *Olympiastadion Berlin: Steine beginnen zu reden*, 88.
25 Volxsport statt Olympia, 'Widerstand gegen Olympia' (undated pamphlet), 37; see also Kluge, *Olympiastadion Berlin* (Berlin: Verl. Das Neue Berlin, 2009), 125.
26 Projekt Historische Kommentierung des Olympiastadions: 1. Sitzung der Expertenkommission. Protokoll, 17 (HEM: Uncatalogued personal papers).
27 Projekt Historische Kommentierung des Olympiastadions: 2. Sitzung des Wissenschaftliches Beirats. Protokoll, 13 (HEM: Uncatalogued personal papers).
28 Arbeitsgemeinschaft Reinald Eckert und Wolfgang Schäche, 33.
29 Stelae erected in 1936 honour gold medal winners at the games in 1896, 1900, 1904, 1906, 1908, 1912, 1928, 1932 and 1936. Those erected between 1957 and 2010 commemorate the gold medal winners at the games in 1952, 1956, 1960, 1964, 1968, 1972, 1976, 1984, 1988, 1992, 1994/6, 1998/00 and 2002/04. Four additional stelae were installed in 1998 to retrospectively honour all GDR gold medal winners. Note that in 1994 the winter games began to be held separately to the summer games, hence the two sets of years that appear from this point.

30 Kluge, *Olympiastadion Berlin*, 85.
31 Projekt Historische Kommentierung des Olympiastadions: 1. Sitzung der Expertenkommission. Protokoll, 9. It is not clear why this board would only address these two post-war stelae and not the full eleven that were then standing.
32 Projekt Historische Kommentierung des Olympiastadions: 2. Sitzung des Wissenschaftliches Beirats. Protokoll, 9 (HEM: Uncatalogued personal papers).

Chapter 8

1 Donath, 'Konservieren und kommentieren', 83.
2 Benjamin Ziemann, *Contested Commemorations: Republican War Veterans and Weimar Political Culture* (Cambridge: Cambridge University Press, 2016), 256-7.
3 See, for example, Aleida Assmann, *Die Lange Schatten der Vergangenheit: Erinnerungskultur und Geschichtspolitik* (Munich: Verlag C. H. Beck, 2006), 66-7; Donath, 'Garden Guide: The Olympic Grounds Former Reichssportfeld', 5-6; Kluge, *Olympiastadion Berlin: Steine beginnen zu Reden*, 140-3; Rödiger, *The Olympic Stadium Berlin: From the German Stadium to the Reichssportfeld*, 34.
4 Kluge, *Olympiastadion Berlin: Steine beginnen zu reden*, 89.
5 Reichssportfeld Verwaltung, *Führer durch das Reichssportfeld* (Berlin: Reichssportfeld-Verwaltung, 1937), 1.
6 March, 'Das Reichssportfeld', 269-77 (276e).
7 Gerhard Krause, *Das Reichssportfeld* (Berlin: Reichssportverlag GmbH, 1936), 12.
8 In English: 'You grey and holy phalanxes march under clouds of glory and bear the bloody sacrifice for king and fatherland'. Translation: Marg, *Choreography of the Masses*, 78.
9 In English: 'The battle is ours! So that you may live, oh Fatherland, and do not count the dead! Dearest! Not one too many has fallen for you'. Translation: Marg, *Choreography of the Masses*, 78.
10 March, 'Das Reichssportfeld', 276e.
11 Mittig, 'Kunst und Propaganda im NS-System', 448.
12 March, 'Das Reichssportfeld', 272.
13 Kluge, *Olympiastadion Berlin: Steine beginnen zu reden*, 146.
14 Schmidt, *Werner March*, 59.
15 Ibid.
16 Schäche and Szymanski, *Das Reichssportfeld: Architektur im Spannungsfeld von Sport und Macht*, 129.
17 Kluge, *Olympiastadion Berlin: Steine beginnen zu reden*, 151.
18 Schmidt, *Werner March*, 59.
19 Bauentwurf für das Bauvorhaben Reichsportsfeld Berlin-Charlottenburg: Glockenturm, 16 June 1958 LAB B126/ 63531.
20 Bauentwurf für das Bauvorhaben Reichsportsfeld Berlin-Charlottenburg: Glockenturm, 16 June 1958 BARch (Koblenz) B126/ 63531.
21 Schäche and Szymanski, *Das Reichssportfeld: Architektur im Spannungsfeld von Sport und Macht*, 132.
22 Schmidt, *Werner March*, 59.
23 Cited in Schäche and Szymanski, *Das Reichssportfeld: Architektur im Spannungsfeld von Sport und Macht*, 132.

24 Letter from Sondervermögens-und Bauverwaltung bei der Oberfinanzdirektion Berlin to the Bundeschatzminister and to the Deutschen Bundestag – Petitionsausschuß, 7 March 1967 BArch (Koblenz) B/157/ 6609.
25 Volxsport statt Olympia, 'Widerstand gegen Olympia' (undated pamphlet), 27.
26 Schäche and Szymanski, *Das Reichssportfeld: Architektur im Spannungsfeld von Sport und Macht*, 133.
27 Senatsverwaltung für Bildung, Jugend und Sport, *Leitkonzept für das Olympiagelände*, June 2004, 8, https://www.parlament-berlin.de/ados/UASport/vorgang/0085.pdf [accessed 21 January 2019].
28 Stefanie Endlich, 'Vom Reichssportfeld zum Olympiapark: Ein Baudenkmal aus der NS-Zeit wird Kommentiert', in *Gedächtnis, Kultur und Politik,* ed. Ingeborg Siggelkow (Berlin: Frank und Timme Verlag für wissenschaftliche Literatur, 2006), 12.
29 Ibid., 15–16 (footnote 8).
30 Hans Stimmann, 'Stadtplanung: Koloseen der Moderne', *Architektur + Bauphysik* No 7, June 2006, 8–9, 9.
31 Werner March, 1936 cited in Schmidt, *Werner March*, 58.
32 March, 'Das Reichssportfeld', 274.
33 Meeting minutes. Session of the Abgeordnetenhaus von Berlin, Ausschuss für Bauen, Wohnen und Verkehr, 10 May 2000, 4, http://pardok.parlament-berlin.de/starweb/adis/citat/VT/14/AusschussPr/bwv/bwv14006.i.pdf [accessed 25 January 2019].
34 March, 'Das Reichssportfeld', 272.
35 Werner Durth and Paul Siegel, *Baukultur: Spiegel gesellschaftlichen Wandels* (Berlin: Jovis Verlag GmbH, 2009), 31.
36 Meeting Minutes, 26. Session of the Abgeordnetenhaus von Berlin, Ausschuss für Jugen, Familie, Schule und Sport, 21 January 1999. 18 LAB D Rep 001 Nr 13266.
37 48. Sitzung des Abgeordnetenhauses am 18. March 2004 DRs Nr 15/ 2551 (II.A. 2) Auflagenbeschlüsse 2004. LAB D Rep 002 Nr 13650.
38 Ibid.
39 Ibid.
40 Senatsverwaltung für Bildung, Jugend und Sport, *Leitkonzept für das Olympiagelände*, June 2004, 30–1, https://www.parlament-berlin.de/ados/UASport/vorgang/0085.pdf [accessed 21 January 2019].
41 Der Senat von Berlin, 'Kapitel 12 50, Titel 714 02 Sanierung im Bereich der Langemarckhalle zu Ausstellungszwecken', 15 February 2005, http://www.parlament-berlin.de/ados/Haupt/vorgang/h15-2894-v.pdf [accessed 3 December 2012].
42 Endlich, 'Vom Reichssportfeld zum Olympiapark', 13–14.
43 gmp Architekten von Gerkan Marg and Partner, 'Projects: Langemarck Hall, Olympic Stadium' (undated webpage), http://www.gmp-architekten.com/projects/langemarck-hall-olympic-stadium.html [accessed 12 December 2012].
44 For a more developed discussion of 'transparency ideology' in the Federal Republic of Germany, see Ascher Barnstone, *The Transparent State*.
45 Hettlage and Reiher, *Olympiastadion Berlin*, 10.
46 Odenthal, 'Denkmalpflege: Die Geschichtswahrende Modernisierung des Olympiastadions', 3.
47 Dean, *Governmentality*, 155–74.
48 Macdonald, 'Undesirable Heritage', 20.
49 Ibid., 20.
50 Senat von Berlin, 'Kapitel 12 50, Titel 714 02 Sanierung im Bereich der Langemarckhalle zu Ausstellungszwecken', 2.

51 Niven, *Facing the Nazi Past*, 36–7.
52 Chloe Paver, 'You Shall Know Them by Their Objects: Material Culture and Its Impact in Museum Displays about National Socialism', in *Cultural Impact in the German Context*, ed. Rebecca Braun and Lyn Marven (New York: Camden House, 2010), 171.
53 Ibid., 171–3.

Part 4

1 Part 4 uses material from an earlier journal article on this topic: Clare Copley, 'Curating Tempelhof: Negotiating the Multiple Histories of Berlin's "Symbol of Freedom"', *Urban History*, 44 (4) (2017). Many thanks to Cambridge University Press for their permission to reuse this.

Introduction to Part 4

1 Meuser, *Vom Fliegerfeld zum Wiesenmeer*, 28.
2 Paul Smith and Bernard Toulier, 'Introduction', *Berlin Tempelhof, Liverpool Speke, Paris Le Bourget: Airport Architecture of the Thirties*, ed. Paul Smith and Bernard Toulier (Paris: Editions du Patrimoine, 2000), 10.
3 Gabi Dolff-Bonekämper, 'Berlin-Tempelhof', in *Berlin Tempelhof, Liverpool Speke, Paris Le Bourget: Airport Architecture of the Thirties*, ed. Smith and Toulier, 52.
4 Ibid.
5 Ibid.
6 Ibid, 60.

Chapter 9

1 David Kaminski-Morrow, 'Last-Ditch Referendum Fails to Support Keeping Historic Berlin Tempelhof Open', *Flightglobal: Aviation Connected*, 28 April 2008, http://www.flightglobal.com/news/articles/last-ditch-referendum-fails-to-support-keeping-historic-berlin-tempelhof-223306/ [accessed 27 July 2014].
2 Michael Thiele, 'Der Architekt und sein Bauwerk', in *Landing on Tempelhof: 75 Jahre Zentralflughafen 50 Jahre Luftbrücke. Ausstellungskatalog*, ed. Matthias Heisig and Michael Thiele (Berlin: Bezirksamt Tempelhof von Berlin, 1998), 76.
3 Hecker, 'Berlin-Tempelhof: A City Airport of the 1930s', 93.
4 Thies Schröder, *Flughafen Tempelhof*, information leaflet produced by the Senatsverwaltung für Stadtentwicklung und Umweltschutz (December 1994). No pagination.
5 Dittrich, *Ernst Sagebiel: Leben und Werk 1892-1970*, 159.
6 Hecker, 'Berlin-Tempelhof: A City Airport of the 1930s', 92.
7 Dolff-Bonekämper, 'Berlin-Tempelhof', 57.
8 See, for example, Axel Drieschner, 'Ernst Sagebiel's Tempelhof Airport', 104; Dolff-Bonekämper, 'Berlin-Tempelhof', 57.

9 See, for example, Drieschner, 'Ernst Sagebiel's Tempelhof Airport', 103–5; Hecker, 'Berlin-Tempelhof: A City Airport of the 1930s', 96–7.
10 Hecker, 'Berlin-Tempelhof: A City Airport of the 1930s', 93.
11 Werner Jockeit and Cornelia Wendt, 'Approaching the Built Heritage: The Conservation Plan for Berlin-Tempelhof', in *Proceedings of the International L'Europe de L'Air conferences on Aviation Architecture: Liverpool (1999), Berlin (2000), Paris (2001)*, ed. Bob Hawkins, Gabriele Lechner and Paul Smith (London: English Heritage, 2005), 61.
12 Thiele, 'Der Architekt und sein Bauwerk', 78–9.
13 Be Berlin, 'Airport Building: The Mother of All Airports' (undated webpage), http://www.tempelhoferfreiheit.de/en/about-tempelhofer-freiheit/airport-building [accessed 17 June 2013].
14 See, for example, Hecker, 'Berlin-Tempelhof: A City Airport of the 1930s', 96–7.
15 Meuser, *Vom Fliegerfeld zum Wiesenmeer*, 34.
16 Drieschner, 'Ernst Sagebiel's Tempelhof Airport', 103.
17 Ibid., 103.
18 Dolff-Bonekämper, 'Berlin-Tempelhof', 54.
19 Some of many examples of this kind of language can be found in K. Westphal and D. Schölkopf, 'Goodbye Tempelhof', *Welt Am Sonntag*, 26 October 2008; C. van Lessen, 'Im Sinkflug', *Tagesspiegel*, 28 April 2008; N. Bernau, 'So viel Flughafen wird nie wieder sein in Berlin', *Berliner Zeitung*, 16 November 2006.
20 Jörg Schindler, 'Schwingen im Körper der Stadt', *Frankfurter Rundschau*, 2 November 2004.
21 Dirk Westphal, 'Neue Chance für Tempelhof', *Welt am Sonntag*, 21 November 2004.
22 B. Möller, 'Bewundert und erledigt: Die "Mutter aller Flughäfen"', *Hamburger Abendblatt*, 11 January 2007.
23 Torsten Krauel, 'Tempelhof: Der schönste Flughafen der Welt', *Welt am Sonntag*, 23 August 2009.
24 Schindler, 'Schwingen im Körper der Stadt'.
25 T. Schmid, 'Klägliches Ende eines großen Traums', *Die Welt*, 30 October 2008.
26 Bernau, 'So viel Flughafen wird nie wieder sein in Berlin'.
27 Michael Thiele, 'Tempelhof, das Tor zur Welt', in *Landing on Tempelhof: 75 Jahre Zentralflughafen 50 Jahre Luftbrücke. Ausstellungskatalog*, ed. Matthias Heisig and Michael Thiele (Berlin: Bezirksamt Tempelhof von Berlin, 1998), 137.
28 Schmitz, *Flughafen Tempelhof – Berlins Tor zur Welt*, 105.
29 Dolff-Bonekämper, 'Berlin-Tempelhof', 60.
30 Schmitz, *Flughafen Tempelhof - Berlins Tor zur Welt*, 110.
31 Ibid., 111.
32 S. Endlich, M. Geyler-von Bernus and B. Rossié, 'Flow of Refugees' (undated webpage), http://www.tempelhoferfreiheit.de/nc/en/about-tempelhofer-freiheit/history/symbol-of-freedom/flow-of-refugees/?page=1 [accessed 15 June 2013].
33 Matthias Donath, Gabriele Schultz and Michael Hoffmann, *Denkmale in Berlin-Bezirk Tempelhof-Schoeneberg Orsteile Tempelhof, Mariendorf, Marienfelde und Lichtenrade* (Berlin: Michael Imhof for the Landesdenkmalamt Berlin, 2007), 80.
34 In English: 'They gave their lives for the freedom of Berlin serving in the airlift 1948/9.'
35 Stefanie Endlich, 'Geschichte des Tempelhofer Feldes und des Flughafens Tempelhof. Ortsbegehung, Pläne, Diskussionen', in *Verein Aktives Museum: Mitgliederrundbrief* 66 (January 2012), 4–7, 4.

36 Damm, Siebenhaar and Zang, *Schauplatz Berlin 1933. 1945. 1961. Heute*, 81; Stefanie Endlich and Bernd Wurlitzer, *Skulpturen und Denkmäler in Berlin* (Berlin: Stapp Verlag Berlin, 1990).
37 Gedenkstätte Deutscher Widerstand and Aktives Museum Faschismus und Widerstand in Berlin e.V., 'Luftbrückenflugzeug C- 47' (undated webpage), http://www.gedenktafeln-in-berlin.de/nc/gedenktafeln/gedenktafel-anzeige/bz/tempelhof-schoeneberg/tid/luftbrueckenflugzeug-1/ [accessed 1 March 2013].
38 Elke Dittrich, *Der Flughafen Tempelhof in Entwurfszeichnungen und Modellen 1934-44* (Berlin: Lukas Verlag, 2005), 26–7.
39 Endlich, 'Geschichte des Tempelhofer Feldes und des Flughafens Tempelhof', 5.
40 Endlich and Wurlitzer, *Skulpturen und Denkmäler in Berlin*.
41 Stefanie Endlich, 'Geschichte des Tempelhofer Feldes und des Flughafens Tempelhof', 4.
42 Norbert Huse, 'Verloren, gefährdet, geschützt – Baudenkmale in Berlin', in *Verloren, gefährdet, geschützt: Baudenkmale in Berlin. Ausstellung im ehemaligen Arbeitsschutzmuseum Berlin-Charlottenberg 7 Dez. 1985 - 5 Maerz 1989*, ed. Gruhn-Zimmerman (Berlin: Argon Verlag Gmbh, 1989), 13.
43 Among many examples, see *Bild*, 13 May 2009, '160 000 Berliner feierten Flughafen Tempelhof'; *Tagesspiegel*, 30 April 2011, 'Freiheit für Tempelhof'; CDU-Fraktion Berlin, *Pro-Tempelhof*, 1; SPD–Fraktion Berlin, *Tempelhofer Feld*.
44 CDU-Fraktion des Abgeordnetenhauses von Berlin, *Pro-Tempelhof*, information flyer ed. F. Henkel (Berlin: CDU-Fraktion des Abgeordnetenhauses von Berlin, undated).
45 CDU-Fraktion des Abgeordnetenhauses von Berlin, *Pro-Tempelhof*, Bold in original.
46 Peter Hahne, 'Über Rosinenbomber und den Kampf David gegen Goliath', *Bild*, 26 April 2008. Unless otherwise indicated all *Bild* articles were accessed at www.bild.de.
47 See, for example, Hahne, 'Über Rosinenbomber und den Kampf David gegen Goliath'.
48 CDU-Fraktion Berlin, *Pro-Tempelhof*.
49 SPD Berlin, *Für ein flugfreies Tempelhof*, information flyer (Berlin: SPD Berlin, undated).
50 Tempelhof Aufmachen. Für Alle, *Als Flughafen viel zu Schade!*, Information flyer (Berlin: Tempelhof Aufmachen. Für Alle, undated).
51 M. Sauerbier, 'Wieder 11 285-mal JA für den Flughafen', *Bild*, 19 January 2008.
52 K. Colmenares, 'Wowereit bleibt Stur: Tempelhof – Jetzt erst recht!', *Bild*, 12 December 2007; see also Franz Josef Wagner, 'Lieber Klaus Wowereit', *Bild*, 21 April 2008.
53 R. Senftleben and F. Hartmann, 'Wir halten Tempelhof am Leben', *Bild*, 18 December 2007; Anon., 'Mehrheit der Berliner ist für den Erhalt von *Tempelhof*', *Bild*, 22 April 2008.
54 Anon., 'Ganze Berliner FDP sagt JA zu *Tempelhof*', *Bild*, 12 December 2007.
55 C. Müll, '100 Berliner und Ihr Ja zu *Tempelhof*', *Bild*, 22 April 2008.
56 Anon., '100 Dachdecker kämpfen für Tempelhof', *Bild*, 8 February 2008.
57 O. Santen, 'Rettet den Berliner City-Airport! 67 Top-Manager für Tempelhof', *Bild*, 15 April 2008.
58 See, for example, Sauerbier, 'Wieder 11 285-mal JA für den Flugahfen'; Anon., 'Nur noch 49 403 Stimmen bis zur Landung', *Bild*, 22 December 2007; Anon., '529 053 Stimmen für City-Airport', *Bild*, 28 April 2008.
59 M. Sauerbier, 'Berlin braucht Tempelhof. Berlin will Tempelhof', *Bild*, 16 January 2008.
60 H. Bruns, 'Senatorin ätzt gegen Tempelhof-Freunde', *Bild*, 6 March 2008.
61 Anon., 'Warum Die Legende Nicht Sterben Darf', *Bild*, 23 April 2008.

62 Axel Brüggemann, '100 Gründe für den Flughafen der Herzen', *Bild*, 25 April 2008.
63 Anon., 'Berliner, rettet Tempelhof!', *Bild*, 27 April 2008; Anon., 'Der Rosinenbomber darf nicht sterben!', *Bild*, 26 April 2008.
64 SPD Berlin, 'Für ein flugfreies Tempelhof'.
65 K. Schölkopf, 'Tempelhof-Gegner starten Offensive', *Die Welt*, 28 February 2008; see also Anon., 'Tempelhof-Gegner: Volksbegehren Ja, Volksentscheid Nein,' *Der Tagesspiegel*, 21 December 2007; Anon., 'Tempelhof-Gegner werben für Nein-Stimmen', *Die Welt*, 8 March 2008.
66 Amt für Statistik Berlin-Brandenburg, *Volksentscheid 'Tempelhof bleibt Verkehrsflughafen' am 27. April 2008: Endgültiges Ergebnis*, https://www.wahlen-berlin.de/historie/abstimmungen/Landeswahlleiterbericht_VE08.pdf [accessed 5 December 2018]. Averages calculated by author from provided district-by-district breakdown.

Chapter 10

1 Alexandra Handrack and Werner Jockeit, *Flughafen Berlin-Tempelhof: Erfassung und Bestandsaufnahme der Denkmalsubstanz. Band 1 Textteil-Historische Fotodokumentation- Quellenkatalog* (Berlin: Arbeitsgemeinschaft Alexandra Handrack und Werner Jockeit, 1995), see, for example, the analysis of different parts of the building, 33–6.
2 Ibid., 48.
3 Jockeit and Wendt, 'Approaching the Built Heritage: The Conservation Plan for Berlin-Tempelhof', 167.
4 Jockeit and Wendt, 'Approaching the Built Heritage: The Conservation Plan for Berlin-Tempelhof', 166–70.
5 Stefanie Endlich and Beate Rossié, 'Geschichte des Tempelhofer Feldes, Zweiter Teil: Ein weiterer Rundgang, diesmal zu Resten und Spuren des Alten Flughafens', *Verein Aktives Museum: Mitgliederrundbrief*, 67 (August 2012), 13.
6 Gürgen and Itzek, 'Tempelhofs dunkle Seite', *TAZ.de*, 2 April 2012, http://www.taz.de/!90845/ [accessed 15 July 2014].
7 Nikolaus Wachsmann, *KL: A History of the Nazi Concentration Camps* (London: Abacus, 2016), 31–8.
8 As the two are commonly confused it should be noted that Tempelhof's Columbia-Haus should not be mistaken for the Columbus Haus, the ten-storey glass and steel building designed by Sagebiel's tutor Erich Mendelsohn, which was erected on Potsdamer Platz in 1932 and destroyed during the demonstrations of 1953. See James Howard Kunstler, *The City in Mind: Meditations on the Urban Condition* (New York: Free Press, 2003), 119.
9 Kurt Schilde, *Vom Columbia-haus zum Schulenburgring: Dokumentation mit Lebensgeschicten von Opfern des Widerstandes und der Verfolgung von 1933 bis 1945 aus dem Bezirk Tempelhof* (Berlin: Bezirksamt Tempelhof von Berlin, 1987), 43.
10 Karoline Georg and Kurt Schilde, '"Warum schweigt die Welt?" Häftlinge des Berliner Konzentrationslagers Columbia-Haus 1933-1936', *Museums Journal*, 3 (2013), 32–3, 32.
11 Wachsmann, *KL: A History of the Nazi Concentration Camps*, 92–7.
12 Schilde, *Vom Columbia-haus zum Schulenburgring*, 52.
13 Richard J. Evans, *The Third Reich at War* (London: Allen Lane, 2008), 348.

14 Susan Pollack and Reinhard Bernbeck, 'The Limits of Experience: Suffering, Nazi Forced Labour Camps, and Archaeology', *Archaeological Papers of the American Anthropological Association*, 27 (2016), 22–39, 23.
15 Evans, *The Third Reich at War*, 348.
16 Ibid., 348–51.
17 Detlev Peukert, *Inside Nazi Germany* (New York: Penguin, 1989), 127.
18 Maria Theresia Starzmann, 'Excavating Tempelhof Airfield: Objects of Memory and the Politics of Absence', *Rethinking History*, 18 (2) (2014), 211–29, 215.
19 Ibid., 216.
20 Ibid., 220.
21 Berliner Geschichtswekstatt e. V. *Projektgrüppe NS-Zwangsarbeit*, http://www.berliner-geschichtswerkstatt.de/zwangsarbeit.html [accessed March 2016].
22 M. Heisig, 'Die "Weser" Flugzeugbau GmbH auf dem Flughafen Tempelhof: Rüstungsproduktion und Zwangsarbeit für den Krieg', in *Kein Ort der Freiheit: Das Tempelhfer Feld 1933-45*, ed. F. Böhne and B. Winzer (Berlin, 2012), 43–61, 44.
23 Jordan, *Structures of Memory*, 153.
24 Thea Fleischhauer , 'Gedächtnisgeschichte Tempelhofer Feld: Förderverein für ein Gedenken an die Naziverbrechen auf dem Tempelhofer Feld e. V.' http://www.tempelhofer-unfreiheit.de/de/gedaechtnisgeschichte-tempelhofer-feld-f oerderverein-fuer-ein-gedenken-die-naziverbrechen-auf-dem-tempelhofer-feld-e-v [accessed March 2016].
25 Kurt Schilde, *Erinnern- und nicht vergessen: Dokumentation zum Gedenkbuch für die Opfer des Nationalsozialismus aus dem Bezirk Tempelhof* (Berlin: Bezirksamt Tempelhof von Berlin, 1988).
26 Schilde, *Vom Columbia-haus zum Schulenburgring*.
27 Jordan, *Structures of Memory*, 158–9.
28 In English: 'Remember, commemorate, warn: the Columbia-Haus was a prison from 1933 and, between 8.1.1935 and 5.11.1936, a National Socialist concentration camp, People were imprisoned, debased, tortured and murdered here'.
29 Chloe Paver, 'Exhibiting the National Socialist Past: An Overview of Recent German Exhibitions', *Journal of European Studies*, 39 (2009), 169–88, 233.
30 Uwe Doering, *Aktuelles aus dem Abgeordnetenhaus* (2010) Left Party political flyer, http://www.dielinke-treptow-koepenick.de/fileadmin/tk/thematisch/doering/info_ag h_januar_2010.pdf [accessed September 2018].
31 Bezirksverordnetenversammlung Tempelhof-Schöneberg von Berlin, *Antrag Drucks. Nr: 1494/XVIII Fraktion der SPD Informations-und- Gedenkort am Columbiadamm*, 16 June 2010, https://www.berlin.de/ba-tempelhof-schoeneberg/politik-und-verwal tung/bezirksverordnetenversammlung/online/___tmp/tmp/45081036951808623 /951808623/00032508/08-Anlagen/01/1_Version_vom_08_06_2010.pdf [accessed September 2018].
32 http://thf33-45.de/verein-2/ [accessed 9 July 2016].
33 Progress report from the round table to the Abgeordnetenhaus Berlin, Vorlage-zur Kenntnisnahme: Sachstandsbericht des Runden Tisches 'Historische Markierung Tempelhofer Feld' Drucksache 17/ 2354 18 June 2015, https://www.parlament-berlin.d e/ados/17/IIIPlen/vorgang/d17-2354.pdf.
34 Endlich and Rossié, 'Geschichte des Tempelhofer Feldes, Zweiter Teil', 13.
35 Progress report from the round table to the Abgeordnetenhaus Berlin, Vorlage-zur Kenntnisnahme: Sachstandsbericht des Runden Tisches 'Historische Markierung

Tempelhofer Feld' Drucksache 17/ 2354, 18 June 2015, https://www.parlament-berlin.de/ados/17/IIIPlen/vorgang/d17-2354.pdf

36 Susan Pollack and Reinhard Bernbeck, 'Gate to a Darker World', in *Ethics and the Archaeology of Violence*, ed. Alfredo González-Ruibal and Gabriel Moshenska (London: Springer, 2014), 137–52, 144.
37 Susan Pollack and Reinhard Bernbeck, 'Archäologische Ausgrabungen auf dem Tempelhofer Flugfeld (2012)', http://www.ausgrabungen-tempelhof.de/Ausgrabungen%20Tempelhofer%20Flugfeld.pdf [accessed 12 January 2019].
38 Ibid.
39 Progress report from the round table to the Abgeordnetenhaus Berlin, Vorlage-zur Kenntnisnahme: Sachstandsbericht des Runden Tisches, 'Historische Markierung Tempelhofer Feld' Drucksache 17/ 2354', 18 June 2015. Appendix: Susan Pollack and Reinhard Bernback, 'Bisherige Forschungs Aktivitäten Rund um den Ehemaligen Flughafen Tempelhof: Ausgrabungen auf dem Tempelhofer Feld' 2012–2014, https://www.parlament-berlin.de/ados/17/IIIPlen/vorgang/d17-2354.pdf.
40 Pollack and Bernbeck, 'The Limits of Experience', 26.
41 Ibid.
42 Pollack and Bernbeck, 'Gate to a Darker World', 147.
43 Pollack and Bernbeck, 'The Limits of Experience', 26.
44 Ibid., 146–7.
45 Ibid., 26.
46 Ibid., 33.
47 Starzmann, 'Excavating Tempelhof Airfield', 221.
48 Starzmann, 'The Fragment and the Testimony: Reflections on Absence and Time in the Archaeology of Prisons and Camps', *International Journal of Historical Archaeology*, 22 (2018), 574–92, 581.
49 Peukert, *Inside Nazi Germany*, 129–44
50 Pollack and Bernbeck, 'The Limits of Experience', 33.
51 Progress report from the round table to the Abgeordnetenhaus Berlin, Vorlage-zur Kenntnisnahme: Sachstandsbericht des Runden Tisches 'Historische Markierung Tempelhofer Feld' Drucksache 17/ 2354, 18 June 2015. Appendix: Susan Pollack and Reinhard Bernback, Bisherige Forschungs Aktivitäten Rund um den Ehemaligen Flughafen Tempelhof: Ausgrabungen auf dem Tempelhofer Feld 2012-2014 https://www.parlament-berlin.de/ados/17/IIIPlen/vorgang/d17-2354.pdf
52 Progress report from the round table to the Abgeordnetenhaus Berlin, Vorlage-zur Kenntnisnahme: Sachstandsbericht des Runden Tisches "Historische Markierung Tempelhofer Feld" Drucksache 17/ 2354, 18 June 2015, https://www.parlament-berlin.de/ados/17/IIIPlen/vorgang/d17-2354.pdf.
53 Report for the Runder Tisch Historische Markierung Tempelhofer Feld, *Sachstandsbericht zur bisherigen Arbeit*, 1 July 2014. Appendix: Berliner Forum für Geschichte und Gegenwart e.V.:Geschichte des Tempelhofer Feldes und des Flughafens Tempelhof. First written 31 March 2011, updated June 2014, https://tempelhofer-feld.berlin.de/documents/23/sachstandsbericht-rundertisch2014.pdf. 4.
54 Report for the Runder Tisch Historische Markierung Tempelhofer Feld, *Sachstandsbericht zur bisherigen Arbeit*, 1 July 2014. Appendix: Berliner Forum für Geschichte und Gegenwart e.V.:Geschichte des Tempelhofer Feldes und des Flughafens Tempelhof. First written 31 March 2011, updated June 2014, https://tempelhofer-feld.berlin.de/documents/23/sachstandsbericht-rundertisch2014.pdf. 9.

55 Report for the Runder Tisch Historische Markierung Tempelhofer Feld, *Sachstandsbericht zur bisherigen Arbeit*, 1 July 2014. Appendix: Berliner Forum für Geschichte und Gegenwart e.V.:Geschichte des Tempelhofer Feldes und des Flughafens Tempelhof. First written 31 March 2011, updated June 2014, https://tempelhofer-feld.berlin.de/documents/23/sachstandsbericht-rundertisch2014.pdf. 14.
56 Report for the Runder Tisch Historische Markierung Tempelhofer Feld, *Sachstandsbericht zur bisherigen Arbeit*, 1 July 2014. Appendix: Berliner Forum für Geschichte und Gegenwart e.V.:Geschichte des Tempelhofer Feldes und des Flughafens Tempelhof. First written 31 March 2011, updated June 2014, https://tempelhofer-feld.berlin.de/documents/23/sachstandsbericht-rundertisch2014.pdf. 5.
57 Text on the information boards is attributable to Stefanie Endlich, Monica Geyler-von Bernus and Beate Rossié. Translation by Robin Benson (Berlin, 2013).
58 Report for the Runder Tisch Historische Markierung Tempelhofer Feld, *Sachstandsbericht zur bisherigen Arbeit*, 1 July 2014. Appendix: Berliner Forum für Geschichte und Gegenwart e.V.:Geschichte des Tempelhofer Feldes und des Flughafens Tempelhof. First written 31 March 2011, updated June 2014, https://tempelhofer-feld.berlin.de/documents/23/sachstandsbericht-rundertisch2014.pdf. 12.
59 Progress report from the round table to the Abgeordnetenhaus Berlin, Vorlage-zur Kenntnisnahme: Sachstandsbericht des Runden Tisches "Historische Markierung Tempelhofer Feld" Drucksache 17/ 2354, 18 June 2015, https://www.parlament-berlin.de/ados/17/IIIPlen/vorgang/d17-2354.pdf.
60 See, for example, Dirk Westphal, 'Neue Chance für Tempelhof', *Welt am Sonntag*, 21 November 2004; Westphal and Schölkopf, 'Goodbye Tempelhof'; Peter von Becker, 'Ja, macht nur einen Masterplan', *Der Tagesspiegel*, 7 December 2008.
61 Tempelhof Projekt GmbH, *Tempelhofer Freiheit Unlimited: Event Location Tempelhof Airport* (Berlin: Tempelhof Projekt GmbH, 2011), 5.
62 Ibid., 7.
63 Ibid., 8–9.
64 Ibid., 10–11.
65 Ibid., 59.
66 Ibid.
67 Ibid., 14–18.
68 Tempelhof Projekt GmbH, 'Available Space: Airport Building' (undated webpage), http://www.tempelhoferfreiheit.de/en/organize-events-rent-invest/event-location/available-space-airport-building [accessed 20 November 2013].
69 Ibid.
70 Tempelhof Projekt GmbH, *Tempelhofer Freiheit Unlimited: Event Location Tempelhof Airport*, 49.
71 Pollack and Bernbeck, 'Gate to a Darker World', 140.
72 See, for example, *Berliner Zeitung So leben die Flüchtling im Containerdorf*, 29 May 2018, https://www.berliner-zeitung.de/berlin/tempelhofer-feld-so-leben-die-fluechtlinge-im-containerdorf-30519934
73 Tempelhof Projekt GmbH, *Events und Messen*, https://www.thf-berlin.de/de/aktuelles/veranstaltungen/ [accessed 22 March 2019].
74 Tempelhof Projekt GmbH, Nutzungskonzept für das Flughafengebäude, Report to the Runder Tisch Historische Markierung Tempelhofer Feld, *Sachstandsbericht zur bisherigen Arbeit*, 1 July 2014, https://tempelhofer-feld.berlin.de/documents/23/sachstandsbericht-rundertisch2014.pdf.

75 Speech by Staatsministerin Professor Monika Grütters, *Anlässlich der Eröffnung der Ausstellung 'Ein Weites Feld: Der Flughafen Tempelhof und seine Geschichte' im Rahmen des Europäischen Kulturerbejahres* delivered 4 September 2018 in Berlin, https://www.topographie.de/fileadmin/topographie/public/Presse/Reden_und_ Vortraege/Gruetters-180904_Rede_Tempelhof_Ausstellung_ECHY.pdf [accessed 24 April 2019].
76 Der Tagesspiegel, *Der Flughafen Tempelhof und seine Geschichte*, 4 September 2018, https://www.tagesspiegel.de/berlin/neue-ausstellung-in-berlin-der-flughafen-temp elhof-und-seine-geschichte/22995348.html [accessed 24 April 2019].
77 See, for example, Berliner Woche, *Neue Ausstellung über den Flughafen stellt NS-Zeit in den Mittelpunk* [14 September 2018]; Berliner Morgenpost, *Ein weites Feld: neue Ausstellung im Flughafen Tempelhof* [4 September 2018], https://www.morgenpost.de/ berlin/article215251273/Ein-weites-Feld-neue-Ausstellung-im-Flughafen-Tempelhof .html both [accessed 24 April 2019].
78 Berlin SPD Antrag 40/01/2014 Historisches Gesamtkonzept für das Tempelhofer Feld umgehend entwickeln, 25 April 2016, https://parteitag.spd-berlin.de/cvtx_ant rag/historisches-gesamtkonzept-fuer-das-tempelhofer-feld-umgehend-entwickeln/ [accessed 24 April 2019].
79 http://thf33-45.de/2016/03/14/aktuell/ [accessed 24 April 2019].
80 Berliner Morgenpost, *Ab Ende Juni keine Flüchtlinge mehr am Flughafen Tempelhof*, 19 March 2019, https://www.morgenpost.de/bezirke/tempelhof-schoeneberg/article21 6695983/106-neue-Stellen-fuer-das-Fluechtlingsamt.html [accessed 24 April 2019].
81 Tempelhof Project GmbH, *Ideal Conditions for Events*, April 2018, https://www.thf -berlin.de/fileadmin/user_upload/Ideal_Conditions_for_Events.pdf [accessed 24 April 2019].

Chapter 11

1 As well as the 'Planung und Entwicklung' section of the Tempelhofer Freiheit website, http://www.tempelhoferfreiheit.de/ueber-die-tempelhofer-freiheit/planu ng-entwicklung/planungsgeschichte [accessed 16 March 2013], see flyers such as Be Berlin, Senatsverwaltung für Stadtentwicklung und Umwelt and Tempelhofer Freiheit, *Tempelhofer Freiheit: Planung zur Parklandschaft*, June 2011; Be Berlin, Senatsverwaltung für Stadtentwicklung und Umwelt and Tempelhofer Freiheit, *Park Landscape Development: Free Space for the City of Tomorrow*, March 2012.
2 Foucault, 'Of Other Spaces', 24. There are multiple translations of this text in circulation. Most notable are those by Miskowiek (1986), Leach (1986) and Hurley (1998). Dehaene and De Cauter describe all three as 'fine but imperfect' (Michiel Dehaene and Lieven De Cauter, *Heterotopia and the City: Public Space in a Postcivil Society* [Oxon: Routledge, 2008]), 14. Given that the conceptualization of heterotopia in this chapter has much in common with that of Hetherington (1997) it will use the same translation – that by Jan Miskowiek which featured in *Diacritics* in 1986.
3 Michel Foucault, *The Order of Things: An Archaeology of the Human Sciences* (London: Tavistock Publications, 1970), xv–xviii.
4 Foucault, 'Of Other Spaces', 22 (footnote 1).
5 Ibid., 25.
6 Ibid.

7 Ibid., 26.
8 Ibid., 27.
9 Ibid.
10 Catherine Collins and Alexandra Opie, 'When Places Have Agency: Roadside Shrines as Traumascapes', *Continuum: Journal of Media and Cultural Studies*, 24 (2010), 107-18; Xavier Guillot, 'The "Institutionalisation" of Heterotopias in Singapore', in *Heterotopia and the City: Space in a Postcivil Society*, ed. Michiel Dehaene and Lieven De Cauter (Abingdon, Oxon: Routledge, 2008).
11 Edward W. Soja, *Thirdspace: Journeys to Los Angeles and Other Real-and-Imagined Places* (Oxford: Blackwell, 1996), 162.
12 Michiel Dehaene and Lieven De Cauter, 'Heterotopia in a Postcivil Society', in *Heterotopia and the City: Space in a Postcivil Society*, ed. Michiel Dehaene and Lieven De Cauter (Abingdon, Oxon: Routledge, 2008).
13 Peter Johnson, 'Unravelling Foucault's "Different Spaces"', *History of the Human Sciences*, 19 (2006), 75-90, 75.
14 Robert Topinka, 'Foucault, Borges, Heterotopia: Producing Knowledge in Other Spaces', *Foucault Studies*, 9 (2010), 54-70, 57.
15 See, for example, A. Arias, 'Fernando Vallejo's Ruinous Heterotopias: The Queer Subject in Latin America's Urban Spaces', in *Telling Ruins in Latin America*, ed. M. Lazzara and V. Unruh (New York: Palgrave Macmillan, 2008); P. Billingham, *Sensing the City through Television: Urban Identities in Fictional Drama* (Bristol: Intellect, 2000); Sally Munt, *Queer Attachments: The Cultural Politics of Shame* (Aldershot: Ashgate, 2007).
16 Hetherington, *The Badlands of Modernity: Heterotopia and Social Ordering*.
17 Joyce, *The Rule of Freedom*, 188.
18 C. Orillard, 'Between Shopping Malls and Agoras: A French History of "Protected Public Space"', in *Heterotopia and the City: Space in a Postcivil Society*, ed. Michiel Dehaene and Lieven De Cauter (Abingdon, Oxon: Routledge, 2008).
19 Setha Low, 'The Gated Community as Heterotopia', in *Heterotopia and the City: Space in a Postcivil Society*, ed. Michiel Dehaene and Lieven De Cauter (Abingdon, Oxon: Routledge, 2008).
20 Myra Shackley, 'Space, Sanctity and Service; The English Cathedral as Heterotopia', *International Journal of Tourism Research*, 4 (2002), 345-52.
21 Jane Juffer, 'Why We Like to Lose: On Being a Cubs Fan in the Heterotopia of Wrigley Field', *The South Atlantic Quarterly*, 105 (2006), 289-301.
22 Joshua Samuels, 'Of Other Scapes: Archaeology, Landscape, and Heterotopia in Fascist Sicily', *Archaeologies: Journal of the World Archaeological Congress*, 6 (2010), 62-81.
23 Sarah Chaplin, 'Heterotopia Deserta: Las Vegas and Other Spaces', in *Intersections: Architectural Histories and Critical Theories*, ed. Iain Borden and Jane Rendell (London: Routledge, 2000).
24 Soja, *Thirdspace*.
25 Jia Lou, 'Revitalizing Chinatown into a Heterotopia: A Geosemiotic Analysis of Shop Signs in Washington, D.C.'s Chinatown', *Space and Culture*, 10 (2007) 170-94.
26 Arun Saldanha, 'Heterotopia and Structuralism', *Environment and Planning A*, 40 (2008), 2080-96, 2082.
27 Benjamin Genocchio, 'Discourse, Discontinuity, Difference: The Question of "Other" Spaces', in *Postmodern Cities and Spaces*, ed. Sophie Watson and Katherine Gibson (Oxford: Blackwell, 1995), 36.

28 Topinka, 'Foucault, Borges, Heterotopia: Producing Knowledge in Other Spaces', 58, referring to Edward W. Soja, 'Heterotopologies: A Remembrance of Other Spaces in the Citadel-La', in *Postmodern Cities and Spaces*, ed. Sophie Watson and Katherine Gibson (Oxford: Blackwell, 1995), 13–34.
29 Soja, *Thirdspace*, 162–3.
30 Genocchio, 'Discourse, Discontinuity, Difference', 39.
31 Saldanha, 'Heterotopia and Structuralism', 2083.
32 David Harvey, 'Cosmopolitanism and the Banality of Geographical Evils', *Public Culture*, 12 (2000), 529–64.
33 Saldanha, 'Heterotopia and Structuralism'.
34 David Harvey, 'The Kantian Roots of Foucault's Dilemmas', in *Space, Knowledge and Power: Foucault and Geography*, ed. Jeremy W. Crampton and Stuart Elden (Aldershot: Ashgate, 2007), 45.
35 Topinka, 'Foucault, Borges, Heterotopia: Producing Knowledge in Other Spaces'.
36 Foucault, 'Of Other Spaces', 27.
37 Matthew Philpotts, 'The Ruins of Dictatorship: Prora and Other Spaces', *Central Europe*, 12 (2014), 47–61.
38 Foucault, *Discipline and Punish*, 201.
39 Ibid., 201.
40 Hetherington, *The Badlands of Modernity: Heterotopia and Social Ordering*, 39.
41 Catherine Ward Thompson, 'Urban Open Space in the 21st Century', *Landscape and Urban Planning*, 60 (2002), 59–72, 69.
42 See, for example, Be Berlin and Tempelhof Projekt GmbH, 'Planung und Entwicklung' (undated webpage), http://www.tempelhoferfreiheit.de/ueber-die-tempelhofer-frei heit/planung-entwicklung/planungsgeschichte [accessed 16 March 2013].
43 Michael Müller, *Park Landscape Development: Free Space for the City of Tomorrow*, leaflet produced by the Senatsverwaltung für Stadtentwicklung und Umwelt (March 2012), unpaginated.
44 See, for example, Thomas Loy, 'Kein "Designerpark" für Tempelhofer Flugfeld', *Der Tagesspiegel*, 14 August 2012; dpa/ds, 'Berlin plant einen See auf dem Tempelhofer Feld', *Die Welt*, 7 March 2013.
45 Meuser, *Vom Fliegerfeld zum Wiesenmeer*, 64.
46 Galen Cranz, *The Politics of Park Design: A History of Urban Parks in America* (London: MIT Press, 1982).
47 Tempelhof Projekt GmbH, 'Tasks' (undated webpage), http://www.tempelhoferfreiheit .de/en/about-tempelhofer-freiheit/project-partners/tempelhof-projekt-gmbh/task [accessed 25 February 2013].
48 Aperto AG, *Mehr Freiheit fürs Feld: Aperto gibt ehemaligem Flughafengelände Berlin-Tempelhof ein neues Gesicht*, press release (4 April 2011), https://www.aperto.de/sta rt/presse/Pressemitteilungen-Archiv/pressemitteilungen-2011/Aperto-gestaltet-Tem pelhofer-Freiheit.html [accessed 25 February 2013].
49 Tempelhof Projekt GmbH, Senatsverwaltung für Stadtentwicklung and Grün Berlin, 'Zwischen- und Pionierenutzer der Tempelhofer Freiheit' (2010), 2, http://www.tempelhoferfreiheit.de/fileadmin/user_upload/Mitgestalten/Pioniere_ der_Tempelhofer_Freiheit_Broschuere_Stand_Dezember_2010.pdf [accessed 27 May 2013].
50 DPA/ The Local, 'Tempelhof to become Enormous City Park', *The Local*, 31 August 2009, http://www.thelocal.de/20090831/21611 [accessed 27 April 2013].

51 U. Paul, 'Macht auf das Tor', *Berliner Zeitung*, 8 May 2010; S. Flatau and A. Klesse, 'Riesiger Andrang auf dem Flugfeld Tempelhof', *Berliner Morgenpost*, 9 May 2010.
52 Anon., 'Schwungvoller Start, abendliche Turbulenzen. 100 000 feiern Eröffnung des Tempelhofer Parks. Protestler klettern über die Umzäunung', *Der Tagesspiegel*, 9 May 2010.
53 Senatsverwaltung für Stadtentwicklung und Umwelt, 'Pressebox: Ergebnisse Online-Dialog Tempelhof vorgestellt', 22 August 2007, http://www.stadtentwicklung.berlin.de/aktuell/pressebox/archiv_volltext.shtml?arch_0708/nachricht2763.html [accessed 15 March 2013].
54 Online-Dialog Flughafen Tempelhof, 'Bustour und Online-Dialog Flughafen Tempelhof', 6 October 2007, http://www.youtube.com/watch?v=NZn7NNYskXs [accessed 6 June 2013]; See also ZebralogTHF, *Prämierung Ideen Online-Dialog Flughafen* Tempelhof, 21 November 2007, http://www.youtube.com/watch?v=XZsQ-tB8DY8 [accessed 6 June 2013].
55 Senatsverwaltung für Stadtentwicklung und Umwelt, 'Pressebox: 2. Phase Online-Dialog zum Flughafen-Tempelhof beendet', 8 November 2007, http://www.stadtentwicklung.berlin.de/aktuell/pressebox/archiv_volltext.shtml?arch_0711/nachricht2862.html [accessed 15 March 2013]. For press coverage, see, for example, J. Voigt, 'Der Flughafen Tempelhof als großer Gemeinschaftsgarten', *Berliner Zeitung*, 23 August 2007; 'Die Grundkriterien sind nicht verhandelbar', *Tageszeitung*, 2 November 2007.
56 Be Berlin and Tempelhof Projekt GmbH, 'Planung und Entwicklung' (undated webpage), http://www.tempelhoferfreiheit.de/ueber-die-tempelhofer-freiheit/planung-entwicklung/planungsgeschichte [accessed 16 March 2013].
57 Be Berlin and Tempelhof Projekt GmbH, 'Planung und Entwicklung' (undated webpage), http://www.tempelhoferfreiheit.de/ueber-die-tempelhofer-freiheit/planung-entwicklung/planungsgeschichte [accessed 16 March 2013].
58 Ibid.
59 Tempelhof für Alle, 'Zu diesem Blog', 6 May 2012, http://tfa.blogsport.de [accessed 6 June 2013].
60 Tempelhof für Alle, 'Tempelhof Pioniere', 17 May 2010, http://tfa.blogsport.de/2010/05/17/tempelhof-pioniere [accessed 6 June 2013].
61 Aperto, 'Tempelhofer Freiheit' (undated webpage), https://www.aperto.de/start/referenzen/tempelhofer-freiheit.html [accessed 25 February 2013].
62 Harald Simons, Annabell Reinel and Frank Kühn, 'Volkswirtschaftliche Auswirkungen eines Verzichts auf eine Teilbebauung des Tempelhofer Flugfeldes', October 2012, http://www.tempelhoferfreiheit.de/nc/ueber-die-tempelhofer-freiheit/aktuelles/veroeffentlichungen/?page1 [accessed 6 June 2013].
63 Be Berlin and Tempelhof Projekt GmbH, 'Standortkonferenz' (undated webpage), http://www.tempelhoferfreiheit.de/ueber-die-tempelhofer-freiheit/aktuelles/nachrichten/standortkonferenz [accessed 10 March 2013].
64 Unless otherwise stated, references to the 'masterplan' are taken from Senatsverwaltung für Stadtentwicklung und Umwelt, et al., 'Freiraum für die Stadt von Morgen: Informationen zur Entwicklung des Ehemaligen Flughafens Tempelhof' (2013), http://www.tempelhoferfreiheit.de/fileadmin/user_upload/Ueber_die_Tempelhofer_Freiheit/Aktuelles_neu/Downloads/2013-04_Faltblatt_Tempelhofer_Freiheit.pdf [accessed 16 July 2013].

65　Senatsverwaltung für Stadtentwicklung und Wohnen, Be Berlin and Tempelhof Projekt GmbH, 'Planung und Entwicklung: Masterplan' (undated webpage), www.thf-berlin.de/planung-und-entwicklung/masterplan-tempelhofer-freiheit/ [accessed 3 September 2013].
66　Martin Rank, 'Müller wirbt mit günstigem Wohnen', *Die Tageszeitung*, 6 March 2013.
67　Be Berlin and Tempelhof Projekt GmbH, 'Freiraum für die Stadt von Morgen' (2013), http://www.tempelhoferfreiheit.de/fileadmin/user_upload/Presse/Standortkonferenz/Freiraum-für-die-Stadt-von-morgen.pdf [accessed 9 March 2013].
68　Almut Jirku, 'Historic Transport Landscapes in Berlin', in *Proceedings of the International L'Europe de L'Air Conferences on Aviation Architecture:Liverpool (1999), Berlin (2000), Paris (2001)*, ed. Bob Hawkins, Gabriele Lechner and Paul Smith (London: English Heritage, 2005), 210–15 (210).
69　Cranz, *The Politics of Park Design*, 1–56.
70　Jirku, 'Historic Transport Landscapes in Berlin', 210–11.
71　Cranz, *The Politics of Park Design*, 1–56 especially 42–6.
72　Joyce, *The Rule of Freedom*, 222–4.
73　Be Berlin and Tempelhof Projekt GmbH, 'Freiraum für die Stadt von Morgen' (2013), http://www.tempelhoferfreiheit.de/fileadmin/user_upload/Presse/Standortkonferenz/Freiraum-für-die-Stadt-von-morgen.pdf [accessed 9 March 2013].
74　Ibid.
75　Joyce, *The Rule of Freedom*, 222–4.
76　Ibid., 222.
77　'Be Berlin and Tempelhof Projekt GmbH, 'Freiraum für die Stadt von Morgen' (2013), http://www.tempelhoferfreiheit.de/fileadmin/user_upload/Presse/Standortkonferenz/Freiraum-für-die-Stadt-von-morgen.pdf [accessed 9 March 2013].
78　Grün Berlin GmbH, *Tempelhofer Park: Besucherinformation/ Visitor Information* (Berlin: Be Berlin, April 2010), unpaginated leaflet.
79　Anon., 'Park in Tempelhofer Feld wird abends dicht gemacht', *Welt Kompakt*, 23 April 2010; Anon., 'Tempelhofer Feld schließt abends seine Tore', *Berliner Morgenpost*, 23 April 2010.
80　Eva Kalwa, 'Rasenspiele statt Rosinenbomber', *Die Tagesspiegel*, 7 May 2010; M. Falkner, C. Brüning, and S. Pletl, 'Die neue Rollbahn: Der ehemalige Flughafen Tempelhof ist jetzt Berlins größter Park. Zehntausende Berliner erkunden das riesige Gelände', *Berliner Morgenpost*, 9 May 2010.
81　K. Pezzei, 'Der Zaun fällt-ein bisschen', *Die Tageszeitung*, 29 December 2009.
82　Reclaim Tempelhof, 'Auswertung vom 8. Mai', 25 May 2010, http://tempelhof.blogsport.de/2010/05/25/auswertung-vom-8-mai-2010/#more-111 [accessed 10 March 2013].
83　Initiatives include Nachrichten aus Nord- Neukölln, http://nk44.blogsport.de [accessed 17 May 2013; 100% Tempelhofer Feld, http://www.thf100.de/start.html [accessed 17 May 2013]; and Tempelhof für Alle http://tfa.blogsport.de [accessed 17 May 2013].
84　Amt für Statistik Berlin-Brandenburg, 'Volksentscheids 'Tempelhofer Feld' am 24. Mai 2014: Ergebnis des Volksentscheids', www.wahlen-berlin.de/abstimmungen/ve2014_tfeld/ergebnisprozent.asp?sel1=6053&sel2=0798 [accessed 12 July 2016].
85　https://thf100.de/news-initiative.html.
86　Tempelhof Projekt GmbH, Senatsverwaltung für Stadtentwicklung and Grün Berlin, 'Zwischen- und Pioniernutzer der Tempelhofer Freiheit' (2010), http://www.tempelhoferfreiheit.de/fileadmin/user_upload/Mitgestalten/Pioniere_der_Tempelhofer_Freiheit_Broschuere_Stand_Dezember_2010.pdf [accessed 27 May 2013], 2.

87 Till, 'Interim Use at a Former Death Strip?', 106.
88 Karen Franck and Quentin Stevens, *Loose Space: Possibility and Diversity in Urban Life* (Abingdon, Oxon: Routledge, 2007), 273.
89 Lange, 'From Cool Britannia to Generation Berlin?', 155.
90 Louekari, 'The Creative Potential of Berlin', 470.
91 Lanz, 'Be Berlin! Governing the City through Freedom', 1314.
92 Louekari, 'The Creative Potential of Berlin', 463.
93 Lange, 'From Cool Britannia to Generation Berlin?', 148.
94 Colomb, *Staging the New Berlin*, 240–3.
95 Studio Urban Catalyst, 'Urban Catalyst Final Report: Strategies for Temporary Uses – Potential Development of Urban Residual Areas in European Metropolises', September 2003, https://cordis.europa.eu/docs/publications/6579/65794761-19_en.doc, 5.
96 Tempelhof Projekt GmbH, Senatsverwaltung für Stadtentwicklung and Grün Berlin, 'Zwischen- und Pioniernutzer der Tempelhofer Freiheit' (2010), http://www.tempelhoferfreiheit.de/fileadmin/user_upload/Mitgestalten/Pioniere_der_Tempelhofer_Freiheit_Broschuere_Stand_Dezember_2010.pdf [accessed 27 May 2013].

Conclusion

1 See, for example, Maiken Umbach, 'How Similar Are Donald Trump and Adolf Hitler?' *International Business News,* 3 March 2017, https://www.ibtimes.co.uk/what-are-similarities-between-donald-trump-adolf-hitler-1582136?utm_campaign=Echobox&utm_medium=Social&utm_source=Twitter#link_time=1474302704 [accessed 14 April 2019]; Richard Evans, Mary Fulbrook, et al. 'Repeating History', in *The Times Literary Supplement,* 13 November 2018, https://www.the-tls.co.uk/articles/public/repeating-history-trump-fascist/ [accessed 14 April 2019].
2 David Art, 'The AfD and the End of Containment in Germany?' *German Politics and Society,* 127, 36 (3), (2018), 76–86, 78–9.
3 See, for example, Jasmin Siri, 'The Alternative for Germany after the 2017 Election', *German Politics,* 27 (1), (2018), 141–5.
4 Cited in Art, 'The AfD and the End of Containment in Germany?', 127, 36 (3), 81.
5 Evans, 'From Nazism to Never Again', 15.
6 'German fury at AfD Höcke's Holocaust Memorial Remark', *BBC,* 18 January 2017, https://www.bbc.co.uk/news/world-europe-38661621
7 Der Tagesspiegel, *'Denkmal der Schande' vor der Haustür von Höcke,* 22 November 2017, https://www.tagesspiegel.de/politik/protest-gegen-rechten-afd-politiker-denkmal-der-schande-vor-der-haustuer-von-hoecke/20616902.html [accessed 10 April 2019].
8 See, for example, 'Breiter Protest gegen die AfD in Münster', *Weltfälische Nachrichten* 22 February 2019, https://www.wn.de/Muenster/3665739-Demonstrationen-gegen-Meuthen-Auftritt-Breiter-Protest-gegen-die-AfD-in-Muenster; 'Lauter, friedlicher Protest gegen die AfD', *Stuttgarter Zeitung,* 18 May 2019, https://www.stuttgarter-zeitung.de/inhalt.demo-in-backnang-lauter-friedlicher-protest-gegen-die-afd.499da434-382f-4d31-b27b-8ae685733eef.html; 'In Berlin 20,000 detractors shout down 5,000 AfD protestors, *D.W.,* 27 May 2018. https://www.dw.com/en/in-berlin-20000-detractors-shout-down-5000-afd-protesters/a-43948489

9. Art, 'The AfD and the End of Containment in Germany', 84–5.
10. Evans, 'From Nazism to Never Again', 15
11. Caroline Gay, 'Remembering for the Future, Engaging with the Present: National Memory Management and the Dialectic of Normality in the Berlin Republic', in *Politics and Culture in Twentieth Century Germany,* ed. William Niven and James Jordan (Suffolk: Camden House, 2003), 205.
12. Ruth A. Starkman, 'Perpetual Impossibility? The Normalisation of German-Jewish Relations in the Berlin Republic', in *Transformations of the New Germany,* ed. Ruth A. Starkman (Basingstoke: Palgrave Macmillan, 2006).
13. Stefan Berger, *The Search for Normality: National Identity and Historical Consciousness in Germany since 1800* (Oxford: Berghahn Books, 2007); Glenn H. Penny, 'German Polycentrism and the Writing of History', *German History,* 30 (2012), 265–82.
14. Rainer Baumann and Gunther Hellmann, 'Germany and the Use of Military Force: "Total War", the "Culture of Restraint" and the Quest for Normality', *German Politics,* 10 (2001), 61–82; Adrian Hyde-Price and Charlie Jeffery, 'Germany in the European Union: Constructing Normality', *JCMS: Journal of Common Market Studies,* 39 (2001), 689–717.
15. Abel outlines and rejects this view as a criterion of 'good' German cinema. Marco Abel, *The Counter-Cinema of the Berlin School* (Suffolk: Camden House, 2013), 303.
16. Felix Lutz, 'Evolution and Normalization: Historical Consciousness in Germany', *German Politics and Society,* 30 (2012), 35–63.
17. Konrad H. Jarausch, 'Beyond the National Narrative: Implications of Reunification for Recent German History', *German History,* 28 (2010), 498–514.

Bibliography

Archives consulted:

Bundesarchiv Berlin-Lichterfelde (BArch)
Bundesarchiv Koblenz (BArch (Koblenz))
Landesarchiv, Berlin (LAB)
Landesdenkmalamtarchiv Berlin (LDA)
National Football Museum Archive, Preston, UK (NFMA)
Personal papers of Prof. Dr. Hans-Ernst Mittig (uncatalogued) (HEM)

Online archives:

Abgeordnetenhaus Berlin, online document archives https://www.parlament-berlin.de/de/Dokumente and at http://pardok.parlament-berlin.de/starweb/AHAB/

European Commission, Community Research and Development Information Service (CORDIS) https://cordis.europa.eu/en

Flughafen Tempelhof online document archive https://www.thf-berlin.de/en/news/downloads/ and previously at www.tempelhofer-feld.berlin.de/documents

Stiftung Topographie des Terrors, speeches archive https://www.topographie.de/presseservice/reden/

Individual files are cited in the footnotes only

Other websites, blogs, pamphlets and leaflets

100% Tempelhofer Feld, http://www.thf100.de/start.html, accessed 17 May 2013.

Amt für Statistik Berlin-Brandenburg. 'Volksentscheids "Tempelhofer Feld" am 24. Mai 2014: Ergebnis des Volksentscheids', www.wahlen-berlin.de/abstimmungen/ve2014_tfeld/ergebnisprozent.asp?sel1=6053&sel2=0798, accessed 12 July 2016.

Amt für Statistik Berlin-Brandenburg. 'Volksentscheid "Tempelhof bleibt Verkehrsflughafen" am 27. April 2008: Endgültiges Ergebnis', https://www.wahlen-berlin.de/historie/abstimmungen/Landeswahlleiterbericht_VE08.pdf, accessed 5 December 2018.

Aperto. 'Tempelhofer Freiheit' (undated webpage), https://www.aperto.de/start/referenzen/tempelhofer-freiheit.html, accessed 25 February 2013.

Aperto AG. *Mehr Freiheit fürs Feld: Aperto gibt ehemaligem Flughafengelände Berlin-Tempelhof* ein neues Gesicht, press release (4 April 2011), https://www.aperto.de/start/

presse/Pressemitteilungen-Archiv/pressemitteilungen-2011/Aperto-gestaltet-Tempelhofer-Freiheit.html, accessed 25 February 2013.
Be Berlin. 'Airport Building: The Mother of All Airports' (undated webpage), http://www.tempelhoferfreiheit.de/en/about-tempelhofer-freiheit/airport-building, accessed 17 June 2013.
Be Berlin and Tempelhof Projekt GmbH. 'Freiraum für die Stadt von Morgen' (2013), http://www.tempelhoferfreiheit.de/fileadmin/user_upload/Presse/Standortkonferenz/Freiraum-für-die-Stadt-von-morgen.pdf, accessed 9 March 2013.
Be Berlin and Tempelhof Projekt GmbH. 'Planung und Entwicklung' (undated webpage), http://www.tempelhoferfreiheit.de/ueber-die-tempelhofer-freiheit/planung-entwicklung/planungsgeschichte, accessed 16 March 2013.
Be Berlin and Tempelhof Projekt GmbH. 'Standortkonferenz' (undated webpage), http://www.tempelhoferfreiheit.de/ueber-die-tempelhofer-freiheit/aktuelles/nachrichten/standortkonferenz, accessed 10 March 2013.
Be Berlin, Senatsverwaltung für Stadtentwicklung und Umwelt and Tempelhofer Freiheit. *Tempelhofer Freiheit: Planung zur Parklandschaft* (June 2011).
Be Berlin, Senatsverwaltung für Stadtentwicklung und Umwelt and Tempelhofer Freiheit. *Park Landscape Development: Free Space for the City of Tomorrow* (Leaflet, March 2012).
Berlin SPD Antrag 40/01/2014 Historisches Gesamtkonzept für das Tempelhofer Feld umgehend entwickeln, 25. April 2016, https://parteitag.spd-berlin.de/cvtx_antrag/historisches-gesamtkonzept-fuer-das-tempelhofer-feld-umgehend-entwickeln/, accessed 24. April 2019.
Berliner Forum für Geschichte und Gegenwart. 'Denkmal für die Ereignisse des 17. Juni 1953' (undated webpage), http://www.bfgg.de/projekte/denkmal-17-juni-1953.html, accessed 29 August 2013.
Berliner Geschichtswerkstatt e.V., http://www.berliner-geschichtswerkstatt.de/, accessed 17 May 2013.
Bundesfinanzministerium. '"Platz des Volksaufstandes von 1953" – Bezirksamt Mitte befürwortet Benennungsvorschlag des BMF' (3 April 2013), http://www.bundesfinanzministerium.de/Content/DE/Standardartikel/Ministerium/20130303-Platzbenennung.html, accessed 2 October 2013.
Bundesfinanzministerium. 'Blick hinter die Kulissen', 7 March 2011, http://www.bundesfinanzministerium.de/Content/DE/Video/2011-03-07-blick-hinter-die-kulissen-textfassung.htm, accessed 21 September 2013.
Bundesfinanzministerium. 'Virtueller Besuch im BMF' (undated webpage), http://www.bundesfinanzministerium.de/Web/DE/Ministerium/Virtueller_Besuch/virtueller_besuch.html, accessed 17 November 2013.
Bundesregierung. 'Einladung zum Staatsbesuch: 150.000 beim Tag der offenen Tür' (undated webpage), http://www.bundesregierung.de/Webs/Breg/DE/Themen/Tag_der_offenen_Tuer/_node.html, accessed 22 September 2013.
Bundesstiftung Aufarbeitung. 'Plakatausstellung "Wir wollen freie Menschen sein! Der DDR-Volksaufstand vom 17. Juni 1953"' (16 January 2013), http://www.bundesstiftung-aufarbeitung.de/uploads/2013-pdf/17juni-ausstellung-stadt-gemeinde.pdf, accessed 20 February 2013.
CDU-Fraktion des Abgeordnetenhauses von Berlin. Pro-*Tempelhof*, information flyer ed. by F. Henkel (Berlin: CDU-Fraktion des Abgeordnetenhauses von Berlin, undated).

Doering, Uwe. *Aktuelles aus dem Abgeordnetenhaus* (2010), Left Party political flyer http://www.dielinke-treptow-koepenick.de/fileadmin/tk/thematisch/doering/info_agh_januar_2010.pdf, accessed September 2018.

Evans, Richard, Mary Fulbrook et al. 'Repeating History', *The Times Literary Supplement*, 13 November 2018, https://www.the-tls.co.uk/articles/public/repeating-history-trump-fascist/, accessed 14 April 2019.

Förderverein zum Gedenken an Nazi-Verbrechen um und auf dem Tempelhofer Flugfeld e.V., http://thf33-45.de/verein-2/, accessed 9 July 2016

Gedenkstätte Deutscher Widerstand and Aktives Museum Faschismus und Widerstand in Berlin e.V. 'Luftbrückenflugzeug C-47' (undated webpage), http://www.gedenktafeln-in-berlin.de/nc/gedenktafeln/gedenktafel-anzeige/bz/tempelhof-schoeneberg/tid/luftbrueckenflugzeug-1/, accessed 1 March 2013.

gmp Architekten von Gerkan Marg and Partner. 'Projects: Langemarck Hall, Olympic Stadium' (undated webpage), http://www.gmp-architekten.com/projects/langemarck-hall-olympic-stadium.html, accessed 12 December 2012.

Grün Berlin GmbH. *Tempelhofer Park: Besucherinformation/ Visitor Information* (Berlin: Be Berlin, April 2010), unpaginated leaflet.

Hübner, Holger, with the Gedenkstätte Deutscher Widerstand. 'Gedenktafeln in Berlin' (undated website), http://www.gedenktafeln-in-berlin.de/nc/gedenktafeln/gedenktafel-anzeige/tid/harro-schulze-boysen, accessed 13 June 2013.

Müller, Michael. *Park Landscape Development: Free Space for the City of Tomorrow*, leaflet produced by the Senatsverwaltung für Stadtentwicklung und Umwelt (March 2012), unpaginated.

Nachrichten aus Nord- Neukölln, http://nk44.blogsport.de, accessed 17 May 2013.

Online-Dialog Flughafen Tempelhof. 'Bustour und Online-Dialog Flughafen Tempelhof', 6 October 2007, http://www.youtube.com/watch?v=NZn7NNYskXs, accessed 6 June 2013.

Presse- Und Informationsamt des Landes Berlin. 'Leitkonzept für das Olympiagelände Berlin: Pressemitteilung', 29 April 2004, https://www.berlin.de/rbmskzl/aktuelles/pressemitteilungen/2004/pressemitteilung.47994.php, accessed 2 November 2017.

Schröder, Thies. *Flughafen Tempelhof*, information leaflet produced by the Senatsverwaltung für Stadtentwicklung und Umweltschutz, December 1994. No pagination.

Senatsverwaltung für Bildung, Jugend und Sport. *Leitkonzept für das Olympiagelände*, June 2004, https://www.parlament-berlin.de/ados/UASport/vorgang/0085.pdf, accessed 21 January 2018.

Senatsverwaltung für Stadtentwicklung und Umwelt. 'Pressebox: Ergebnisse Online-Dialog Tempelhof vorgestellt', 22 August 2007, http://www.stadtentwicklung.berlin.de/aktuell/pressebox/archiv_volltext.shtml?arch_0708/nachricht2763.html, accessed 15 March 2013.

Senatsverwaltung für Stadtentwicklung und Umwelt. 'Pressebox: 2. Phase Online-Dialog zum Flughafen-Tempelhof beendet', 8 November 2007, http://www.stadtentwicklung.berlin.de/aktuell/pressebox/archiv_volltext.shtml?arch_0711/nachricht2862.html, accessed 15 March 2013.

Senatsverwaltung für Stadtentwicklung und Umwelt et al. 'Freiraum für die Stadt von Morgen: Informationen zur Entwicklung des Ehemaligen Flughafens Tempelhof' (2013), http://www.tempelhoferfreiheit.de/fileadmin/user_upload/Ueber_die_Tempelhofer_Freiheit/Aktuelles_neu/Downloads/2013-04_Faltblatt_Tempelhofer_Freiheit.pdf, accessed 16 July 2013.

Senatsverwaltung für Stadtentwicklung und Wohnen, Be Berlin and Tempelhof Projekt GmbH. 'Planung und Entwicklung: Masterplan' (undated webpage), www.thf-berlin.de/planung-und-entwicklung/masterplan-tempelhofer-freiheit/, accessed 3 September 2013.

Simons, Harald Annabell Reinel and Frank Kühn. 'Volkswirtschaftliche Auswirkungen eines Verzichts auf eine Teilbebauung des Tempelhofer Flugfeldes' (October 2012), http://www.tempelhoferfreiheit.de/nc/ueber-die-tempelhofer-freiheit/aktuelles/veroeffentlichungen/?page1, accessed 6 June 2013.

SPD Berlin. *Für ein flugfreies Tempelhof*, information flyer (Berlin: SPD Berlin, undated).

Tempelhof Aufmachen. *Für Alle, Als Flughafen viel zu Schade!*, information flyer (Berlin: Tempelhof Aufmachen. Für Alle, undated).

Tempelhof für Alle homepage, http://tfa.blogsport.de, accessed 17 May 2013.

Tempelhof für Alle. 'Tempelhof Pioniere', 17 May 2010, http://tfa.blogsport.de/2010/05/17/tempelhof-pioniere, accessed 6 June 2013.

Tempelhof für Alle. 'Zu diesem Blog', 6 May 2012, http://tfa.blogsport.de, accessed 6 June 2013.

Tempelhof Projekt GmbH. 'Available Space: Airport Building' (undated webpage), http://www.tempelhoferfreiheit.de/en/organize-events-rent-invest/event-location/available-space-airport-building, accessed 20 November 2013.

Tempelhof Projekt GmbH. *Events und Messen*, https://www.thf-berlin.de/de/aktuelles/veranstaltungen/, accessed 22 March 2019.

Tempelhof Projekt GmbH. 'Ideal Conditions for Events', April 2018, https://www.thf-berlin.de/fileadmin/user_upload/Ideal_Conditions_for_Events.pdf, accessed 24 April 2019.

Tempelhof Projekt GmbH. 'Tasks' (undated webpage), http://www.tempelhoferfreiheit.de/en/about-tempelhofer-freiheit/project-partners/tempelhof-projekt-gmbh/task, accessed 25 February 2013.

Tempelhof Projekt GmbH. *Tempelhofer Freiheit Unlimited: Event Location Tempelhof Airport* (Berlin: Tempelhof Projekt GmbH, 2011).

Tempelhof Projekt GmbH, Senatsverwaltung für Stadtentwicklung and Grün Berlin. 'Zwischen- und Pionierenutzer der Tempelhofer Freiheit', 2010, http://www.tempelhoferfreiheit.de/fileadmin/user_upload/Mitgestalten/Pioniere_der_Tempelhofer_Freiheit_Broschuere_Stand_Dezember_2010.pdf, accessed 27 May 2013.

Umbach, Maiken. 'How Similar Are Donald Trump and Adolf Hitler?' *International Business News*, 3 March 2017 https://www.ibtimes.co.uk/what-are-similarities-between-donald-trump-adolf-hitler-1582136?utm_campaign=Echobox&utm_medium=Social&utm_source=Twitter#link_time=1474302704, accessed 14 April 2019.

Vereinigung 17 Juni 1953. 'Endlich: "Platz des Volksaufstandes von 1953"', 29 March 2013, http://17juni1953.wordpress.com/2013/03/29/endlich-platz-des-volksaufstandes-von-1953, accessed 1 October 2013.

Volxsport statt Olympia. 'Widerstand gegen Olympia' (undated pamphlet).

ZebralogTHF. *Prämierung Ideen Online-Dialog Flughafen Tempelhof* (21 November 2007), http://www.youtube.com/watch?v=XZsQ-tB8DY8, accessed 6 June 2013.

Newspaper articles

B.Z. 'Finanzministerium Klagt gegen Arbeitsgemeinschaft 13. August', 9 September 2004.*

B.Z. 'Sollen die Nazi-Skulpturen am Olympia-Stadion Verhüllt werden?', 30 May 2006.

BBC. 'German Fury at AfD Höcke's Holocaust Memorial Remark', 18 January 2017, https://www.bbc.co.uk/news/world-europe-38661621
Berger, Ursel. 'Die Athleten Von Olympia-Berlin', *Der Tagesspiegel*, 19 February 1993.
Berliner Morgenpost. 'Ab Ende Juni keine Flüchtlinge mehr am Flughafen Tempelhof', 19 March 2019, https://www.morgenpost.de/bezirke/tempelhof-schoeneberg/article21 6695983/106-neue-Stellen-fuer-das-Fluechtlingsamt.html, accessed 24 April 2019.
Berliner Morgenpost. 'Ein weites Feld: neue Ausstellung im Flughafen Tempelhof', 4 September 2018, https://www.morgenpost.de/berlin/article215251273/Ein-weites-Feld-neue-Ausstellung-im-Flughafen-Tempelhof.html
Berliner Morgenpost. 'Tempelhofer Feld schließt abends seine Tore', 23 April 2010.
Berliner Woche. 'Neue Ausstellung über den Flughafen stellt NS-Zeit in den Mittelpunkt', 14 September 2018.
Berliner Zeitung. 'Ein Bau so dunkel wie das Nazi Reich', 23 May 1997.
Berliner Zeitung. 'Gedenktafel zur Diamantenen Hochzeit', 27 July 1997, http://www.berliner-zeitung.de/archiv/gedenktafel-zur-diamantenen-hochzeit,10810590,9158320.html.
Berliner Zeitung. 'So leben die Flüchtling im Containerdorf', 29 May 2018, https://www.berliner-zeitung.de/berlin/tempelhofer-feld-so-leben-die-fluechtlinge-im-containerdorf-30519934
Berliner Zeitung. 'Widerstandsgruppe Rote Kapelle geehrt', 21 November 1994, http://www.berliner-zeitung.de/archiv/widerstandsgruppe-rote-kapelle-geehrt,10810590,8886012.html.
Bernau, N. 'Bildersturm am Olympiastadion', *Berliner Zeitung*, 31 May 2006.
Bernau, N. 'So viel Flughafen wird nie wieder sein in Berlin', *Berliner Zeitung*, 16 November 2006.
Bild. '100 Dachdecker kämpfen für Tempelhof', 8 February 2008.**
Bild. '529 053 Stimmen für City-Airport', 28 April 2008.
Bild. 'Berliner, rettet Tempelhof!', 27 April 2008.
Bild. 'Der Rosinenbomber darf nicht sterben!', 6 April 2008.
Bild. 'Ganze Berliner FDP sagt JA zu *Tempelhof*, 12 December 2007.
Bild. 'Mehrheit der Berliner ist für den Erhalt von *Tempelhof*, 22 April 2008.
Bild. 'Nur noch 49 403 Stimmen bis zur Landung', 22 December 2007.
Bild. 'Warum Die Legende Nicht Sterben Darf', 23 April 2008.
Borgelt, Hans. 'Olympia 2000 - eine Ideenfabrik', *Der Tagesspiegel*, 25 October 1992.
Brüggemann, Axel. '100 Gründe für den Flughafen der Herzen', *Bild*, 25 April 2008.
Bruns, H. 'Senatorin ätzt gegen Tempelhof-Freunde', *Bild*, 6 March 2008.
Buchholz. 'Entfernen hilft auch nichts', *Stuttgarter Zeitung*, 2 June 2006.
Buddensieg, Tilmann. 'Hierzulande ein Stildiktat', *Frankfurter Allgemeine Zeitung*, 23 January 1993.
Buddensieg, Tilmann. 'Olympia 1936-Olympia 2000: Anmerkungen zum Reichssportfeld/ auf dem Wege zum Metropole (12) Berlin-Krisen, Kräfte und Konzepte', *Der Tagesspiegel*, 13 December 1992.
Colmenares, K. 'Wowereit bleibt Stur: Tempelhof - Jetzt erst recht!', *Bild*, 12 December 2007.
DPA/DS. 'Berlin plant einen See auf dem Tempelhofer Feld', *Die Welt*, 7 March 2013.
DPA/ The Local. 'Tempelhof to become enormous city park', *The Local*, 31 August 2009, http://www.thelocal.de/20090831/21611.
DW. 'Gauland bezeichnet NS-Zeit als "Vogelschiss in der Geschichte"', 2 June 2018, https://www.dw.com/de/gauland-bezeichnet-ns-zeit-als-vogelschiss-in-der-geschichte/a-44054219.

DW. 'In Berlin 20, 000 detractors shout down 5, 000 AfD protestors', 27 May 2018, https://www.dw.com/en/in-berlin-20000-detractors-shout-down-5000-afd-protesters/a-439 48489.
Falkner, M., C. Brüning and S. Pletl. 'Die neue Rollbahn: Der ehemalige Flughafen Tempelhof ist jetzt Berlins größter Park. Zehntausende Berliner erkunden das riesige Gelände', *Berliner Morgenpost*, 9 May 2010.
Fischer, Vera. '"Maskenball" für Sportler-Kolosse?', *Berliner Morgenpost*, 7 March 1993.
Flatau, S. and A. Klesse. 'Riesiger Andrang auf dem Flugfeld Tempelhof', *Berliner Morgenpost*, 9 May 2010.
Gürgen and Itzek. 'Tempelhofs dunkle Seite', *TAZ.de*, 2 April 2012, http://www.taz.de/!90845/.
Hahne, Peter. 'Über Rosinenbomber und den Kampf David gegen Goliath', *Bild*, 26 April 2008.
Haubrich, Rainer. 'Bulldozer Gegen Breker', *Die Welt*, 31 May 2006.
Herzinger, Richard. 'Sollen Nazi-Skulpturen verhüllt werden?', *Welt am Sonntag*, 5 June 2006.
Kalwa, Eva. 'Rasenspiele statt Rosinenbomber', *Der Tagesspiegel*, 7 May 2010.
Kaminski-Morrow, David. 'Last-Ditch Referendum Fails to Support Keeping Historic Berlin Tempelhof Open', *Flightglobal: Aviation Connected*, 28 April 2008, http://www.flightglobal.com/news/articles/last-ditch-referendum-fails-to-support-keeping-historic-berlin-tempelhof-223306/.
kla. 'Luxury Project Suspended: Protests in Berlin Save the Wall for Now', *Spiegel International Online*, 4 March 2013, http://www.spiegel.de/international/germany/investor-seeks-compromise-in-controversial-berlin-wall-a-886714.html
Kotte, Hans-Hermann and Hans Monath. 'Künstlerische Entnazifizierungsversuche zur Rettung der "Jahrtausendspiele"', *Die Tageszeitung*, 27 January 1993.
Krauel, Torsten. 'Tempelhof: Der schönste Flughafen der Welt', *Welt am Sonntag*, 23 August 2009.
Lambrecht, M. 'Rexrodt Mag den Treuhand-Sitz', *Berliner Zeitung*, 30 January 1993.
Lang-Lendorff, Antje. 'Bis die Fotos Wieder Hängen', *Berliner Zeitung*, 23 June 2005.
Lautenschläger, Rolf. 'Lea Rosh mag keine Nackten Nazis', *Die Tageszeitung*, 31 May 2006.
Lessen, C. van. 'Im Sinkflug', *Der Tagesspiegel*, 28 April 2008.
Loy, Thomas. 'Kein "Designerpark" für Tempelhofer Flugfeld', *Der Tagesspiegel*, 14 August 2012.
Mittig, Hans Ernst interviewed by Gerd Nowakowski published as 'Ein Ort des militanten Totenkults', in *Die Tageszeitung*, 17 January 1994.
Möller, B. 'Bewundert und erledigt: Die "Mutter aller Flughäfen"', *Hamburger Abendblatt*, 11 January 2007.
Müll, C. '100 Berliner und Ihr Ja zu Tempelhof', *Bild*, 22 April 2008.
Paul, U. 'Macht auf das Tor', *Berliner Zeitung*, 8 May 2010.
Pezzei, K. 'Der Zaun fällt-ein bisschen', *Die Tageszeitung*, 29 December 2009.
Prelinger, Dieter. 'Olympiadenkmale von 1936', *Der Tagesspiegel*, 8 November 1992.
Rank, Martin. 'Müller wirbt mit günstigem Wohnen', *Die Tageszeitung*, 6 March 2013.
Ruppert, Wolfgang. 'In Stein gehauener Rassenwahn', *Die Zeit*, 17 September 1993.
Santen, O. 'Rettet den Berliner City-Airport! 67 Top-Manager für Tempelhof', *Bild*, 15 April 2008.
Sauerbier, M. 'Berlin braucht Tempelhof. Berlin will Tempelhof', *Bild*, 16 January 2008.
Sauerbier, M. 'Wieder 11 285-mal JA für den Flugafen', *Bild*, 19 January 2008.
Schindler. 'Schwingen im Körper der Stadt', *Frankfurter Rundschau*, 2 November 2004.

Schmid, T. 'Klägliches Ende eines großen Traums', *Die Welt*, 30 October 2008.
Schölkopf, K. 'Tempelhof-Gegner starten Offensive', *Die Welt*, 28 February 2008.
Senftleben, R. and F. Hartmann. 'Wir halten Tempelhof am Leben', *Bild*, 18 December 2007.
Siedler, Wolf Jobst. 'Anstössige Athleten. Überflüssige Diskussion: Die Skulpturen des Olympiageländes', *Frankfurter Allgemeine Zeitung*, 12 January 1993.
Der Spiegel. 'Ein Kapitaler Selbstbetrug', 5/1993, February 1993, 49–51.
Der Spiegel. 'Gauland provoziert mit Rede zu Deutschlands Nazi-Vergangenheit', 14 September 2017, https://www.spiegel.de/politik/deutschland/alexander-gauland-provoziert-mit-rede-zu-deutschlands-nazi-vergangenheit-a-1167750.html.
Der Spiegel. 'Herrenmenschen in Cellophan', 14/1993, April 1993, 62–70.
Spiegel Online International. 'In East Germany the Neo-Nazis are Winning', 21 August 2002, http://www.spiegel.de/international/germany/press-review-on-the-german-far-right-20-years-after-the-rostock-riots-a-851193.html.
Spiegel Online International. Christopher Stoltzenberg, 'Debunking Hitler: Marking the Site of the Führer's Bunker', 9 June 2006, http://www.spiegel.de/international/debunking-hitler-marking-the-site-of-the-fuehrer-s-bunker-a-420483.html.
Stuttgarter Zeitung. 'Lauter, friedlicher Protest gegen die AfD', 18 May 2019, https://www.stuttgarter-zeitung.de/inhalt.demo-in-backnang-lauter-friedlicher-protest-gegen-die-afd.499da434-382f-4d31-b27b-8ae685733eef.html
Der Tagespiegel. '"Denkmal der Schande" vor der Haustür von Höcke', 22 November 2017, https://www.tagesspiegel.de/politik/protest-gegen-rechten-afd-politiker-denkmal-der-schande-vor-der-haustuer-von-hoecke/20616902.html.
Der Tagespiegel. 'Der Flughafen Tempelhof und seine Geschichte', 4 September 2018, https://www.tagesspiegel.de/berlin/neue-ausstellung-in-berlin-der-flughafen-tempelhof-und-seine-geschichte/22995348.html.
Der Tagespiegel. 'Oppermann über Gauland: "Geschmacklose Geschichtsklitterung"', 15 September 2017, https://www.tagesspiegel.de/politik/rede-des-afd-spitzenkandidaten-oppermann-ueber-gauland-geschmacklose-geschichtsklitterung/20332986.html.
Der Tagesspiegel. 'Schwungvoller Start, abendliche Turbulenzen. 100 000 feiern Eröffnung des Tempelhofer Parks. Protestler klettern über die Umzäunung', 9 May 2010.
Der Tagesspiegel. 'Tempelhof-Gegner: Volksbegehren Ja, Volksentscheid Nein', 21 December 2007.
Die Tageszeitung. 'Die Grundkriterien sind nicht verhandelbar', 2 November 2007.
Vehlewald, Hans-Jörg. 'Riesenstreit um Figuren am Berlin WM-Stadion: Ist das Nazi-Kunst?', *Bild*, 31 May 2006.
Voigt, J. 'Der Flughafen Tempelhof als großer Gemeinschaftsgarten', *Berliner Zeitung*, 23 August 2007.
von Becker, Peter. 'Ja, macht nur einen Masterplan', *Der Tagesspiegel*, 7 December 2008.
Wagner, Franz Josef. 'Lieber Klaus Wowereit', *Bild*, 21 April 2008.
Die Welt. 'Tempelhof-Gegner werben für Nein-Stimmen', 8 March 2008.
Welt Kompakt. 'Park in Tempelhofer Feld wird abends dicht gemacht', 23 April 2010.
Weltfälische Nachrichteni. 'Breiter Protest gegen die AfD in Münster', 22 February 2019, https://www.wn.de/Muenster/3665739-Demonstrationen-gegen-Meuthen-Auftritt-Breiter-Protest-gegen-die-AfD-in-Muenster.
Westphal, Dirk. 'Neue Chance für Tempelhof', *Welt am Sonntag*, 21 November 2004.
Westphal, D. and S. Schölkopf. 'Goodbye Tempelhof', *Welt Am* Sonntag, 26 October 2008.

*Unless otherwise indicated (such as by the inclusion of page numbers or a different url), all articles were accessed via LexisNexis Academic.
**Unless otherwise indicated (such as by the inclusion of page numbers), all *Bild* articles were accessed at www.bild.de.

Books and journal articles:

Abel, Marco. *The Counter-Cinema of the Berlin School* (Suffolk: Camden House, 2013).
Allinson, Mark. *Politics and Popular Opinion in East Germany, 1945–1968* (Manchester: Manchester University Press, 2000).
Anon. '"Reichstagslösung" für das Berliner Olympiastadion? - Senat bringt neue Umbauvariante ins Gespräch', *BauNetz*, 24 November 1997, http://www.baunetz.de/meldungen/Meldungen_Senat_bringt_neue_Umbauvariante_ins_Gespraech_27 57.html, accessed 13 November 2013.
Anon. 'Zur Neugestaltung der Reichshauptstadt', *Bauen-Siedeln-Wohnen*, 18 (1938), 246.
Arbeitsgemeinschaft Reinald Eckert und Wolfgang Schäche. 'Das Ehemalige Reichssportfeld, Geschichte und Bestand', in *Thies Schröder, Senatsverwaltung für Stadtentwicklung und Umweltschutz*, ed. Kooperatives Gutachterverfahren Olympisches Dorf Und Olympiagelände (Berlin: Kulturbuchverlag, 1993), 32–48, 43.
Arias, A. 'Fernando Vallejo's Ruinous Heterotopias: The Queer Subject in Latin America's Urban Spaces', in *Telling Ruins in Latin America*, ed. M. Lazzara and V. Unruh (New York: Palgrave Macmillan, 2008), 229–40.
Art, David. 'The AfD and the End of Containment in Germany?' *German Politics and Society*, 127, 36:3, (2018), 76–86.
Ascher Barnstone, Deborah. *The Transparent State: Architecture and Politics in Postwar Germany* (London: Routledge, 2005).
Assmann, Aleida. *Die Lange Schatten der Vergangenheit: Erinnerungskultur und Geschichtspolitik* (Munich: Verlag C. H. Beck, 2006).
Assmann, Jan. 'Collective Memory and Cultural Identity', *New German Critique*, 65 (1995), 125–33.
Atelier für Lichtplanung Kress und Adams. 'Das Lichtkonzept', in *Das Detlev-Rohwedder-Haus: Architektur und Nutzung*, ed. Hans-Joachim Henzgen and Andrea Ulrich for the Bundesministerium der Finanzen Referat Presse und Information (Berlin: Bundesbauamt III, 1999), 22–3.
Azharyu, Maoz. 'German Reunification and the Politics of Street Names: The Case of East Berlin', *Political Geography*, 16 (1997), 479–93.
Baker, Mona. *Translation and Conflict: A Narrative Account* (London: Routledge, 2006).
Baumann, Rainer and Gunther Hellmann. 'Germany and the Use of Military Force: "Total War", the "Culture of Restraint" and the Quest for Normality', *German Politics*, 102001), 61–82.
Bauman, Zygmunt. *Modernity and the Holocaust* (Cambridge: Polity, 1989).
Beckett, Katherine and Steve Herbert. 'Dealing with Disorder: Social Control in the Post-industrial City', *Theoretical Criminology*, 12 (1) (2008), 5–30.
Berger, Stefan. *The Search for Normality: National Identity and Historical Consciousness in Germany since 1800* (Oxford: Berghahn Books, 2007).
Billingham, P. *Sensing the City through Television: Urban Identities in Fictional Drama* (Bristol: Intellect, 2000).

Blüm, Norbert. 'Die Hauptstadt-Debatte des Deutschen Bundestages vom 20. Juni 1991', in *Broschüre*: Dokumente zur Bundeshauptstadt Berlin, ed. Presse- und Informationsamt des Landes Berlin (Berlin: Presse- und Informationsamt des Landes Berlin, 1994).

Bodenschatz, Harald, Friedhelm Fischer and Engelbert Luetke-Daldrup. 'Berlin: Hauptstadt mit Vergangenheit - zur Geschichte der Standorte für Regierungsfunktionen', in *Architektur in Berlin - Jahrbuch,* ed. Lothar Juckel for the Architektenkammer Berlin (Hamburg: Junius Verlag GmbH, 1992).

Bodenschatz, Harald, Johannes Geisenhof and Dorothea Tscheschner. Report, 'Gutachten zur Bau-, Stadtbau- und Nutzungsgeschichtlichen Bedeutung des "Hauses der Parlementarier" (ehem. Reichsbankgebäude bzw. Zk-Gebäude der SED), des Treuhandgebäudes (Detlev-Rohwedder-Haus, ehem. Gebäude des Reichsluftfahrtministerium bzw. Haus Der Ministerien) und des ehemaligen Staatsratsgebäudes' (Berlin: Planungsbüro Gruppe DASS, 1993).

Bröckling, Ulrich, Susanne Krasmann and Thomas Lemke, eds. *Governmentality: Current Issues and Future Challenges* (London: Routledge, 2010).

Buddensieg, Tilmann. *Berliner Labyrinth: Preußische Raster; vom Lustgarten zum Alexanderplatz, vom Reichstag ins Reichssportfeld, von Moabit nach Britz, vom Kemperplatz zum Waldsängerpfad - 'Ich sehe keinen Ausweg aus diesem Labyrinth' (Schinkel, 1829)* (Berlin: Wagenbach, 1993).

Bundesministerium der Finanzen. *The Detlev Rohwedder Building - German History Reflected* ed. D. Hansen and M. Jachmann (Berlin: Bundesministerium der Finanzen, 2008).

Burg, Annegret and Senatsverwaltung für Bau- und Wohnungswesen. *Neue Berlinische Architektur: Eine Debatte* (Berlin: Birkhäuser Verlag, 1994).

Bushart, Magdalena. 'Dem Bildwerke auf dem Reichssportfeld in Berlin', in *Das Kunstwerk als Geschichtsdokument: Festschrift für Hans-Ernst Mittig*, ed. Annette Tietenberg (Munich: Klinkhardt und Biermann, 1999), 129–43.

Caldwell, Peter C. and Karrin Hanshew. *Germany since 1945: Politics, Culture and Society* (London: Bloomsbury, 2018).

Campbell John L. and Ove Kaj Pedersen. *The Rise of Neo-liberalism and Institutional Analysis* (Oxford: Princeton University Press, 2001).

Castillo, Greg. 'The Nylon Curtain: Architectural Unification in Divided Berlin', in *Berlin: Divided City 1945-1989*, ed. Philip Broadbent and Sabine Hake (Oxford: Berghahn Books, 2010), 46–55.

Cesarani, David. *After Eichmann: Collective Memory and Holocaust Since 1961* (London: Routledge, 2013).

Chaplin, Sarah. 'Heterotopia Deserta: Las Vegas and Other Spaces', in *Intersections: Architectural Histories and Critical Theories*, ed. Iain Borden and Jane Rendell (London: Routledge, 2000).

Childs, David. *The GDR: Moscow's German Ally* (Oxon: Routledge ,2015).

Cicchini, Marco. 'A New "Inquisition"? Police Reform, Urban Transparency and House Numbering in Eighteenth-Century Geneva', *Urban History,* 39 (4) (2012), 614–23.

Collins, Catherine and Alexandra Opie. 'When Places Have Agency: Roadside Shrines as Traumascapes', *Continuum: Journal of Media and Cultural Studies*, 24 (2010), 107–18.

Colomb, Claire. 'Requiem for a Lost *Palast*: "Revanchist Urban Planning" and "Burdened Landscapes" of the German Democratic Republic in the New Berlin', *Planning Perspectives*, 22 (2007), 283–323.

Colomb, Claire. *Staging the New Berlin: Place Marketing and the Politics of Urban Reinvention Post-1989* (London: Routledge, 2012).

Conradi, Peter. 'Gastvortrag: Parlaments- und Regierungsbauten in Bonn und Berlin', in *Machtarchitekturen: Beiträge zur Diskussion Politischer Bauten u.a. von Bruno Flierl, Peter Conradi, Werner Sewing, Axel Schultes und Charlotte Frank*, ed. Florian Dreher and Klaus-Tilman Fritzsche (Berlin: Universität der Künste, 2004), 67–77.

Cooke, Paul. *Representing East Germany since Unification: From Colonisation to Nostalgia* (Oxford: Berg, 2005).

Copley, Clare. 'Curating Tempelhof: Negotiating the Multiple Histories of Berlin's Symbol of Freedom', *Urban History*, 44 (4) (2017), 698–717. doi:10.1017/S0963926816000869.

Copley, Clare. 'Stones Do Not Speak for Themselves': Disentangling Berlin's Palimpsest', *Fascism*, 8 (2) (2019), 219–49. doi: https://doi.org/10.1163/22116257-00802006.

Coppi, Hans. *Dieser Tod paßt zu mir: Harro Schulze-Boysen, Grenzgänger im Widerstand, Briefe 1915 – 1942* (Berlin: Aufbau-Verlag, 1999).

Cowan, D. and A. Marsh. 'From Need to Choice, Welfarism to Advanced Liberalism? Problematics of Social Housing Allocation', *Legal Studies*, 25 (2005), 22–48.

Crampton, Jeremy W. and Stuart Elden. 'Introduction: Space, Knowledge and Power: Foucault and Geography', in *Space, Knowledge and Power: Foucault and Geography*, ed. Jeremy W. Crampton and Stuart Elden (Oxon: Routledge, 2016), 1–19.

Crang, M. 'Envisioning Urban Histories: Bristol as Palimpsest, Postcards and Snapshots', *Environment and Planning A*, 28 (1996), 429–52.

Cranz, Galen. *The Politics of Park Design: A History of Urban Parks in America* (London: MIT Press, 1982).

Czaplicka, John. 'History, Aesthetics and Contemporary Commemorative Practice in Berlin', *New German Critique*, 65 (1995), 155–87.

Damm, Stefan, Klaus Siebenhaar and Karsten Zang, *Schauplatz Berlin 1933. 1945. 1961. Heute* (Berlin: Bostelmann and Siebenhaar, 2005).

Dean, Mitchell. *Governmentality: Power and Rule in Modern Society* (London: Sage, 2010).

Dehaene Michiel and Lieven de Cauter. *Heterotopia and the City: Public Space in a Postcivil Society* (Oxon.: Routledge, 2008).

Demps, Laurenz, Eberhard Schultz and Klaus Wettig. *Das Bundesfinanzministerium: Ein Belasteter Ort?* (Berlin: Parthas, 2001).

Dittrich, Elke. *Der Flughafen Tempelhof in Entwurfszeichnungen und Modellen 1934–44* (Berlin: Lukas Verlag, 2005).

Dittrich, Elke. *Ernst Sagebiel: Leben und Werk 1892–1970* (Berlin: Lukas Verlag, 2005).

Dolff-Bonekämper, Gabi. 'Berlin-Tempelhof', in *Berlin Tempelhof, Liverpool Speke, Paris Le Bourget: Airport Architecture of the Thirties*, ed. Paul Smith and Bernard Toulier (Paris: Editions du Patrimoine, 2000), 30–62.

Donath, Matthias. *Architektur in Berlin 1933–1945 - Ein Stadtführer* (Berlin: Lukas Verlag for the Landesdenkmalamt Berlin, 2004).

Donath, Matthias. *Garden Guide: The Olympic Grounds - Former Reichssportfeld* (Berlin: Landesdenkmalamt (Berlin) and Museumspädagogischer Dienst (Berlin), 2001).

Donath, Matthias. 'Konservieren und kommentieren – Denkmalvermittlung für das Olympiagelände', in *Sport Stätten Kultur / Sport Sites Culture,* ed. Fiona Laudamus, Michael Petzet and John Ziesemer (Munich: ICOMOS Nationalkomitee der Bundesrepublik Deutschland, 2002), 81–8.

Donath, Matthias, Gabriele Schultz and Michael Hoffmann. *Denkmale in Berlin-Bezirk Tempelhof-Schoeneberg Orsteile Tempelhof, Mariendorf, Marienfelde und Lichtenrade* (Berlin: Michael Imhof for the Landesdenkmalamt Berlin, 2007).
Dreher, Florian and Klaus-Tilman Fritzsche. 'Vorwort: Architektur und Repräsentation - Demokratie als Bauaufgabe', in *Machtarchitekturen: Beiträge zur Diskussion Politischer Bauten u.a von Bruno Flierl, Peter Conradi, Werner Sewing, Axel Schultes und Charlotte Frank*, ed. Florian Dreher and Klaus-Tilman Fritzsche (Berlin: Universität der Künste, 2004), 6–7;
Drieschner, Axel. 'Ernst Sagebiel's Tempelhof Airport: Typology, Iconography and Politics', in *Historic Airports: Proceedings of the International L'Europe de L'Air Conferences on Aviation Architecture Liverpool (1999), Berlin (2000), Paris (2001)*, ed. Bob Hawkins, Gabriele Lechner and Paul Smith (London: English Heritage, 2005), 100–11.
Durth, Werner and Paul Siegel. *Baukultur: Spiegel gesellschaftlichen Wandels* (Berlin: Jovis Verlag GmbH, 2009).
Eisenstadt, S. N. 'Multiple Modernities', *Daedalus*, 129 (Winter 2000), 1–29.
Elden, Stuart. 'Governmentality, Calculation, Territory', *Environment and Planning D: Society and Space*, 25 (3) (2007), 562–80.
Endlich, Stefanie. 'Berlin', in *Gedenkstätten für die Opfer des Nationalsozialismus. Eine Dokumentation. Band II: Bundesländer Berlin, Brandenburg, Mecklenburg-Vorpommern, Sachsen-Anhalt, Sachsen, Thüringen*, ed. Ulrike Puvogel (Bonn: Bundeszentrale für politische Bildung, 2000), 27–228 (119).
Endlich, Stefanie. 'Geschichte des Tempelhofer Feldes und des Flughafens Tempelhof. Ortsbegehung, Pläne, Diskussionen', in *Verein Aktives Museum: Mitgliederrundbrief* 66, January 2012, 4–7
Endlich, Stefanie. '"Historische Kommentierung" am Berliner Olympiastadion', in *Verein Aktives Museum: Mitgliederrundbrief 53* (Berlin, June 2005), 12–16.
Endlich, Stefanie. 'Historische-Kommentierung' des Olympiageländes Berlin' *Gedenkstättenrundbrief* 132 (2006), pp 3–9, https://www.gedenkstaettenforum.de/nc/gedenkstaettenrundbrief/rundbrief/news/historische_kommentierung_des_olympiagelaendes_berlin/, 11 April 2018.
Endlich, Stefanie. 'Open-Air-Installation im Olympiastadion "Historische Kommentierung" endlich realisiert', in *Stadtkunst Kunststadt: Informationsdienst der Kulturwerk des BBK Berlins GmbH* 53, 2006, 22.
Endlich, Stefanie. 'Vom Reichssportfeld zum Olympiapark: Ein Baudenkmal aus der NS-Zeit wird Kommentiert', in Gedächtnis, Kultur und Politiki, ed. Ingeborg Siggelkow (Berlin: Frank und Timme Verlag für wissenschaftliche Literatur, 2006), 7–18.
Endlich, Stefanie and Beate Rossié. 'Geschichte des Tempelhofer Feldes, Zweiter Teil: Ein weiterer Rundgang, diesmal zu Resten und Spuren des Alten Flughafens', *Verein Aktives Museum: Mitgliederrundbrief* 67, August 2012.
Endlich, Stefanie and Beate Rossié. 'Zum Umgang mit den Skulpturen von Breker, Thorak und anderen Bildhauern auf dem Berliner Olympiagelände', in *Zeitgeschichte-online, Thema: Wohin mit Breker? Zum Umgang mit NS-Kunst in Museen und im öffentlichen Raum*, hrsg. von Jan-Holger Kirsch, Dezember 2006, http://www.zeitgeschichte-online.de/portals/_rainbow/documents/pdf/endlich_rossie_breker.pdf, accessed 1 March 2018.
Endlich, Stefanie and Bernd Wurlitzer. *Skulpturen und Denkmäler in Berlin* (Berlin: Stapp Verlag Berlin, 1990).

Endlich, Stefanie, Geyler-von Bernus Monica, and Rossié, Beate. 'Flow of Refugees' (undated webpage), http://www.tempelhoferfreiheit.de/nc/en/about-tempelhofer-fr eiheit/history/symbol-of-freedom/flow-of-refugees/?page=1 , accessed 15 June 2013.

Engel, Helmut and Wolfgang Reuß, *Berlin - Woher Wohin? Oder: Dicht daneben ist auch vorbei!* (Berlin: Mann, 1995)

Epstein, Catherine A. *Nazi Germany: Confronting the Myths* (Chichester: John Wiley & Sons, 2015).

Evans, Richard J. 'From Nazism to Never Again: How Germany Came to Terms with Its Past', *Foreign Affairs*, 97 (2018), 8–15.

Evans, Richard J. *The Third Reich at War* (London: Allen Lane, 2008).

Faulenbach, Jürgen and Carola Schüller. *Informationen zur Politischen Bildung: Hauptstadt Berlin* (Bonn: Bundeszentrale für Politische Bildung, 1993).

Fleischhauer, Thea. 'Gedächtnisgeschichte Tempelhofer Feld: Förderverein für ein Gedenken an die Naziverbrechen auf dem Tempelhofer Feld e. V.' http://www.temp elhofer-unfreiheit.de/de/gedaechtnisgeschichte-tempelhofer-feld-foerderverein-fuer-ei n-gedenken-die-naziverbrechen-auf-dem-tempelhofer-feld-e-v, accessed March 2016.

Flierl, Bruno. *Berlin baut um - wessen Stadt wird die Stadt?: Kritische Reflexionen 1990– 1997* (Berlin: Verlag für Bauwesen, 1998).

Flierl, Thomas. 'Government Buildings of the GDR: On Dealing with Their History and Architecture', in *Bau und Raum Jahrbuch / Building and Regions Annual*, ed. Annegret Burg (Tübingen: Ernst Wasmuth Verlag GmbH & Co, 2001/2002), 91–3.

Foot, Sarah. 'Remembering, Forgetting and Inventing: Attitudes to the Past at the End of the First Viking Age', *Transactions of the Royal Historical Society* (Sixth Series) 9 (1999), 185–200.

Foucault, Michel. 'Of Other Spaces', *Diacritics*, 16 (1986), 22–7.

Foucault, Michel. *Discipline and Punish: The Birth of the Modern Prison* (London: Penguin, 1991).

Foucault, Michel. *Power/ Knowledge: Selected Interviews and Other Writings 1972-1977*, ed. Colin Gordon (New York: Pantheon Books, 1980).

Foucault, Michel. *Security, Territory, Population: Lectures at the Collège de France 1977 -1978* ed. Michel Senellart, François Ewald, Alessandro Fontana and Arnold I. Davidson and trans. Graham Burchell (New York: Palgrave Macmillan, 2009).

Foucault, Michel. *Society Must Be Defended: Lectures at the Collège de France 1975-1976*, ed. by Mauro Bertani, François Ewald, Alessandro Fontana and Arnold I. Davidson and trans. David Macey (New York: Picador, 2003).

Foucault, Michel. 'Space, Knowledge, and Power', in *The Foucault Reader*, ed. Paul Rabinow (London: Penguin, 1991), 239–56 (242).

Foucault, Michel. *The History of Sexuality Volume 1: An Introduction*, trans. Robert Hurley (New York: Pantheon Books: 1978).

Foucault, Michel. *The Order of Things: An Archaeology of the Human Sciences* (London: Tavistock Publications, 1970), xv–xviii.

Foucault, Michel. '"Truth and Power" Interview with Alessandro Fontana and Pasquale Pasquino', in *Power/ Knowledge*, ed. Colin Gordon (New York: Pantheon, 1980), 109–33.

Franck, Karen and Quentin Stevens. *Loose Space: Possibility and Diversity in Urban Life* (Oxon: Routledge, 2007).

François, Etienne and Hagen Schultze. *Deutsche Erinnerungsorte Bände 1–3* (Munich: Verlag C. H. Beck, 2002, 2003 and 2009 respectively).

Frick, Wilhlem. 'Gleichwort', in *Das Reichssportfeld: Eine Schöpfung des Dritten Reiches für die Olympischen Spiele und die Deutschen Leibesübungen*, Hrsg Reichsministerium des Innern (Berlin: Reichsparteiverlag, 1936).

Fulbrook, Mary. *Anatomy of a Dictatorship: Inside the GDR 1949–1989* (Oxford: Oxford University Press, 1995).

Fulbrook, Mary. *Reckonings: Legacies of Nazi Persecution and the Quest for Justice* (Oxford: Oxford University Press, 2018).

Füller, Henning, Georg Glasze and Robert Pütz. 'Shaping the Urban Renaissance: New-Build Luxury Developments in Berlin', *Urban Studies*, 50 (2013), 1540-56.

Garland, David. '"Governmentality" and the Problem of Crime: Foucault, Criminology, Sociology', *Theoretical Criminology*, 1 (2) (1997), 173-214.

Gassert, Philipp, and Alan E. Steinweis, eds. *Coping with the Nazi Past: West German Debates on Nazism and Generational Conflict, 1955–1975*, (Oxford: Berghahn Books, 2007).

Gay, Caroline. 'Remembering for the Future, Engaging with the Present: National Memory Management and the Dialectic of Normality in the Berlin Republic', in *Politics and Culture in Twentieth Century Germany*, ed. William Niven and James Jordan (Suffolk: Camden House, 2003), 201-21.

Gedi, Noa and Yigal Elam. 'Collective Memory - What Is It?', *History and Memory*, 8 (1996), 30-50.

Genocchio, Benjamin. 'Discourse, Discontinuity, Difference: The Question of "Other" Spaces', in *Postmodern Cities and Spaces*, ed. Sophie Watson and Katherine Gibson (Oxford: Blackwell, 1995), 35-46.

Georg, Karoline and Kurt Schilde. '"Warum schweigt die Welt?" Häftlinge des Berliner Konzentrationslagers Columbia-Haus 1933-1936', *Museums Journal* 3, (2013), 32-3.

Gerz, Joachim. 'Das Geld, die Liebe, der Tod, die Freiheit - was Zählt am Ende?', in *Das Detlev-Rohwedder-Haus: Architektur und Nutzung*, ed. Hans-Joachim Henzgen and Andrea Ulrich for the Bundesministerium der Finanzen Referat Presse und Information (Berlin: Bundesbauamt III, 1999), 44-5.

Geyer, Michael and Sheila Fitzpatrick. *Beyond Totalitarianism: Stalinism and Nazism Compared* (Cambridge: Cambridge University Press, 2009).

Gillies, Donald. 'Developing Governmentality: Conduct and Education Policy', *Journal of Education Policy*, 23 (4) (2008), 415-27.

Girra, Dagmar. *Gedenktafeln in Mitte, Tiergarten und Wedding: Band 1* (Berlin: Edition Luisenstadt, 2000).

Girra, Dagmar. *Gedenktafeln in Mitte, Tiergarten und Wedding: Band 2* (Berlin: Edition Luisenstadt, 2000).

Görtemaker, Manfred, Michael Bienert and Marko Leps. *Orte der Demokratie in Berlin: Ein Historisch-Politischer Wegweiser* (Bonn: BpB, 2004).

Gregor, Neil. *Haunted City: Nuremberg and the Nazi Past* (London: Yale University Press, 2008).

Griffin, Roger. 'Modernity, Modernism, and Fascism. A "Mazeway Resynthesis"', *Modernism/ modernity*, 15 (January 2008), 9-24.

Guillot, Xavier. 'The "Institutionalisation" of Heterotopias in Singapore', in *Heterotopia and the City: Space in a Postcivil Society*, ed. Michiel Dehaene and Lieven De Cauter (Oxon: Routledge, 2008), 179-88.

Güldner, Bettina and Wolfgang Schuster. 'Das Reichssportfeld', in *Skulptur und Macht Figurative Plastik in Deutschland der 30er und 40er Jahre – Eine Ausstellung im Rahmen des Gesamtprojektes der Akademie der Künste 'Das war ein Beispiel nur ...' vom 8. Mai bis 3. Juli 1983* (Berlin: Fröhlich and Kaufmann GMbG, 1983), 37–60.

Gumbert, Heather. 'Constructing a Socialist Landmark: The Berlin Television Tower', in *Berlin: Divided City 1945–1989*, ed. P. Broadbent and S. Hake (Oxford: Berghahn Books, 2010), 89–99.

Gunn, Simon. *The Public Culture of the Victorian Middle Class: Ritual and Authority and the English Industrial City*, 1840–1914 (Manchester: Manchester University Press, 2000).

Halbwachs, Maurice and Lewis A. Coser. *On Collective Memory* (Chicago: University of Chicago Press, 1992).

Handrack, Alexandra and Werner Jockeit. *Flughafen Berlin-Tempelhof: Erfassung und Bestandsaufnahme der Denkmalsubstanz. Band 1 Textteil-Historische Fotodokumentation- Quellenkatalog* (Berlin: Arbeitsgemeinschaft Alexandra Handrack und Werner Jockeit, 1995)

Hannah, Matthew G. *Governmentality and the Mastery of Territory in Nineteenth-century America*, Vol. 32 (Cambridge: Cambridge University Press, 2000).

Hannah, Matthew. 'State Knowledge and Recurring Patterns of State Phobia: From Fascism to Post-politics', *Progress in Human Geography*, 40 (4) (2016), 476–94.

Hansen, D. and M. Jachman. *Das Detlev-Rohwedder-Haus: Spiegel der deutschen Geschichte* (Berlin: Bundesministerium der Finanzen, 2015).

Hansen, D. and M. Jachmann. *The Detlev Rohwedder Building - German History Reflected* (Berlin: Bundesministerium der Finanzen, 2008).

Harris, Anita. 'Discourses of Desire as Governmentality: Young Women, Sexuality and the Significance of Safe Spaces', *Feminism & Psychology*, 15 (1) (2005), 39–43.

Harvey, David. 'Cosmopolitanism and the Banality of Geographical Evils', *Public Culture*, 12 (2000), 529–64.

Harvey, David. 'The Kantian Roots of Foucault's Dilemmas', in *Space, Knowledge and Power*: Foucault and Geography, ed. Jeremy W. Crampton and Stuart Elden (Aldershot: Ashgate, 2007), 41–7.

Haspel, Jörg. 'Vorwort: Architekturzeugnisse der NS-Zeit Erhalten, um zu Erinnern', in *Architektur in Berlin 1933–1945 - Ein Stadtführer*, ed. Matthias Donath (Berlin: Lukas Verlag for the Landesdenkmalamt Berlin, 2004), 9–13.

Hebbert, Michael. 'The Street as Locus of Collective Memory', *Environment and Planning D*, 23 (2005), 581–96.

Hecker, Manfred. 'Berlin-Tempelhof: A City Airport of the 1930s', in *Historic Airports: Proceedings of the International L'Europe de L'Air Conferences on Aviation Architecture Liverpool (1999), Berlin (2000), Paris (2001)*, ed. Bob Hawkins, Gabriele Lechner and Paul Smith (London: English Heritage, 2005), 92–9.

Heckner, Elke. 'Berlin Remake: Building Memory and the Politics of Capital Identity', *The Germanic Review: Literature, Culture, Theory*, 77 (2002), 304–25.

Heisig, M. 'Die "Weser" Flugzeugbau GmbH auf dem Flughafen Tempelhof: Rüstungsproduktion und Zwangsarbeit für den Krieg', in *Kein Ort der Freiheit: Das Tempelhfer Feld 1933 -45*, ed. F. Böhne and B. Winzer (Berlin, 2012), 43–61.

Herf, Jeffrey. *Divided Memory* (London: Harvard University Press, 1997).

Hesse, Frank Pieter. 'Die Standorte von Parlament und Regierung. Wege der Denkmalpflege', in *Hauptstadt Berlin: Denkmalpflege für Parlament, Regierung und Diplomatie 1900–2000. Beiträge zur Denkmalpflege in Berlin*, ed. Frank Pieter Hesse and Jürgen Tietz (Berlin: Verlag Bauwesen for the Landesdenkmalamt Berlin, 2000), 15–24.

Hetherington, Kevin. *The Badlands of Modernity: Heterotopia and Social Ordering* (London: Routledge, 1997).
Hettlage, Bernd and Wolfgang Reiher. *Olympiastadion Berlin: Die Neuen Architekturführer* (Berlin: Stadtwandel, 2006).
Higgins, Vaughan. 'Calculating Climate: "Advanced Liberalism" and the Governing of Risk in Australian Drought Policy', *Journal of Sociology*, 37 (2001), 299–316.
Hoffmann, Hans Wolfgang. 'Licht ins Dunkel: Ein sperriges Erbstück für den Finanzminister', *Stadtforum*, 25 (1997), 24–5
Hoffmann, Hilmar. 'Kultur als Signal der Völkerverständigung', *Berlin 2000: Das Olympia Magazin*, (May 1992), 15.
Hoffmann, Hilmar. *Mythos Olympia: Autonomie und Unterwerfung von Sport und Kultur: Hitlers Olympiade, Olympische Kultur, Riefenstahls Olympia-Film*, 1st edn (Berlin: Aufbau-Verlag, 1993).
Hoffmann-Axthelm, Dieter. 'Former Government Buildings in Berlin and Their Future', in *Bau und Raum Jahrbuch / Building and Regions Annual*, ed. Annegret Burg (Tübingen: Ernst Wasmuth Verlag GmbH & Co, 2001/2002), 88 – 91 (.
Hoh-Slodczyk, Christine. 'Original- Veränderung-Bestand', in *Das Detlev-Rohwedder-Haus: Architektur und Nutzung*, ed. Hans-Joachim Henzgen and Andrea Ulrich for the Bundesministerium der Finanzen Referat Presse und Information (Berlin: Bundesbauamt III, 1999), 13–17.
Hoss, Christiane and Martin Schönfeld. *Gedenktafeln in Berlin: Orte der Erinnerung an Verfolgte des Nationalsozialismus 1991–2001. Schriftenreihe Band 9* (Berlin: Verein Aktives Museum und Widerstand in Berlin, 2002).
HPP International. 'Der Eingang Wilhelmstrasse', in *Das Detlev-Rohwedder-Haus: Architektur und Nutzung*, ed. Hans-Joachim Henzgen and Andrea Ulrich for the Bundesministerium der Finanzen Referat Presse und Information (Berlin: Bundesbauamt III, 1999), 26–7.
HPP International. 'Der Kleine Saal', in *Das Detlev-Rohwedder-Haus: Architektur und Nutzung*, ed. Hans-Joachim Henzgen and Andrea Ulrich for the Bundesministerium der Finanzen Referat Presse und Information (Berlin: Bundesbauamt III, 1999), 34–5.
Hübinger, Petra and Joachim G. Jacobs. 'Die Steinernen Innenhöfe als Inszenierung der Macht', in *Das Detlev-Rohwedder-Haus: Architektur und Nutzung*, ed. Hans-Joachim Henzgen and Andrea Ulrich for the Bundesministerium der Finanzen Referat Presse und Information (Berlin: Bundesbauamt III, 1999), 10–11.
Huse, Norbert. 'Verloren, gefährdet, geschützt - Baudenkmale in Berlin', in *Verloren, gefährdet, geschützt: Baudenkmale in Berlin. Ausstellung im ehemaligen Arbeitsschutzmuseum Berlin-Charlottenberg 7 Dez. 1985 - 5 März 1989*, ed. Gruhn-Zimmerman (Berlin: Argon Verlag Gmbh, 1989), 11–19 (139).
Huxley, Margo. 'Geographies of Governmentality', in *Space, Knowledge and Power: Foucault and Geography*, ed. Jeremy Crampton and Stuart Elden (Oxon: Routledge, 2016), 185–204.
Huxley, Margo. 'Space and Government: Governmentality and Geography', *Geography Compass*, 2 (5) (2008) 1635–58.
Huyssen, Andreas. *Present Pasts: Urban Palimpsests and the Politics of Memory* (Stanford: Stanford University Press, 2003).
Hyde-Price, Adrian and Charlie Jeffery. 'Germany in the European Union: Constructing Normality', *JCMS: Journal of Common Market Studies*, 39 (2001), 689–717.
James-Chakraborty, Kathleen. *German Architecture for a Mass Audience* (New York: Routledge, 2000).

James-Chakraborty, Kathleen. 'Memory and the Cityscape: The German Architectural Debate About Post-Modernism', *German Politics and Society*, 17 (1999), 71–83.
Jampol, Justinian. 'Problematic Things: East German Materials after 1989', in *Divided Dreamworlds? The Cultural Cold War in East and West*, ed. Peter Romijn, Giles Scott-Smith and Joes Segal (Amsterdam: Amsterdam University Press, 2012).
Jarausch, Konrad H. *After Hitler: Recivilizing Germans, 1945–1995* (Oxford: Oxford University Press, 2008).
Jarausch, Konrad H. 'Beyond the National Narrative: Implications of Reunification for Recent German History', *German History*, 28 (2010), 498–514.
Jarausch, Konrad H., and Michael Geyer. *Shattered Past: Reconstructing German Histories* (Oxford: Princeton University Press, 2009).
Jaroskinski, Eric. 'Building on a Metaphor: Democracy, Transparency and the Berlin Reichstag', in *Berlin: The Symphony Continues: Orchestrating Architectural, Social and Artistic Change in Germany's New Capital*, ed. C. Costabile-Henning, R. Halverson and K. Foell (Berlin: Walter de Gruyter GmbH, 2004), 59–77.
Jaskot, Paul B. *The Architecture of Oppression: The SS, Forced Labour and the Nazi Building Economy* (London: Routledge, 2000).
Jessop, Bob. 'From Micro-powers to Governmentality: Foucault's Work on Statehood, State Formation, Statecraft and State Power', *Political Geography* 26, (2007), 34–40.
Jirku, Almut. 'Historic Transport Landscapes in Berlin', in *Proceedings of the International L'Europe de L'Air Conferences on Aviation Architecture: Liverpool (1999), Berlin (2000), Paris (2001)*, ed. Bob Hawkins, Gabriele Lechner and Paul Smith (London: English Heritage, 2005), 210–15.
Jockeit, Werner and Cornelia Wendt. 'Approaching the Built Heritage: The Conservation Plan for Berlin-Tempelhof', in *Proceedings of the International L'Europe de L'Air conferences on Aviation Architecture: Liverpool (1999), Berlin (2000), Paris (2001)* ed. Bob Hawkins, Gabriele Lechner and Paul Smith (London: English Heritage, 2005), 158–70.
Johnson, Peter. 'Unravelling Foucault's "Different Spaces"', *History of the Human Sciences*, 19 (2006), 75–90.
Jordan, Jennifer. 'A Matter of Time: Examining Collective Memory in Historical Perspective in Postwar Berlin', *Journal of Historical Sociology*, 18 (2005), 37–71.
Jordan, Jennifer. *Structures of Memory: Understanding Urban Change in Berlin and Beyond* (Stanford, CA: Stanford University Press, 2006).
Joyce, Patrick. *The Rule of Freedom: Liberalism and the Modern City* (London: Verso, 2003).
Juffer, Jane. 'Why We Like to Lose: On Being a Cubs Fan in the Heterotopia of Wrigley Field', *The South Atlantic Quarterly*, 105 (2006), 289–301.
Kaelber, Lutz. 'New Analyses of Trauma, Memory, and Place in Berlin and Beyond. A Review Essay', *Canadian Journal of Sociology Online* (May–June 2007), 1–10.
Kaminsky, Annette. 'Gedenkzeichen, Gedenkstätten und Museen zur Diktator in SBZ und DDR: Berlin', in *Orte Des Erinnerns: Gedenkzeichen, Gedenkstätten und Museen Zur Diktatur in SBZ und DDR*, ed. Annette Kaminsky (Berlin: Ch. Links Verlag, 2007), 45–144.
Kerr, Derek. 'Beheading the King and Enthroning the Market: A Critique of Foucauldian Governmentality', *Science and Society*, 63, no. 2 (1999), 173 – 202.
Kidd, Alan J. and Kenneth W. Roberts. *City, Class and Culture: Studies of Social Policy and Cultural Production in Victorian Manchester* (Manchester: Manchester University Press, 1985).

Kluge, Volker. *Olympiastadion Berlin: Steine Beginnen zu Reden* (Berlin: Parthas Verlag, 1999).

Knittel, Susanne C. 'Remembering Euthanasia, Grafeneck in the Past, Present, and Future', in *Memorialisation in Germany since 1945*, ed. Bill Niven and Chloe Paver (Basingstoke: Palgrave Macmillan, 2010), 124–33.

Koch, Habbo. 'The Return of the Images: Photographs of Nazi Crimes and the West German Public in The "Long 1960s"', in *Coping with the Nazi Past: West German Debates on Nazism and Generational Conflict 1955–1975*, ed. P. Gassert and A. Steinweis (Oxford: Berghahn Books, 2006), 31–50.

Koepnick, Lutz. 'Redeeming History? Foster's Dome and the Political Aesthetics of the Berlin Republic', *German Studies Review*, 24 (2001), 303–23.

Koshar, Rudy. *From Monuments to Traces: Artefacts of German Memory, 1870–1990*, Vol. 24 (London: University of California Press, 2000).

Koshar, Rudy. *Germany's Transient Pasts: Preservation and National Memory in the Twentieth Century* (London: University of North Carolina Press, 1998).

Krause, Gerhard. *Das Reichssportfeld* (Berlin: Reichssportverlag GmbH, 1936).

Kunstler, James Howard. *The City in Mind: Meditations on the Urban Condition* (New York: Free Press, 2003).

Ladd, Brian. *The Ghosts of Berlin: Confronting German History in the Urban Landscape* (London: University of Chicago Press, 1997).

Lange, Bastian. 'From Cool Britannia to Generation Berlin? Geographies of Culturepreneurs and their Creative Milieus in Berlin', in *Cultural Industries: The British Experience in International Perspective*, ed. C. Eisenberg, R. Gerlach and C. Handke (Online: Humboldt University Berlin Edoc- Server, 2006), 145–72, http://edoc.hu-berlin.de/conferences/culturalindustries/lange-bastian/PDF/lange.pdf, accessed 20 March 2013.

Lanz, Stefan. 'Be Berlin! Governing the City through Freedom', *International Journal of Urban and Regional Research*, 37 (3013), 1305–24.

Larner, Wendy and William Walters, eds. *Global Governmentality: Governing International Spaces* (London: Routledge, 2004).

Larsen, Laragh. 'Re-placing Imperial Landscapes: Colonial Monuments and the Transition to Independence in Kenya', *Journal of Historical Geography*, 38 (1) (2012), 45–56.

Legg, Stephen. 'Foucault's Population Geographies: Classifications, Biopolitics and Governmental Spaces', *Population, Space and Place*, 11 (2005), 137–56.

Legg, Stephen. 'Governmentality, Congestion and Calculation in Colonial Delhi', *Social and Cultural Geography*, 7 (5) (2006), 709–29.

Legg, Stephen . 'Subjects of Truth: Resisting Governmentality in Foucault's 1980s', *Environment and Planning D: Society and Space*, 31 (1) (2019), 27–45

Lemke, Thomas. '"The Birth of Bio-Politics": Michel Foucault's Lecture at The Collège de France on Neo-Liberal Governmentality', *Economy and Society*, 30 (2001), 190–207.

Lemke, Thomas. 'Foucault, Governmentality and Critique', *Rethinking Marxism*, 14 (3) (2002), 46–64.

Lemke, Thomas. *Foucault, Governmentality and Critique* (London: Routledge, 2015).

Light, Duncan. 'Gazing on Communism: Heritage Tourism and Post-Communist Identities in Germany, Hungary and Romania', *Tourism Geographies*, 2 (2) (2000), 157–76.

Lord, Beth. 'Foucault's Museum: Difference, Representation, and Genealogy', *Museum and Society*, 4 (March 2006), 1–14.

Lou, Jia. 'Revitalizing Chinatown into a Heterotopia: A Geosemiotic Analysis of Shop Signs in Washington, D.C.'s Chinatown', *Space and Culture*, 10 (2007), 170–94.

Louekari, Meri. 'The Creative Potential of Berlin: Creating Alternative Models of Social, Economic and Cultural Organisation in the Form of Network Forming and Open-Source Communities', *Planning Practice and Research*, 21 (2006), 463–81.

Low, Setha. 'The Gated Community as Heterotopia', in *Heterotopia and the City: Space in a Postcivil Society*, ed. Michiel Dehaene and Lieven De Cauter (Abingdon, Oxon: Routledge, 2008), 153–64.

Lutz, Felix. 'Evolution and Normalization: Historical Consciousness in Germany', *German Politics and Society*, 30 (2012), 35–63.

Macdonald, Sharon. *Difficult Heritage: Negotiating the Nazi Past in Nuremberg and Beyond* (London: Routledge, 2010), 1–7.

Macdonald, Sharon. 'Undesirable Heritage: Fascist Material Culture and Historical Consciousness in Nuremberg', *International Journal of Heritage Studies*, 12 (2006), 9–28.

Macdonald, Sharon. 'Words in Stone? Agency and Identity in a Nazi Landscape', *Journal of Material Culture* 11 (1–2) (2006), 105–26.

March, Werner. 'Das Reichssportfeld', *Monatshefte für Baukunst und Städtebau* No. 20, 1936, 269–77.

March, Werner. 'Die baukünstlerische Gestaltung des Reichssportfeldes', in *Das Reichssportfeld: Eine Schöpfung des Drittes Reiches für die Olympischen Spiele und die Deutsche Leibseübungen*, ed. Reichsministerien des Innern (Reichssportverlag: Berlin, 1936), 27–55.

Marcuse, Harold. *Legacies of Dachau: the uses and abuses of a concentration camp*, 1933–2001 (Cambridge: Cambridge University Press, 2001).

Marcuse, Peter. 'Reflections on Berlin: The Meaning of Construction and the Construction of Meaning', *International Journal of Urban and Regional Research*, 22 (1998), 331–8.

Marg, Volkwin. *Choreography of the Masses: In Sport. In the Stadium. In a Frenzy* (Berlin: Jovis and the Akademie der Künste, 2012).

Maur, Hans. *Traditionstätte der Arbeiterbewegung in Zentrum Berlins, der Haupstadt der Deutsche Demokratischen Republik* (Berlin: Museum für Deutsche Geschichte, 1971).

McDonald, Catherine and Greg Marson. 'Workfare as Welfare: Governing Unemployment in the Advanced Liberal State', *Critical Social Policy*, 25 (2005), 374–401.

McGarr, Paul M. '"The Viceroys Are Disappearing from the Roundabouts in Delhi": British Symbols of Power in Post-colonial India', *Modern Asian Studies*, 49 (3) (2015), 787–831.

McGowan, Lee. *The Radical Right in Germany 1870 to the Present* (London: Routledge, 2014).

McKee, Kim. 'Post-Foucauldian Governmentality: What Does It Offer Critical Social Policy Analysis?' *Critical Social Policy*, 29 (3) (2009), 465–86.

Meuser, Philipp. *Vom Fliegerfeld zum Wiesenmeer: Geschichte und Zukunft des Flughafens Tempelhof* (Berlin: Quintessenz Verlags GmbH, 2000).

Meyer, Ulf. *Bundeshauptstadt Berlin / Capital City Berlin* (Berlin: Jovis Verlag, 1999).

Miller Lane, Barbara. *Architecture and Politics in Germany* 1918 -1945 (Cambridge, MA: Harvard University Press, 1968).

Mittig, Hans-Ernst. 'Kunst und Propaganda im NS-System', in *Moderne Kunst 2: Das Funkkolleg zum Verständnis der Gegenwartskunst,* ed. Monika Wagner (Hamburg: Rowohlt Taschenbuch Verlag GmbH, 1991), 443–66.

Moeller, Robert. 'The Politics of the Past in the 1950s: Rhetorics of Victimisation in East and West Germany', in *Germans as Victims: Remembering the Past in Contemporary Germany*, ed. Bill Niven (Basingstoke: Palgrave Macmillan, 2006), 26–42.

Morris, R. J. 'The Middle Class and British Towns and Cities of the Industrial Revolution, 1780-1870', in *Pursuit of Urban History*, ed. Fraser and Sutcliffe (London: Edward Arnold, 1983), 286-306.
Munt, Sally. *Queer Attachments: The Cultural Politics of Shame* (Aldershot: Ashgate, 2007).
Newsinger, John. 'Why Rhodes Must Fall', *Race & Class*, 58 (2) (2016), 70-8.
Nicolai, Bernd. 'The Berlin Olympic Stadium: How to Deal with the First 'Gesamtkunstwerk' of the Third Reich Today?', in *Sport Stätten Kultur / Sport Sites Culture*, ed. Fiona Laudamus, Michael Petzet and John Ziesemer (Munich: ICOMOS Nationalkomitee der Bundesrepublik Deutschland, 2002), 37-9.
Nienhoff, H. 'Faszination Des Raumes', *architektur + bauphysik*, 7 (2006), 18-22.
Niven, Bill. *Facing the Nazi Past: United Germany and the Legacy of the Third Reich*, 4th edn (Hoboken, USA: Taylor and Francis (online access), 2001).
Niven, Bill. *Facing the Nazi Past: United Germany and the Legacy of the Third Reich* (London: Routledge, 2002).
Niven, Bill and Chloe Paver. 'Introduction', in *Memorialisation in Germany since 1945*, ed. Bill Niven and Chloe Paver (Basingstoke: Palgrave Macmillan, 2010), 1-13.
Nora, Pierre. 'Between Memory and History: Les *Lieux de Mémoire*', *Representations*, 26 (1989), 7-24.
Nora, Pierre. *Realms of Memory, vol 1: Conflicts and Divisions* (New York: Columbia University Press, 1996).
Odenthal, Anna Maria. 'Denkmalpflege: Die Geschichtswahrende Modernisierung des Olympiastadions', *architektur + bauphysik*, 7 (2006), 2-8.
O'Malley, Pat, Lorna Weir and Clifford Shearing. 'Governmentality, Criticism, Politics', *Economy and Society*, 26 (4) (1997), 501-17.
Orillard, C. 'Between Shopping Malls and Agoras: A French History of 'Protected Public Space', in *Heterotopia and the City: Space in a Postcivil Society*, ed. Michiel Dehaene and Lieven De Cauter (Oxon: Routledge, 2008), 117-36.
Osborne, Thomas. 'Bureaucracy as a Vocation: Governmentality and Administration in Nineteenth-Century Britain', *Journal of Historical Sociology*, 7 (1994), 289-313.
Osborne Thomas and Nikolas Rose. 'Governing Cities: Notes on the Spatialisation of Virtue', *Environment and Planning D: Society and Space*, 17 (1999), 737-60.
Otter, Chris. 'Making Liberalism Durable: Vision and Civility in the Late-Victorian City', *Social History*, 27 (2002), 1-15.
Overbeek, Henk. *Restructuring Hegemony in the Global Political Economy: The Rise of Transnational Neo-liberalism in the 1980s* (London: Routledge, 1993).
Parton, Nigel. 'Risk, Advanced Liberalism and Child Welfare: The Need to Rediscover Uncertainty and Ambiguity', *British Journal of Social Work*, 28 (1998), 5-27.
Paver, Chloe. 'Exhibiting the National Socialist Past: An Overview of Recent German Exhibitions', *Journal of European Studies*, 39 (2009), 225-49.
Paver, Chloe. 'You Shall Know Them by Their Objects: Material Culture and Its Impact in Museum Displays about National Socialism', in *Cultural Impact in the German Context*, ed. Rebecca Braun and Lyn Marven (New York: Camden House, 2010), 169-88.
Pehnt, Wolfgang. 'Der Wunsch, zu sein wie Andere auch: Zur Architektur der Deutschen Hauptstadt', in *Ein Neues Deutschland? Zur Physiognomie Der Berliner Republik*, ed. Karl Heinz Bohrer and Kurt Scheel (Berlin: Klett-Cotta, 2006), 758-70.
Pehnt, Wolfgang. *Deutsche Architektur Seit 1900* (Munich: Deutsche Verlags-Anstalt, 2005).
Pendas, Devin O. *The Frankfurt Auschwitz Trial, 1963-1965: Genocide, History, and the Limits of the Law* (Cambridge: Cambridge University Press, 2006).

Penny, Glenn H. 'German Polycentrism and the Writing of History', *German History*, 30 (2012), 265–82.
Petrescu, Corina. *Against All Odds: Models of Subversive Space in National Socialist Germany* (Bern: Peter Lang, 2010).
Petropoulos, Jonathan. *Artists Under Hitler: Collaboration and Survival in Nazi Germany* (London: Yale University Press, 2014).
Petropoulos, Jonathan. *Art as Politics in the Third Reich* (University of North Carolina Press: London, 1999).
Petsch, Joachim. *Baukunst und Stadtplanung im Dritten Reich: Herleitung, Bestandsaufnahme, Entwicklung, Nachfolge* (Munich: Hanser, 1976).
Peukert, Detlev. *Inside Nazi Germany* (New York: Penguin, 1989).
Pfundtner, Hans. 'Die Gesamtleitung der Errichtung des Reichssportfeldes', in *Das Reichssportfeld: Eine Schöpfung des Dritten Reiches für die Olympischen Spiele und die deutschen Leibesuebungen*, ed. Reichsministerium des Innern (Berlin: Reichsspartei Verlag, 1936), 11–26.
Philpotts, Matthew. 'Cultural-Political Palimpsests: The Reich Aviation Ministry and the Multiple Temporalities of Dictatorship', *New German Critique*, 117 (39) (2012), 207–30.
Philpotts, Matthew. 'The Ruins of Dictatorship: Prora and Other Spaces', *Central Europe*, 12 (2014), 47–61.
Pollack, Susan and Reinhard Bernbeck. 'Archäologische Ausgrabungen auf dem Tempelhofer Flugfeld' (2012), http://www.ausgrabungen-tempelhof.de/Ausgrabungen%20Tempelhofer%20Flugfeld.pdf, accessed 12 January 2019.
Pollack, Susan and Reinhard Bernbeck. 'Gate to a Darker World', in *Ethics and the Archaeology of Violence*, ed. Alfredo González-Ruibal and Gabriel Moshenska (London: Springer, 2014), 137–52.
Pollack, Susan and Reinhard Bernbeck. 'The Limits of Experience: Suffering, Nazi Forced Labour Camps, and Archaeology', *Archaeological Papers of the American Anthropological Association*, 27 (2016), 22–39.
Poly, Regina. 'Die Außenanlagen', in *Das Detlev-Rohwedder-Haus: Architektur und Nutzung*, ed. Hans-Joachim Henzgen and Andrea Ulrich for the Bundesministerium der Finanzen Referat Presse und Information (Berlin: Bundesbauamt III, 1999), 38–9.
Poovey, Mary. *Making a Social Body: British Cultural Formation, 1830–1864* (London: University of Chicago Press, 1995).
Potter, Hilary. 'Rosenstraße: A Complex Site of German-Jewish Memory', in *Memorialisation in Germany since 1945*, ed. Bill Niven and Chloe Paver (Basingstoke: Palgrave Macmillan, 2010), 214–23.
Powell, Kimberly. 'Remapping the City: Palimpsest, Place, and Identity in Art Education Research', *Studies in Art Education*, 50 (2008), 6–21.
Pratt, Anna and Sara K. Thompson. 'Chivalry, "Race" and Discretion at the Canadian Border', *The British Journal of Criminology*, 48 (5) (2008), 620–40.
Pujolar, Joan. 'African Women in Catalan Language Courses: Struggles over Class, Gender and Ethnicity in Advanced Liberalism', in *Words, Worlds, and Material Girls: Language, Gender, Globalization*, ed. Bonnie McElhinny (Berlin: Walter de Gruyter GmbH, 2007), 305–48.
Rabinow, Paul. *French Modern: Norms and Forms of the Social Environment* (London: The MIT Press, 1989).
Rakower, Lauren. 'Blurred Lines: Zooming in on Google Street View and the Global Right to Privacy', *Brooklyn Journal of International Law*, 37 (2011), 317–47.
Reichssportfeld Verwaltung. *Führer durch das Reichssportfeld* (Berlin: Reichssportfeld-Verwaltung, 1937).

Riera, Monica. 'How Should We Build? Architecture, History and the Post-Cold War Context in Germany', *National Identities*, 8 (2006), 383–400.

Roesler, Jorg. 'Privatisation in Eastern Germany: Experience with the Treuhand', *Europe-Asia Studies*, 14 (3) (1994), 505–17

Rose, Nikolas. 'Government, Authority and Expertise in Advanced Liberalism', *Economy and Society*, 22 (1993), 283–99.

Rose, Nikolas. *Powers of Freedom: Reframing Political Thought* (Cambridge: Cambridge University Press, 1999).

Rosenfeld, Gavriel. 'The Architects' Debate: Architectural Discourse and the Memory of Nazism', *History and Memory*, 9 (1997), 189–225.

Rosenfeld, Gavriel D. *Munich and Memory: Architecture, Monuments, and the Legacy of the Third Reich* (London: University of California Press, 2000).

Rosenfeld, Gavriel D. and Paul B. Jaskot, 'Introduction', in *Beyond Berlin: Twelve German Cities Confront the Nazi Past*, Gavriel D. Rosenfeld and Paul B. Jaskot (Ann Arbour: University of Michigan Press, 2008).

Rosol, Marit. 'On Resistance in the Post-political City: Conduct and Counter-Conduct in Vancouver', *Space and Polity*, 18 (1) (2014), 70–84.

Rousso, Henry and Arthur Goldhammer. *The Vichy Syndrome: History and Memory in France since 1944* (Cambridge, MA: Harvard University Press, 1994).

Sagebiel, Ernst. 'Vom Bau des Reichsluftfahrtministeriums', *Monatshefte für Baukunst und Städtebau*, 20 (1936), 81–92.

Saldanha, Annette. 'Heterotopia and Structuralism', *Environment and Planning A*, 40 (2008), 2080–96.

Salwa, Ismail. 'Authoritarian Government, Neoliberalism and Everyday Civilities in Egypt', *Third World Quarterly*, 32 (2011), 845–62.

Samuels, Joshua. 'Of Other Scapes: Archaeology, Landscape, and Heterotopia in Fascist Sicily ', *Archaeologies: Journal of the World Archaeological Congress*, 6 (2010), 62–81.

Saunders, Anna. 'Challenging or Concretising Cold War Narratives? Berlin's Memorial to the Victims of 17 June 1953', in *Memorialisation in Germany since 1945*, ed. Bill Niven and Chloe Paver (Basingstoke: Palgrave Macmillan, 2010), 298–307.

Saunders, Anna. *Memorializing the GDR: Monuments and Memory after 1989* (Oxford: Berghahn Books, 2018).

Saunders, Anna. 'Remembering Cold War Division: Wall Remnants and Border Monuments in Berlin', *Journal of Contemporary European Studies*, 17 (2009), 1–19.

Schäche, Wolfgang. *Architektur und Städtebau in Berlin zwischen 1933 und 1945: Planen und Bauen unter der Ägide der Stadtverwaltung* (Berlin: Gerbr. Mann Verlag, 1992).

Schäche, Wolfgang. 'Der "Zentralflughafen Tempelhof" in Berlin', in *Berlin in Geschichte und Gegenwart: Jahrbuch des Landesarchivs Berlin*, ed. Sigurd H. Schmidt (Berlin: Gebr. Mann Verlag, 1996), 151–64.

Schäche, Wolfgang and Norbert Szymanski. *Das Reichssportfeld: Architektur im Spannungsfeld von Sport und Macht* (Berlin: be.bra-Verlag, 2001).

Schilde, Kurt. *Erinnern- und nicht vergessen: Dokumentation zum Gedenkbuch für die Opfer des Nationalsozialismus aus dem Bezirk Tempelhof* (Berlin: Bezirksamt Tempelhof von Berlin, 1988).

Schilde, Kurt. *Vom Columbia-haus zum Schulenburgring: Dokumentation mit Lebensgeschichten von Opfern des Widerstandes und der Verfolgung von 1933 bis 1945 aus dem Bezirk Tempelhof* (Berlin: Bezirksamt Tempelhof von Berlin, 1987).

Schlusche, Günter. 'Die Parlaments- und Regierungsbauten des Bundes im Kontext der Berliner Stadtentwicklung', *Aus Politik und Zeitgeschichte*, B 34–35 (2001), 16–24.

Schmitz, Frank. *Flughafen Tempelhof - Berlins Tor zur Welt* (Berlin: be.bra, 1997).

Schulte-Sasse, Linda. 'Retrieving the City as Heimat: Berlin in Nazi Cinema', in *Berlin: Culture and Metropolis*, ed. Charles Haxthausen and Heidrun Suhr (Oxford: University of Minnesota Press, 1990), 166–86.
Schultz, Eberhard. 'Abriss oder Sanierung? Umgang mit einem Historischen Ort / Demolition or Renovation: Handling an Historic Site', in *Das Bundesfinanzministerium: Ein Belasteter Ort?*, ed. Laurenz Demps, Eberhard Schultz and Klaus Wettig (Berlin: Parthas, 2001), 52–77.
Schweitzer, Eva. *Großbaustelle Berlin: Wie Die Hauptstadt Verplant Wird* (Berlin: Nicolai, 1996).
Shackley, Myra. 'Space, Sanctity and Service: the English Cathedral as Heterotopia', *International Journal of Tourism Research*, 4 (2002), 345–52.
Sigley, Gary. 'Chinese Governmentalities: Government, Governance and the Socialist Market Economy', *Economy and Society*, 35 (2006), 487–508.
Siri, Jasmin. 'The Alternative for Germany after the 2017 Election', German *Politics* 27 (1), (2018), 141–5.
Smith, Paul and Bernard Toulier. 'Introduction', in *Berlin Tempelhof, Liverpool Speke, Paris Le Bourget: Airport Architecture of the Thirties*, ed. Paul Smith and Bernard Toulier (Paris: Editions du Patrimoine, 2000), 10–30.
Soederberg, Susanne, Georg Menz and Philip G. Cerny. *Internalizing Globalization: The Rise of Neo-liberalism and the Decline of National Varieties of Capitalism* (Basingstoke: Palgrave Macmillan, 2005).
Soja, Edward W. 'Heterotopologies: A Remembrance of Other Spaces in the Citadel-La', in *Postmodern Cities and Spaces*, ed. Sophie Watson and Katherine Gibson (Oxford: Blackwell, 1995), 13–34.
Soja, Edward W. *Thirdspace: Journeys to Los Angeles and Other Real-and-Imagined Places* (Oxford: Blackwell, 1996).
Sontag, Susan. *Regarding the Pain of Others* (New York: Farrar, Straus and Giroux, 2003).
Speer, Albert. *Inside the Third Reich* (London: Phoenix, 2003).
Stack, Heather M. 'The "Colonization" of East Germany?: A Comparative Analysis of German Privatization', *Duke Law Journal*, 46 (5) (1997), 1211–53.
Starkman, Ruth A. 'Perpetual Impossibility? The Normalisation of German-Jewish Relations in the Berlin Republic', in *Transformations of the New Germany*, ed. Ruth A. Starkman (Basingstoke: Palgrave Macmillan, 2006), 233–50.
Starzmann, Maria Theresia. 'Excavating Tempelhof Airfield: Objects of Memory and the Politics of Absence', *Rethinking History*, 18 (2) (2014), 211–29.
Starzmann, Maria Theresia . 'The Fragment and the Testimony: Reflections on Absence and Time in the Archaeology of Prisons and Camps', *International Journal of Historical Archaeology*, 22 (2018), 574–92.
Stimmann, Hans. 'Stadtplanung: Koloseen der Moderne', *Architektur + Bauphysik* No. 7, June 2006, 8–9.
Straub, Jakob and Andreas Fecht, *Schatten der Macht: Architektur des Nationalsozialismus in Berlin* (Berlin: Jovis Verlag, 2006).
Taylor, Robert. *The Word in Stone: The Role of Architecture in the National Socialist Ideology* (Berkeley and London: University of California Press, 1974).
Thiele, Michael. 'Der Architekt und sein Bauwerk', in *Landing on Tempelhof: 75 Jahre Zentralflughafen 50 Jahre Luftbrücke. Ausstellungskatalog*, ed. Matthias Heisig and Michael Thiele (Berlin: Bezirksamt Tempelhof von Berlin, 1998), 74–85.
Thiele, Michael. 'Tempelhof, das Tor zur Welt', in *Landing on Tempelhof: 75 Jahre Zentralflughafen 50 Jahre Luftbrücke. Ausstellungskatalog*, ed. Matthias Heisig and Michael Thiele (Berlin: Bezirksamt Tempelhof von Berlin, 1998), 132–46.

Thomas Schmidt. *Das Berliner Olympia Stadion und seine Geschichte* (Berlin: Express Edition, 1983).
Thomas Schmidt. *Werner March: Architekt des Olympia-Stadions 1894–1976* (Berlin: Birkhäuser Verlag, 1992).
Till, Karen. 'Interim Use at a Former Death Strip? Art, Politics and Urbanism at *Skulpturenpark Berlin_Zentrum*', in *The German Wall: Fallout in Europe*, ed. Marc Silberman (New York: Palgrave Macmillan, 2011), 99–122.
Topinka, Robert. 'Foucault, Borges, Heterotopia: Producing Knowledge in Other Spaces', *Foucault Studies*, 9 (2010), 54–70.
Umbach, Maiken. *German Cities and Bourgeois Modernism, 1890–1924* (Oxford: Oxford University Press, 2009).
Urban, Florian. *Neo-Historical East Berlin: Architecture and Urban Design in the German Democratic Republic 1970–1990* (Farnham: Ashgate, 2009).
Vanolo, Alberto. '"Smartmentality": The Smart City as Disciplinary Strategy', *Urban Studies*, 51 (5) (2014): 883–98.
van Pelt, Robert-Jan. 'Auschwitz: From Architect's Promise to Inmate's Perdition', *Modernism/ modernity*, 1 (1994), 80–120.
Wachsmann, Nikolaus. *KL: A History of the Nazi Concentration Camps* (London: Abacus, 2016).
Ward Thompson, Catherine. 'Urban Open Space in the 21st Century', *Landscape and Urban Planning*, 60 (2002), 59–72.
Watson, Virginia. 'Liberalism and Advanced Liberalism in Australian Indigenous Affairs', *Alternatives: Global, Local, Political*, 29 (2004), 577–98.
Webber, Andreas. *Berlin in the Twentieth Century: A Cultural Topography* (Cambridge: Cambridge University Press, 2008).
Weitz, Eric. *Creating German Communism 1890–1990* (Princeton, NJ: Princeton University Press, 1997).
Wiedmer, Caroline Alice. *The Claims of Memory: Representations of the Holocaust in Contemporary Germany and France* (London: Cornell University Press, 1999).
Wilderotter, Hans. *Das Haus am Werderschen Markt: Von der Reichsbank zum Auswärtigen Amt / The History of the New Premises of the Federal Foreign Office* (Berlin: Jovis, 1999).
Wise, Michael Z. *Capital Dilemma: Germany's Search for a New Architecture of Democracy* (New York: Princeton Architectural Press, 1998).
Young, James. 'The Counter Monument: Memory Against Itself in Germany', *Critical Inquiry*, 18 (1992), 267–96.
Zehfuss, Maja. *Wounds of Memory: The Politics of War in Germany* (Cambridge: Cambridge University Press, 2007).
Ziemann, Benjamin. *Contested Commemorations: Republican War Veterans and Weimar Political Culture* (Cambridge: Cambridge University Press, 2016).
Zlonicky, Peter. 'Ein Zwischen-Resümee', in *Hauptstadt Berlin: Festung, Schloss, Demokratischer Regierungssitz. Städtbau und Architektur Bericht 10*, ed. Hans Stimmann (Berlin: Senatsverwaltung für Bau-und Wohnungswesen, 1992).
Zuckerwise, Gail M. 'Governmentality in Amsterdam's Red Light District', *City*, 16 (1–2) (2012), 146–57.

Index

Note: Concepts and topics that underpin the analysis throughout the book, such as post-authoritarian governmentality, power and resistance and post-unification memory politics are not included in the index.

100% Tempelhofer Feld   156, 168, 172, 217 n.83
17 June 1953 uprising   55
  memory and memorialisation of 56, 57–62, 66–8
17 June Association   60, 66–7

Active Museum of Fascism and Resistance in Berlin (Aktives Museum für Faschismus und Widerstand in Berlin)   21, 99
Air Lift Memorial   137–9, *see also* Platz der Luftbrücke
Albiker, Karl   81, 88–9, 107–8
Allied Control Council   29
Alternative for Germany (Alternative für Deutschland (AfD))   23, 178
antiquity   25
  allusions to in art and architecture 30, 81, 87, 94–5, 101, 119
  Hitler's admiration of   31
Architects' Debate   32, 36
architecture
  in divided Germany   32, 36 (*see also* transparency ideology)
  in the Third Reich
    architectural policy   30
    forced labourers   31
    Hitler's views on   4, 30–1, 83
    housing   31
    industrial   30, 134
    international style   31, 93–4, 96–7, 134
    modern style and techniques   4, 29–31, 41, 83, 89, 120, 133, 136
    monumentality   4, 30–1, 41, 71, 83, 95, 98, 114, 134, 156
    neoclassical   30, 87, 93, 133–4

  prestige buildings   2, 3, 30–1, 41, 72, 120, 132, 136, 139
  and propaganda   2, 3, 28, 30–1, 41, 44, 88–9, 95, 98–9, 132
  Völkisch   30–1
  use of in the Berlin Republic as challenges to Nazi structures 48, 69, 72–3, 119–20
  in the Weimar Republic   3, 30, 82, 131
Assmann, Aleida   34, 149
Assmann, Jan   34, 191
Association for the Commemoration of Nazi Crimes around and on Tempelhofer Feld (Förderverein zum Gedenken an die Nazi-Verbrechen um und auf dem Tempelhofer Feld (THF 1933–45))   150, 157
Auschwitz Trials (Frankfurt)   20
aviation history   3, 131, 153, 155
Aviation Ministry (Reichsluftfahrtministerium) (building)
  aesthetics of   29, 41, 46, 48–50, 53–5, 70–1
  debates over demolition   2, 44, 46–8
  design and construction of   2, 29, 41
  Lingner mural   51–2, 61–2
  post-unification renovation of   48–54, 71–2
  Soviet use of   2, 43, 50
  use in GDR   2, 43–4, 49, 50–3, 55
  use in Third Reich   2, 41–3, 69–71

Barlach, Ernst   91
Battle of Langemarck   3, 111, 113–14, 120–1, *see also* Langemarck myth; Olympic Stadium, Langemarck Hall

Bauhaus 30
Berghain 174
Berlin Air Lift 16, 129, 131, 137–40, 143, 148, 153, 155, 157
Berlin blockade 4, 137, 141, 153, 155
Berlin Brandenburg International airport (BBI) 133
Berlin Bridge Association (Verein Berliner Brücke) 66–7
Berlin Forum for History and Present (Berliner Forum für Geschichte und Gegenwart) 60, 99, 100, 150
Berlin History Workshop (Berliner Geschichtswerkstatt) 21, 148
Berlin Republic, *see* Federal Republic of Germany
Berlin Television Tower 32
Berlin Wall 1, 2, 35, 44, 64, 131, 137, 154
Berufsband Bildener Künstler (BBK) 99
biopolitics 14–16
Bitburg controversy 21
Blaupunkt 84
Bodenschatz Harald 36, 47, 71
Bonn Republic, *see* Federal Republic of Germany
Brandt, Willy 21
Breker, Arno 89, 94–5
British Administration of Berlin 3, 84–5, 115, *see also* Air Lift Memorial
Bubis, Ignatz 92
Bundeshaus, Bonn 32

Central Council of Jews in Germany 92, 97
Christo 91
colonisation
  British in India 16, 27
  theory of German unification 22, 44, 51
Columbia-Haus concentration camp
  excavation of 151
  memorialisation and marking of 148–50, 152–4, 157–8, 179
  use in the Third Reich 146–7
Corbusierhaus (Unité d'Habitation) 115
Cranz, Galen 166, 169
Cremer, Fritz 91

Crimes of the Wehrmacht exhibition 21–2
Critical Reconstruction of Berlin 36

Dean, Mitchell 14–16, 120
De Cauter, Lieven 162, 213 n.2
Dehaene, Michiel 162, 213 n.2
denazification
  of buildings 29
  of people/ society 20–1
Detlev Rohwedder House (Detlev-Rohwedder-Haus), *see* Aviation Ministry (building)
Deutscher Werkbund 99
Diem, Carl
  controversy over plaque 104–6
  and the Langemarck Hall 114–15
  speech to the *Volksturm* 3
Diepgen, Eberhard 60, 92, 93
Dietrich Eckart Stage 81–2, *see also* Olympic Stadium, Waldbühne
Domenig, Günther 69
Donath, Matthias 70

East Germany, *see* German Democratic Republic
Eckert, Reinald 90
Eichel, Hans 61
Eichmann Trial 20
Elden, Stuart 25
Endlich, Stefanie 97, 99, 100, 118
Engler, Paul and Klaus 131
Evans, Richard 147, 178

Federal Finance Ministry (institution) 2, 41, 44, 46, 48–50, 52–4, 59–63, 67, 73–7
Federal Finance Ministry, *see* Aviation Ministry (building)
Federal Republic of Germany
  architecture in (*see* architecture)
  Basic Law 17, 84
  electoral system 17
  far right politics in 21, 93, 177–8
  founding of 17
  and the GDR (*see* German Democratic Republic)
  memory of Third Reich (1949–1990) 19–22, 29, 32–6
  referendum responses 143

Federal Strategy for Memorial Sites 22, 24
Flatow brothers 109
Flex, Walter 113, 120, 122
Flughafen Tempelhof, *see* Tempelhof Airport
forced labourers 31, 146, 147–8, 150–4, 157
Foro Mussolini 87
Foucault, Michel
  on biopower 15–16
  on the Bonn Republic 17–19
  on France 23
  on the GDR 18
  on governmentality 11–16, 24–7
  on heterotopia 160–4
  on space 25–7, 76
France
  Haussmann's Paris 31
  legacy of Vichy 23
  and neoclassical sculptures and architecture 93, 96
Frankfurt School 18
Freiburg School 18
Frick, Wilhelm 43, 83
Fuhlsbüttel airport (Hamburg) 136

Gauland, Alexander 23
Gebhardt, Willy 103
Gehrts, Erwin 65
Gerkan, Marg and Partners (gmp) 85, 117–19
German Democratic Republic (GDR)
  architecture in (*see* architecture)
  built traces of 2, 22, 33, 35, 44, 46–54, 176
  Foucault on 18
  founding of 2, 43,
  memory of the Third Reich in 19–20
  Olympic champions 108–9
  referendum responses 143
  refugees from 137
  unification 22, 44 (*see also* Treuhand)
German Economic Commission 43
Germania 4, 31, 89, 134
German Stadium (Detusches Stadion) 2, 82, 103–5, *see also* March, Otto
Gerz, Jochen 74–5

Gestapo 55, 63–4, 146
  site of former headquarters of 21, 64
Giordano, Ralph 95, 97
Göring, Hermann 41–4, 69, 70
Gropius, Walter 115
GROSS.MAX 168–70

Hackesche Höfe 174
Halbwachs, Maurice 34
Hannah, Matthew 25
Hansa Quarter 32
Harvey, David 162–3
Haspel, Jörg 54, 93
Hentrich-Petschnigg and Partner (HPP) 47, 48
Hertha Berlin 84, 125, 179
heterotopia 7, 132, 160–5, 169, 175, *see also* Tempelhofer Feld as heterotopia
Historians' Debate (*Historikerstreit*) 21
History Workshop movement 21, *see also* Berlin History Workshop
Hitler, Adolf
  and architecture 4, 30, 31, 83 (*see also* Germania)
  bunker 1, 2, 181 n.1
  Olympic opening ceremony 84, 114
  Olympic Stadium design 3, 83, 89, 112, 114, 117
  Tempelhof 4, 131
Hoffmann, Hilmar 91–4
Hoffmann-Axthelm, Dieter 54
Hohenzollern Palace 32, *see also* Stadtschloss
Hölderlin, Friedrich 113, 115–16, 120, 122
Holocaust 33, 92
  and biopolitics 16
  memory and memorialisation of 20–2, 92, 123, 178
Holocaust television show 21
House of German Art (Munich) 30
House of Ministries (Haus der Ministerien), *see* Aviation Ministry (building)
Hrdlicka, Alfred 91
Huyssen, Andreas 28

industrial Revolution   26
Interbau exhibition   115
interim spaces   172–5
International Society for Human Rights   58, 59

Jaskot, Paul   31, 33
Jews   20, 22, 41, 43, 84, 92, 95, 97, 146–7, 178
Jordan, Jennifer   35, 148,
Joyce, Patrick   24–5, 70, 73, 169, 170

Karrenberg, Katherina   60–1
Kay, Ella   109
Koch, Karl   146–7, 157
Kohl, Helmut   21, 22, 47
Kolbe, Georg   88, 89
Kollwitz, Käthe   91
Koshar, Rudy   22, 35
Kosina, Heinrich   3, 131

Ladd, Brian   31, 36
Landesdenkmalamt Berlin, *see* Office of Monument Preservation of the State of Berlin
Lane, Barbara Miller   30
Langemarck myth   111–14, 120–2, *see also* Battle of Langemarck; Olympic Stadium, Langemarck Hall
Le Corbusier   115, 134
Legg, Stephen   12, 16, 27
Lemcke, Walter E.   130, 139
Lemke, Thomas   12, 13
Lewald, Theodor   104–6
Lingner, Max   51, *see also* Aviation Ministry, Lingner's mural
Ludwig, Eduard   137–8
Lufthansa   133
  and forced labourers   147–8, 151–2
Luftwaffe   41

Macdonald, Sharon   33, 122
Mages, Josef 'Sepp'   89
Mahlberg, Paul   3, 131
Manchester   26
March, Otto   2, 29, 82, 193
March, Werner
  career after 1945   11–15, 83–5, 105–6, 115

German Sports Forum   82
  plans for the 1936 Olympic Stadium   3, 29, 81–5, 87–9, 93–4, 101, 104–5, 113–14, 117, 124
Meller, Willy   89
Memorials and memorialisation   1, 5, 13, 22–2, 33, 55–6, 180, *see also* Federal Strategy for Memorial Sites
  contingent nature of   35, 45, 56, 177
  for discussions of the development of specific memorials (*see* 17 June 1953; Air Lift Memorial; Columbia-Haus; Harro Schulze-Boysen; Langemarck Hall; Libertas Schulze-Boysen)
Memorials Forum (Gedenkstättenforum)   97
Memorial to the Murdered Jews of Europe   22, 95, 96, 178
Mendelsohn, Erich   134, 209 n.8
Merkel, Angela   76, 178
Mittig, Hans-Ernst   83, 98–9, 139
Möhring, Bruno   29
Müller Reimann Architekten   69

Nagel, Wolfgang   46
National Democratic Party of Germany (Nationaldemokratische Partei Deutschlands (NPD))   21
New Objectivity (Neue Sachlichkeit)   30
Night of Broken Glass (Kristallnacht)   43, 53, 151
NOlympic city movement   104–5
Nora, Pierre   35
Nuremberg International Military Tribunal   20
Nuremberg rally grounds   30, 33, 48, 69, 89, 122

Occupying powers, *see* British Administration of Berlin; Soviet Union, Soviet Administration of Berlin; United States Air Force
Office of Monument Preservation of the State of Berlin (Landesdenkmalamt Berlin)   48, 60, 99, 150
Olmsted, Frederick Law   169, 170

Olympia (film)   90
Olympic Games   107
   1916 (cancelled) Olympics   2, 82, 100, 103
   1936 Olympics   2, 3, 82, 84, 114
      engagement with the legacy of   91, 92, 98–110, 120–5
      opening ceremony of   84, 87, 122
      organisation of   3, 104, 106
      as propaganda   3, 82–4, 93, 114
   2000 Olympic bid   90, 91–4
      fears of parallels with 1936   93–4
      opposition to   104–5, 116
Olympic Stadium
   aesthetics of   3, 29, 81–3, 85, 87–90, 100, 111–14, 117–20
   design and construction of   2–3, 81–3, 112–14
   Flex and Hölderlin inscriptions   111, 113, 115–16, 122
   Langemarck Hall   3, 7, 81, 86, 100, 101, 111–25
   Maifeld   3, 81–2, 85, 89–91, 101, 111–14, 117, 120
   Marathon Gate   82–4, 89, 100, 103–6, 111, 117
   1960s renovations of   104–6, 115–16, 118
   1970s renovations of   84–5
   Olympic Bell   84, 100, 113, 115
   Otto March's Stadium for the 1916 Olympics (*see* German Stadium; March, Otto)
   post-unification renovations of   85, 117–20
   Sport Forum   3, 82, 100–1
   Stelae for Olympic Champions   81, 103, 107–10
   use in West Germany   84–5, 115
Open Door Day (Tag der offenen Tür)   73–4, 76–7

Palast der Republik   1, 51
panopticon   164
Pfundtner, Hans   83
Philpotts, Matthew   29, 49, 51, 163
Pitz and Hoh   48–50, 71–2
Platz der Luftbrücke   129, 134, 138, 142, *see also* Air Lift Memorial
Platz des Volksaufstandes von 1953   67
Podbielski Oak   100–1
Poelzig, Hans   134
Prinz-Albrecht-Strasse   55, 146
public parks   165–6, 169–70

Reclaim Tempelhof   171
Red Army Faction (RAF)   44
Red Orchestra (Rote Kapelle)   55, 57
referenda
   on closure of Tempelhof (2008)   133, 138, 140–3
   on development of Tempelhofer Feld (2014)   5, 156, 168, 172
Reich Bank   47–8, 69
Reich Ministry of Popular Enlightenment and Propaganda   48
Reichsluftfahrtministerium, *see* Aviation Ministry (building)
Reichstag   1, 85, 174
   Reichstag Fire   146
   wrapping of   91
Riefenstahl, Leni   90, 93
Ringstrasse, Vienna   31
Rohwedder, Detlev   2, 44
Rose, Nikolas   14–16, 25, 27
Rosenfeld, Gavriel   33
Rosh, Lea   95–7
Rüppel, Wolfgang   58, 61–2, 66

Sagebiel, Ernst
   and Aviation Ministry   2, 4, 29, 41, 42, 48, 69, 70, 131
   and Tempelhof   4, 131, 134–8, 139, 146–7, 151, 153–6
Schäche, Wolfgang   36, 90, 99, 115, 116
Schäuble, Wolfgang   76
Schinkel, Karl Friedrich   32, 134
Schulze-Boysen, Harro   45, 55
   memory and memorialisation of   56–7, 62–8
Schulze-Boysen, Libertas   55, 66–7
Schutzstaffel (SS)   21, 31, 146
Schwaetzer, Irmgard   46–7
Schwerbelastungskörper   32
Schwippert, Hans   32
Socialist Realism   49, 51, 58

Socialist Unity Party of Germany (Sozialistische Einheitspartei Deutschlands (SED)) 20, 22
Soja, Edward 162
Soviet Union 20
   and 17 June 1953 uprising 55, 59
   Soviet Military Administration of Berlin 2, 32, 42, 43–4
   Soviet prisoners of war in Nazi Germany 147, 151–2
Space Pioneers 175
Speer, Albert 4, 30, 83,
Staatsratsgebäude 47
Stadtschloss 1, see also Hohenzollern Palace
Stalinallee 32, 55, 58, 59
Steibert, Georg 148–9, 154
Süssmuth, Rita 21

Tacheles 173
Tannenbergdenkmal 134
Taut, Max 115
Tegel airport 131
Tempelhof Airport, see also Air Lift Memorial; Tempelhofer Feld
   aesthetics 4, 29, 134–6, 138, 139, 156
   American use of 131, 144–5 (see also Berlin Air Lift)
   closure of 4, 131, 133, 140–3, 145, 152, 154–5, 159, 167
   design and construction of 4, 131–2, 133–7
   eagle's head 130, 139
   events location 155–8
   first airport on site 3, 131, 151, 153
   refugees 4, 5, 137, 157
   technical elements 134–6, 140–3
Tempelhofer Feld
   concentration camp (see Columbia-Haus concentration camp)
   excavation of 150–2
   fence, controversy over 170–2
   forced labourer barracks (see forced labourers)
   as heterotopia 159–75
   history trail 150, 152–14
   memorial 148–50, 154
   as park 142, 145, 159, 163–72
   proposed development of 165–72
   referenda over (see referenda)

Tempelhofer Freiheit
   name, controversy over 145, 157, 159, 165
   as park (see Tempelhofer Feld)
Tempelhof Für Alle 168
13 August Working Group (Arbeitsgemeinschaft 13. August) 59, 67
Thorak, Josef 88, 89
Töpfer, Klaus 47
Topography of Terror Foundation 99, 149, 150
Topography of Terror Museum 1, 21, 41, 64
transparency ideology 32, 119
Treaty of Versailles 3, 41, 131
Tresor 173
Treuhand 2, 22, 29, 44
Troost, Paul 30

Ulbricht, Walter 44, 53
United States Air Force 4, 129, 131, 133, 137, 139, 144, 155, 156, see also Berlin Air Lift; Tempelhof Airport
Urban Catalysts 175

von der Asseburg, Graf Egbert 103
von Podbielski, Viktor 100, 103
von Semper, Gottfried 31
von Tshammer und Osten, Hans 114
von Weizsäcker, Richard 21, 178

Wackerle, Joseph 88, 89, 96
Waigel, Theodor 59–60
Waldbühne 82, 94, 100, 115
Waldschmidt, Arnold 51, 62
Walter Bau AG 99–101
Wehrmacht 20, 22, 41, 43
Welthaupstadt Germania 4, 31, 89, 134
Weser Flugzeugbau GmbH (Weser Flug) 147, 152
West Germany, see Federal Republic of Germany
Wolff, Heinrich 69
World Cup
   1974 World Cup 84–5
   2006 World Cup 1, 85–6, 90, 94–9, 116–19
Wowereit, Klaus 141

Zwischennutzung 174–5

www.ingramcontent.com/pod-product-compliance
Lightning Source LLC
Chambersburg PA
CBHW052112010526
44111CB00036B/1920